AF506033

THE ABSENT MUSEUM

Blueprint for a Museum of Contemporary Art for the Capital of Europe

Edited by
Dirk Snauwaert

Essays by
Manuel Borja-Villel
Charles Esche
Dirk Snauwaert

WIELS
Mercatorfonds
Distributed by
Yale University Press,
New Haven and London

PIERRE ISERBYT

It is with great pleasure and pride in what WIELS has achieved over the past decade that I write these words of introduction. A decennial existence is a milestone for a cultural institution; this is a perfect opportunity to evaluate the rightness of the choices made and the objectives in mind. But although we may look back with satisfaction on the road travelled, this anniversary is especially an opportunity for WIELS to look towards the future, towards new formulas and new, as yet unexplored, territory. This anniversary must therefore also be the starting signal for a new scenario: an interdisciplinary collaboration with a range of cultural players in the region. This renewed approach opens up perspectives on a promising future.

Our hope is that WIELS can now be called, without reservation, 'an institute' and will no longer be dogged, like many institutions in the Brussels-Capital Region, by instability and a lack of public support. From the start, WIELS was built on several pillars, both public and private. That was a deliberate choice, as were its multilingualism and openness to all communities. It has proved that it is possible in the Brussels-Capital Region to strive after new forms of cooperation, over and beyond language communities and formal administrative demarcations. This is what WIELS derives its scope and ambition from, and this is what enables it to grow sustainably and democratically.

'The Absent Museum' recalls a number of elements from the initial phase of WIELS, starting with 'W!', its first exhibition, in 2003. At the time, we were still desperately searching for a suitable framework for the future arts centre. That first show took place in the Métropole building, where the offices of the Wielemans brewery had been located. From the start, the artistic component was closely related to an industrial background: an important site that was undergoing transformation from a manufacturing and production industry to a service economy, from a brewery to artistic and sociocultural activities. That thought was clearly present in WIELS, and that is why it sought to combine heritage, socio-economic reconstruction and experimental art.

For the ambitious programme that the initiators of WIELS had in mind within the unique historical context of the old brewery – a mix of contemporary forms, erudition and a critical approach – inspiring examples were already present in Brussels. On the one hand, there was Anne Teresa De Keersmaeker's dance school P.A.R.T.S., which turned Brussels into the world centre of contemporary dance. On the other, there was the Kunstenfestivaldesarts, a transdisciplinary city festival with a critical perspective on global relationships, rooted in local urban narratives. Both organisations have demonstrated an ongoing commitment in their respective programmes and both have highlighted outstanding, high-profile, leading artists. Thanks to their reputations and their openness, they have contributed to the dissemination of new experiences and ideas. In the coming decade we wish to achieve the same with WIELS in the field of visual art, and build on the solid foundation that has been laid for that purpose over the past decade.

Great variety and a cosmopolitan outlook are essential characteristics of contemporary art, which is a reflection of today's society. Variety, both socially and as regards origin and background, also characterises the population of Brussels. Over the past decade WIELS has mobilised and integrated local unskilled workers in everyday activities, in communications and in pedagogical responsibilities; they have taken part in the social life of the arts centre. With these and other innovative forms of collaboration, the centre has contributed to the area's redevelopment. For artists as well as for the public, art is a step towards individual emancipation and a fully-fledged life of self-fulfilment.

'The Absent Museum' has created a new challenge and offered new opportunities to make contacts and establish new relationships. With this in mind we have looked at other cities such as Amsterdam, Cologne–Düsseldorf, London and Paris and their well-structured cultural institutions. The exhibition raises the following question: on the basis of what common starting points could the European Union imagine a museum for contemporary art? A museum where the global and the local can have an unimpeded chance, which is not squeezed into the straitjacket of administrative measures and organisation. An institution tailored to the multilingual artistic expression of the leading artists that are active both in Brussels plus its surrounding area and in the EU.

The selection of artists for this exhibition includes artists from the WIELS residency programme. They are the living proof of the effectiveness of this exchange programme for young artists. The globalisation that is taking place in society as a whole and therefore also in the art world is inescapable and irreversible. For the authorities that must trace out programmes for their institutions, this forms an unprecedented challenge.

The local economies of art markets and collectors will have to show great openness to ensure that all these talented artists can acquire a reason to stay here in the long term.

Like in 2015, for the very ambitious 'Work/Travail/Arbeid' by Anne Teresa De Keersmaeker, this year too we sought a mixed source of funding for this project. Besides our subsidising authorities, we were able to win over a group of committed art enthusiasts for this project: the WIELS Patrons, with Jean-Pierre and Katherine Berghmans, Michel and Virginie Cigrang, Emilie De Pauw, Pieter and Olga Dreesmann, Dean Johnson and James Van Damme, Catherine Lagrange, Sophie Le Clercq, Wolfgang and Martine de Limburg Stirum, Jean-Claude and Nicole Marian, Michel and Stéphanie Moortgat, Corinne and Alexandre Van Damme, Christian and Nathalie Van Thillo, Jean and Chantal Vandemoortele, and Sylvie Winckler.

'The Absent Museum' exhibition was also made possible thanks to the support of the Willame Foundation. We wish to extend our heartfelt thanks to them, in particular to the members Luc Boellaert, Xavier Donck, Michel Delfosse, André Gordts and Jacques Verhaegen. We are also grateful to FABA Fundación Almine y Bernard Ruiz-Picasso para el Arte for their support. We acknowledge the foreign partners that have lent us their assistance and support: the Mondriaan Fund, the Kunststiftung NRW, the Institut français and Service de Coopération et d'Action Culturelle de l'Ambassade de France en Belgique, the Embassy of the Kingdom of the Netherlands in Brussels, Pro Helvetia, and Peter and Nathalie Hrechdakian.

If the authorities work together in a constructive manner, society itself will also deliver its share of the efforts and means. Today Brussels has already acquired an international reputation as an open, creative and artistic city. We wish to contribute to the discussion that must lead to a European institute for contemporary art. No small ambition, but this illustrates well the spirit that thrives in the creative neighbourhoods of Brussels.

President, WIELS

THE ABSENT [MUSEUM]

ABSENCES
FELT AND UNFELT

CHARLES ESCHE

Museums are places where a society tells stories to itself. Art museums in particular, because they attempt to materialise the imagination, touch on about how a place wants to be seen and why it deserves to be significant among the cultures of the world. New York's Museum of Modern Art; London's Tates Britain and Modern; the National Gallery Singapore; the Museum of Modern Art of Rio de Janeiro (to name only a few) all reflect their host nation or city's unique contribution to the world as seen from inside that location. Understanding this, it is perhaps unsurprising that Brussels has no national museum of contemporary art. The Belgian state is not a nation and its myths of origin and identity are fraught and divided, as well as less institutionalised than other European countries. The city museums that do exist are somewhat archaic structures that owe their existence to royal patronage rather than to the drive for national identity formation sponsored by an emerging bourgeoisie. There are important Flemish and Walloon equivalents of course, but they are not to be found in the capital city, and there is little contact between the institutions or official incentive for coordinating their activities across the country. Indeed, there was a time in the 1970s and 80s when the Van Abbemuseum was, slightly jokingly, considered as the displaced Flemish museum of modern art, though never the Belgian one.

Today, the absence of the museum of modern and contemporary art is seen not in terms of completing an unfinished national narrative or establishing a sense of what art might contribute to what Brussels might be or become as an urban imaginary, but as a gap in the necessary touristic infrastructure of a major European destination. This is the reason, presumably, why importing an outpost of Paris's Centre Georges Pompidou as the missing contemporary art institution is seen as the perfect political solution.

It avoids having to confront the lack of a contemporary national mythology that an independent Brussels institution would have to face, while providing the formal needs and investment opportunities that are considered vital to the future success of Brussels as a top destination. So, Brussels continues to deal with the absence of a museum that might offer it a way to understand itself anew in the face of changing ideas of Europe, the nation state, participating communities and the various different publics that form the ground on which any museum stands.

While it is not within the remit of this text to speculate on what kind of institution that imagined autochthonic Brussels museum might be, I hope it is useful to explain how the Van Abbemuseum, once a significant player within the Flemish cultural ecology, has developed in the past decade as a way to think about what choices a museum in a particular location can and perhaps must make in the twenty-first century. To do so, I have to start with a story of the Van Abbemuseum as an example of a European organisation that was, at the turn of this century, almost entirely orientated towards a western European, modern, white and largely male, heterosexual narrative, and how that changed as the challenges of economic globalisation and cultural pluralism were faced. In this story, which cannot avoid being subjective, I am particularly interested in how a constructed narrative transforms into a description of reality and eventually into a dogma, and how to wind back the dogma so that it becomes just one way of looking at history or one choice among others.

At the start of my directorship in 2004 the geography and ideology of the collection had changed little since my predecessor, but one, Rudi Fuchs, so eloquently described it in 1982 in his preface to the catalogue for Documenta 7 as stretching from New York to Vienna.[1] It was this geography that was understood to drive invention, discovery and innovation globally. It took responsibility for modernity and the task of the museum was to represent and preserve the best artistic examples of this world-forming project – one that extended back to the roots of aesthetic modernism and, in some accounts, to the birth of the great European colonial adventure. To a large degree, this position was shared with the vast majority of European and American institutions, so no criticism is implied here – rather an attempt to understand what was often naturalised and taken for granted.

On arrival, my question, and my dilemma, was how to respond to the post-1989 expansion of the cultural map in a way that suited the position and capacities of a Dutch provincial museum that had maintained an unusually high profile in the western art world. I am fairly sure it was not a dissimilar question to the one Fuchs's successor Jan Debbaut sought to answer when he investigated new geographies (including Scotland) and eventually settled on Los Angeles as a place that was breaking new ground in a way that was consequent for the museum's existing western art collection.[2]

1
documenta 7, catalogue, Kassel 1982.

2
Fascinatingly, Jan Debbaut was invited to join the team developing what became the exhibition 'Magiciens de la terre' but withdrew at some point. It's a nice speculation to imagine what the collection would have become had that experience filtered through into the Van Abbemuseum collection's purchasing policy.

To me, the acceptance of a Euro-American geography for the collection – a NATO collection if you will – was not sufficient in an increasingly diverse and divided Dutch society. The privileging of the United States based, however unconsciously, on the loyalties of the Dutch state after 1945 no longer seemed the only way to support the values of individualism, free exchange, aesthetic experimentation and internationalism. Other values, such as social justice, community cohesion and a new accounting of recent history, also felt like they were emerging as issues within the art world.

The changes we made in the early days were driven more by gut feeling and dissatisfaction with the status quo than with a clear plan of what the museum's programmes needed to address. The collection policy was initially directed towards gender and geographic imbalances in the collection by focusing on women and the former socialist states of Europe, as well as works questioning artistic autonomy and the dominance of economic growth in western society. In retrospect, we were discovering the effects of what we were doing as we went and I would now want to inscribe a subsequent understanding of colonialism and decolonial theory as a way to understand the discomfort and the most significant motivation to change the operationally successful modes the museum had developed. To do so is best done in the words of Uruguayan writer Eduardo Galeano.

> On his deathbed, Copernicus published the book that founded modern astronomy. Three centuries before, Arab scientists Mu'ayyad al-Din al-'Urdi and Nasir al-Din Tusi had come up with the theorems crucial to that development. Copernicus used the theorems but did not cite the source.
>
> Europe looked in the mirror and saw the world.
>
> Beyond that lay nothing.
>
> The three inventions that made the Renaissance possible, the compass, gunpowder, and the printing press, came from China. The Babylonians scooped Pythagoras by fifteen hundred years. Long before anyone else, the Indians knew the world was round and had calculated its age. And better than anyone else, the Mayans knew the stars, eyes of the night, and the mysteries of time.
>
> Such details were not worthy of Europe's attention.
>
> from Eduardo Galeano, 'Euroeverything'[3]

If we Europeans are to take this story seriously, we need to reconsider our place and our culture's place in the twenty-first-century world. Not to do so would not only be irresponsible to the current age but also reveals our ignorance to the diversity of people who increasingly make up the public of the museum. Secondly, any attempt to ignore such conditions in the world simply reaffirms its imbalance and inequality. As Europeans, we could simply continue to keep on looking in the mirror and see the whole world… but would we not increasingly have to turn a blind eye, squint or turn away in order to maintain that pernicious fiction? Eventually, I fear, our peripheral vision would overwhelm the comfort of our own reflection.

There is a consequence to Galeano's challenge however, and that is that we not only have to look at the rest of the picture, but we have to take the focus off what was previously the whole view. New forms of social responsibility and understandings of the political potential of art and its institutions emerge when we choose to think, talk and look elsewhere. To ignore them and the artists that proclaim them is perhaps to maintain an established modernist lineage that was the prime motivation of the modern art museum, but it means to turn away from the world as it has become and to limit our curiosity. It is therefore hard to avoid the conclusion that incorporating decolonial thinking means dismantling the core of the modern assumptions on which the institution has been built. Decolonial thinking endangers the validity of artistic autonomy as a public good, recognises the deliberate alienation in the aesthetics of post-1945 modernism and its intention to appeal solely to a progressive, moneyed, European elite, removes the privilege of the ocular over the bodily and questions the neutrality of the sterile white cube – to name a few of the fundamental modern protocols that underpinned the historic value of a collection like the Van Abbemuseum's. In short, it threatens the basic justification of the museum as it stands, especially as any notional new settlement needs to be negotiated with contemporary users and new, potential stakeholders of the museum who might not assume the intrinsic value of modern art as an *a priori* given. This process of negotiation is already underway but what will emerge is still unclear.

At the same time, it must be evident to anyone with a grasp of historical change that in 2017 the world lacks the collective, common platforms adequate to deal with the multiple ethical, aesthetic and political questions that arise today. The forms of representative democracy developed in the nineteenth century are falling apart. The risk and the hope is that one of the few functional public sites left for those much-needed common platforms to be re-established and flourish is within culture more than within the existing political and economic fields, and specifically that the unexploited potential of the modern and contemporary art museum offers a public forum where the idea of the artistic and the educational can override the tendency to factionalism and operating within bubbles of mutual agreement. One of the main pleasures of the last ten years has been the discovery of how much the existing collection put together by my predecessors offers the contemporary moment once the works are removed from their modernist straightjacket and liberated for use in the here and now. How we learn anew from history, as well as how we rewrite it for the needs of the present, have therefore become the strategic tools to apply to the collection and its forms of display. In doing so, two works of art and literature have been consistently significant. Both dwell on history, its purpose and what might be its effect on the contemporary moment.

3
Eduardo Galeano, 'Euroeverything' in *Mirrors: Stories of Almost Everyone*, trans. Mark Fried, Philadelphia 2009, p. 111.

One is a short passage by Walter Benjamin in his essay 'Theses on the Philosophy of History' and the second a film by the Lebanese artist Rabih Mroué. Benjamin talks about working with history in these terms: 'To articulate the past historically does not mean to recognize it "the way it really was" (Ranke). It means to seize hold of a memory as it flashes up at a moment of danger. […] The danger affects both the content of the tradition and its receivers. The same threat hangs over both: that of becoming a tool of the ruling classes. In every era the attempt must be made anew to wrest tradition away from a conformism that is about to overpower it.'[4] The museum is clearly often the instrument of that conformism but also potentially its opponent in that it has an independent if limited agency based on the modern idea of freedom of art and its institutions to critique and challenge the status quo. Making use of this space for action is what Benjamin's address to tradition anticipates. His past is a phenomenon with different aspects – in history, memory and tradition – and these nuances are crucial to how a museum might address its archives and collections. By looking at objects and relationships within the museum as elements within a history; as keys to unlock memory; and as traditions to be broken and/or upheld – we get closer to how the collections might be deployed precisely in the interests of wresting them away from the conformism that threatens to neutralise their potential. These Benjaminian conceptions of the past are given further shape in a short film by Rabih Mroué, *The Old House* (2003).

The artist films a building in a slow-motion process of collapse that is frozen and looped so that it oscillates between wholeness and disintegration. A voice-over by the artist describes the process by which memories are made and remade over and again. Of a story, Mroué says, 'I retell it. Not to remember it, no, but to make sure that I have forgotten it', and later on he repeats the incantation 'remembering and forgetting' not as a loop but as a refusal to go back to the beginnings, and what we know of beginnings. Throughout the short film, Mroué seeks a way to free memory from its truth and locatedness and in doing so he liberates us from one of the most persistent of modern images – that of the arrow of time shooting out of the present in a predetermined direction that must lead to improvement, development and justice. Mroué, in his work, turns the arrow back into the wheel of time of a pre-modern age in which the beginning is connected to its end. Modernity, in this moment, becomes a fictional option among others, its relevance depending on how we choose to remember and forget.

Benjamin and Mroué's form of thinking, of connecting and disconnecting times and locations and relaying narratives as emancipatory potentialities, can be understood as a kind of instruction to museums in how they can best use their resources for the public interest by taking a position as an active agent within a maelstrom of potential relationships. When they work best, art museums allow the members of the society that host them or use them to think collectively about relationships and social organisations that might tell the most effective and emancipatory stories possible. Ideally, they might practise those forms of being together inside the museum before applying them in the world. It is important that the archives and artworks engaged in this process remain independent of such narratives because they will need to be reused by others – this is the cycle that Mroué evokes. The museum is then a place where interrelationships between people and objects are temporarily forged and deployed to address particular questions, needs or antagonisms. Art museums seen through this one possible lens are tools to rewrite the past from a located, contemporary position as well as to suggest relationships with other places for the needs of the present, both without losing sight of how the one is shaped by the other. In this process, the public art museum can identify a plurality of social and political roles that it can fulfil within its remit of presenting modern and contemporary art. Partly, its task is to test these roles experimentally and find the most effective one.

In the Van Abbemuseum, experimenting with the uses and displays of the collection have been and remain one of our primary focuses. There are various stages to the story of how our approach to the collection has developed and only a summary is given here. Initially, the existing modern and typological narrative of the collection was broken up and the fragments were revealed through a programme of discrete single room presentations ('Plug-Ins'). After a couple of years, the 'Play Van Abbe' series was developed as whole museum narratives in which works were connected to each other in new ways, differences were magnified and the public was equipped with new requests and expectations. Finally, a temporary coherence was reconstructed through the displays we called 'Once Upon a Time' and later simply 'The Collection Now'. Other collection-inspired projects that sometimes happened elsewhere and found their way back to Eindhoven include Superflex's 'Free Sol LeWitt', 'Picasso in Palestine' and Li Mu's 'A Man, A Village, A Museum'.[5] Often these projects shared a quite overt desire to deviate from the established codes of handling the works in the collection: from agreeing to loans, to reconfiguring installation protocols with regards to copying and reproducing. This helped us to learn what we were doing and why we were doing it.

The paradox here is that in taking a position for the museum as a socially engaged institution that operates on behalf of a local and international public as well as artists, we were sometimes accused of alienating a public or abandoning art by the establishment art world. While we were certainly guilty of breaking certain protocols around copying, distributing or loaning works, for instance, these actions facilitated new ways of thinking about a modernist heritage and how it could be put to use in the early twenty-first century. Our recent experience in Eindhoven is that building relationships with the interests of specific local and not-so-local social groups in mind effectively minimises these criticisms by gaining the support of different users. A focus on a very literal conception of accessibility – for instance, working with small groups of people with Alzheimer's or aphasia, blind and partially sighted, deaf and others with different capacities – has grown the local and national affection for the museum and become a significant demonstration of our social relevance from which other inclusive programmes such as 'Queering the Collection' or 'Deviant Practice' can stem.

4
Walter Benjamin, 'Theses on the Philosophy of History' (1940) in *Illuminations*, ed. and with intro. by Hannah Arendt, trans. Harry Zohn, New York 1968, p. 255.

5
Charles Esche et al., *De collectie nu*, Eindhoven 2015; Charles Esche et al., *Plug in to Play*, Eindhoven 2009; Christiane Berndes, *Free Sol LeWitt*, Berlin 2010; 'Picasso in Palestine' in *A Prior Magazine*, no. 22 (2011); Li Mu, *A Man, A Village, A Museum: Qiuzhuang Project*, Eindhoven 2015.

These latter initiatives bring new temporary voices into the management of the museum's activities, and collaborations with universities and academies speak to specific groups. In this process, the position of privilege enjoyed by the artist is shared with other actors who can claim the attention of the museum as institution in a similar way.

At a more abstract level, the narrow protocols of exhibition-making and collection-forming are part of a particular conservative understanding of modernity and its claim on the future. Where once modernity was disruptive, it has become nostalgic and narrow. As we learn to resist the urge to conform to the modern imperative, we can also begin to think beyond old modernist dualities – mind or body, west or rest, public or private, state or corporation. To do so, we can call on the much more profound and unanswerable critique of modernity developed by decolonial thinkers such as Walter Mignolo or Boaventura de Sousa Santos. Their understanding of the unity between modernity and coloniality at a fundamental level (that one cannot be named, discussed or thought without the other) is a crucial act of recognition that impels museums with modern art collections to action. 'Decolonial thinking', as poetically invoked by Galeano, is a challenge to deeply-inbuilt assumptions about ethics and progress – assumptions that often find their expression in the ways that modern art has been presented and collected by a museum like the Van Abbe. Decoloniality questions much of the basis of a western European education, and thus Europeans' unconscious decision-making. It equally puts a bomb under comfortable post-Marxist positions and their tendency towards a disembodied criticality.

And yet, it remains hard to let go entirely of modernity as a system of potential emancipation. To discuss an alternative at this juncture in the world arguably strengthens the religious conservatives of all creeds that want to reassert theocratic control. Indeed, part of the appeal of Daesh or the Israeli and the US religious right are their anti-modern, anti-secular positions. But, just as resisting fascism did not mean simply defending the corrupt status quo, so the current monotheist revival is not the only way to demodernise our societies. It is simply a fact that 'there is no alternative (to modernity)' no longer works as a mantra for too much of the world. Above all, modernity's intimacy, not to say lack of distinction from colonialism, is something that renders it no longer fit for purpose across the planet.

For its next steps, the museum collection can therefore do little else but seek to leave modernity behind and move into an unclear future. In doing so, it seems right to remember and applaud what was modern as well as criticise and debunk. Modernity was a complex and often misunderstood condition and honouring its energy, wit, perseverance and capacity to support the ideas of individuality, emancipation and equality, even if relevant to only a small part of the world, is vital. At the same time, its universal claims to a single truth, its patriarchy, its white privilege, its refusal to recognise other forms of knowledge, and its destructive occupation of others' territories have to be reckoned with. To do so suggests something I believe we could call 'demodern thinking', as a parallel and subsidiary aspect to decoloniality. While our task is certainly to offer visibility, employment, power and platforms to decolonial possibility within the hegemonic west, it is the construction of a demodern discourse that might emerge as a way to follow suit and engage in internal western processes of coming to terms with the past differently.

What happens then once decoloniality and its younger sibling demodernity are centrally addressed? There is the potential to unmake the modernist form and its assumptions – not through critique but by turning away from its internal aesthetic languages and expectations. It would throw into question the modern rhetoric of a utopian order that is always postponed. It would attempt to include the peoples, classes and subjects, knowledge and understanding that modernism defined as backward or marginal. In the Van Abbemuseum, demodern thinking is our proposition for telling new narratives. It starts by looking anew at modern artworks and recognising their place within the belief system of modernity and how they are subject to their time and place. In doing so, the process of applying demodern thinking is not only intended to create a distance between modern works and the world of today, but also to help liberate them from the mythologies of progress and universality and to create the space for new interpretations and understandings based on located and contingent criteria. The demodern rejects claims to universalism and the singular story of modern art's development originating in the international hegemony of New York's Museum of Modern Art. Rather, it pursues pluralist forms and narratives in which queer, deviant and intersectional thinking is given a place and the museum seeks to act in the present and with the people that are local to it, as least as much as the national or international art world. The only reasonable way to do so is to reach out to constituencies that are not yet constituted – to the refugees in your neighbourhood; to the indigenous and the excluded internationally; to teachers and schoolchildren whose school visits are reduced or abolished as a result of austerity; to the differently abled, the sick and the growing disadvantaged everywhere. It is through those who occupy the edges of our white, patriarchal, western vision that a decolonial, demodern perspective might begin to open up – or at least how the art museum might combine contemporary experiences, desires and struggles articulated by these people with the modern and contemporary legacies of art and its potential for imaginative emancipation. This is the only way to imagine that a possible horizon beyond the exhausted liberal mantra of 'there is no alternative (to modernity)' is to become visible. Such a horizon must deal with the consequences of globalisation (and not its rejection), and therefore includes the difficult task of imagining a global civil society-in-becoming, which emerges from a single geographic though socially plural location in which all protagonists are subject to the legacies of coloniality/modernity.

To return to Brussels, it is the potential inherent in the locally grounded, modestly-but-reliably funded, in-it-for-the-long-haul art institution that the city is missing. Although it might perhaps be a little unfashionable today, it is this kind of institution with a collection that can make a difference to the way groups within a place identify with it and among themselves. I have seen that happen on a small scale but to a transformative dimension in Eindhoven. Not all the time, and not with random visitors walking in for an art experience, but through the constituencies we build locally and internationally. That is the absence that Brussels would perhaps be well advised to recognise and to open a debate on how best to provide.

TOWARDS A MUSEUM OF THE COMMON

MANUEL BORJA-VILLEL

The screen shows us a scene characteristic of Elizabethan theatre. A young woman and a man in blackface appear to be arguing. The dialogue makes it very clear that we are deal-ing with a production of *Othello*, the great play in which Shakespeare takes us into the very heart of jealousy. The film is, in fact, a short by Pier Paolo Pasolini entitled *Che cosa sono le nuvole?* However, the Italian filmmaker incorporates a number of elements into the Shakespearean drama that radically transform it. In the first place, the charac-ters do not represent real people but puppets, moved by threads, which perform a preset script. Second, the Othello character does not understand why he has to kill Desdemona, and Desdemona is incapable of understanding Othello's perplexity. She is very pleased with her role and with being the object of jealousy. The dilemma is resolved by the revolt of the public. The spectators invade the stage and, in an outburst of riotous fun, carry the performers out onto the street, breaking all the rules of theatrical representation in what amounts to a genuine carnival reversal. Lucid as ever, in just twenty minutes Pasolini gives us the keys to appreciating the place that art occupies in contemporary society and how the poetic can be understood in political terms. And, moreover, how we can cast off the fetters that constantly shackle us.

Pasolini presents us with protagonists bound to a destiny, the script to which they keep on clinging. Like our relationships, those between the characters in the film have their origins in texts. But these texts are never neutral or politically aseptic. Each culture produces a set of foundational narratives that are its own, which define and 'defend' it against every threat of dissolution as well as from any external enemy, and exert on us an undeniable influence. There is a certain fateful connection between these narratives and the form in which we perceive our destinies, in that, to a great extent, they bestow meaning on our lives, at the same time as they model and coerce them. But why does Pasolini want Othello to rebel against his character? What is the meaning of the public uprising and its transgression of the rules of theatre? What the film suggests is that while the texts or the language we speak do indeed determine us, it is equally true that we have the capacity to rewrite them and act upon them to transform them. Like the marionette of the Moor of Venice, we too can subvert the story.

A society is alive when it interprets and upsets its narratives. This implies an active political subject, capable of rethinking the stories that condition the future and altering the integrative force of myths and ideologies. When we in a cultural institution recognise our nature as 'agents' of our publics, we are acknowledging that they have the capacity to compare texts, to translate them and posit them anew. Through this process we free ourselves from the fateful weight of destiny. As in the case of Walter Benjamin's storyteller, history is memorised by those who receive it: by those who, in reciting it, complete it and invent it.[1] Pasolini's work is, in this sense, deeply anti-modern. While modernity promised people happiness without taking them into account, Pasolini's story unfolds thanks to the spectator.

Theatre – the theatrical, as understood by the Italian writer and director – fulfils the modern desire for liberation, but by way of the insurrection of the spectator and the overflowing of institutional limits. As Artaud pointed out, the theatre enables a liberation in the social sphere of the pathologies engendered by the violence of this normalised life which it is our lot to endure: 'Perhaps the theatre's poison, injected into the social body, disintegrates it.'[2] Modernity, in its pursuit of utopia, that imaginary non-place, imposes a supposedly universal language on a passive and homogeneous audience. Today, by contrast, it is not possible to propose any kind of social change other than through the conception of new forms of sociability, and these can only be in relation and agency.

One of the mysteries of Greek drama was the way in which children were predestined to expiate the sins of the parents. It mattered not at all that they themselves were pure and pious: if their parents had sinned, they would be punished. Whether we class ourselves as conservative or pride ourselves on being progressive, when we decline to question our ways of knowing we load ourselves with a kind of original sin that we pass on to our children. The guilt of the parents comes not only from the violence of power, but also from the belief in the goodness and necessity of our social structures and structures of knowledge. There is an idea that is common to all of us: that the worst of the world's ills is poverty and consequently that the culture of the less affluent classes must be replaced by that of the dominant classes and that history cannot be anything other than bourgeois history.

1
Walter Benjamin, 'The Storyteller: Reflections on the Works of Nikolai Leskov' in *Illuminations*, ed. Hannah Arendt, trans. Harry Zohn, New York 1969, pp. 83–109.

2
Antonin Artaud, *The Theater and Its Double* (1938), trans. Mary Caroline Richards, New York 1958, p. 31.

At present we are witnessing a 'realistic' acceptance of the status quo. We believe that in the last analysis it is always preferable for people to learn and be educated in this bourgeois history than in none. We will say that it is better for people to read books or go to museums than to stop doing these things. However useful it may be for mollifying consciences and moving forwards, this is a culpable manoeuvre. Our society is devoted to the indiscriminate consumption of images and ideas. Everything that is new is susceptible of being converted into merchandise. If in the first half of the twentieth century modernity based its strategies on the exclusion of difference, of whatever threatened a break with the original canon, today the opposite is true: its inclusion has become the norm. But this new norm is as problematic as its predecessor, in that they both ignore the spectator, who is rendered passive, reduced now to a pure consumer of images.

The artistic – the artistic fact – supposes a shared place, between subversion and absorption, between contemplative passivity and the active break, between the state and the multitude, between creation and the market. While it is evidently very difficult to believe that artistic forms can sweep away borders, it is just as hard to think that they serve to shift them. At a time when all museums are caught up in a spiralling rush towards the expansion of spaces and franchises, in an age in which consumerist hedon-ism has entered into a proliferation that knows no end, perhaps the time has come for us to draw back a little and question our own habits. The attention to the fragile life of bodies, the hostility towards the reification of our existence and the explicit manifestation of the disappearance of the boundary between the public and the private, which the theatre of Pasolini provides, may be among the most incisive elements of political intervention today.

Although they retain their importance in the network of creative industries, as public institutions museums have lost much of their mediatory power and, further, have lost their privileged position in defining what we understand to be culture. This is partly because those who shape the cultural scene most definitively today are prominent figures in the communications industries, as well as a diffuse magma of cultural producers, who typically subordinate creative singularity to the selling or expropriation of creative capacity. At the same time, we are immersed in a profound systemic crisis to which museums are not immune: just as an economic paradigm based on speculation and easy money has proved itself to be unsustainable, so the primacy of a museum's building and spectacle over its artistic programme is bereft of validity. There is therefore a pressing need to invent new models.

To make such a statement is to suggest that changes must be made to the very structure of the museum. Institutions have long been the principal structures for inventing the social and for generating affirmative and non-limiting action. This significant historical function is even more important now because governance in modern western society no longer consists of applying repressive measures, but rather of getting citizens to interiorise them. In other words, with the advent in recent decades of artistic criticism as a characteristic form of labour relations – to borrow Luc Boltanski and Ève Chiapello's phrase for the articulated desire for an authentic, non-alienated life based on creativity and non-dependence on the Fordist prototype (with a boss and fixed working hours) – people are no longer forced to behave as they once were. Instead, such criticism now plays an active role in our subjection to governmental rule; it promotes the subordination of the subject to a labour structure in which the cultural producer contributes to his or her own precarious status.[3]

Cultural producers may seek greater freedom and flexibility, but it comes only at the cost of the expropriation of their work by those who wield the capital or the legal tools needed to dispossess them – the tools, in short, that mould creativity to the logic of the marketplace or to those forms of cultural domination intended to serve projects for appropriating public space.

In this regard, it is very difficult to maintain the defence of the public institution today because the dichotomy between 'public' and 'private' – on which social organisation has rested for the past century and a half – no longer works. The creative dimension that defines our society now lies in both the private and public spheres, which are separated in an illusory fashion. Casting the public sphere as the disinterested administrator of creativity does not guarantee that such creativity will not be expropriated for profit. 'Public' now signifies a management regime founded on property, whose goods are thus transferable no matter how accessible they are to a broad sector of the population, and despite the fact that they may be administered by the state.

It is therefore necessary to rethink the institution in terms of a communality that constitutes neither a state public sphere nor a private one, but instead resides at the edge of both. This calls for breaking the dynamic of franchises so attractive to those in charge of museums. Moved by the imperious need to attract the largest public possible, as well as to manage their economic (and cultural) resources more effectively, many museums have chosen to open subsidiary centres, branch divisions of the head office. Bilbao, Abu Dhabi, Dubai and many other cities are witnesses to a globalisation process in which cultural interests intermingle with commercial and even political ones. The job is done within the network, not to create subjectivities but to construct publicity spaces and to establish flows that favour people's and objects' mobility.

In opposition to this trend, we must instead propose a sort of universal archive, a confederation of institutions that share the works stored in their centres and, most of all, the experiences and narratives that are generated around them. Only then will we be able to assert that making 'me' a plural word depends on my commitment to others in the world, rather than on my access to them. The place between the Other and me is where the sphere of the common emerges. It is different from the public sphere because, in the final analysis, what is public does not belong to us. The public sphere offered by the state lies only in the economic management assigned to the political class by all of us, collectively. The common is not an extension of the individual and will never be complete. It only develops through and for others, in a common realm, a shared being, to use Blanchot's terms.[4]

We often imagine an artistic construction in which the Other speaks to us, which is not actually the case. When art pedagogy is

3
Luc Boltanski and Ève Chiapello, *The New Spirit of Capitalism*, trans. Gregory Elliott, London and New York 2005, *passim*.

4
Maurice Blanchot, *The Unavowable Community*, trans. Pierre Joris, Barrytown, NY 2006.

institutionalised, art becomes pure rhetoric directed against what is perceived as social chaos.[5] The museum and the city become a kind of republic of letters, and the artist a national patriarch. It is not enough to represent the Other; it is necessary to find forms of mediation that are both models and specific practices of new forms of solidarity between the intellectual and subordinate communities, and with the various collectives that constitute social movements.

Most of humankind is the South of which Enrique Dussel speaks, constituting the 'other face' of modernity.[6] This South is not situated in a prior postmodern period, the time previous to a modern age that will be realised by applying the same criteria that served for Europe and the United States. It is not a less evolved stage in the same process. Quite the opposite: we live in a world where the centre presupposes the periphery and vice versa; and the development of the former is totally related to that of the latter. The problem lies in the fact that this other modernity is subordinate; it has no say. It obeys the rules of the Western European world, since they have been declared universal. Our laws and our moral doctrine tend to justify their own principles from the inside. Slavery, for example, would be unfair in the bourgeois system, but fair in a pro-slavery society; paid work is unfair in socialism because it robs the worker of the surplus value of his labour, but not in capitalism. The only way of breaking with this discursive order is if the instrumental reason is accompanied by an ethical criterion, which is always exterior to the established power and allows the Other to question Totality. Rather than denying the community, this exteriority discovers it as a place of convergence of persons and groups who are free to disagree.

Interpellation, the act of speaking that gives a voice to those who are outside our discursive construction – that is, outside our system of intelligibility – becomes a necessarily ethical position. It requires a degree of exteriority, of being Other, different to the official institutional community, which only defends its own interests. Emerging, as it always does, from outside the prevailing law, the act of interpellation by definition opposes consensus and exclusive history, and its line of argument is always radical and rarely accepted. Whereas the official discourse declares the dominator of the centre entirely innocent of any acts of cruelty committed on the periphery during modernity, interpellation denounces them. This implies changing the linear, univocal and exclusive narrative to which we have been accustomed into a plural and rhizomatic narrative in which differences are not only not annulled but are intertwined. This also entails the transgression of established genres and canons, as well as the broadening of artistic experience beyond mere contemplation, and the incorporation of projects that are not exhausted within the artistic circuit and are not confined to the established institutional world.

If the main objective of cultural and even artistic institutions is to seek beyond, searching out innovation and what emerges anywhere in order to tame it and transform it into merchandise, then the new institutional sphere should have an open and explicitly political dimension. It should be open to that multiplicity, simultaneously protecting its interests and favouring ethical, political and creative surpluses that are antagonistic in a shared space. It is very important to seek out legal forms appropriate to the production and promotion of what is common through network structures, rather than industrial ones. It is fundamental to get institutions to return to society what they take from it, so that what is common is not usurped by the individualities that make up that magma.

At the Reina Sofía museum, we have been developing various approaches aimed precisely at transforming a public institution into one of the common sphere:

First, *the collection* does not create a compact and exclusive narrative, although it is not a hotchpotch of multiculturalism either. We think of it in terms of setting up multiple forms of relating that challenge our mental structures and our established hierarchies. We advocate a relational identity that is neither unique nor atavistic, but has multiple roots. This situation permits opening up to the Other, and contemplates the presence of other cultures and ways of doing in our own practices, without fear of a hypothetical danger of loss of identity. Obviously, the poetics of relation cannot be understood without taking into account the notion of place. A dependence on the centre–periphery duality no longer makes sense, and the periphery's claim on the centre – so common in Spain's recent history – no longer holds. The relationship does not go from the particular to the general, or vice versa, but from the local to the world as a whole, which is not a universal, homogeneous reality but a plural one. In it, art simultaneously seeks the absolute and its opposite – that is, both writing and orality. We understand that the stories a collection tells us are also history, given that they have the capacity to act as a historical agent. This serves to establish a common element that is shared by the works that compose the collection and the collection itself, by the artistic fact and the museum, by the narrative we write and our actions as historical agents. Politics and art construct 'fictions': that is to say, material rearrangements of signs and images, and of the relations between seeing and knowing, of what is done and what can be done. These 'fictions' are the way we think the real: reconfiguring the map of the sensible and discovering new relationships between the modes of being, doing and saying.[7]

Second, we are working on the creation of a *common archive*. A kind of archive of archives. We are aware that 'the archive' has become a recurring notion in contemporary artistic practice; a rhetorical figure that serves to group together the most disparate efforts, and is often simply a build-up of unrelated documentation. Following Derrida, we could ask ourselves whether the archive does not perhaps pose a certain risk of memory saturation, or even of the negation of the narrative. Nonetheless, in the common archive, the story or stories that its members originate are as important as the document itself. There is no fetishist desire to preserve and conserve everything, but only that which members of the community consider relevant, or that which forms part of their actions. Derrida explains that the archive is both *topos*, a place, and *nomos*, the law that organises it. In the archive of the common, this law is shared; it is not instituted but instituent. It is not based on a genealogy of power, and it does not hierarchically order the knowledge of society. Its role goes further than cataloguing

5
John Beverley, *Against Literature*, Minnesota 1993, p. 11.

6
Enrique Dussel and Karl-Otto Apel, *Ética del discurso y ética de la liberación*, Madrid 2005, p. 144.

7
Jacques Rancière, *La división de lo sensible*, Salamanca 2002, p. 67. (Published in English as *The Politics of Aesthetics: The Distribution of the Sensible*, ed. and trans. Gabriel Rockhill, London and New York 2004.)

data and works and making it available to the community. The opinions, comments and judgements of its users are shared, but so are the norms that order these opinions.

The common archive entails breaking with the notion of the museum as the sole owner of a heritage collection, and replacing it with the idea of a custodian of assets that belong to all of us, one that favours the creation of shared knowledge. The production of memory is social; memory is configured through the experience of remembering together. A period of general amnesia like our own, which appears to have replaced an era in which history was omnipresent (the era of national and imperial delusions), needs productive memory more than ever. It is important that these stories spread and multiply as much as possible. While our society's economic system is based on scarcity, which allows art objects to reach exorbitant values, the common archive is based on excess, on an ordering that defies countable criteria. In this case, the person who receives stories is certainly richer, but he who gives (recounts) them is no poorer.

Finally, Museo Reina Sofía is involved in organising a heterogeneous network of collectives, social movements, universities, and so on, who question the museum and generate spheres of negotiation that are not merely representative. This space is produced through the recognition of these other agents – regardless of their institutional complexity – as valid interlocutors or peers when it comes to defining objectives and managing resources. On the other hand, it is essential to leave aside conventional, *a priori* notions of legitimacy – nobody can claim more legitimacy than anybody else – and the use of culture to justify ends other than this open process of construction of the common sphere. There is no doubt that all of this implies questioning the authority and the exemplary role of the museum, in order to endow this collective quest with non-authoritarian, non-vertical modes of cultural action.

Nor is the idea to avoid ties with institutions, but to establish networks and discover new fields for differing practices. It is not enough to say that the mass media lies or to complain about the way consensus is engineered and imposed; we have to manage its lies, by offering myths and pre-constituting the terrain on which the facts are distorted, with the aim of redressing this distortion and producing displacements of meaning.[8]

8
Wu Ming, *Esta revolución no tiene rostro*, Madrid 2002, p. 63. (Published in English as *This Revolution Has No Face*, Madrid 2002.)

THE ABSENT MUSEUM.
A BLUEPRINT FOR
A CONTEMPORARY ART MUSEUM

DIRK SNAUWAERT

In cities around the world there has been much speculation about the creation of new museums. Brussels, where for several years discussions have been ongoing about how to complement national narratives with a new institute, is no exception. However, it is striking that little thought has been devoted to the museum's contents, despite the fact that geopolitical shifts and even local transformations of the metropolitan society should encourage reflection on a number of questions: what should a future institution look like, what should it do and what shouldn't it do, which methodology should be applied, which limitations set?

From the start, WIELS has put the emphasis on ways in which artists can translate today's ideas, questions and debates into lyrical representations and forms. It is therefore natural that WIELS also takes part in this discussion by formulating a project that is about the substance of a new museum rather than about its structure or organisation. 'The Absent Museum' exhibition is a contribution to the thinking exercise that precedes the creation of new institutions – in this case an exercise based on artistic practice, not only on discourse or theory.

That a museum differs in many respects from an arts centre is common knowledge. Is it because of the general erosion of values that the two are confused and that, for instance, an institution such as WIELS is often called the 'WIELS museum'? The word 'museum' evokes respectability and is associated with a nostalgic fixation on the past. This fits with the cliché of Europe as the 'old' continent, where innovation is secondary and where the impression sometimes surfaces that it is a historical theme park full of exceptional artworks and monuments for the global tourist. However, clichés never reflect reality, and one only needs to step outside the historic city centres to discover that European urbanity is a complex sociological and cultural field of experimentation for super-diversity. This urban future and globalisation form the horizon for the new narratives that future art museums must construct.

At WIELS we pay as much attention to a symbolic-theoretical analysis as to an informal, affective, empathic handling of and involvement with issues, topics and questions that the public still often experiences as challenging and controversial. The habitual reflex is generally to avoid such a reaction by continuing to repeat only what is safe and familiar, by honouring tradition. A glimpse of WIELS's programme and of the profiles of its artists in residence over the past decade suffices to conclude that the terms 'tradition' and 'nostalgia' do not apply here, and even less so in the many contemporary art centres that also bear the name 'museum'.

Has the concept of museum been devalued or are we dealing with a linguistic confusion? In any case, the term 'museum' mainly refers to what the public expects from the institution, to the approach and the level of experience, to the concentration of intelligence and attention around a subject, and not so much the rules of the scientific discipline. In art centres, too, production forms of art and knowledge transfer with a recognisable methodical-programmatic intention take centre stage. In that sense 'museum' is rather a general name for a place in which knowledge and information are shared, where debates take place about visual culture and the history of ideas, identities and sensibilities, by means of carefully chosen and well thought-out temporary exhibitions. Dwelling on phenomena of both material and immaterial culture, observing and interpreting them – that is ultimately the function of the museum. A permanent art collection is not a prerequisite for this. Most exhibitions at WIELS, which does not have a collection, meet these demands. Thus public opinion recognises that WIELS in a certain sense fulfils the role of an absent museum for contemporary art in Brussels.

Museums have designated periods, categories and disciplines. However, these are not principles that can have a claim to absolute and eternal validity. Insights gained from history evolve fast, like mentalities and viewpoints. The question is how these insights from public debates about paradigm shifts can penetrate the formal narratives that the museums present to us. The controversial debates of the past decades were about western supremacy, racial prejudices, and gender and social inequality. Decolonisation and migration, two consequences of globalisation, became public focal points. Museums have at their disposal the material and the knowledge to defuse, to 'un-demonise' these debates, to support and refine them. It is therefore all the more remarkable that during these and other populist crises, art museums hide away and absent themselves.

The super-fast evolutions in globalisation, the technological-scientific revolutions, the ecological turning point and especially the unbridled material overproduction that is taking place in almost all areas of human activity automatically raise the question as to whether it is still possible to claim a representative view from a single collection at a single location. Can an art collection still be exemplary and advance a universal claim?

The changes after the end of the Cold War and arising from the digital revolution caused an explosion in terms of dimension, scale and changed relationships. The geopolitical model was completely reshaped. Decolonisation, including that of the Eastern Bloc after 1989, rapidly generated the insight that it was necessary to equalise 'other, global modernities' and to eliminate the difference between centre and periphery. At the same time, the awareness grew that art museums, and certainly ones exhibiting contemporary art, had to tell a fundamentally different story from fine arts museums, which saw the construction of a stable and homogeneous national identity, based on the pattern of *one* language and *one* culture on *one* territory, as *one* fate. The exemplary was replaced by the exception, the norm by the deviation.

Since then, museums in the metropolises have since been working on more subtle interpretations of 'diverse', 'other' and 'plural' modernities. In doing so they proceed from differential thinking, from divergence, and no longer from the idea of diversity where the focus is on exotic difference in form and appearance, with as underlying gist always a 'hidden' homogeneous identity, a fusion that denies any conflict and seeks to neutralise any difference. In today's geopolitical situation of multipolarity and equal rights, institutions face this new undertaking: how can adequate platforms and structures be created for this new distribution of imagination and its rapid transformations – platforms and structures that are speedy and supple as well as precise and penetrating, and which can steer insight and knowledge in one specific place, bounded by generation and geography?

There has been a lot of experimentation within the culture of biennales and world exhibitions. Valid alternatives have been developed, resistant to image politics and signature architecture, and which present a simplified, schematic, globalising approach as the new western universalism, in which once again the differences and sensibilities of asylum-seeking minorities are instrumentalised and dysfunctional actors are excluded. Rapidity and mobility, two pillars of modernity and liberal free trade, form the foundation of the global flows. The West had to realise that it has become impossible to continue protecting the radical 'other' in the 'distance', according to the 'here vs. elsewhere' pattern. Contact with 'the other' now occurs in close proximity, without any distance, not in the past but concurrently and contemporarily, and that renders this process even more complex.

History forms our image of the past by means of fictional narratives about origin and evolution, the fundamental foundational myths, which are recalled, retold and passed on. Events that have a need to be remembered and passed on are compressed in language and in symbols to form the ambivalent narratives that make up our conception of history. However, the past can also coagulate in repetitive actions that become a habit, turn into tradition and ultimately end up as folklorist ceremony.

The argument that it is impossible to enter into contact or in dialogue with 'the other' can be refuted by creating junctions where – in the experiencing and translating, the retelling of stories of a repressed or painful 'history', such as we share it with most 'others' – a connection can emerge between our possible fixation on difference and our many similarities. History shows numerous similarities in the recollections of controversial issues, such as attitudes during and after the Second World War, ideological collaboration in totalitarian systems or the role played in persecution and extermination; or colonisation and decolonisation; the climate of permanent fear and paranoia during the Cold War; the battle for equal rights of women and minorities and the battle for self-determination in terms of gender and sex; the impact of exile, expulsion and the refugee crisis; integration or assimilation as forms of inclusion; recognising and respecting the traumas of minorities. Such a list will always be a schematic and incomplete sample of reactions towards topics that will stir up controversy for a long time still and will even continue to elicit denial reflexes. The broad public opinion is aware of this, the knowledge and literature about it is available.

Because of this, the deep-rooted tensions that linger in these events carry a common universal potential, and turn them into usable catalysts for empathy in those who see the similarities reflected in widely known biographies and emancipation narratives, as they have occurred at most places across the planet. Artworks that give shape to such themes in a symbolic manner invite us to deal with the issues and to determine a position in a process of raising historical consciousness. In this exhibition we have therefore opted for an additional exercise: namely, a reading of the way in which local, Belgian artists deal with sweeping historical developments of their time, and of the habitual reflex to reject global developments as not being applicable to the uniqueness and specificity of the place.

Through identification or non-identification with narratives that do not perfectly fit the canon, a process of recognition and awareness can develop, instead of adaptation or assimilation. The reinterpretation of personal variations on 'original' narratives shifts attention from stereotyping and standardisation to the discovery of a common dimension, which is shared in agreement or in discussion. This common currency lies precisely in the sharing with others and unity-in-difference, in the connection between the individual existence shared with a community and its collective conceptions and suppositions. Sounding out the border between the private and the public, the inner world and reality – the art museum's starting points – also explains the museum's function as a central platform in defining and altering perspectives with regard to new cultural or social insights.

In this context the individual learns how to distinguish and appreciate choices and judgements, definitions and identities. Theories about the museum sometimes play down the fact that this institution, as part of the new public space of the nation state, contributed to the emergence of 'freedom of expression'. Freed from the control of religion and absolutism, freedom of expression in the art museum was asserted on the basis of the power of science over nature and of individual subjectivity with regard to public rule. The museum was the choice venue for the individual experience of symbols and metaphors that accompanied and influenced the shaping of the new society. The encounter with 'other' and equally free opinions and conceptions drew identification as much as rejection, consensus and dissensus, passion and contemplation, and helped shape a whole range of known and still unknown human sensibilities. Not only were new sensations and unknown physical and mental places explored here, but also values and norms, taboos and sore points.

Entirely different symbolic representations of how to make the world meaningful led, then as now, to experience-based opinions that together constitute civil conceptions, common property, the communal and 'the commons'. It is on the polyphony of symbolic systems in which free opinions can develop, and on the private and public voices that reinterpret and renew the symbolic systems each time, that the art museum's ritual and methodology rest. Scientific methods, which were conceived by modern encyclopedic classification to rationally dominate the chaos of nature, can no longer determine the programme for a starting point that presupposes fundamental equality and otherness, an alternative model that was traced out by intellectuals and artists.

Many museums still work on the basis of the conception of the contextless artwork, made by a genius using universal signs and symbols that were floating freely in a vacuum. Against the mystique of the 'autonomous artwork' and the idealism of 'the mystery of the detached creator' stands the dialectic of art as a part of material production. However, the artist is no longer the 'engineer of the human soul', as the constructivists called him, nor the utopian visionary, as the modernists, with their unattainable abstract spaces, saw him. The artist could simply and directly place himself between contemporary existence and the past as it is remembered, not nostalgically but plainly and plurally. It is at that junction that the awareness of history and of identity ties in with tangible reality.

In this revisionist age, every exhibition with a 'global' stake is certainly no non-committal undertaking. Besides, questions of identity sometimes incite unexpected and violent reactions in people that feel personally targeted as objects of discrimination, as dehumanised subjects, but also in people that observe the issue from the point of view of upholders of the existing social order. In this, the transformation process that makes the past into history can be of some methodological help. Thus, in 2015, the Borinage, with its negative self-image as the collapsed industrial heart of the European continent, formed the starting point for the exhibition 'Atopolis'. An important theme of the show was the source of mobility and flows that were set in motion by modernity and industrialisation. The Borinage was a precursor in the search for ways to fit mass labour migration into social and cultural structures. For the participating artists, this subject was a sounding board.

One of the basic observations while putting together the exhibition 'The Absent Museum' was that the mass inflow of artists from Europe and globalisation in the region had brought about only few levers by which to explore this transformation and give it visibility. A contemporary art museum of or for Europe could be the solution, but it should then be prepared to let go of its traditional approach and outlook. Museums, which concentrate on continuous history, do not generally participate in the above questions: they avoid controversial issues, choosing a consensus-oriented programme, due to the demands of economic feasibility. Vulnerable funding situations immediately put the function of such an art museum up for discussion: is the museum a place of contemplation, of pleasure, of status assertion, of poetic action, or can it be a place where various functions coincide, overlap or even clash?

As an alternative to cold abstraction and spectacular montages, one sometimes likes to hark back to the model of magical, mythical or bricolage thinking. The re-transformation of the world with the help of magic and myth coincides with the rediscovery of another dimension of modernity, in which there is renewed interest in the unconscious, the semiconscious and consciousness itself. In historical contexts and relationships one investigates the birth of new social and symbolic forms and the subjective factors related to them. With this idea as leitmotif, art histories are reread worldwide, seen from the periphery. This results in artists being added to the official art history and the museum line-ups, whereby the old order is thrown off balance, and attention focuses on unspectacular and at times unadapted figures that used to stand in the shadow.

These artists, often pioneers of another modernism – which until decolonisation and the collapse in 1989 of the Cold War territorial spheres of influence was still discarded as unimportant and epigonistic – gained recognition for their role as forerunners of an artistic and intellectual attitude that did not follow the dominating vision but chose the perspective of the underling. Against the standardisation, technologising and mediatisation of the world, they too had to choose between adaptation and the loss of their own culture, between assimilation and resistance.

To make recognition of these artists possible it was necessary to detach information about their works from the orthodox doctrine and interpretations of western art history. An interesting observation is that that information was first circulated via the exchange network of global art biennials, and only afterwards via academic channels, art museums and the art market. In recent years we have been working on this narrative at WIELS and subjected various paradigmatic artists to both an empathic and a critical reading. Alina Szapocznikow's show and the exhibition 'Body Talk: Feminism, Sexuality and the Body in the Work of Six African Women Artists' are the most relevant examples, but the same vision also underlied the exhibitions of works by Felix Gonzalez-Torres, Francis Alÿs, Nasreen Mohamedi, Monir Shahroudy Farmanfarmaian, Yto Barrada, Wangechi Mutu and Akram Zaatari.

Over the past decades Brussels, like most metropolises, has changed from a medium-sized city to a hybrid multiform city that, in addition to a continuous stream of financial exchange and trade, includes within its borders a concentration of population groups with their own particular longings and expectations. As the capital of Belgium and the headquarters of NATO, and since the permanent establishment here, in around 2005, of the centres of decision of the European Union, this diverse Brussels is for all these administrative authorities the ideal place in which to establish a building or institution with a symbolic function, where rituals of political representation can take place. The muses of a globalised culture could function in this as a catalyst, background or historical anchor for dialogue, rather than ceremonies and commemorations. Many cities have chosen a 'signature' architecture with which their contemporary art museums can draw attention to themselves. With its late twentieth and early twenty-first-century monument architecture, a city demonstrates that it does not want to lag behind, that it is innovative, is participating in globalisation. It thereby expresses a future-oriented identity and its association with the international main-stream and periphery.

It is therefore strange, to say the least, that precisely in the capital of Europe, after many expansions and reorganisations of administration and delegations, with the exception of the House of European History, not a single plan has been put forward, neither at communal level nor at federal level, to present the city via an arts museum. Brussels has at its disposal representative public and private collections, several sorts of festivals, from grassroots to the prestigious, but has not advanced a single initiative that has had the ambition to gather and reflect on ideas and artistic and cultural expressions with a global dimension. It is striking to observe that a city where so much western power is concentrated is not participating in the global race towards cultural image-building.

Could Brussels, in the heart of Europe, be striving after a different sort of global aura, a soft power, which concentrates more on immaterial art and stimulates the dissemination of ideas? Or is the lack of ambition for an arts museum rather the result of the sheer realisation that in our age, no collection or museum can still make a claim to encyclopedic completeness, representativity and, to a certain extent, totality? Today it is virtually impossible – and moreover geopolitically and ideologically undesirable – to achieve the representativeness of a world museum, a 'universal museum' with a diachronic, transhistorical collection devoted to the 'major' and 'minor' civilisations. A centre of power such as that of the European Union would then ultimately reflect such a museum, following the example of the former imperial superpowers. Thanks to the recent increase in the number of museums and their 'global' acquisition policy, the rarity of exceptional artworks, towering prices on the art market and limited public purchasing budgets, striving after representativity has become illusory.

We could applaud the fact that governments are not going along with the dynamics of a bidding war around the aseptic symbols of a global and interchangeable culture and image politics, and that governments decide, in terms of contemporary art, to abandon their own acquisition policy in favour of varieties of collaboration with private collections or with 'the big five' among the global museums.[1] The challenge here lies no less in striving after completion or listing a multicultural variety, but the objective is to promote awareness: in earlier times how did new patterns and metaphors emerge of open borders and language and culture exchange, stimuli for a radically equivalent ecology?

The designing of a collective meeting place for many heterogeneous transnational and transcultural identities would be a suitable programme for a future museum of contemporary art in the capital of Europe. An exhibition such as 'The Absent Museum' can function as a blueprint, as an exercise to help shape the programme of such a museum, starting out from the reality with which all European cities are confronted today on a cultural, artistic and intellectual level. Artists and thinkers can work on an overall formulation; those involved in creating the exhibition can research common local problems. From the experiences of interdisciplinary experimental arts from the 1960s, we can learn once more how to play with public space, how to embody language again and how to take urban reality as a concrete starting point for human interchange. A collaboration with the interdisciplinary Kunstenfestivaldesarts was therefore ideal and fitting. With the achievements of innovative theatre, language and dance forms as a starting point, one can look for a way of bending aesthetic indifference, the empty signifier, the floating detached sign, to a confrontation and positioning with regard to reality, and to close the theoretical gap between thinking and speaking.

The performances that lead to a new imagination will certainly be influenced by popular culture, which today is intertwined with mass culture. Yet the distribution of that new imagination cannot be given over to the culture of mass consumption and technological visual industry. The imagination belongs in occupied and embodied narratives, which are indissolubly connected with personal and collective biographies and places. The selection of artists for this exhibition ties in with an idea that already formed the guiding principle of 'Expats & Clandestines', the first official exhibition at WIELS. At the time the starting point was the border between visibility and invisibility in public opinion about immigrant minorities; this theme corrected the habitual division, in the existing visual regime, between demonisation and idealisation of 'the other'. In the programming of WIELS there has been ongoing attention on the intercultural and transnational – as theme and programme, but also in the research of visual language and the effects of perception, whereby the turbulences of globalisation are also viewed from non-western perspectives.

Many artists who have lived a long time in Brussels constantly travel to neighbouring cities such as Amsterdam, Cologne, London and Paris, where they hold exhibitions, attend courses and teach. Naturally they closely follow events and activities and also take part in public debate. This European region comprises the megalopolises of London and Paris, crucial centres with a worldwide connectivity, and in addition to them cities such as Cologne and Amsterdam, where, as in Brussels, very large groups of immigrants live, who, through their economic and other activities, are open to cultural and artistic exchanges, digressions and debates on a world level. The capital of Europe is an important partner in this vast region. Via its extensive network, together with the influence of the European Union, it is also the notion of Europe that is transported – a Europe that, thanks to its colonialist past, has spread its values, structures and influence across the planet.

1
The Museum of Modern Art (MoMA), New York; Tate, London; Centre Pompidou, Paris; Museo Nacional Centro de Arte Reina Sofía, Madrid; Moderna Museet, Stockholm.

Although by limiting our selection of artists to this region we risk being suspected of a new sort of neo-Eurocentrism, we have, nevertheless, chosen to concentrate on local connections that can be traced across the planet and in time. Our intention will become clear only after several repetitions of an exhibition with a similar objective. Common patterns will gradually emerge at many places that point to a paradigm shift. In the expectation of achieving that, an exhibition is the ideal moment, firstly, for artists to create intellectually meaningful poetic expressions with their installations, and secondly, for critical viewer-thinkers to crank up the public debate with their comments. No one better describes this horizon to which we are looking forward than Édouard Glissant in *Une nouvelle région du monde*: 'Is beauty both the reflection, the sign within the work, and the intuition, the premonition in us, of this treatment of a difference which has found confirmation by opening up to the probable and of this attraction of a difference which will surpass itself by offering itself in the same way? Treatment turns into attraction, it is the grand circus of the world, and Being, as we have surmised and repeated, is at once the absolute cognition and recognition of their encounter.'[2]

The confrontation with the temporality of other continents and developments that have their own pace leads us to a critical questioning of the European self-image and self-awareness. The selected artists each have their own cultural-specific voice and play their own role in the global artistic imaginative space. From their output we have jointly chosen works that display a certain dissatisfaction and frustration as their theme, works that summon up discomfort and fear or introduce problems that are experienced as controversial or threatening. Via their controversial themes, these artists explore what critical form their 'true' art practice can still assume in the light of propaganda, manipulation and rhetoric argumentation. It is easier to realise the artwork as a poetical-critical stance from a look back on the recent past than from the flickering present. That is why global issues from today's news were combined with recent historical positions of local artists in works that present lastingly controversial and unresolved moments from recent history.

As soon as we begin to sum up and compare sensitive issues in the recent histories of European countries, we encounter more similarities than differences. Common patterns emerge, each with a specific interpretation but still patterns that point to a fundamental commonality, which has become evident through comparable historical events and ensuing debates and controversies. An awareness is taking place here with regard to history. The ultimate metaphor of that awareness is the museum. And is it precisely in that awareness process that the art museum should remain aloof? How does history relate to the raw material, the past? History emerges from an awareness in a moment of danger. As Walter Benjamin declared in his essay 'Theses on the Philosophy of History', 'To articulate the past historically does not mean to recognize it "the way it really was" (Ranke). It means to seize hold of a memory as it flashes up at a moment of danger.'[3]

In the light of the current crises of value in the European space, the development of an instrument for self-analysis and self-criticism is urgently needed. That instrument must be able to sound out deeper, beyond the miasmas of current events, in order to trace recurrent patterns of the common property. This exhibition can develop a discourse for this, on the basis of artworks and authors. It is a temporary and symbolic manifestation, a blueprint for an open, artistic-intellectual critical space that gives a museum for contemporary art the basic elements to become a place where difficult debates can take place in a serene atmosphere – which is in fact the definition of the free public space.

2
Édouard Glissant,
*Une nouvelle région
du monde*, Esthétique I,
Paris 2006, pp. 45–46.

3
Walter Benjamin,
'Theses on the
Philosophy of
History' (1940) in
Illuminations, ed. and
with intro. by Hannah
Arendt, trans. Harry
Zohn, New York 1968,
p. 255.

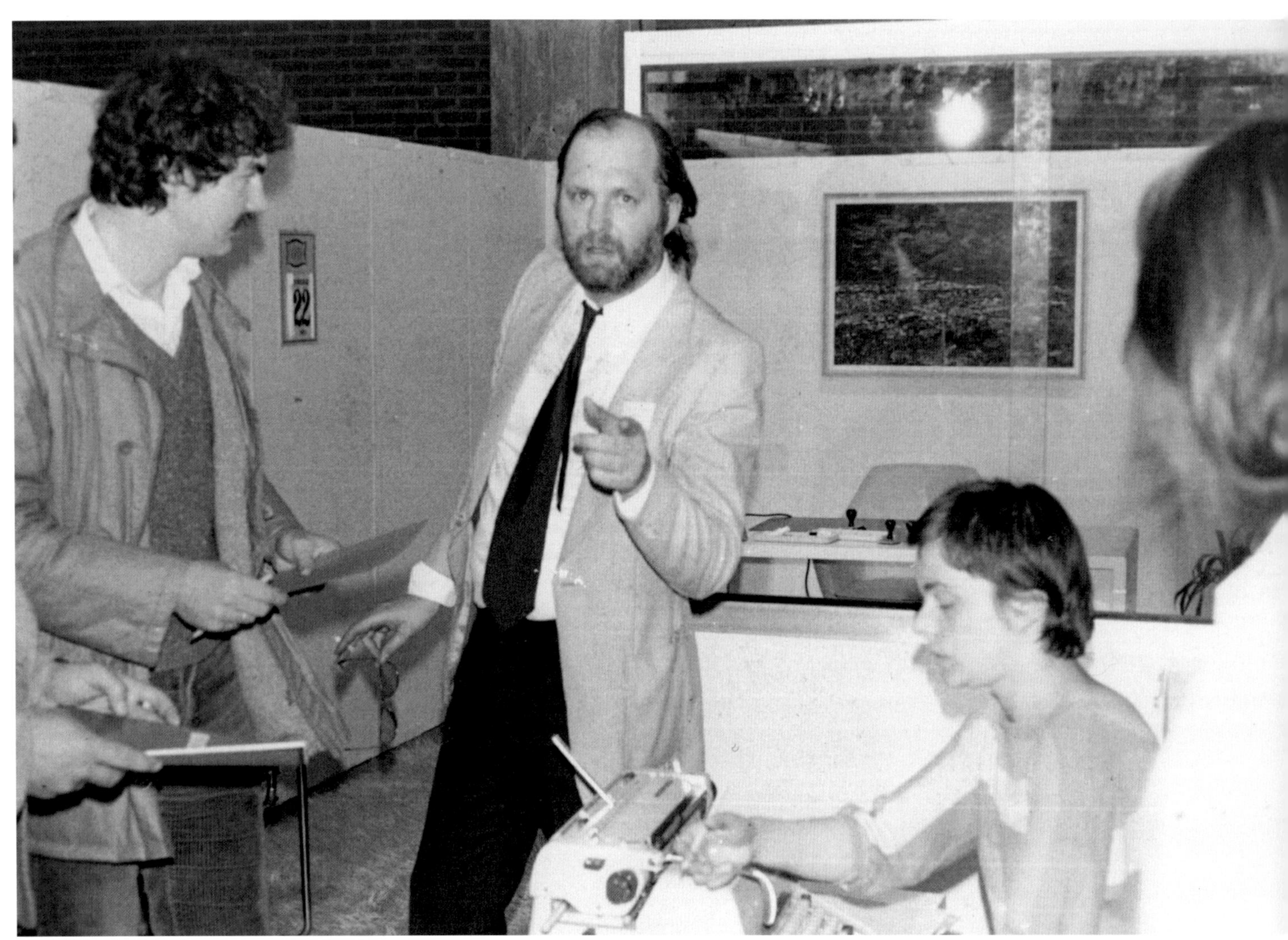

Guillaume Bijl, *Beroepsheroriëntatiecentrum*, views of the installation and 'tableau vivant' happening during the exhibition opening, Cultureel Centrum De Warande, Turnhout, 1980.

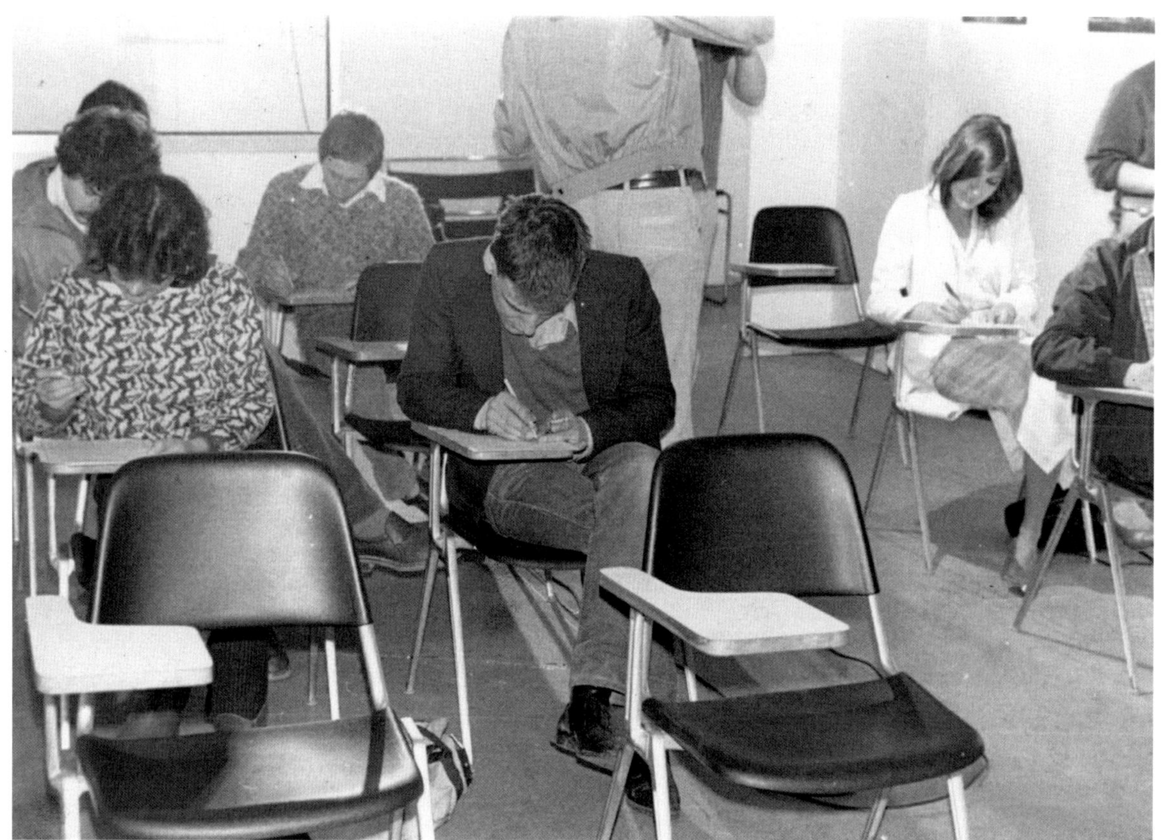

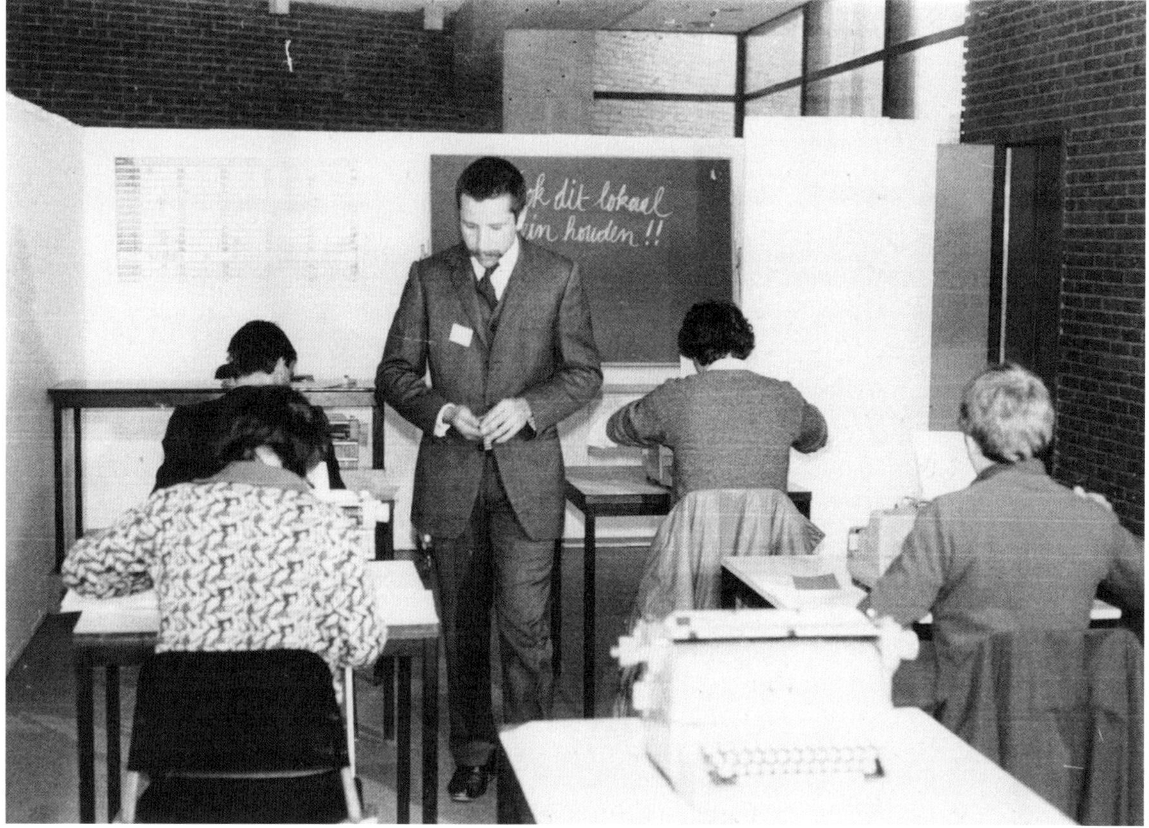
k dit lokael
in houden !!

ART LIQUIDATION project.
BY ORDER OF THE STATE

— Because of the non-functional character of art.

— Because of the lack of space, with which several ministries have recently
  had to contend.

— Because of the uneconomic aspect of the art trade, in which tax evasion is
  the order of the day.

— Because of the annually increasing expenses of the Culture Ministry.

— Because of the growing climate of crisis, for which an urgent solution must
  be found.

— Because of the degrading character of new art trends.

— Because of the anarchistic leanings of many contemporary artists.

WE FIND OURSELVES COMPELLED TO CLOSE ALL MUSEUMS and to turn them, as rapidly
as possible, into a space suitable for more practical objectives.
ART GALLERIES WILL FOLLOW; with the same objective.

THEY WILL BE REPLACED BY, among others:

— revenue offices (department of the ministry of Finance),
— driving schools (department of the ministry of Bridges and Roads),
— retraining centres (department of the ministry of Employment and Work),
— hospital wards (department of the ministry of Health),
— military training centres (department of the ministry of National Defence),
— career guidance offices (department of the ministry of Education),
— databanks (department of the ministry of Justice).

— From the perspective of this measure, in April 1979 Galerie Ruimte Z in
  Antwerp was transformed into DRIVING SCHOOL Z (department of the ministry
  of Bridges and Roads).

— From the perspective of this same measure, part of the exhibition space B
  of the cultural centre De Warande in Turnhout was transformed in May 1980
  into a CAREER GUIDANCE CENTRE (department of the ministry of Employment
  and Work).

— From the perspective of this 'Art liquidation climate', the I.C.C. in
  Antwerp, as a preventive measure and out of financial necessity, has let part
  of the ground floor to a private individual who converted the exhibition
  space in June 1980 into his shoe shop, Chaussures Icécé.

Guillaume Bijl, 'Project m.b.t. Kunstliquidatie' (1977) in *1980*, exhibition catalogue, ICC/Internationaal Cultureel Centrum,
Antwerp, 1980.

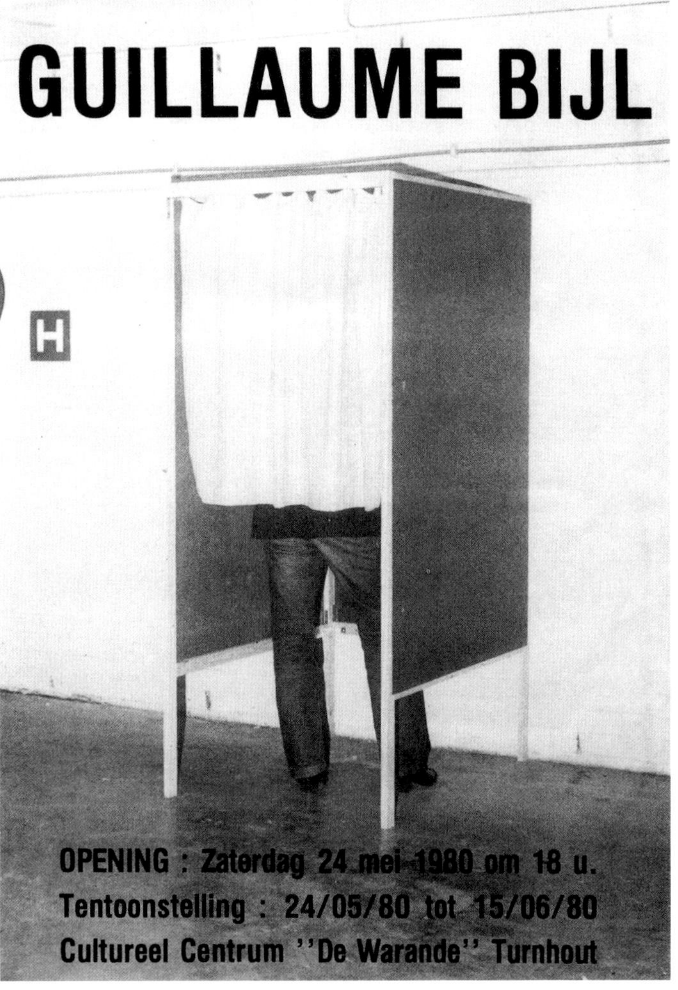

Guillaume Bijl, exhibition poster, Cultureel Centrum De Warande, Turnhout, 1980.

Guillaume Bijl

Guillaume Bijl (b. 1946 in Antwerp) started out, in the 1970s, making text works that described scenarios and scenes. These were soon followed by what he called 'Art Liquidation Projects' – installations that simulated the spaces of utilitarian professions and businesses in museums or cultural centres, acting as *détournements* of the artistic activities that were branded 'useless' and closed, converting the institution into a place with a practical, social 'purpose'. In the later 'Transformation-Installations', that provocative 'anti-art' element is less emphatically present, Bijl favouring an element of surprise. However, for both categories of work he opts for illusionism in which décors and situations are transposed from an everyday reality and economy into spaces that are reserved for art, such as a gallery or a museum room.

The trompe-l'oeil effect of the hyperrealist simulations causes a shock of recognition in visitors but also a surprise: they find themselves in an employment centre, a recruitment agency, a psychiatric hospital – but their logic is of a different order since they question the function of the artworks. Two systems of value are combined, a formal and an informal one, as a result of which the logic of one is not compatible with the syntax of the other. Bijl defines reality as a simulation, a fiction, and makes practical demands on the installation. Rendering art spaces functional is equivalent to the surrendering by western society of specialised spaces for aesthetic judgement, a pessimistic prediction of the influence that the logic of the spectacle and economic profit exert in the field of serious art institutes.

Sculpture trouvée (1980) is one of the few installations that exist from Bijl's early years. It is an exact replica of the voting booth that was used at the time for general elections in Belgium. By installing it in an art space, Bijl shows that freedom of choice and freedom of expression are basic conditions for art and the experience of art. Universal suffrage, by means of which citizens choose their representatives for administrating the country, is a basic principle of parliamentary democracy. For the individual, voting is indeed a modest but effective way of practising personal freedom.

DS

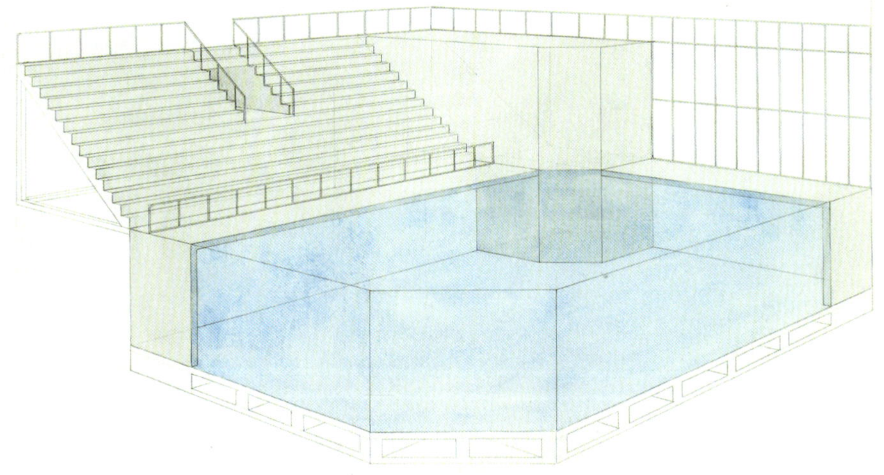

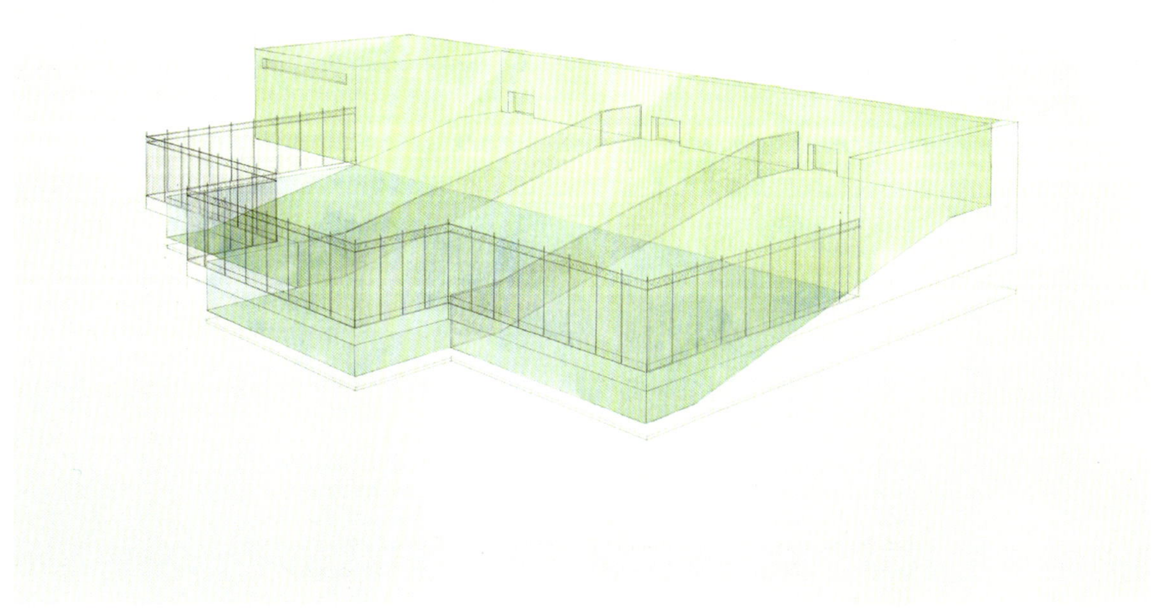

Wesley Meuris, *Aqua Theatre: The Intelligent, Acrobatic Moves of the Bottlenose Dolphin*, 2006, 78 × 84 cm, pencil and watercolour on paper.

Wesley Meuris, *Crocodile Range: A Freshwater Swamp in the Wetlands*, 2006, 78 × 84 cm, pencil and watercolour on paper.

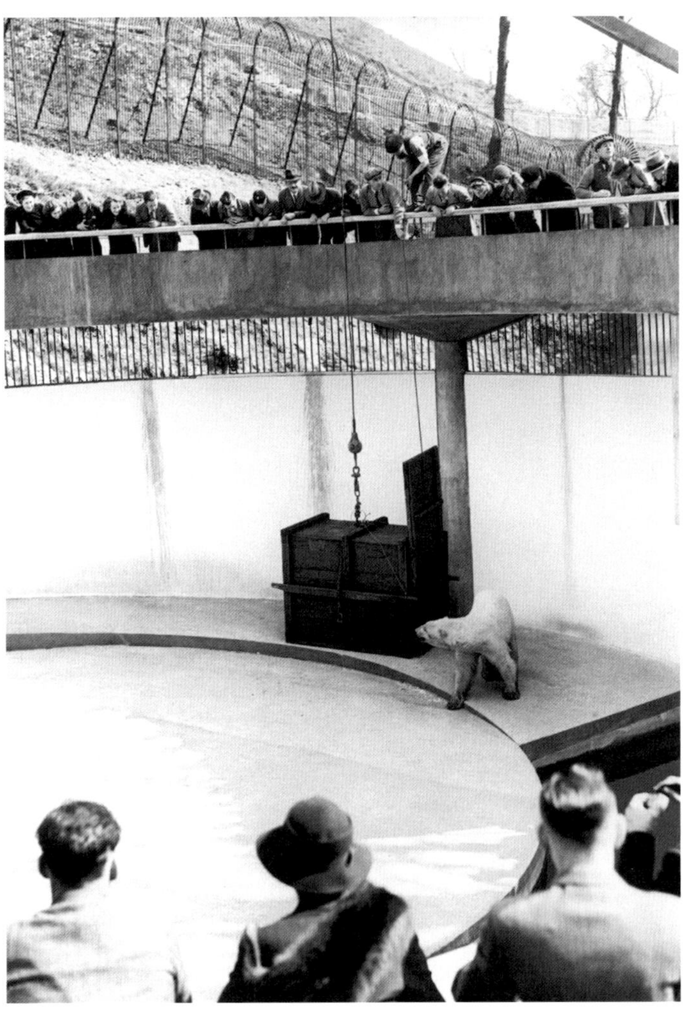

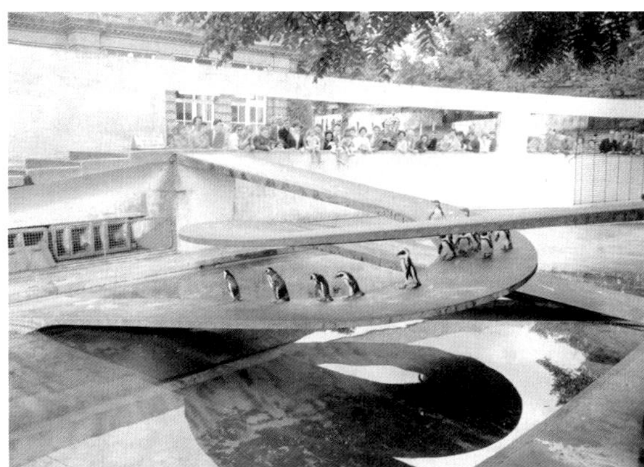

Polar Bear Pit, Dudley
Zoological Gardens,
Worcestershire,
1951. Designed and
built by Berthold
Lubetkin and Tecton
in 1935–37.

Wesley Meuris

Wesley Meuris (b. 1977 in Lier, Belgium) is fascinated by the human urge to rationalise, name, classify and present. In his installations he studies the architecture and infrastructure of museums, exhibition spaces and institutes where various objects are preserved and exhibited. He researches the field of tension between the scientific starting point and the visually attractive presentation, between rational, aesthetic and humane considerations. This also holds for the animal enclosures that he designed for the project *Zoological Classification*, which he launched in 2004: architectural constructions that were initially conceived as a scientifically responsible, artificial translation of the natural habitat, but at the same time met the need to preserve, catalogue, exhibit and observe. His designs for optimised animal shelters are observed especially through a specific 'disciplining' gaze: even though they are designed in an idealistic way and intended to enable the unbridled and spontaneous behaviour of animals, they nevertheless correspond to what Michel Foucault calls controlling and disciplinary institutions. 'Is it surprising that prisons resemble factories, schools, barracks, hospitals, which all resemble prisons?'[1]

With his designs for cages and containers, Meuris approaches the experimental constructivist theories about the experience of interior spaces and geometric forms that were developed in the Vkhutemas art and technical school in Moscow. Berthold Lubetkin (1901–1990) applied the same principles in his designs for animal enclosures in London Zoo and in Dudley Zoo, for which he studied the behaviour of specific animal sorts. Meuris too starts out in his designs for well-defined sorts that live in specific biotopes and circumstances, and takes into account the ensuing demands: safety, visibility for visitors and observers, comfort for the animals through the imitation of their natural habitat. But all that merely confirms the gap between object and spectator, because protection also means surveillance, observation means control, and the imitation of the natural environment is artificial and abstract. Meuris here also implicitly raises questions about the way in which institutional power functions: what forms does it take and what procedures does it follow in the exercise of its authority?

DS

1
Michel Foucault,
*Discipline and Punish:
The Birth of the Prison*,
trans. Alan Sheridan,
New York 1995, p. 228.

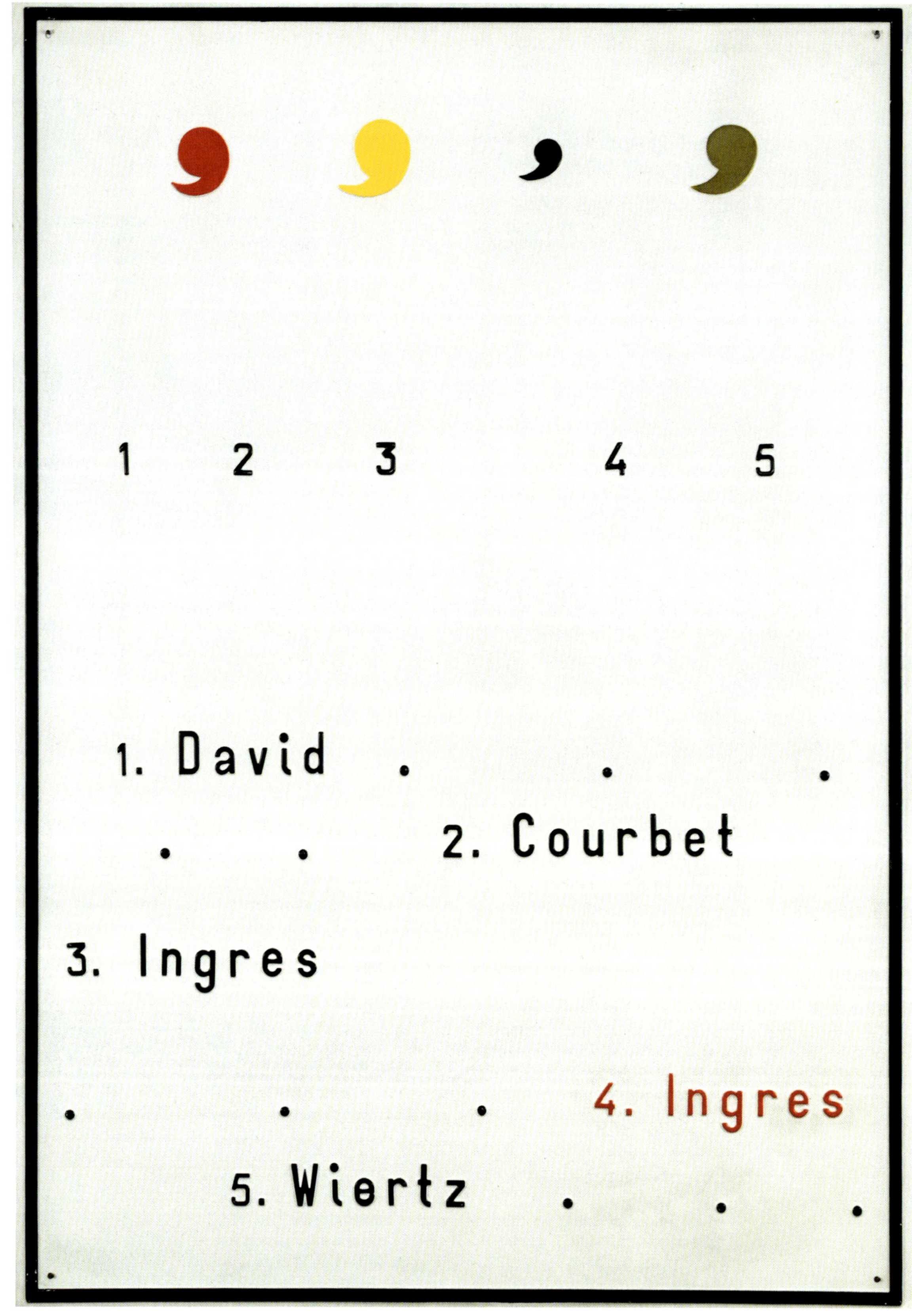

Marcel Broodthaers, *1. David 2. Courbet 3. Ingres 4. Ingres 5. Wiertz*, 1972, 119.4 × 83.8 cm, painted vacuum-formed plastic plate.

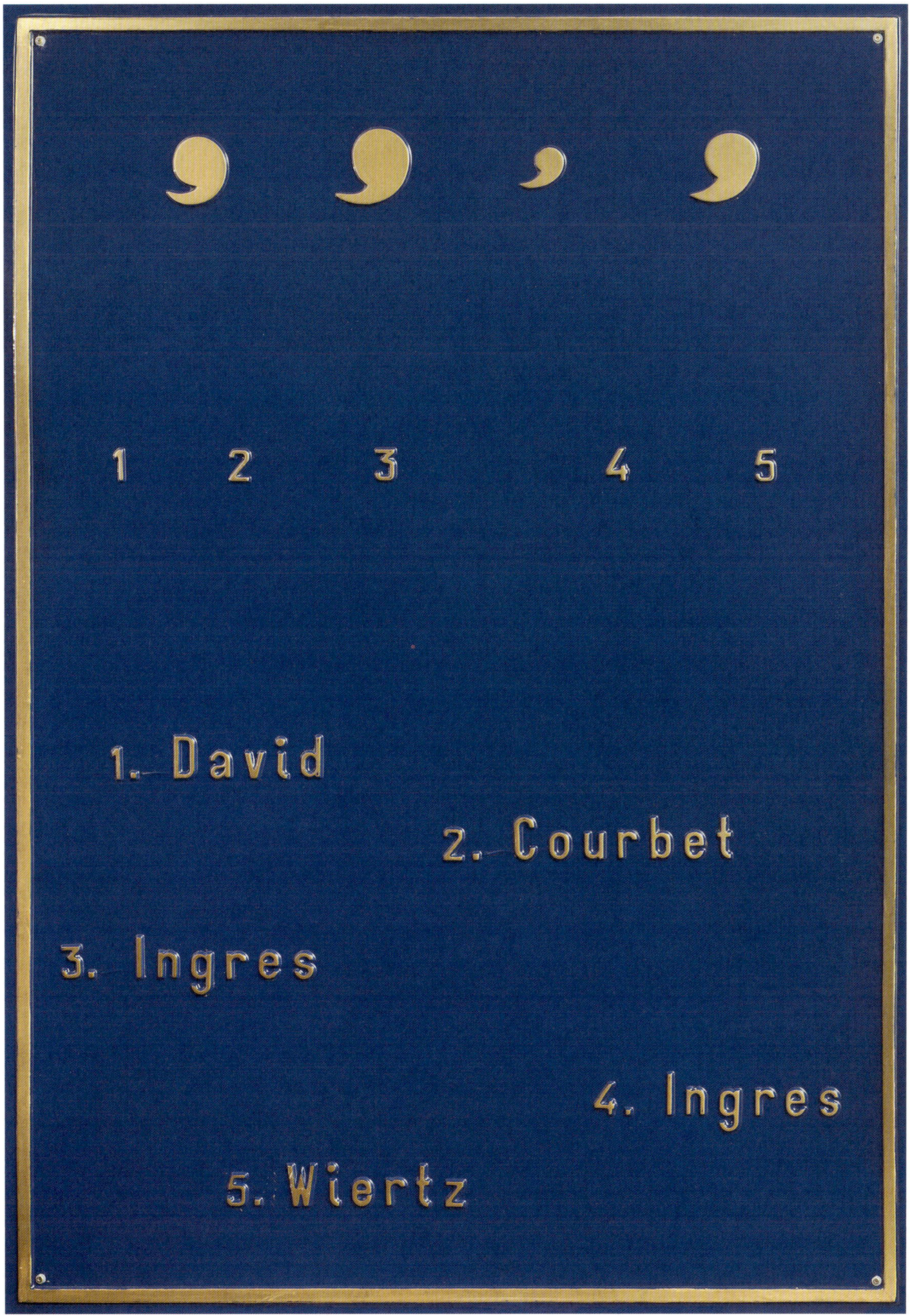

Marcel Broodthaers, *1. David 2. Courbet 3. Ingres 4. Ingres 5. Wiertz*, 1971, 120 × 86 cm, painted vacuum-formed plastic plate.

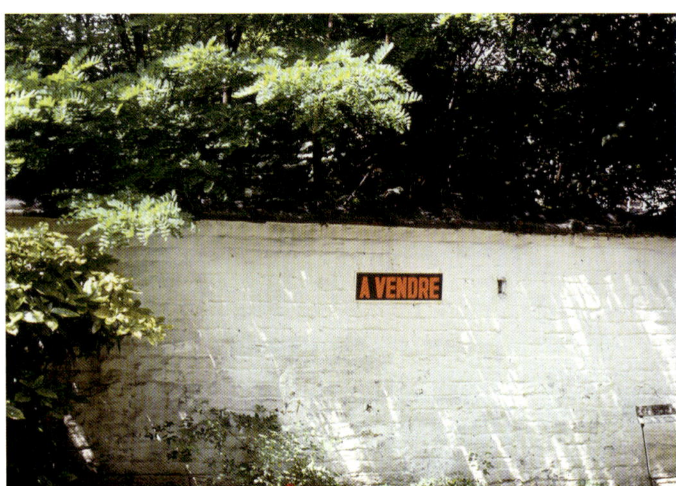

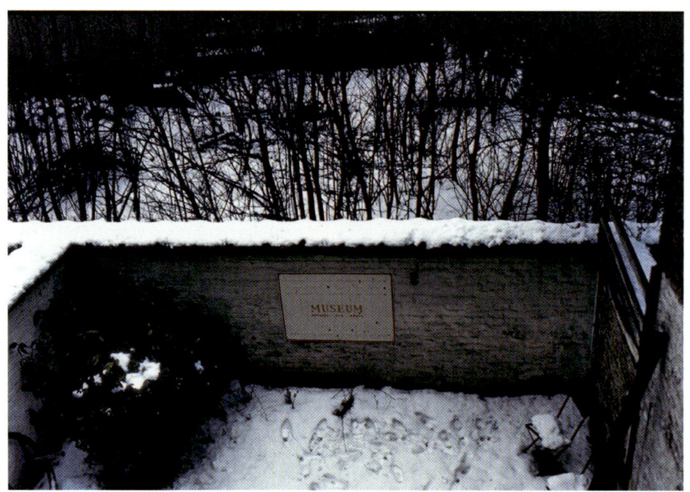

Le jardin du Musée d'Art Moderne, Département des Aigles, Section XIXe siècle, 1968–69. Photo copyright Maria Gilissen.

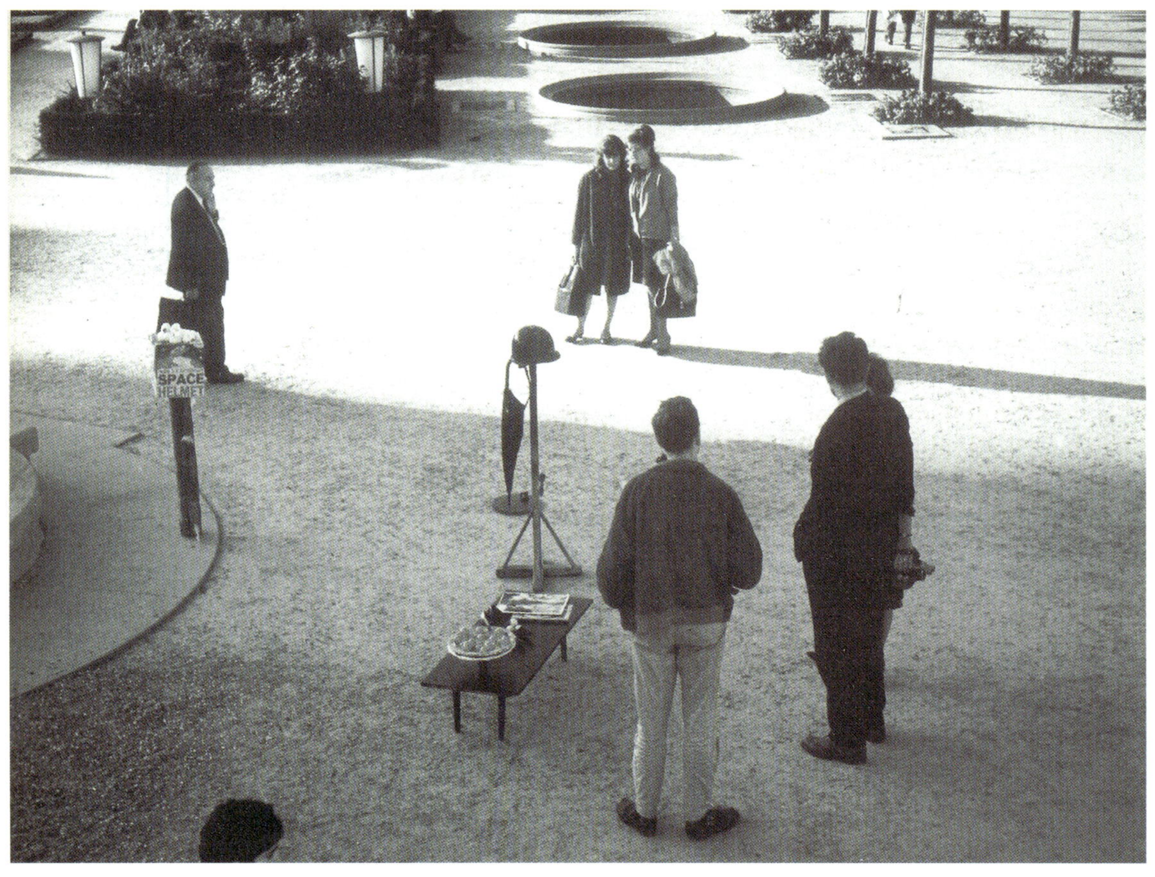

Exposition surprise, Parc du Mont des Arts, Bruxelles, September 1964. Photo copyright Maria Gilissen.

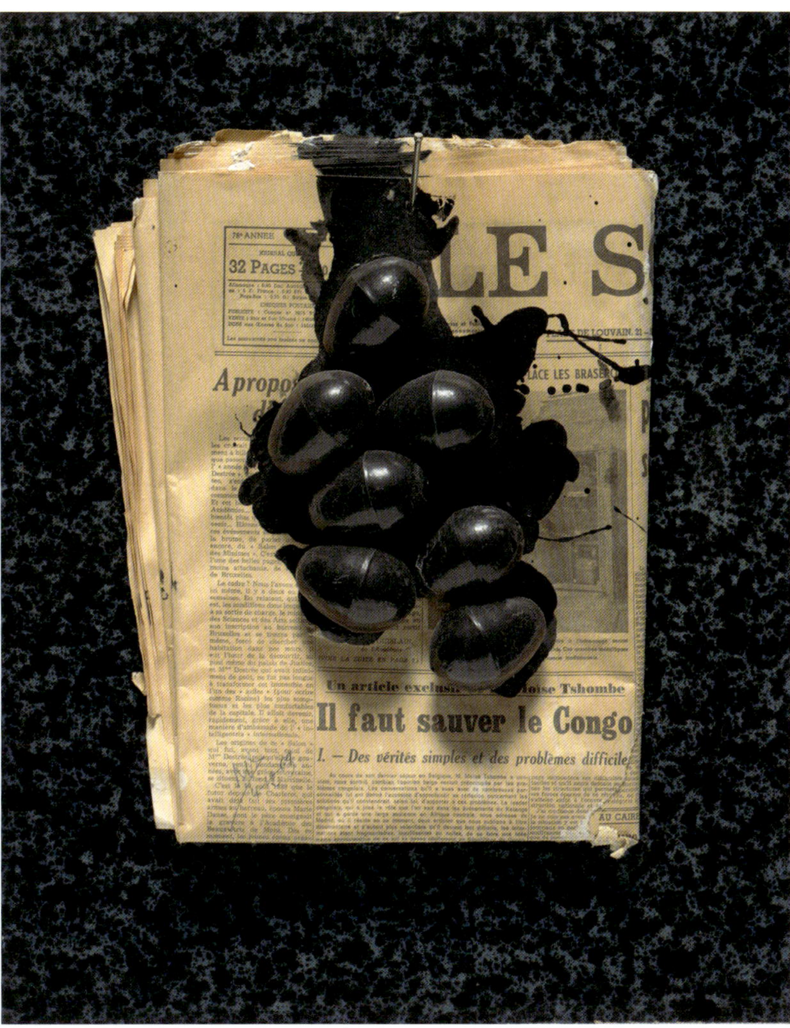

Marcel Broodthaers, *Le problème noir en Belgique*, 1963–64, 48.1 × 39.1 × 6.4 cm, newspaper, manufactured eggs, paint and nail on found decorative paper board.

Marcel Broodthaers

Between 1968 and 1970, the year he left Brussels definitively and moved to Düsseldorf, Marcel Broodthaers (Brussels 1924–1976 Cologne) worked on a series of some thirty-five vacuum-formed plastic reliefs featuring all sorts of inscriptions, numerals, symbols and other signs, with always a positive and a negative image. They belonged to the new category of multiples that challenged the status of the unique and authentic artwork. With their shiny surface, the plates complied entirely with the idea of progress and with utopian aspirations for a fusion of art, technology and social interaction, which pop art and nouveau réalisme championed. The cheap new material and the industrial production process also lent themselves to the manufacture of art in large editions in order to bring them within reach of the masses.

That democratisation would radically alter the perception and the impact of artwork for the people.

In 1968, Broodthaers also created his famous fictional museum, *Musée d'Art Moderne, Département des Aigles*, in his home and studio in Brussels. That concept, an imitation of a one-man institute, set up in the twilight of the May–June protests, was the setting for debates about the role of art in a changing society. Over the course of four years he developed this idea in various spaces and structured it with different departments. With this initiative he drew attention to the role of the museum as a space for perception and analysis, study and method, and also for discussion and the critical questioning of reality. From the *Section littéraire* of his museum he communicated

with friends and acquaintances by means of open letters. In these pamphlet-like writings, as well as formulating political ideas he also put forward opinions about art, such as the division between free, poetical art and art as an object and commodity in a commercialised society.

Such an idea also underlies the plastic reliefs. They constitute a form of poetic writing or sculpting with language and signs, but at the same time act as an intrusive, direct advertising 'messenger'. With their three-dimensional details heightened by paint, they belong to Broodthaers' most explicitly painterly works. The reliefs can be hung as paintings, but also as signboards, sterile plastic imitations of advertising technology. Broodthaers defines the words, signs and symbols that they contain as 'rebuses':

their reading is impeded by the graphic technique, which makes the text visible as image and the image visible as text. The letters and signs bulge in the material, in a sense turning them into 'empty' signs or signifiers. Thus these 'Industrial Poems', as he called them, bear witness both to the directness of the image and to the distance of the language; they have the shape of a rebus that, as a result of the production process, consists of empty signs. They are at once signboard and painting, a commentary on production and the production process of language and communication, in a system that is dominated by forms of business and commercial interaction.

DS

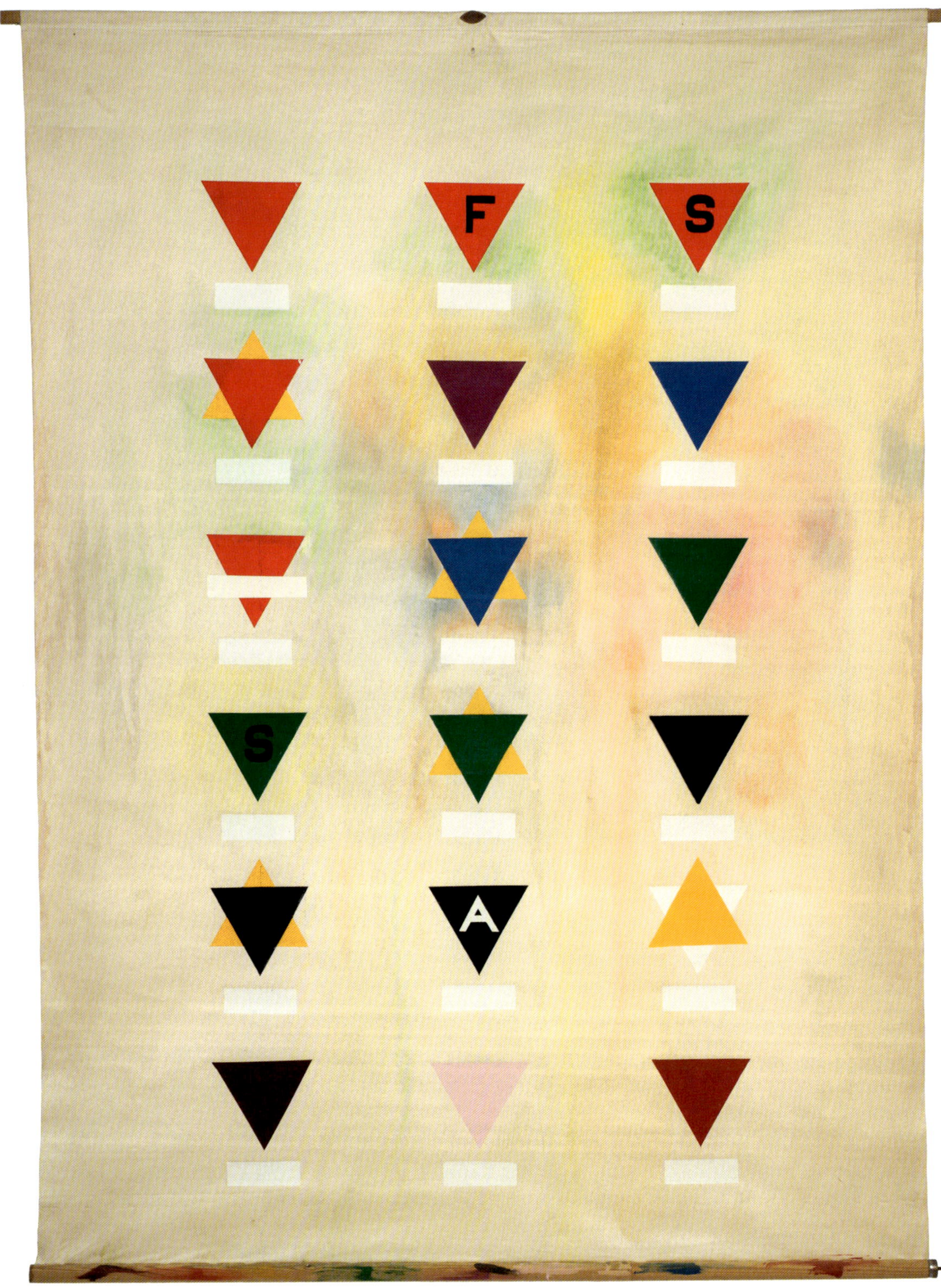

Jef Geys, *Sterrendoek*, 1965, 170 × 140 cm, oil and pastel on canvas.

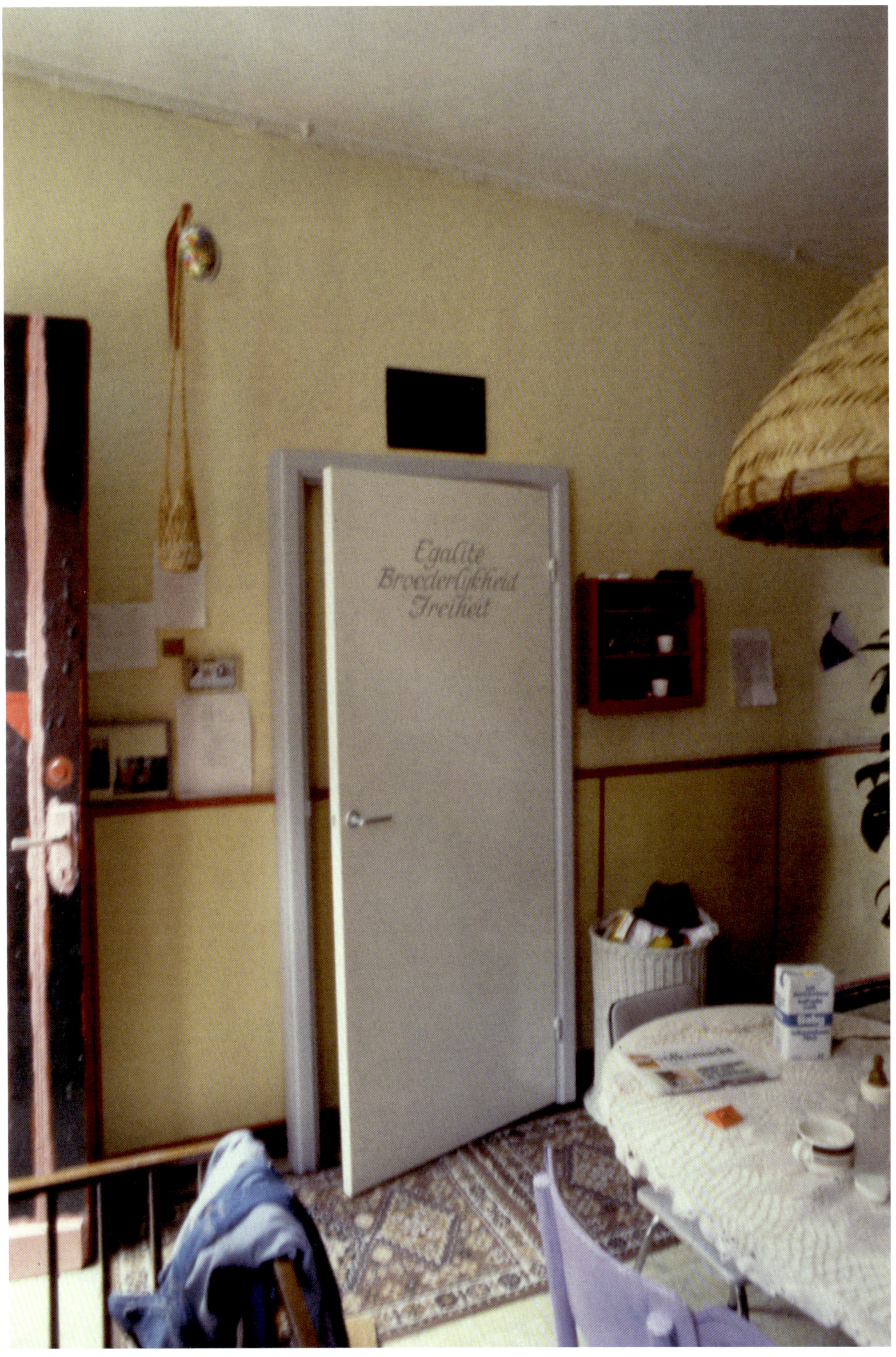

Jef Geys, *Égalité, Broederlijkheid, Freiheit*, 1986, 213.5 × 99 × 11.5 cm, wooden door and frame, paint.

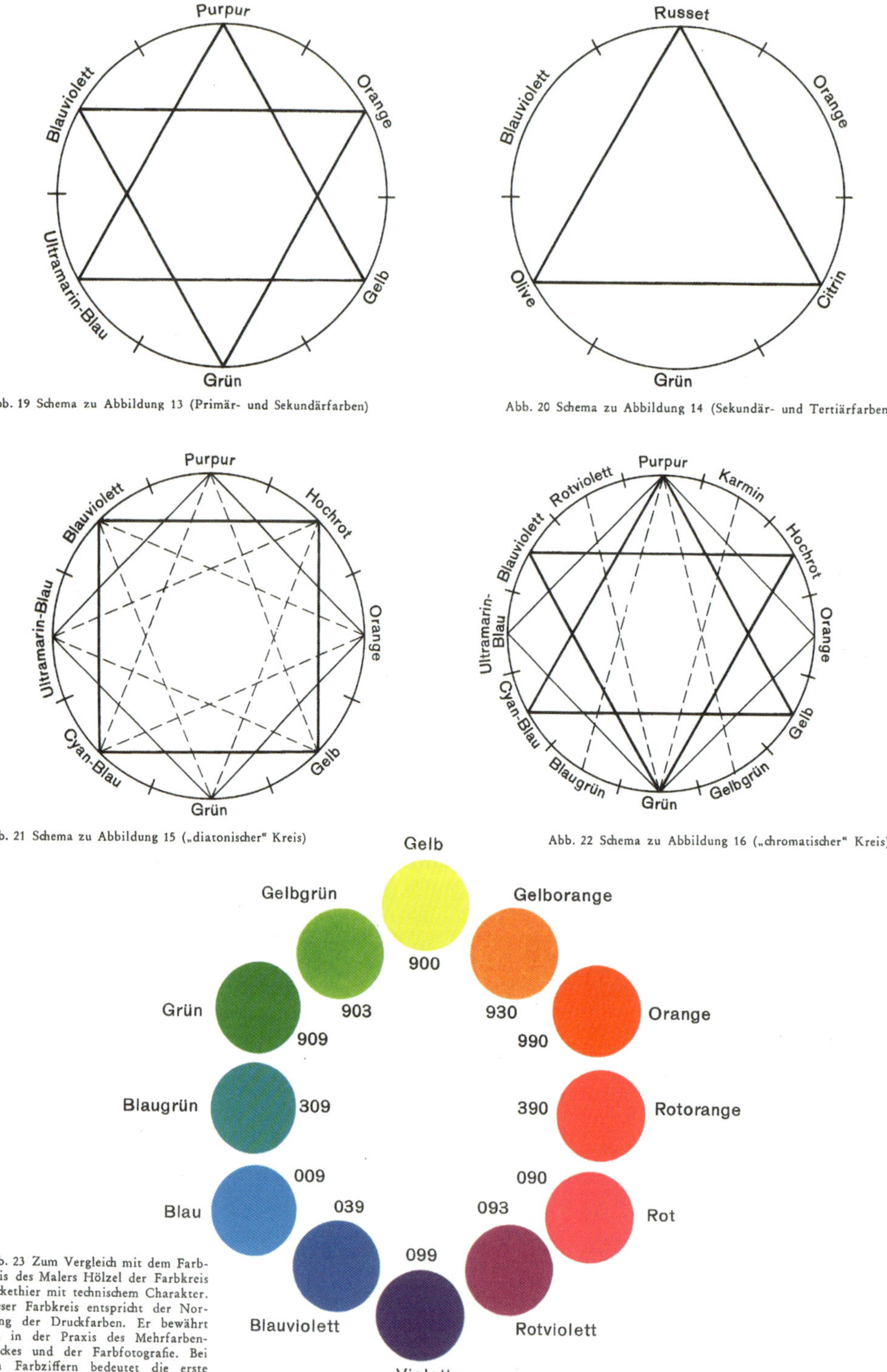

Abb. 19 Schema zu Abbildung 13 (Primär- und Sekundärfarben)

Abb. 20 Schema zu Abbildung 14 (Sekundär- und Tertiärfarben)

Abb. 21 Schema zu Abbildung 15 („diatonischer" Kreis)

Abb. 22 Schema zu Abbildung 16 („chromatischer" Kreis)

Abb. 23 Zum Vergleich mit dem Farbkreis des Malers Hölzel der Farbkreis Hickethier mit technischem Charakter. Dieser Farbkreis entspricht der Normung der Druckfarben. Er bewährt sich in der Praxis des Mehrfarbendruckes und der Farbfotografie. Bei den Farbziffern bedeutet die erste Ziffer den Gelbanteil der Farbe (9 = voller Farbton), die zweite den Rotanteil, die dritte den Blauanteil.

ill. 1

Excerpt from *Jef Geys: Architectuur als begrenzing*, exhibition catalogue, São Paulo Art Biennial, Ghent 1991.

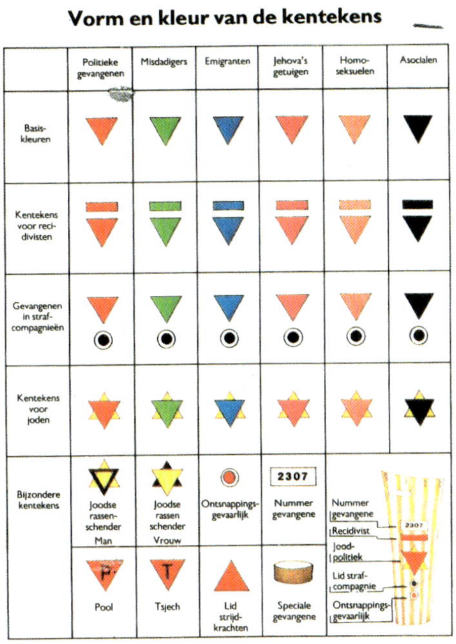

Vorm en kleur van de kentekens

	Politieke gevangenen	Misdadigers	Emigranten	Jehova's getuigen	Homo-seksuelen	Asocialen
Basis-kleuren						
Kentekens voor reci-divisten						
Gevangenen in straf-compagnieën						
Kentekens voor joden						
Bijzondere kentekens	Joodse rassen-schender Man / Pool	Joodse rassen-schender Vrouw / Tsjech	Ontsnappings-gevaarlijk / Lid strijd-krachten	Nummer gevangene / Speciale gevangene	Nummer gevangene / Recidivist / Jood-politiek / Lid straf-compagnie / Ontsnappings-gevaarlijk	

ill. 28

Jef Geys

Opening up for discussion the border between serious, academic art and popular, entertaining, visual culture is a constant in the work of Jef Geys (b. 1934 in Leopoldsburg). The post-war period in which he started producing work was still dominated by the division between formalist abstraction and expressive figuration. New movements emerged in the early 1960s, such as pop art and *nouveau réalisme*, which thematised objects and images from consumer society as motifs in visual art. Geys observes the successive trends and tendencies in thought, politics and art, and launches alternative proposals from the margins, with a lot of scepticism and the necessary humour. At the same time, he demonstrates the insufficiency of language and signs, and the slight disconnect between them; he deconstructs the inadequate relationship between thing, name and representation, and replaces it with an intertextual method that unsettles the claim of totality of hegemonial thought.

Captivated on the one hand by avant-garde geometry and the use of forms standardised through repetition, on the other he develops a sustained interest for images as vehicles for knowledge transfer. His professional activity as a teacher of visual education offers him the opportunity to explore the borders between artistic and everyday reality, between sophisticated visual and artistic views and the utilitarian-didactic function of images.

Geys has always had an interest in the artistic heritage of constructivism and the Bauhaus. In the mid-1960s he made several works in which he methodically used geometric forms and primary colours, like comments on the neutral composition of hard-edge abstraction. This enabled him to map the geometric patterns that underlie the perception of reality, and to try them out on images of mass media, testing their capacity to normalise and erode everything. Geys observes with interest the didactic image and form systems that map out visible reality, but becomes suspicious when intuition hardens into a system or appeals to a mythological legitimacy.

'Precisely during the period 1960–63, I was preoccupied with such things as "form" and what made "form" look different: camouflage and mimicry – in short, the hidden, the things that one seems to see. Images–forms that are shown in a certain way – i.e. in a studied "correct" way, under "correct" guidance, embedded in a "correct" strategy – are readily accepted, as if they have existed all the time. Repetition, while creating habit, at the same time almost leaves a taste of *déjà vu*. The end result is an accepted boredom. Images–forms, no matter how strong they are, may appear perfectly normal, submitted, tame, having reached saturation point. The images are experienced as something purely "retinal", which is also the experience one is looking for: the significance underneath is kept at a distance. We are inclined to dispose of any images that cannot be used to finish our homework, as mere scenery for more important things that we supposedly have on our minds. To demonstrate this obvious wearing out of images, I started looking for basic forms with a very simple structure but a heavily loaded content. Then I discovered the identification badges prisoners had to wear in concentration camps: impersonal geometric forms in primary colours, with a cloud of personal data in contrasting pastel colours in the background. These apparently insignificant things emerging at the surface, the personal daily objects, contrasting with constructions that seemed so easy to prove, utterly confused me. So I went in search of what connected these daily and obvious banalities. I started thinking about standards.'[1]

Gleichheit, Fraternité, Vrijheid (1986) is one of the six works that Geys displayed in the context of the exhibition 'Chambres d'amis' that took place in six rooms in private homes in Ghent. In contrast to other participating artists, who for their contributions preferred homes of wealthy people, Geys showed his works in the homes of people on welfare. He painted on doors the words 'Equality, Fraternity, Liberty' – the ideals of the French Revolution and the bourgeois republic from 1789 onwards – in the three national languages of Belgium. The doors appear to be normal standard models in a frame, but once opened, the visitor faces the blind walls behind them. The intention of the exhibition was to take art outside the walls of the museum, regarded as an impressive, central, public institution. Using the inscriptions and the choice of locations, Geys shows that art is not the exclusive privilege of an elite, and also that freedom, and in particular freedom of expression, is a basic condition for the existence of art and its reception.

DS

1
Jef Geys, excerpt from 'Story' in *Jef Geys: Architectuur als begrenzing,* exh. cat., São Paulo Art Biennial, Ghent 1991, n.p.

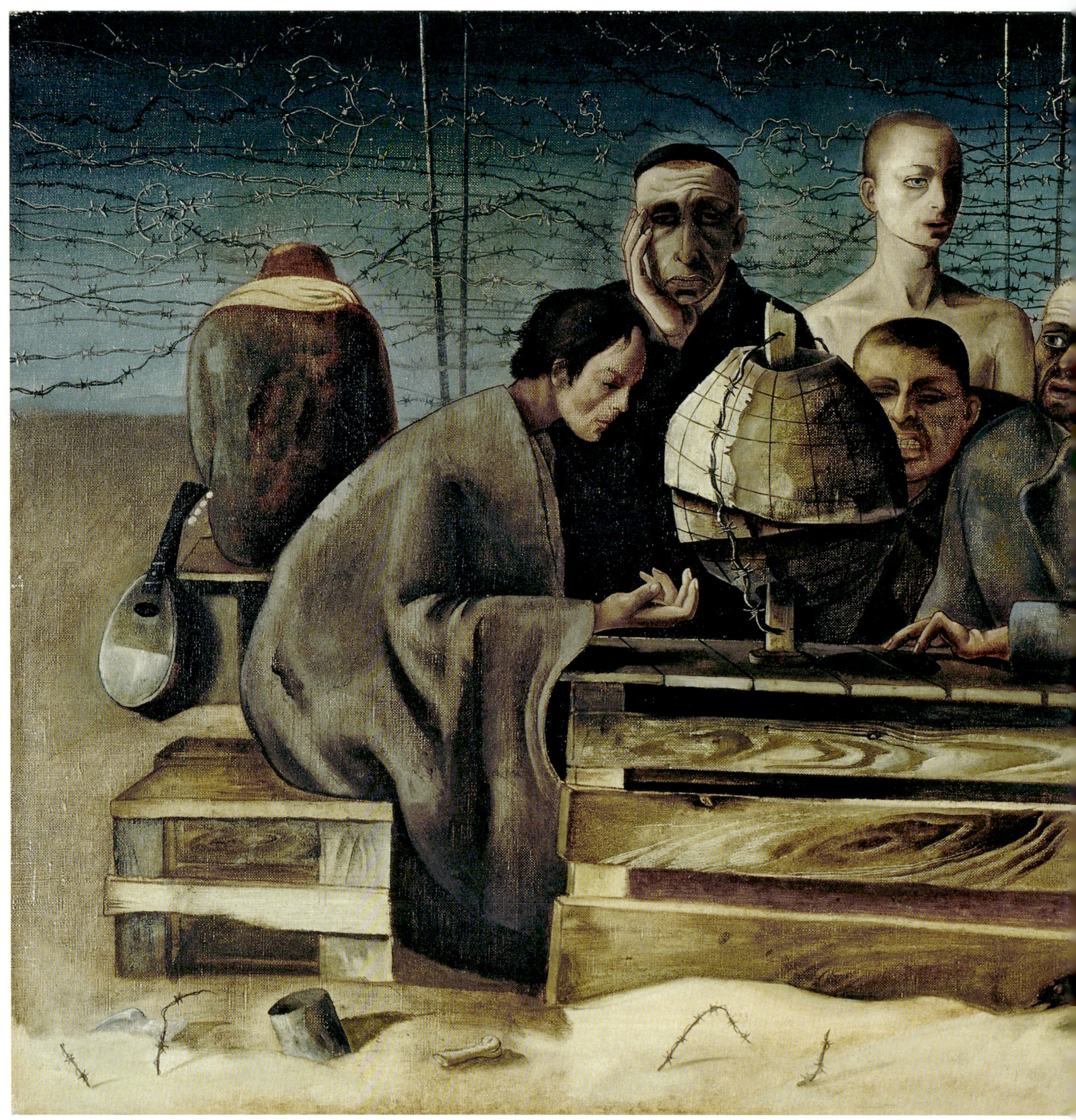

Felix Nussbaum, *St. Cyprien (Gefangene in Saint-Cyprien)*, 1942, 68 × 138 cm, oil on canvas.

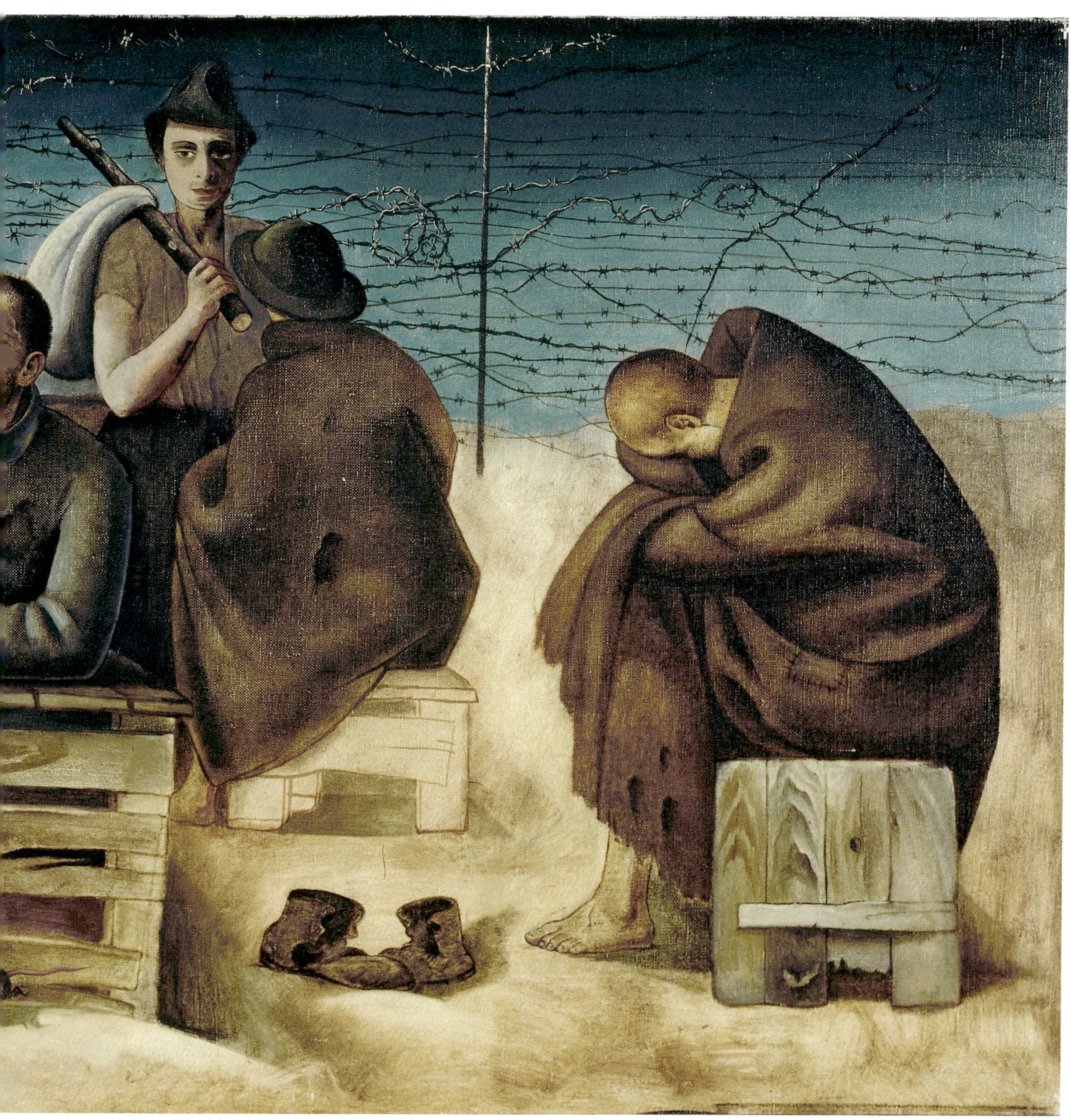

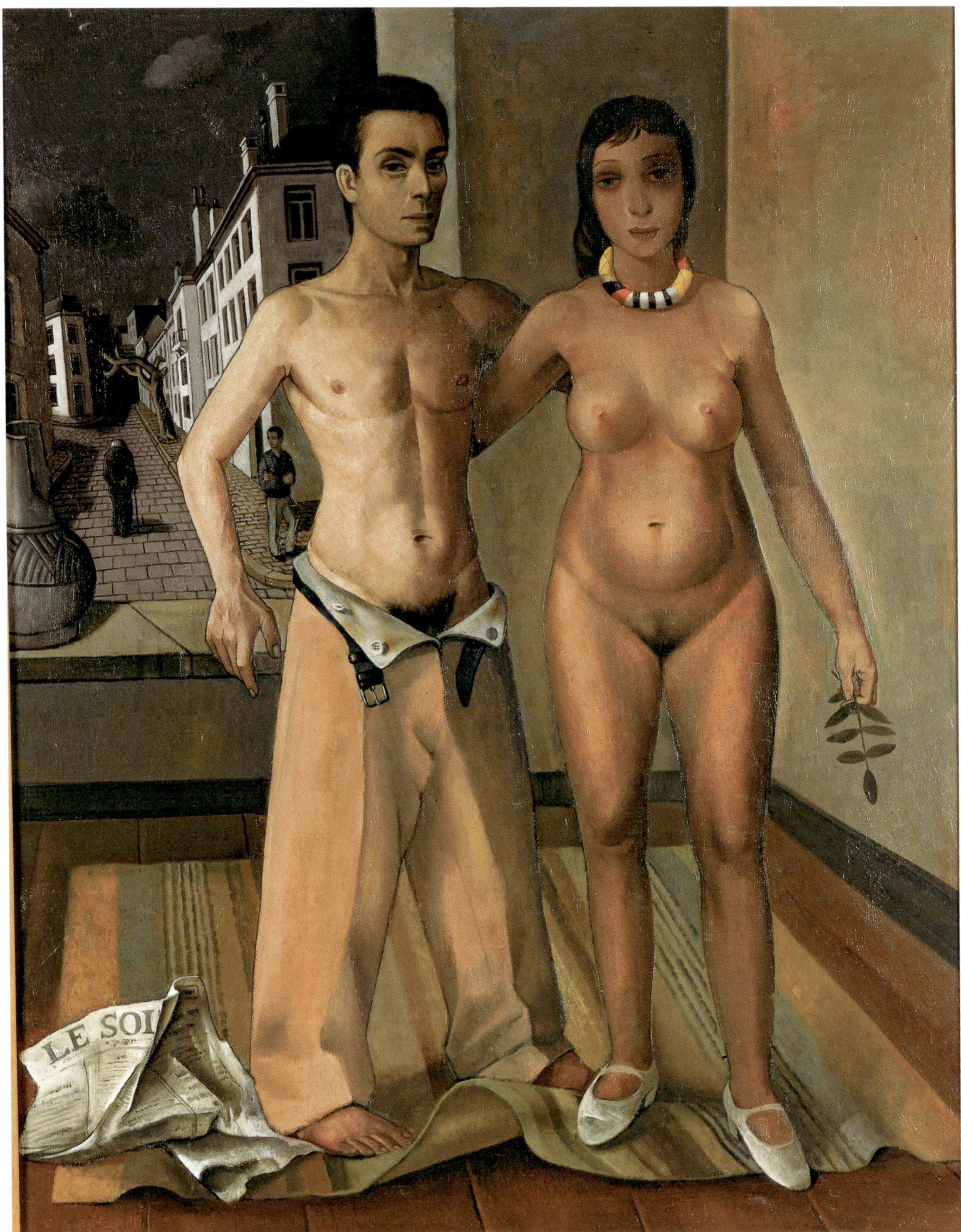

Felix Nussbaum, *Soir (Selbstbildnis mit Felka Platek)*, 1942, 87 × 72 cm, oil on canvas.

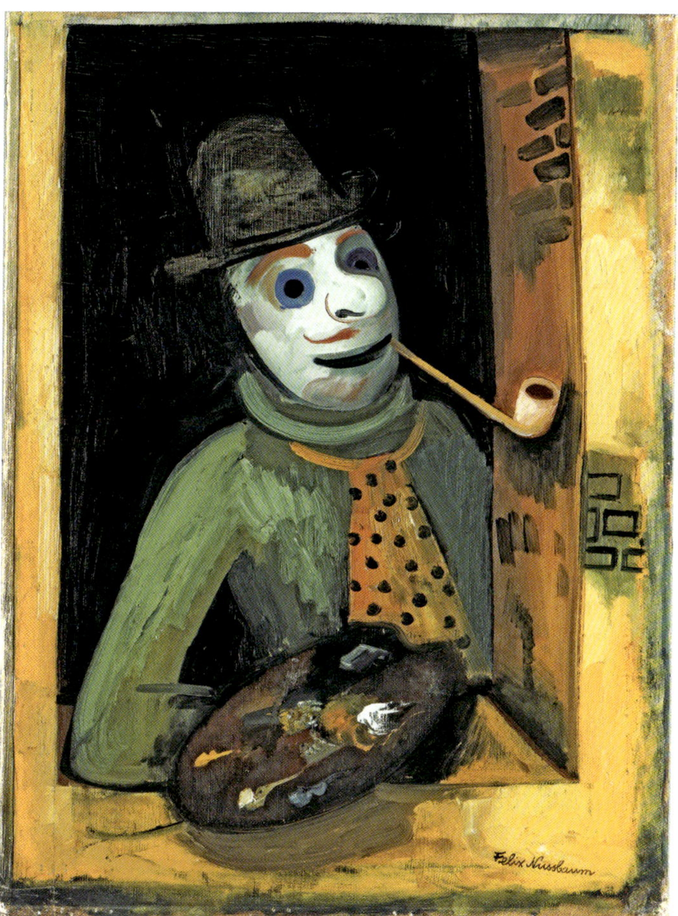

Felix Nussbaum,
Maler mit Maske,
c. 1935, 62 × 47.5 cm,
oil on canvas.

Felix Nussbaum

If I perish, then don't let my paintings die. Show them to the people!

Having travelled from Germany to Rome for study purposes, the German-Jewish painter Felix Nussbaum (Osnabrück 1904–1944 Auschwitz) and his wife Felka Platek were made refugees by Hitler's seizure of power in 1933. After all sorts of detours through Italy and France, they arrived in Ostend in 1935. In 1937 they moved to Brussels where they lived and worked at various addresses. After the invasion by German forces in 1940, Nussbaum was deported by the Belgian authorities because of his German nationality to an internment camp in Saint-Cyprien on the Mediterranean, from where he ultimately managed to escape. He returned to Brussels, where he lived in hiding with Felka until June 1944, when they were denounced and arrested by the Gestapo. Nussbaum and Platek were transported in August 1944 on the last Belgian convoy of Jews to the extermination camp of Auschwitz, where they were both killed.

Although Nussbaum already belonged to the artistic avant-garde in 1920s Berlin, he was completely forgotten after the war and only rediscovered little by little. Thanks to the sustained efforts of surviving family members, his works gradually came to the surface again – both in Germany and in the various cities where he was active during his exile – among which, large groups of important works that he had given to acquaintances in Brussels for safekeeping. At present more than 500 works by Nussbaum are known. The Felix Nussbaum Haus – a museum that has been housed since 1998 in a new building designed by Daniel Libeskind, in the artist's hometown of Osnabrück – contains some 200 paintings and drawings. In Belgium, the Jewish Museum in Brussels and the Kazerne Dossin in Mechelen are the only public collections where work by Nussbaum is on show.

Nussbaum's work attests to an undeniable artistic talent. His portraits, still lifes and grotesque historical scenes are penetrating, surprising and often oppressive. He played an important role in the development of art movements such as Neue Sachlichkeit and magic realism. In his early years he was influenced by expressionism; later by surrealism and Italian new figurative art.

The worldwide interest that his work now enjoys also has to do with the utterly personal manner in which he portrays his experience of life as a migrant and Jewish war refugee. Fear of persecution and betrayal clearly permeates the works of his final years. His works therefore often feature as key examples in publications about racial persecution and genocide. Due to both the great artistic quality of his work and his tragic life, he occupies a particular place in twentieth-century art.

DS

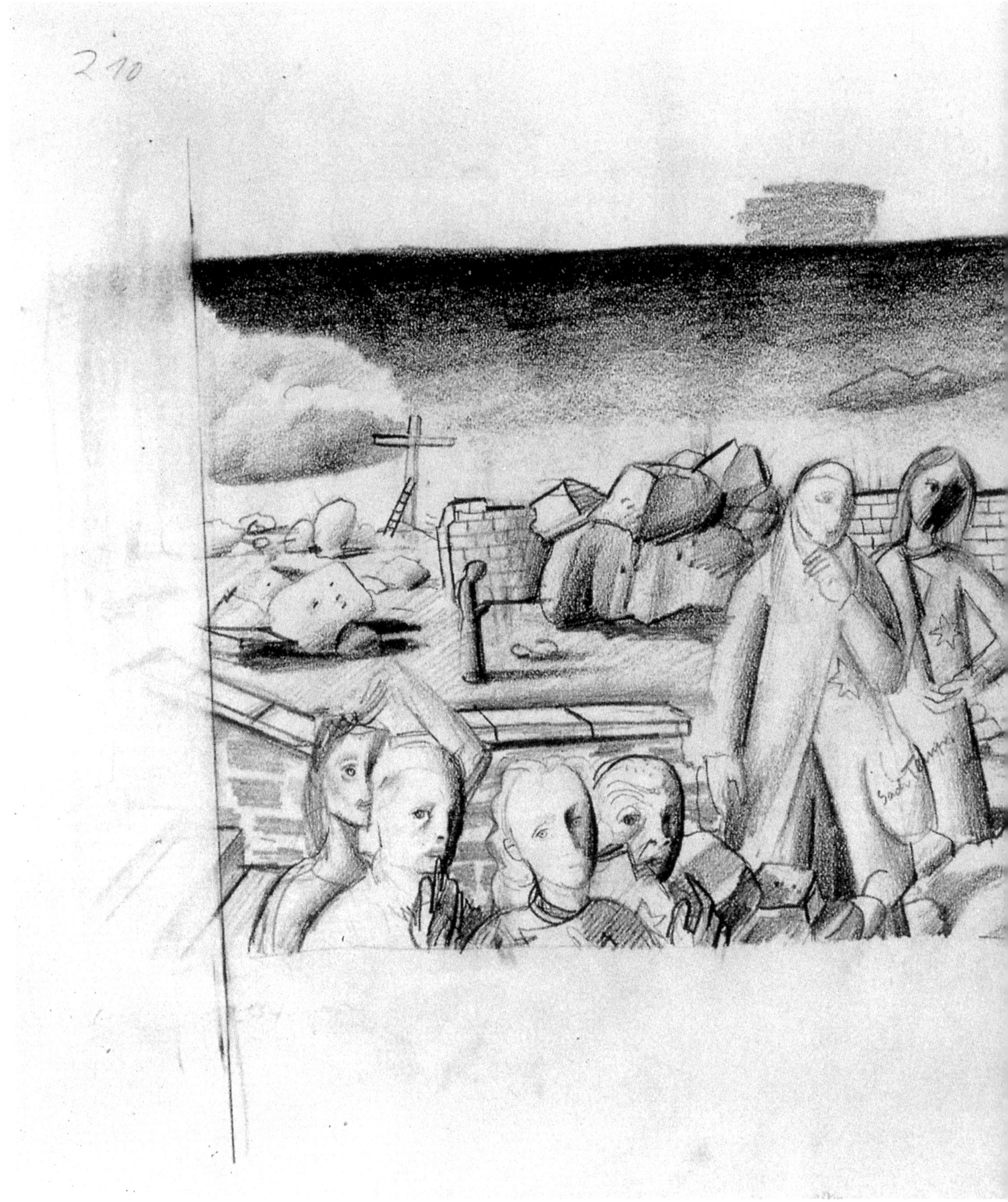

Felix Nussbaum, *Vorzeichnung zu den Verdammten*, c. late 1943, 12.5 × 21 cm, pencil on parchment paper.

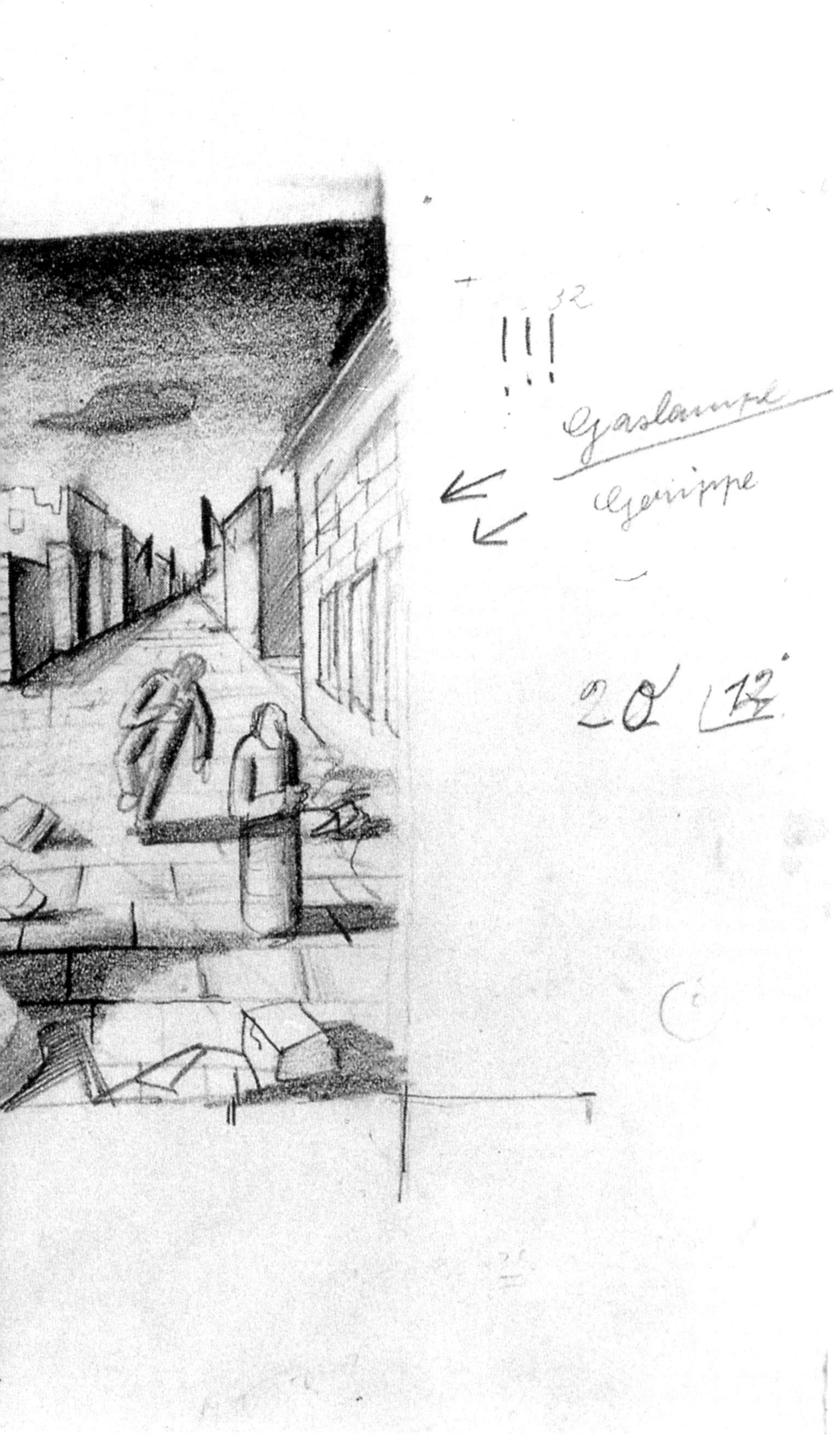

1943

I think about Morandi painting on top of a hill surrounded by fascism,
I think about Picabia finding inspiration in soft-porn magazines on the Côte d'Azur,
I think about Marinetti returning sick from the Russian Front,
I think about Duchamp playing chess in his New York apartment,
I think about Ronald Searle POW in the Kwai jungle,
I think about Ensor playing the harmonium during the bombardment of Ostend,
I think about Otto Dix watching his works being destroyed by the Nazis,
I think about Beckmann under siege in Amsterdam,
I think about Dali, Ernst and Breton reunited in their New York exile,
I think about Magritte painting Fantômas stepping over Paris,
I think about Mondrian painting *Broadway Boogie Woogie*,
I think about Derain much courted by the Nazis in Paris,
I think about Tatlin observing bird flight from his garden in Moscow,
I think about Beuys flying his Stuka dive-bomber over Crimea,
I think about de Chirico copying his paintings in a corner of his studio,
I think about Matisse 'painting with scissors' on the French Riviera,
I think about Soutine dying from an ulcer in Paris while escaping the Gestapo,
I think about Grosz repudiating his past from his new home in Long Island,
I think about Lee Miller photographing English women driving tractors,
I think about Kandinsky in the suburbs of Paris ceasing to write,
I think about Paul Nash once again a war artist for the British Army,
I think about Leni Riefenstahl filming *Tiefland* with extras from concentration camps,
I think about Schlemmer forbidden to paint and dying in a hospital in Baden-Baden,
I think about Picasso making a sculpture out of a bicycle in occupied Paris,
I think about Hannah Höch painting the *Totentanz* triptych in Nazi Germany,
I think about Camille Claudel dying forgotten in the asylum of Montdevergues,
I think about Siqueiros publishing *In War, Art of War* from his Cuban exile,
I think about Emil Nolde painting 'unpainted pictures' in Seebüll,
I think about Schwitters learning from Norway that his *Merzbau* had been destroyed,
I think about Cartier-Bresson escaping from a German labour camp,
I think about Felix Nussbaum hiding from his neighbours in Etterbeek,
I think about Blinky Palermo born in the rubble of Leipzig.

Francis Alÿs, *1943*, 2017.

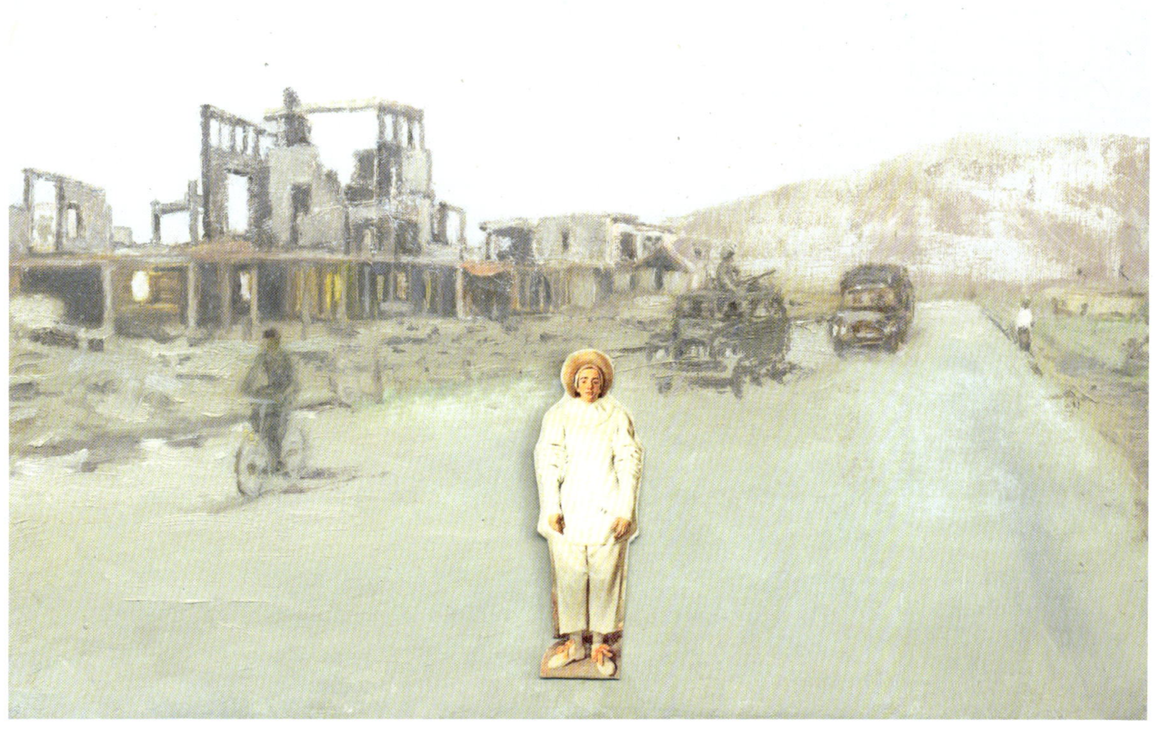

Francis Alÿs,
Untitled (Pierrot), 2010,
13 × 18.1 × 1.2 cm,
oil and collage on
canvas on wood.

Francis Alÿs

Francis Alÿs (b. 1959 in Antwerp) is known for his simple and at the same time intriguing physical actions and interventions in the everyday life of metropolises, at places where geopolitical tensions prevail or where borders are crossed. He makes video recordings of these performances, which he exhibits together with the documentation, maps and notes that preceded and the melancholy oil paintings that he makes during the preparatory trips for his projects.

1943 is a list of artists in different imagined situations in the year 1943. Alÿs first exhibited this work in 2012, at Documenta 13 in Kassel, where it was pinned to a noticeboard as a note next to paintings depicting the West's intervention in Afghanistan and the mediatisation of that war. He displayed a second version in 2016 in Havana, juxtaposed with a painting from 1943 by the communist Mexican muralist David Alfaro Siqueiros.

In response to the invitation to take part in 'The Absent Museum', Alÿs suggested creating *1943* once more, in order to engage in dialogue with the work of Felix Nussbaum. He has added the name 'Nussbaum' to the list and will exhibit this with one of the latter's works from 1943. Alÿs also wishes to display *1943* together with a new work that he is making for the Iraq Pavilion at the 57th Venice Biennale (May–November 2017), which is based on his recent experience on the frontline near Mosul, during the battle of the Iraqi and Kurdish forces against IS.

With *1943* Alÿs explores the attitude of committed avant-garde artists in times of war or life-threatening conflicts. How did artists survive? How did they resist violence and ideological repression? Some sympathised; others collaborated; others waited, resigned, and just carried on with their lives. Are artists obliged to resist and act? Do they have a duty to produce images of the conflict? Do they have to document and denounce it, or, if not, withdraw into an inner exile? Alÿs raises a philosophical question regarding the ethical position of the artist in the face of a tragic event, a deadly war or an unendurable dictatorship, and the consequences for their reputation.

DS

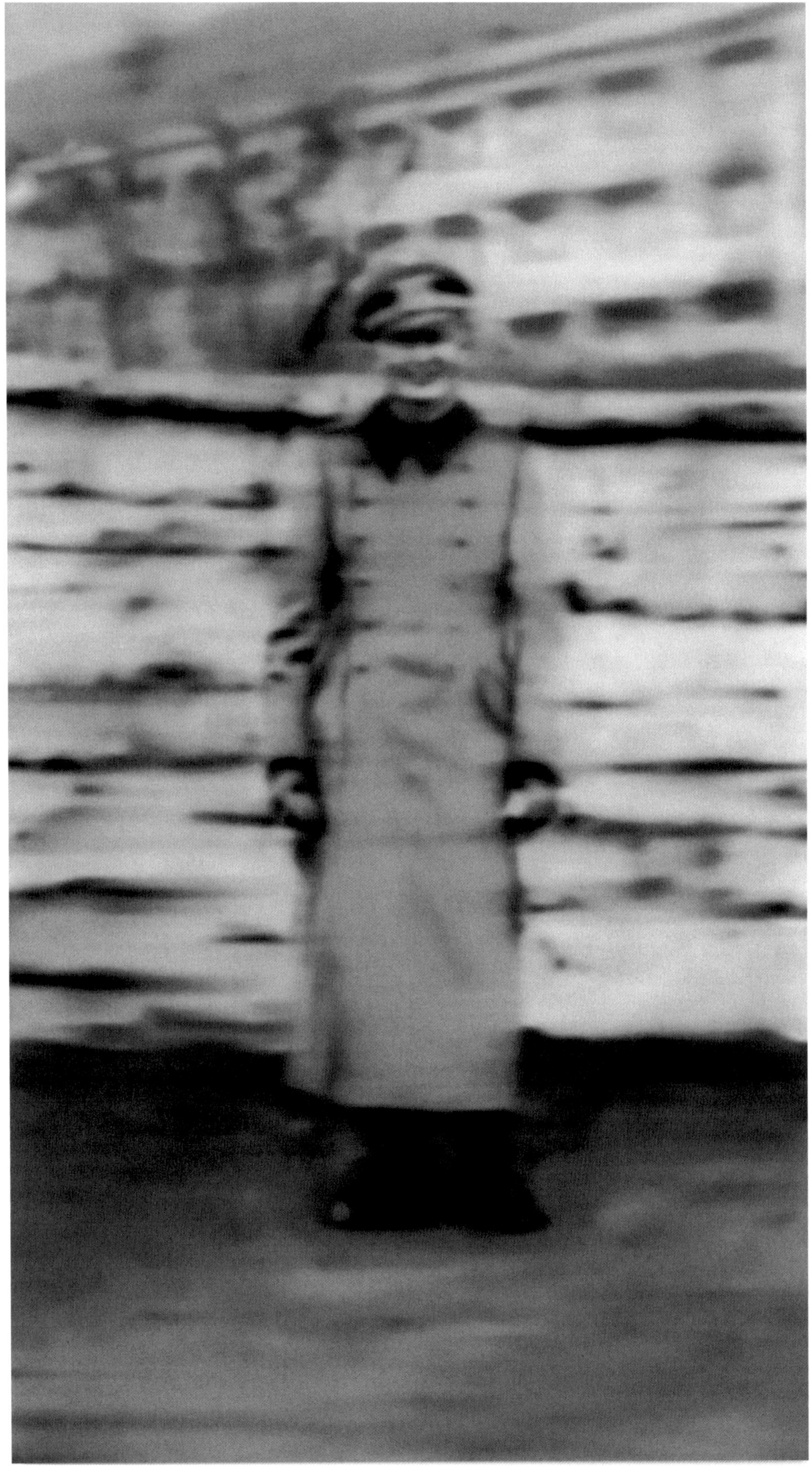

Gerhard Richter, *Onkel Rudi*, 2000, 96 × 58.5 cm, cibachrome mounted on Dibond.

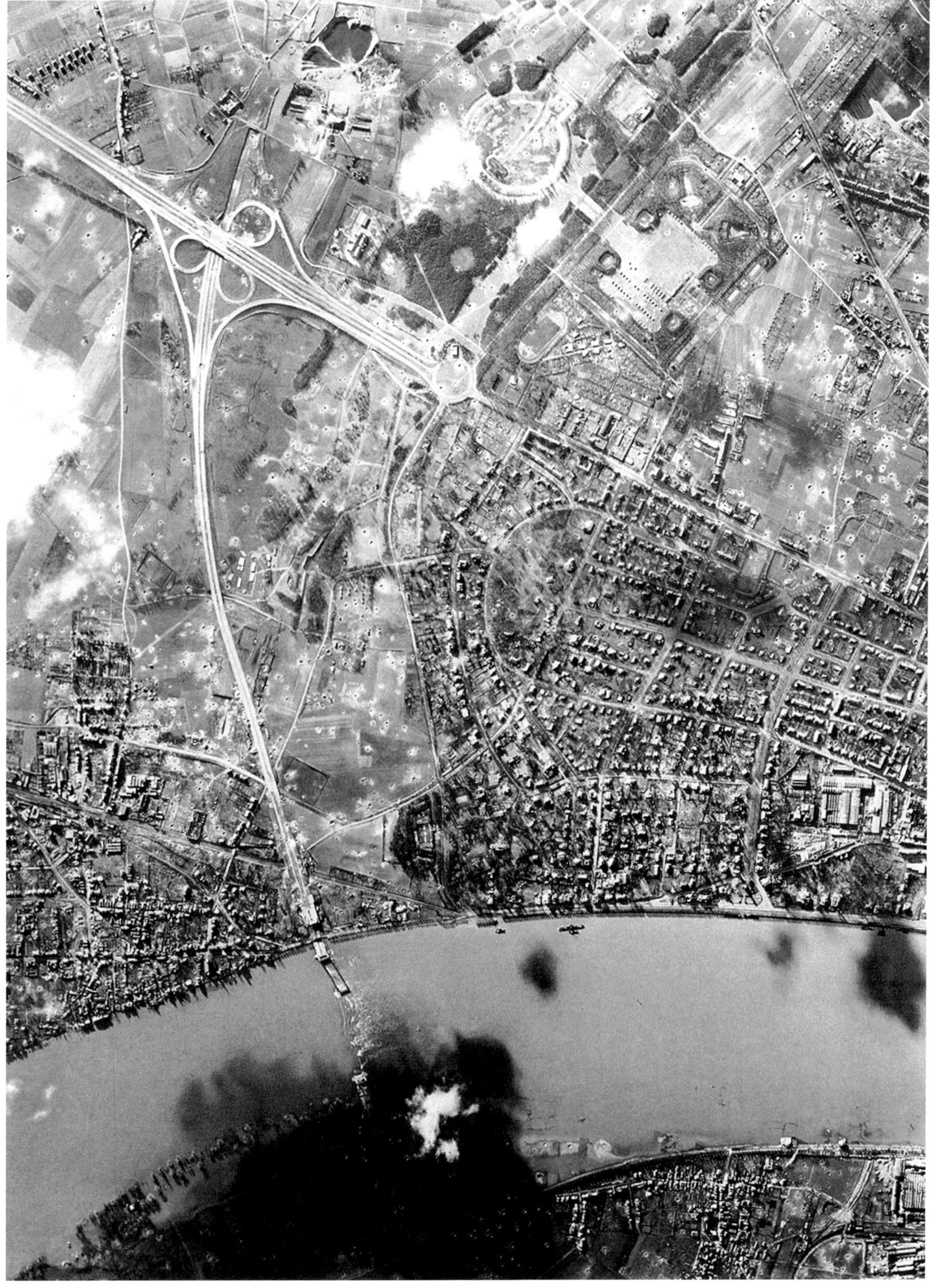

Gerhard Richter, *Bridge 14 FEB 45 (I)*, 2000, 46 × 34.5 cm, offset print on lightweight cardboard, coated with printer's varnish, fixed on cardboard.

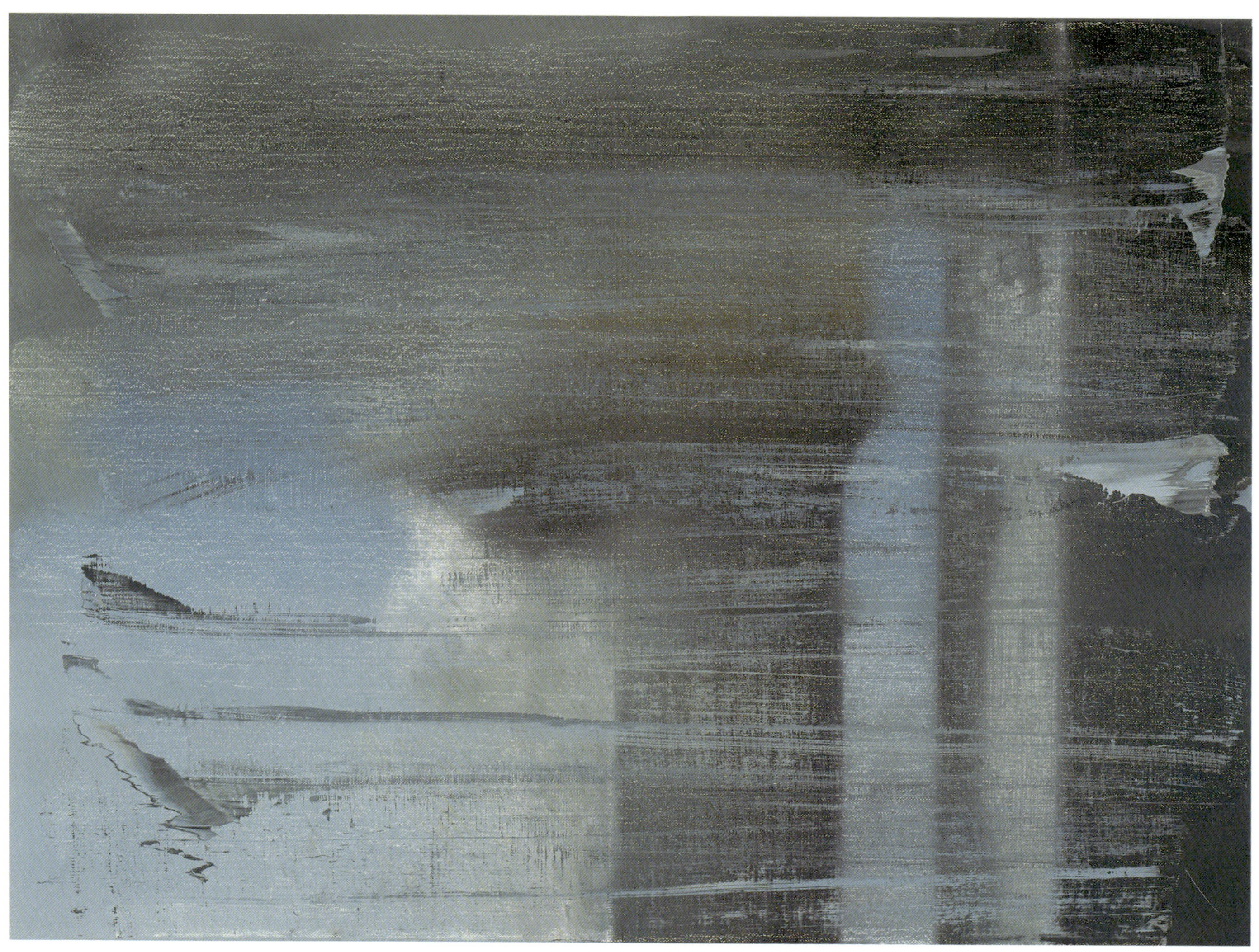

Gerhard Richter, *September*, 2005, 52.1 × 71.8 cm, oil on canvas.

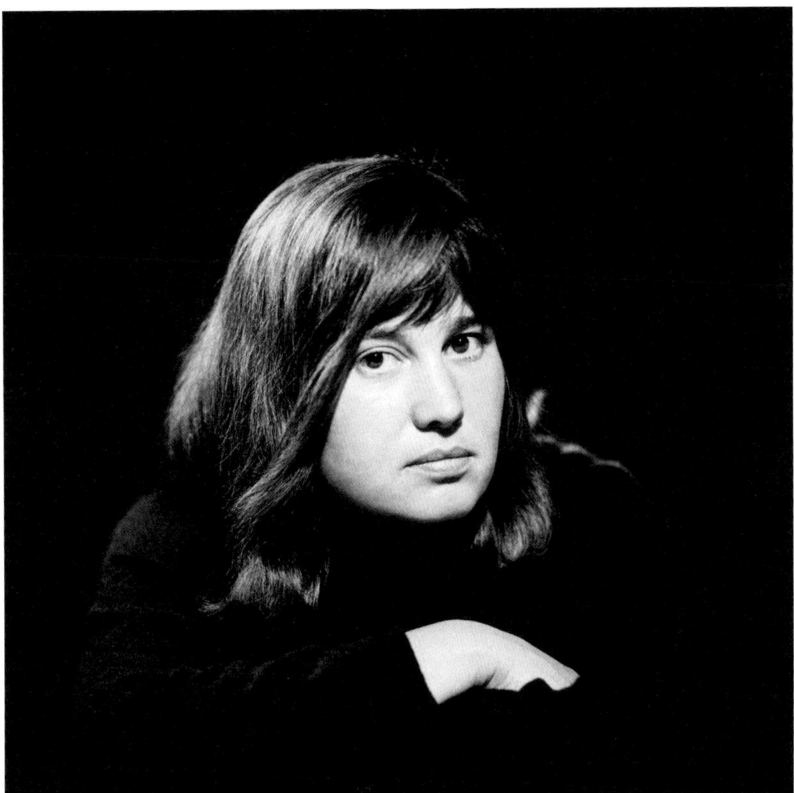

Gerhard Richter, *Ulrike Meinhof*, 2015, 51 × 50 cm, giclée print on Hahnemühle Photo Rag on Alu Dibond.

Gerhard Richter

The contribution of Gerhard Richter (b. 1932 in Dresden) to the visual arts of the past half century can hardly be overestimated. After fleeing the GDR for West Germany in 1961, together with other artists he organised an exhibition that launched the notion of 'capitalist realism'. This was an ironic commentary on the social-realist, edifying aesthetics of the Eastern Bloc, but also a critique of western capitalist society and its mass culture. From 1964 onwards Richter used photographs of everyday objects – newspaper cuttings as well as his own snapshots – as the starting point for abstracting impersonal paintings and drawings. To this day, Richter continues to explore all the possibilities that painting offers as representation, experience and space for critical reflection. His work covers themes such as standardisation and mechanisation, the inevitable issue of authorship in an age of industrial image production and limitless distribution by the media, and the position of art as an object of financial speculation. In his figurative work he also turns his gaze on important moments in history, not with heroic or shocking scenes, but with unremarkable personal pictures that rather tie in with oral history.

In his early years, Richter made works with which he suggested that painting could play a role in the processing of Germany's still recent Nazi past. He went through photo albums to select ambiguous depictions, familiar but still quite charged, of relatives whose lives and fates were related in one way or another to the war, such as the portrait of an uncle wearing the uniform of the Wehrmacht (*Onkel Rudi*, 1965/2000), or souvenir photos that allude to the separation of families in the Germany that was divided by the Iron Curtain (*Hund*, 1965).

Bridge 14 FEB 45 (2000) refers to the air raids that took place during the Second World War. It was a relatively new form of warfare, which raised many questions, given the lack of precision and the terror that was inflicted on the civilian population. The Allied bombing of German cities especially caused a profound trauma and was a taboo subject for many decades. For this work, Richter used an aerial photograph taken from a reconnaissance flight above Cologne, the last big German city that, in March 1945, was the target of a tactical aerial bombardment.

Ulrike Meinhof (2015) is a portrait after a youth photograph of the former journalist, leftist activist and member of the Baader-Meinhof Group, the terrorist movement later called the Red Army Faction (RAF). Richter used the photo as study matter during the preparation of the series of paintings entitled *18 October 1977*, with which he treats one of the most controversial episodes of post-war German history. The series comprises fifteen paintings in tones of grey, made after photos of Baader-Meinhof members who had died in their cells.

DS

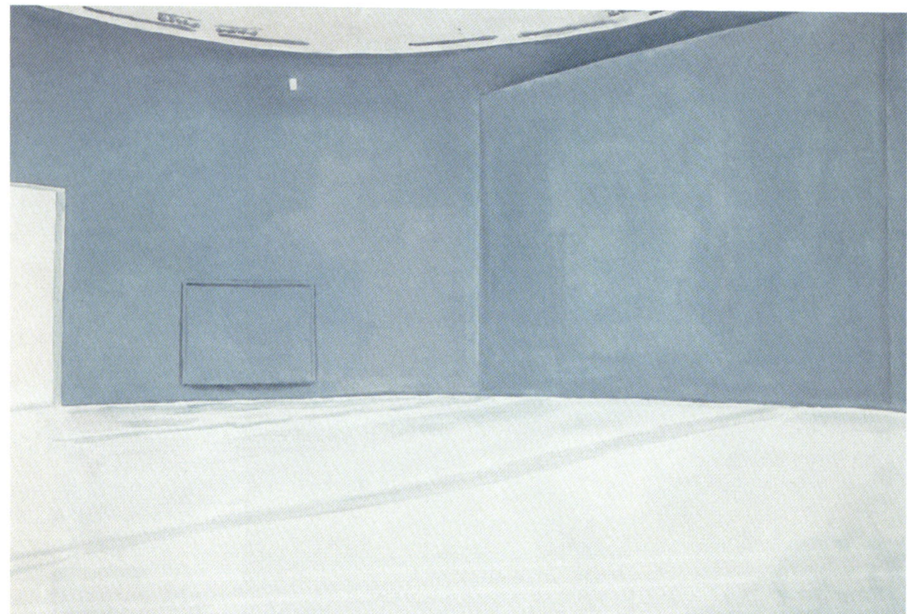 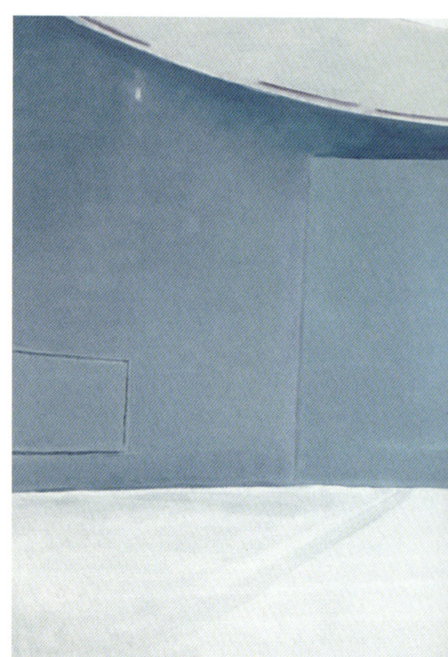

Luc Tuymans, *Doha I, II, III*, 2016, 147.4 × 231.8 cm; 151.7 × 231.8 cm; 154.6 × 232.8 cm, oil on canvas.

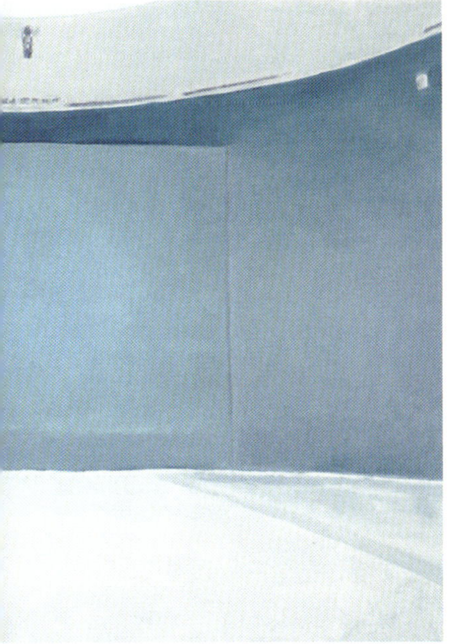 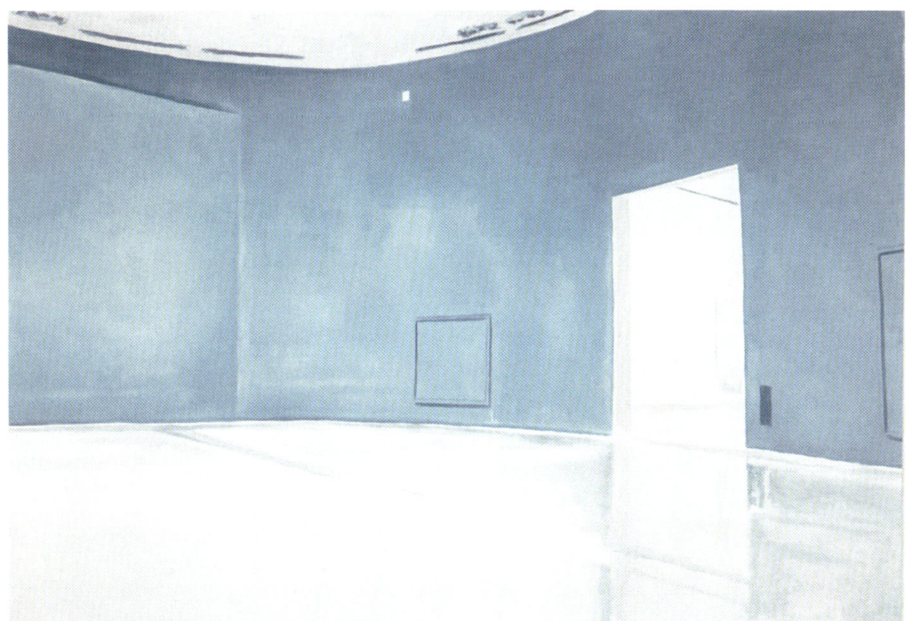

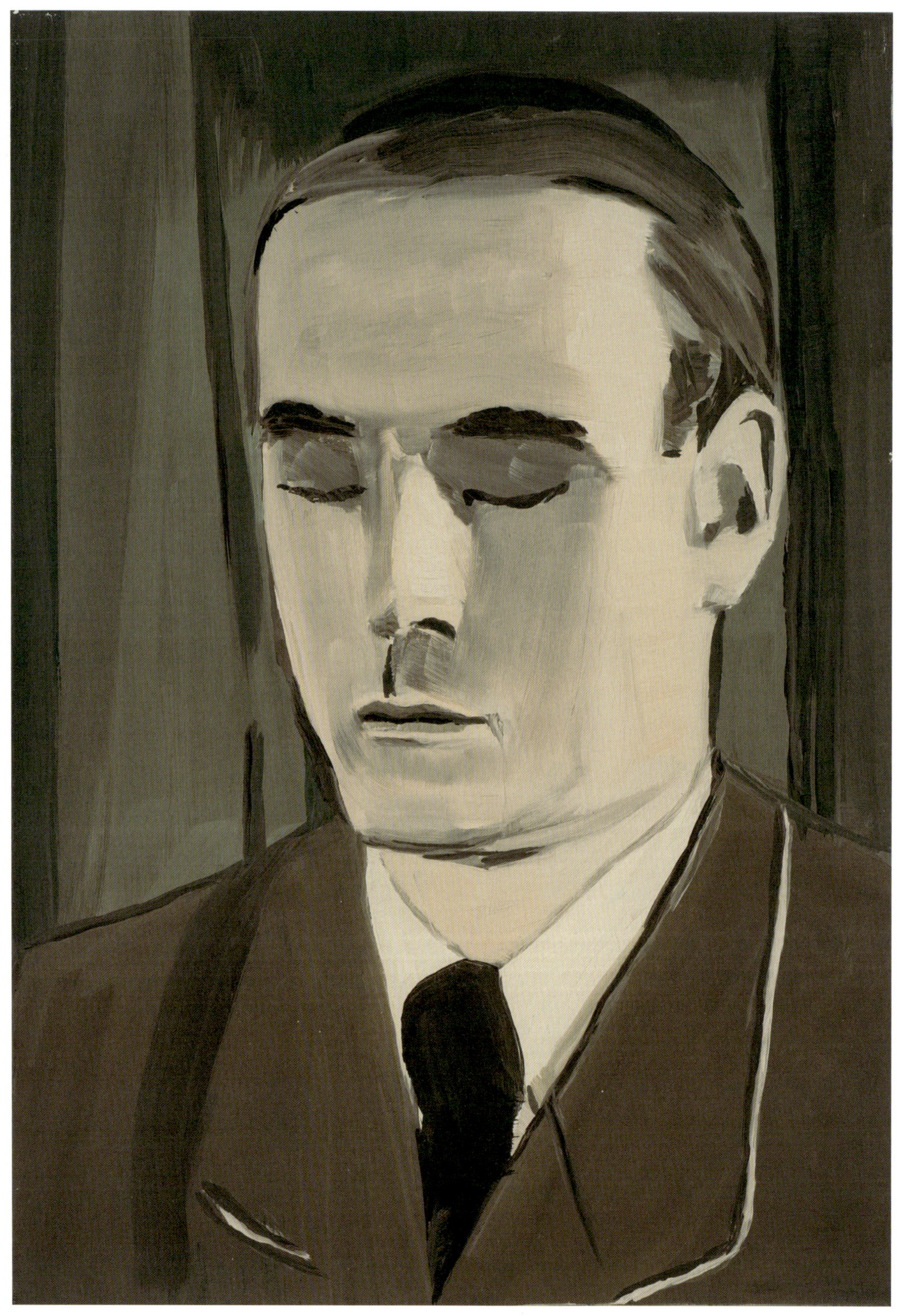

Luc Tuymans, *Secrets*, 1990, 52 × 37 cm, oil on canvas.

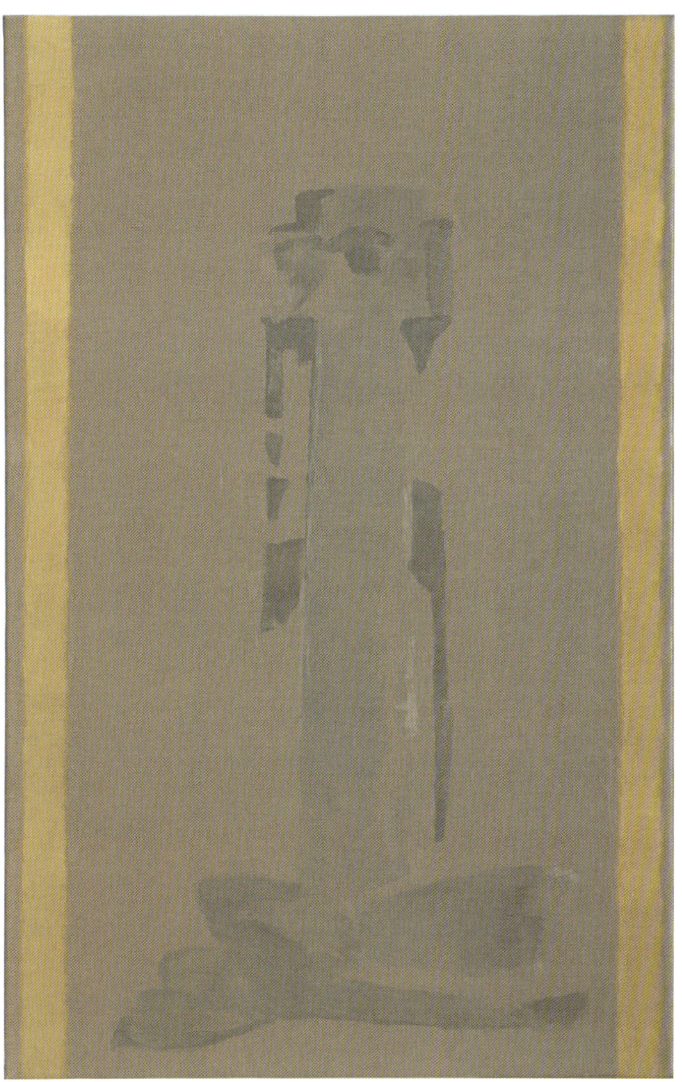

Luc Tuymans

The triptych *Doha I, Doha II, Doha III* came into being in the wake of the 2015–16 retrospective exhibition 'Intolerance' of work by Luc Tuymans (b. 1958 in Mortsel, Belgium) held at the Qatar Museums Gallery Al Riwaq in Doha. It illustrates the artist's work method, both in the choice of motif and in its translation. The paintings are based on photographs taken of the museum's empty rooms after the exhibition. They show the aseptic, clinical character of an architectural type that holds as the global standard for the presentation of contemporary art. As in much corporate architecture, the dimensions are monumental and the feeling of space overwhelming. The bare, sterile spaces are well suited to the rituals and ceremonies attached to the status of its prominent visitors.

In this neo-modernist architecture, the much-discussed white cube with its neutral background has become a sacralising shrine in which everything naturally takes on the fetishist character of a trophy.

Tuymans photographed and painted the slight discoloration that, after several months, his works had produced on the white walls: vague silhouettes, square or rectangular, like negative shadows left behind by time and lighting. They are like after-images on the retina of the museum walls, where the works, although they have been removed, still retain a certain presence. 'After-image' is a key concept in Tuymans' work. In its figurative form, painting is for him not only the reproduction of visually registered reality – it is the result of a process in which the perceived blends with conscious and unconscious images and details drawn from a stock of memories. Thus it is also possible to construct an image from memory, or the brain can complete a missing part of a reproduction; conversely, the viewer can also be blind to clearly visible elements.

The simultaneous processing of perception and memory plays an important role in Tuymans' work as a whole. In his best-known pieces and in thematic exhibitions he often connects the process of repression, forgetting and denial, with symbolic representations of painful, unassimilated or traumatic historical events. Recurrent themes are the problematic handlings of a past of wartime collaboration, the cult of nationalism and the denial of the genocide after the Second World War. In dealing with these issues Tuymans often uses photographs from propaganda magazines that enjoyed a wide circulation at the time. Thus, *Secrets*, an early work from 1990, is based on a photo of a leader of the right-wing movement; it refers to the typology of the archaising leader portrait that is meant to radiate calm and self-confidence, but especially evokes the problematic memory of that period. In individual paintings and drawings, and later also in essayistic exhibitions, Tuymans deals with themes such as the Holocaust, the colonisation of the Congo, nationalist cults and, more recently, the artificial idyll of Disney theme parks, and the power and influence of the Jesuits.

DS

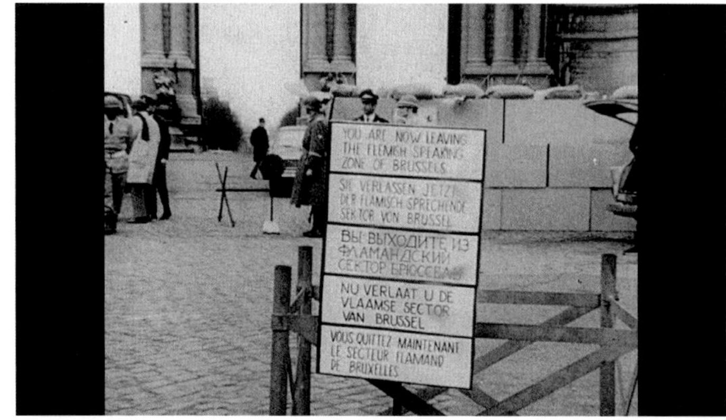

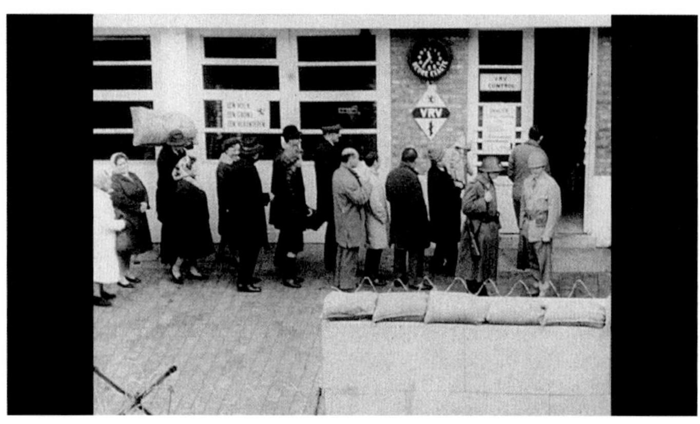

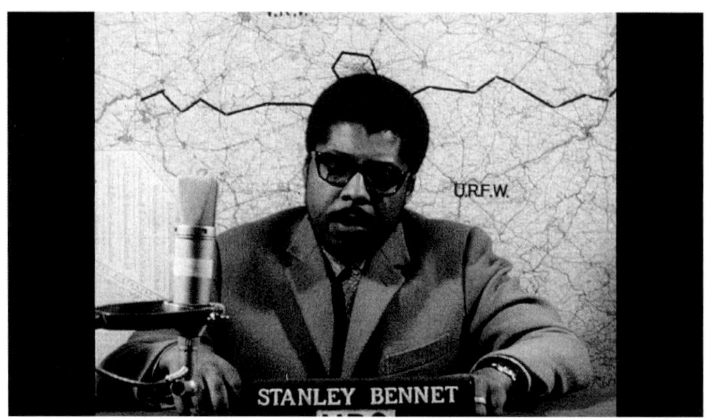

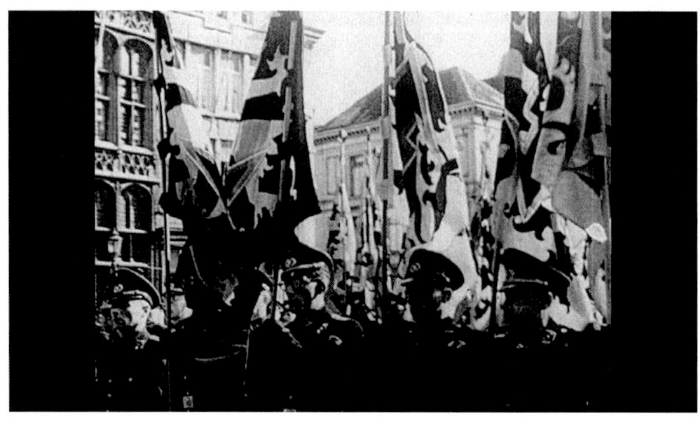

Le Mur, 1968, Belgium, 16mm film transferred to HD video, black and white, sound, 6'42".

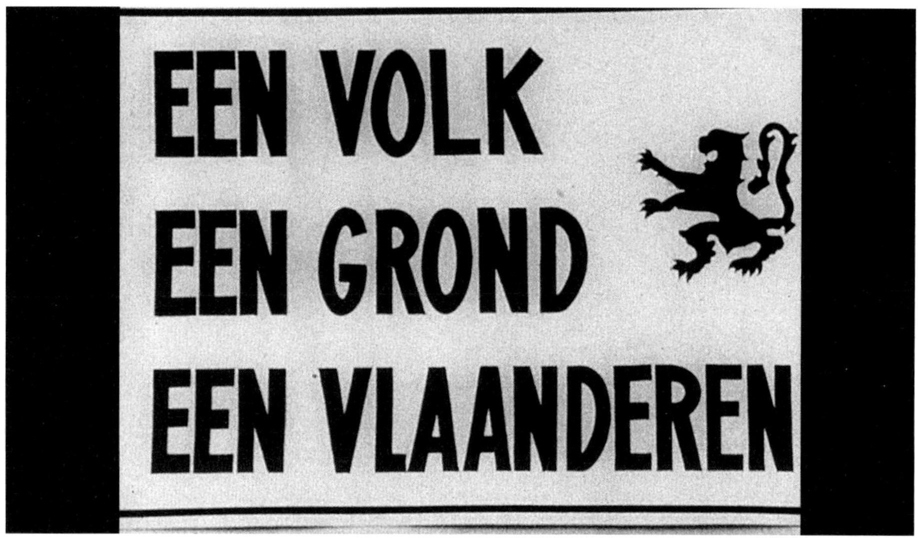

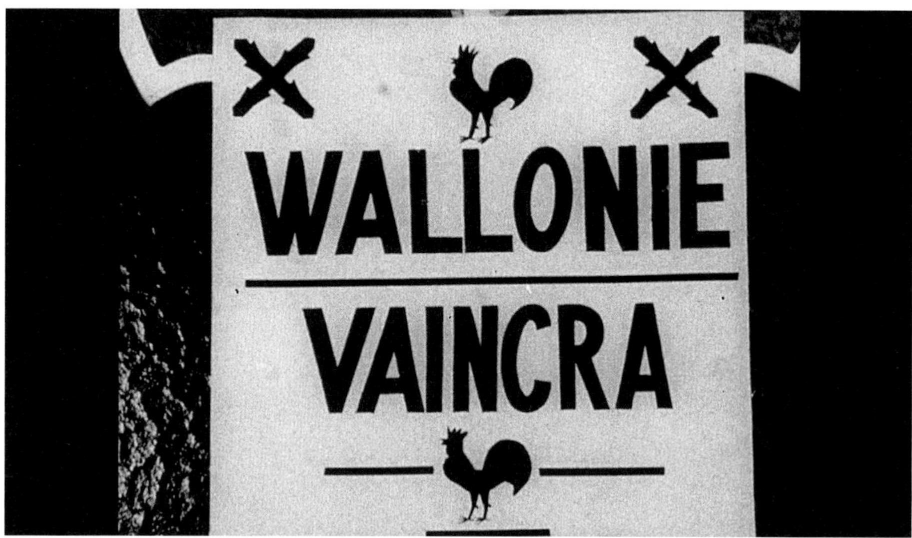

Le Mur

It was in 1968 when a 16mm print of *Le Mur* was brought to London by the Belgian documentary film-maker Henri Storck, who showed it to a small group of students at the Slade Film Department, University College London. The film course was led by his friend Thorold Dickinson, the director of a number of British film classics and first professor of film in the UK. Dickinson and Storck had known each other since the early days of the European Film Society Movement.

I was part of the group of students to whom Storck introduced the film as a timely statement that reflected heated discussions and acts of aggression taking place in Belgium at the time. We students knew from press and TV reports that tensions between the Flemish and Walloon populations in Brussels had led to ethnic clashes in that city. I remember lacing up the film onto the Bell & Howell projector. What we saw on the screen was highly unexpected: a wall was being erected through the centre of Brussels. The film started like a TV reportage but eventually revealed its fictitious character.

Storck explained that the film illuminated a serious crisis in Belgian society and gave us a short account of the history of this conflict. He greatly valued the film as an effective experiment in political education. Its viewing was a sobering experience, as we realised that the construction of a wall through Brussels was not just a theoretical speculation. The film gave a warning of how easily divisiveness between people can be exploited to the point where divisions become physical. The construction of the Berlin Wall, in 1961, was a vivid reminder of how a wall through Brussels could become a political reality.

At the end of the film, the camera tilts up from a young man awaking from the nightmare, towards a calendar showing the date, Sunday 31 March. This in fact was the day the 1968 Belgian general election took place. *Le Mur* was produced to be screened during that critical election campaign and was made at the initiative of the news-reel company Belgavox. It was during the run-up to the 1968 election that it was shown, attached to the regular news reel, in major Brussels cinemas. According to the testimony of Eric van Beuren, the film's cameraman, *Le Mur* was directed by Hugo Mellaerts, a staff editor of Belgavox. It appears that Storck had been one of the initiators of the project and advisor to the production team.

Lutz Becker, 2016

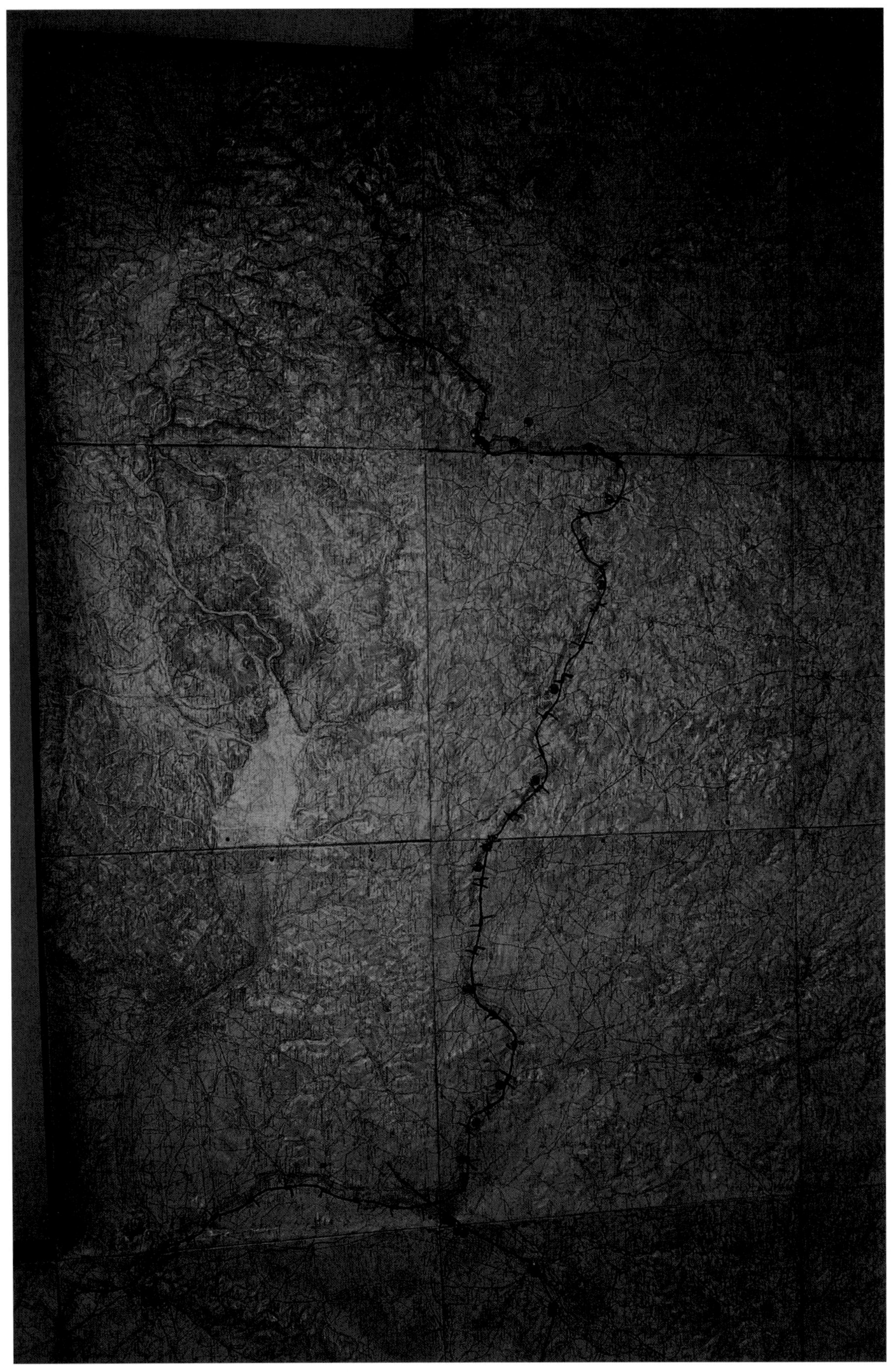

Dirk Braeckman, *R.R.-D.R.-11*, 2011, 180 × 120 cm, gelatin silver print.

Dirk Braeckman

In his idiosyncratic and experimental approach to photography, which he applies consistently, Dirk Braeckman (b. 1958 in Eeklo, Belgium) focuses his attention on the processing of the image – from negative to print that forms the end result – rather than on the shot itself, the 'decisive moment' that records a temporal fragment of reality.

Braeckman often attends to his negatives a long time after the photographs were taken, when the memory of the subject is no longer crystal clear in his mind. His prints are generally grainy, which results in the texture of skin, clothing and other materials showing as suggestive tones of grey. He deliberately avoids the clarity, transparency and precision of detail with which photography is often associated. His dark, impenetrable pictures are never anecdotal; he highlights atmosphere, texture and suggestion. Sometimes details appear in the dark surface – stains, flashes, spots of light – details that bring the dark environment to life, but seem like the result of random factors. His subjects are often indeterminate, abandoned spaces from which he omits any indication of time and place, so that they tend towards symbolism.

In *R.R.-D.R.-11* Braeckman treated the shot of a map fitted with barbed wire and hung on a wall. Where the map is or what region it depicts is unclear; the scar formed by the barbed wire taken from a border or barrier might make it possible for insiders to identify the territory.

Striking and clearly perceptible beside the craggy, milled line of the heavily pronounced border are the relief indications, heights, valleys, mountains, forests, lakes, rivers, which lend the map an organic, uneven surface. The craggy line suggests a border, a demarcation line before or after a conflict; it is almost impossible to read the photo other than as the result of an armed conflict. From a European perspective it suggests a piece of the notorious Iron Curtain or another uncrossable, high-security and dangerous border. The Iron Curtain, which cut across the European continent, is not only burned into memory as that physical, military border, but also as a psychological fracture, with the systematic rivalry of ideological, military and cultural propaganda between the Eastern Bloc and the West. The Cold War divided the planet into two blocs in a global conflict, whereby a military deterrence policy of 'balance of terror' or 'mutual assured destruction' created a climate of permanent fear, paranoia and terror.

However, Braeckman's photograph does not necessarily refer to that historical context. He records the marked graphic designation of one border among many other lines, the heavily accentuated, serrated line of a divide.

DS

The Baudouin/Boudewijn Experiment

The late king of Belgium – Baudouin or Boudewijn – found a remarkable solution to a personal dilemma. As king, he was supposed to ratify every new law established by parliament. His contribution to the actual formulation of the law, however, was nil, thus making the signing of the document a purely formalistic act. In a particular instance, parliament was working out a law that would legalise abortion. Baudouin/Boudewijn, being a confessed Catholic, had moral problems signing the decree; on the other hand, he did not want to obstruct the implementation of a new law. When the time came and his signature was requested, he called upon his 'inability to govern' for one day. Therefore, the parliament could approve the law without his signature. The following day, Baudouin/Boudewijn became king again.

This solution to a dilemma is ingeniously simple. It is a short-term deviation from your usual behaviour, a shift in character for the sake of avoiding producing something you don't want to produce, a refusal during a period of time to be the professional you usually are. It is as if you are cutting off a continuous line of being. Stop, and start again? Not a change in what you do, but the inclusion of an alien moment of not doing. A deviation – even a negative deviation – since the way is shortened by including a moment of motionlessness.

The experiment planned here will be as follows: a space is provided to accommodate 100 people who are willing to step out of their 'usual life' for 24 hours (the amount of time during which the king was not king). The space will be closed from the outside world and mobile phones, radios and TVs will not be allowed. This is to emphasise the group aspect of the experiment and to create a structure in which the 'step-out' can be done commonly. The necessary infrastructure (beds, food, sanitary facilities, safety) will be provided, but no programme or methods of entertainment (people are free to bring what they like). Basically, the experiment will be to see what happens under these conditions; people are freed from their usual constraints, and yet confined to a space and a time.

The Baudouin/Boudewijn Experiment will not be recorded by means of film, video or otherwise (and thus is contrary to any Big-Brother-like set up); the only 'recordings' will be the memories of the participants, and they will be 'broadcast' by the stories they are willing to tell. The experiment will thus be a very unscientific one, as objectivity is not the aim. Rather, it will be a unique opportunity to experience with others the possibility of getting away from what you usually are.

Carsten Höller, 2001

Originally planned for 'Brussels, European Capital of Culture 2000', Carsten Höller's *The Baudouin/Boudewijn Experiment: A Deliberate, Non-Fatalistic Large Scale Group Experiment in Deviation* took place the following year, on 27 September 2001, at the Atomium, organised by Roomade and curated by Barbara Vanderlinden. WIELS and Kunstenfestivaldesarts present the performance again on 8 May 2017 in the Brussels Palais de la Dynastie/Dynastiepaleis.

FOCUS

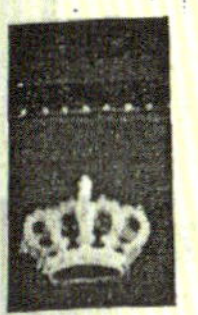

WELKOM, BOUDEWIJN II. Met een perfekt gevoel voor synchroniciteit hebben Frank Swaelen en Charles - Ferdinand Nothomb 'hun' parlementsleden naar een stemming geloodst, die van dit land opnieuw een koninkrijk heeft gemaakt.
Bij de stemming over het besluit om Boudewijns 'onmogelijkheid om te regeren' op te heffen, was er geen enkele neen-stem. Voor de verenigde kamers was voordien door premier Martens de uitzonderlijk expliciete brief voorgelezen, waarin de vorst zijn gewetensnood uitte. Intussen blijkt CVP-voorzitter Van Rompuy veel later dan andere kollega's van de krisis op de hoogte te zijn gebracht.

Historische vergadering vertoont mat verloop

DE KONING IS TERUG
Geen enkele tegenstem

(Brussel. Eigen berichtgeving)

Even na zessen gisteravond maakten 245 ja-stemmen in de verenigde kamers een einde aan 'de onmogelijkheid van de koning om te regeren'. Er waren 93 onthoudingen en geen enkele nee-stem. Anderhalve dag zonder koning was meteen voorbij. Alle partijen vroegen wel 'om een oplossing' om een dergelijke 'kortsluiting' in de toekomst te vermijden.

Bijna stipt om 3 uur schreeuwde een bode boven het geroezemoes van kamerleden en senatoren de komst van senaatsvoorzitter Swaelen (CVP) uit. Protokolair kreeg hij de eer, geflankeerd door kamervoorzitter Nothomb (PSC), om deze historische vergadering te leiden. Na een korte inleiding besteeg eerste minister Martens het spreekgestoelte om het regeringsstandpunt eerst in het Nederlands, dan in het Frans aan de vergadering mee te delen.

De premier gaf een chronologisch overzicht van de gebeurtenissen van de afgelopen dagen en las de briefwisseling voor die tussen de regering en het staatshoofd werd gevoerd. De eerste brief van Boudewijn (zie p. 5) werd drie dagen later door de eerste minister en de vice-premiers met een voorstel van oplossing (het inroepen van grondwetsartikel 82) beantwoord. In het schrijven stelt Martens eveneens "strukturele wijzigingen" voor om te vermijden dat "in de toekomst gelijkaardige problemen zouden rijzen". In een tweede brief aan de regering (gedateerd op 3 april) "stemt" hij (de koning) "in met het inroepen van artikel 82".

Eergisteren schreef het staatshoofd dan zijn laatste brief bij dit konflikt. Boudewijn neemt "akte" van het feit dat de ministerraad het wetsontwerp Lallemand-Michielsens heeft bekrachtigd. "Ten gevolge hiervan heeft de reden van mijn onmogelijkheid te regeren opgehouden te bestaan. Mag ik U verzoeken dit te willen meedelen aan de Regering en aan de Wetgevende Kamers", aldus de koning. Aldus geschiedde, door het samenroepen van de verenigde kamers.

Na deze verklaring werd de vergadering voor drie kwartier geschorst om de frakties in staat te stellen hun houding te bepalen. Vervolgens beten de liberalen de spits af. PRL-voorzitter Duquesne en zijn PVV-kollega Verhofstadt waren van oordeel dat "de koning nooit in de onmogelijkheid was geweest om te regeren daar de uitgewerkte regeling ongrondwettelijk was". De regering kreeg scherpe kritiek omdat ze verzuimd had de oppositiegroepen van meet af aan bij de oplossing van de impasse te betrekken. Ook de grondwettelijke "bri-

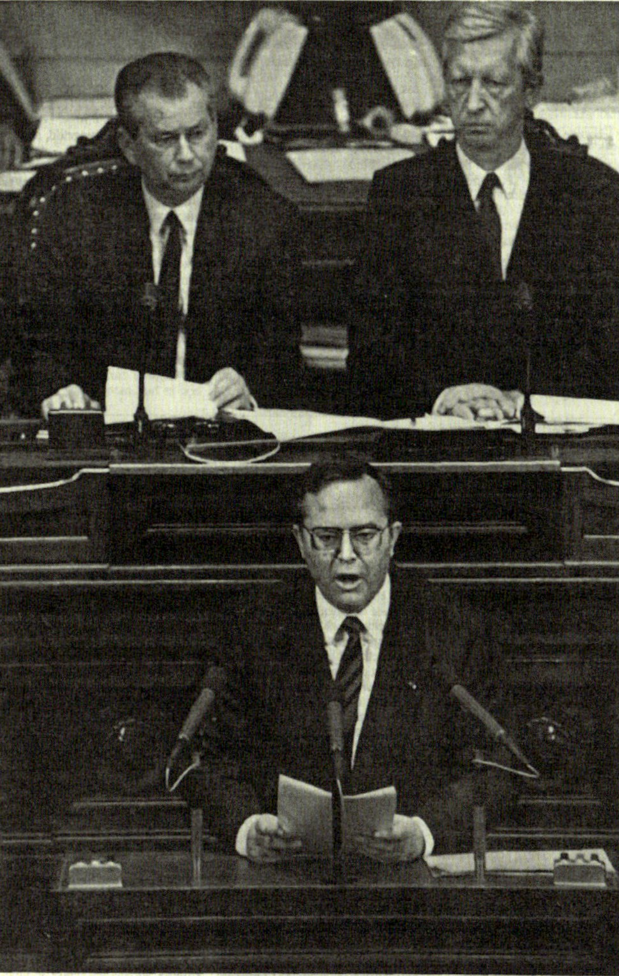

Premier Martens las de verenigde kamers de integrale tekst van de 'noodbrief' van het staatshoofd voor. (Foto Filip Claus)

colage" namen de liberalen stevig op te korrel. "De krisis van vandaag is het gevolg van het volstrekt ongrondwettelijk antwoord van de regering aan de koning", sneerde Verhofstadt. Hij vroeg zich trouwens af hoe een "koning 'in de onmogelijkheid om te regeren' zich akkoord kan verklaren

met een bepaalde procedure". De "trouw aan de monarchie" weerhield de liberalen er echter van tegen te stemmen.

De teneur bij de groenen ging in dezelfde richting. Mieke Vogels (Agalev) voelde zich "misbruikt" en vond de hele toestand gisteren "onwezen-

lijk". De groenen wilde het spel dan ook niet meespelen en hielden het bij een onthouding. Zo verging het ook het FDF.

Bij de meerderheidspartijen was de Volksunie de enige partij die twee onthoudingen in haar rangen moest toestaan (kamerlid Caudron en sena-

tor Luyten). Voorzitter Gabriëls betreurde nogmaals dat er rond het VU-voorstel geen consensus werd bereikt. In een opmerkelijk korte en zakelijke tussenkomst wees hij erop dat een "komplete chaos" moest worden vermeden en "het regeringswerk voortgezet". "Desondanks moet er een grondwettelijke manier gezocht worden om dit soort kortsluitingen in de toekomst te vermijden", stelde Gabriëls.

CVP-voorzitter Van Rompuy vergeleek de gewetensproblemen van de koning met deze van de CVP-parlementsleden. "De koning kon deze gewetensnood niet uiten", betoogde hij. Van Rompuy prees de verantwoordelijkheid die de regeringsleden bij de oplossing van dit konflikt op zich hadden genomen, "het bewijst een hoge politieke moraal en kultuur". Het feit dat ook CVP-ministers de abortuswet hebben ondertekend, vergoelijkte de CVP-voorzitter door erop te wijzen dat ze "niet als persoon maar als instelling hebben gehandeld". "De CVP-ministers gaan in geweten niet akkoord met deze wet maar zij hebbben dit in het parlement kunnen uiten", zei Van Rompuy. "De CVP en de regering hebben het mogelijk gemaakt dat de koning zijn gewetensnood op een uitzonderlijke manier heeft kunnen uiten, de geschiedenis zal hierover oordelen."

Het laatste woord was voor de SP en haar voorzitter Vandenbroucke. Vlaamse en Waalse socialisten waren het trouwens opvallend eens. Twee "verantwoordelijkheden" waren er volgens hem in het spel. De demokratie moest "geëerbiedigd" worden en de bevolking moest een "uitzichtloos konflikt" tussen de instellingen worden bespaard. Net zoals de PS pleitte ook de SP voor "regeringsvoorstellen na rijp beraad om de herhaling van een dergelijk incident in de toekomst te vermijden".

Na een kort antwoord en dankwoord van de premier waarin hij beloofde later op interpellaties te gronde te zullen antwoorden, kon even voor zessen de stemming beginnen. Dit moest bij naamafroeping gebeuren aangezien elektronisch stemmen onmogelijk was. Nelly Maes kreeg de eer alle namen te debiteren terwijl in de zaal een uitgelaten sfeer heerste. Iedereen lachte de spanning weg en keurde gedurende een half uur durende stemming het voorstel van besluit goed of onthield zich. Niemand stemde tegen. Het Vlaams Blok had ostentatief het halfrond verlaten. Na tien minuten cijferwerk waren de hoofden geteld en kreeg Boudewijn zijn bevoegdheden terug.

Bart Brinckman

Bart Brinckman, 'De Koning is terug. Geen enkele tegenstem' (The King is back. Not a single opposing vote), *De Morgen*, 6 April 1990.

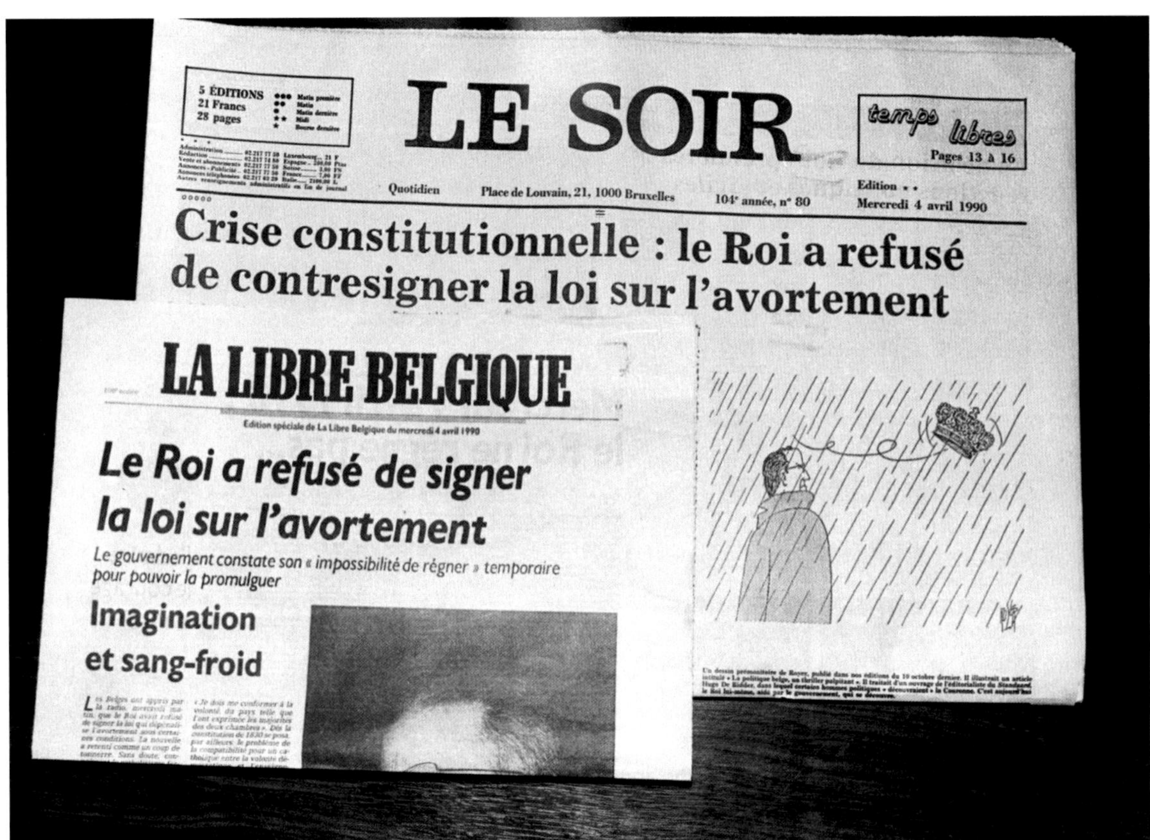

Headlines in *Le Soir* and *La Libre Belgique*, 4 April 1990.

In 1971, almost twenty years before the abortion law was approved by the Belgian Parliament, Senator Willy Calewaert (SP, Flemish Socialist Party) introduced a bill for the partial legalisation of voluntary termination of pregnancy. In 1974 the Tindemans government set up a commission that would tackle ethical questions, including abortion. Between 1974 and 1989 dozens of bills were introduced for a partial decriminalisation of abortion. In 1978, Leona Detiège (SP) even introduced a bill for the full decriminalisation of abortion, which was rejected by a small majority of only two votes. In the same year, Lucienne Michielsens (PVV, Party for Freedom and Progress) drafted a bill in which she tried to reconcile the standpoints of the different parties, but once more unsuccessfully. Wilfried Martens (CVP, Christian People's Party), Prime Minister at the time, wrote later in his memoirs that the CVP in particular blocked the consensus among the various parties.[1]

In 1986, Michielsens and Roger Lallemand (PS, French-speaking Socialist Party) put forward an amended bill that enjoyed the support of many parties, but not of the CVP. Any agreement seemed far off when, on 19 October 1987, the government fell as a result of the increasing tension between the Communities caused by the appointment of a Walloon, José Happart, as mayor of the Flemish town of Voeren. In April 1988, Martens managed with difficulty to assemble a new government composed of Christian Democrats and Liberals. During the government negotiations, Frank Swaelen, the then chairman of the CVP, had made it clear that the Lallemand-Michielsens bill was not acceptable to his party. As a result, the abortion issue was not included in the government programme, and the parties agreed that it would not be on the agenda for several months: this helped gain time for a consultation among the coalition partners. Lallemand would later openly admit that this was the ideal moment to get the law into Parliament without causing a crisis.[2] In February 1989 the negotiations took up again and on 20 June a Senate commission finally approved the bill. Of the fifteen senators who voted against, ten were from the CVP. On 6 November the Senate passed the almost unamended Lallemand-Michielsens bill. The Chamber of Representatives did the same on 29 March 1990.

The bills for a partial decriminalisation of abortion that were submitted between 1970 and 1989 came up against political as well as personal hurdles. For nineteen years the government had repeatedly postponed tackling the abortion law. Equally striking is the fact that Lallemand could get the bill into Parliament thanks to an abstention, a form of 'not-acting' of the government that deliberately ignored the abortion issue in its programme, even though this issue was of enormous interest to the public. The moral dilemma of King Baudouin, which would ultimately lead to the infamous royal crisis and the signing of the law on 3 April 1990, was nothing more than the anticipated final stop of the political slow train that had left the station in 1971. In a draft letter that he presented to Martens, King Baudouin himself wrote: 'Is it normal that I am the only Belgian citizen who is obliged to act against his conscience in such an important matter? Does freedom of conscience apply to everyone except the King?'[3]

Although King Baudouin clearly stated that his moral conscience would never allow him to sign this law, he declared himself open to a legal solution. He did not wish to stand in the way of democracy. Jean-Luc Dehaene was also clear in this respect with Martens: 'The government cannot fall over this, or we will have elections with the monarchy at stake.' Therefore, a solution had to be found since Article 109 of the Belgian Constitution clearly stipulates that 'the King sanctions and promulgates laws'. Of the answers that were imagined, the so-called 'Norwegian' solution was the most interesting. This would ensure that the King would no longer have to ratify all laws. Martens was resolutely against this. His reticence was understandable: such a procedure would take weeks and would plunge the country into political chaos. For the CVP, however, there was more at stake: the party's very identity and credibility. Martens writes: 'Apart from the political objections, this [Norwegian] solution also places my party in an impossible position. Because a two-thirds majority would have been demanded of it to limit the authority of the King – which my party did not want in the least – to ratify a law which it had voted against!'[4]

Nevertheless, the power of the King was temporarily limited. Article 93 (then art. 82) of the Constitution was invoked: 'If the King finds himself unable to reign, the ministers, having noted this inability, immediately convene the Houses. The Regent and Guardian are appointed by the joint Houses.' King Baudouin agreed to this legal solution on 3 April and all the ministers convened that same evening. The Council of Ministers began at 23.20. Wilfried Martens writes: 'I first read out the exchange of correspondence with the King and concluded that the Council of Ministers had to approve three actions: a decision recording the King's inability to reign, dated 3 April; a decision by the Council that the ministers themselves sanctioned and promulgated the bill regarding the voluntary termination of pregnancy; and the decision, to be dated 4 April and to be taken by the Council that would gather after midnight, to convene on 5 April the Chamber of Representatives and the Senate in a joint session of the Houses to ask them to record the end of the King's inability to reign. I explained that after the approval of the first two actions, the King would send me a new letter in which he would inform me that for him his inability to reign had ceased.'[5]

BVB

1
Wilfried Martens, *De Memoires: Luctor et Emergo*, Tielt 2006, p. 482.

2
José-Alain Fralon, *Boudewijn: De man die geen koning wilde zijn*, Antwerp 2001, p. 263 (originally published in French as *Baudouin, l'homme qui ne voulait pas être roi*, Paris 2001).

3
Martens, *De Memoires*, op. cit., p. 487.

4
Ibid., pp. 488–89.

5
Ibid., p. 493.

Walter Swennen, *We/They*, 2010, 90 × 70 cm, oil on canvas.

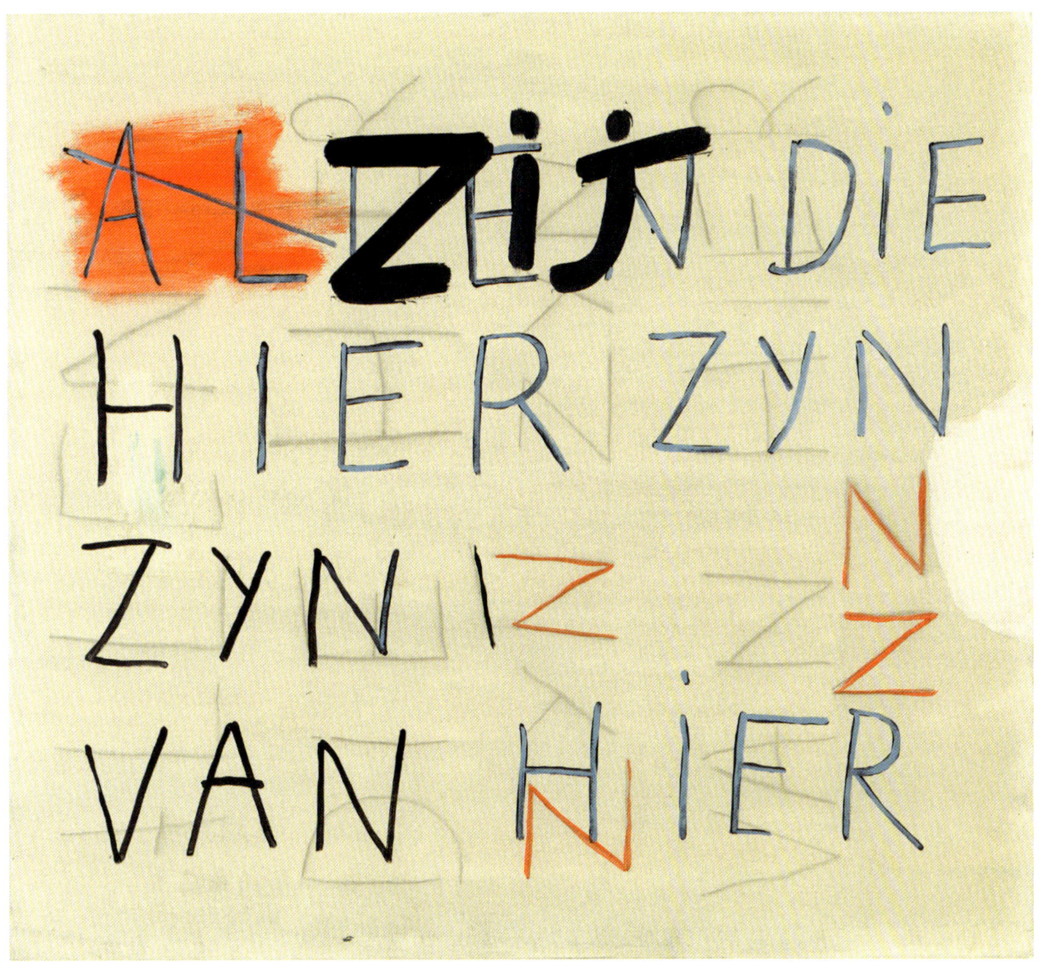

Walter Swennen,
*Ceux qui sont ici,
sont d'ici*, 2013,
136 × 150 cm, oil and
acrylic on canvas.

Walter Swennen

After studying philosophy and psychology in Leuven, Walter Swennen (b. 1946 in Brussels) was active as a poet. In the mid-1960s he took part in public happenings and events in the spirit of the American beat generation. From the early 1980s he devoted himself full-time to painting.

Entirely in line with his earlier activity as a poet, writer and psychologist, Swennen often works with language, words, signs and their translations, in a form of intertextuality to which he adds the specificity of conceptual painting. The material, the support and the painting as process and tradition play an important role in this. The painting as an entity, made up of language and signs, images and symbols, and their painterly depiction or representation, composed of material and the gestures of painting, is remote to the conception of art as unambiguous representation,

as communication and optical fulfilment of expectations.

In his experimental painterly approach, Swennen seeks to strip both text and image of their conventional meaning and to let them appear rid of all utilitarian function, as a fluid form, as substance, as an unstable, free or empty signifier. The motif, when manifested as language, writing, utterance, symbol or pictogram, is unrelated to the background with which it dialogues.

Swennen's attraction to childhood memories, children's drawings and nursery rhymes is connected to the principles of modernist poetry, with its unexpected rhythms and musicality, and contrary to rigid, academic language. In order to break open the rules of grammar and syntax, the modernist poets often sought and found examples in children's rhymes, snippets of conversations that they picked up

during their wanderings through the city or in the headlines of popular magazines. The result was a free and flexible use of language with nonsense, absurd and semantic ambiguities free of logic.

Swennen first used the inscription '*Zij die hier zijn zijn van hier*' (Those who are here are from here) in a drawing he made on the occasion of 'Black Sunday', 24 November 1991, when the far-right party Vlaams Blok made significant gains in Belgium's general elections. The text is a variation, in the Dutch vernacular, of the medieval legal principle *Quidquid est in territorio est etiam de territorio* (Whatever is in the territory is indeed of the territory). According to Hannah Arendt, as stated in her *Origins of Totalitarianism*, this principle, with its 'holy history', underlies the right of asylum that was undermined and violated by the nation states.

The musical repetition of words and sounds brings to mind the Dadaist poetry of Paul van Ostaijen. This is not the only time that Swennen has used a drawing as the basis for a painting – in this case two paintings that emerged over an interval of several years. The text itself (which is neither printed nor written, but painted) becomes the motif, the image and the painting. In *We/They* the text, painted in manuscript, is the literal naming of a border, of distinction, difference, otherness – not individually but, rather, in relation to a group identity. The motif is derived from the heading in a notebook used for recording games of bridge.

DS

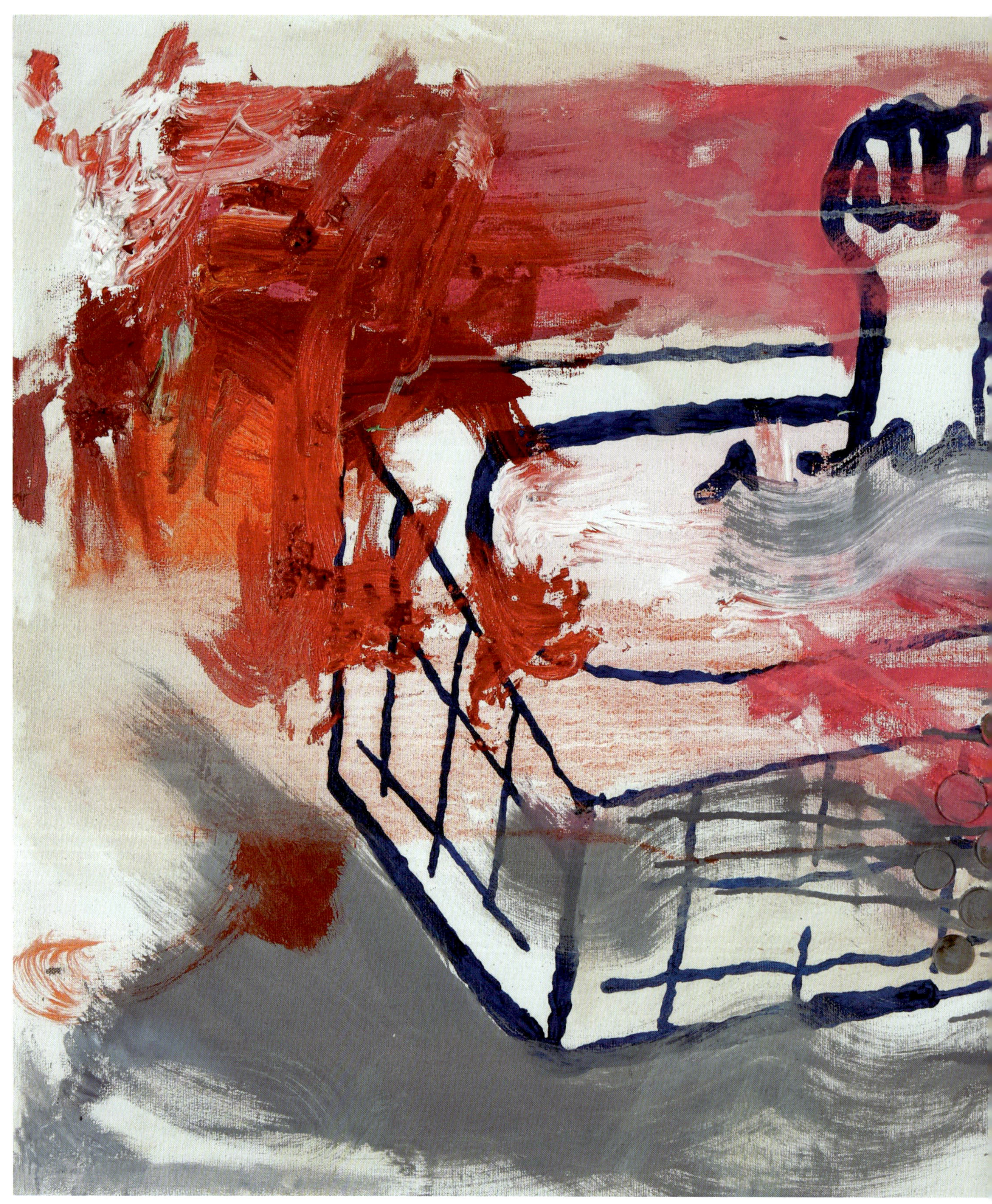

Martin Kippenberger, *Untitled*, 1988, 63 × 92 cm, oil and coins on canvas.

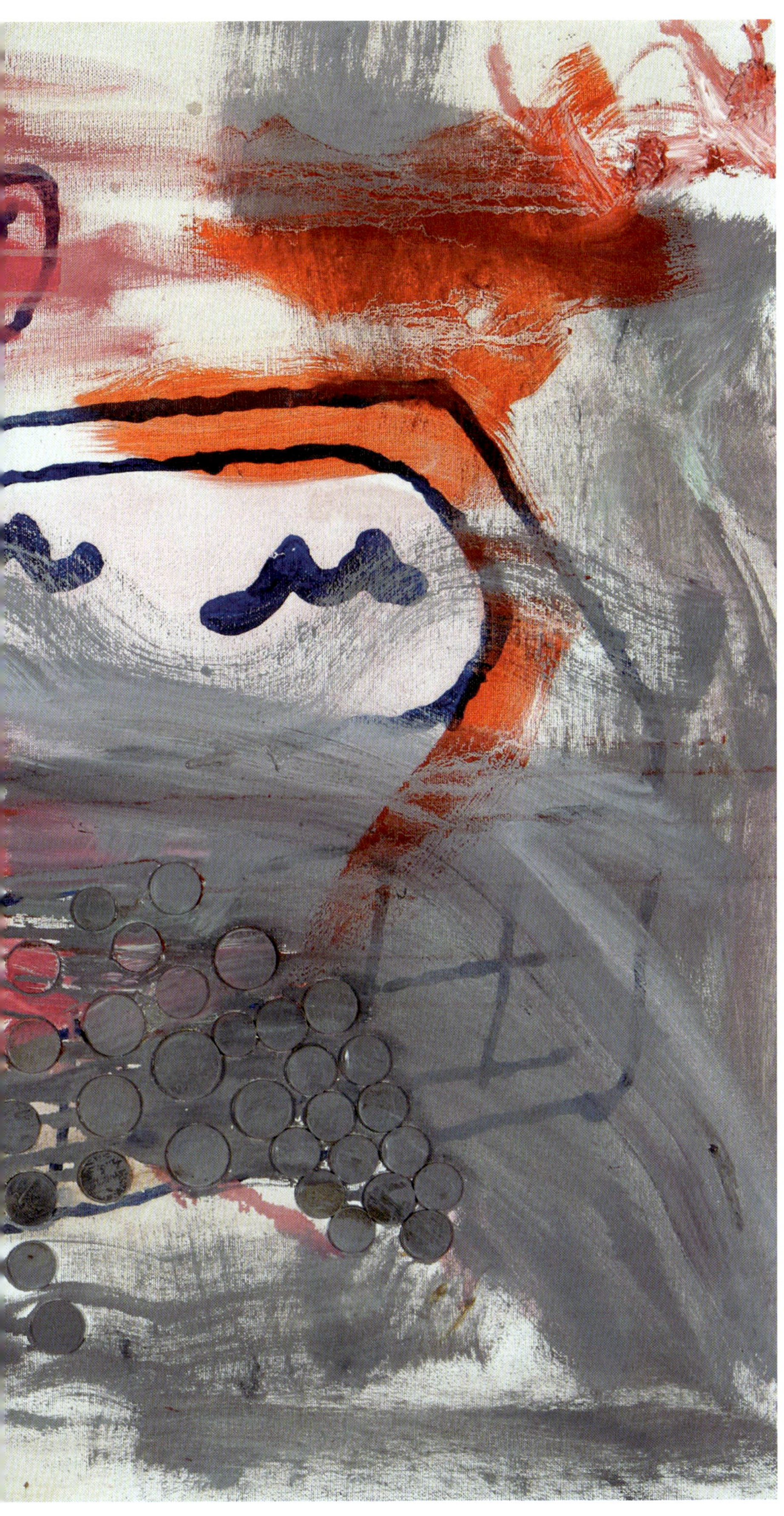

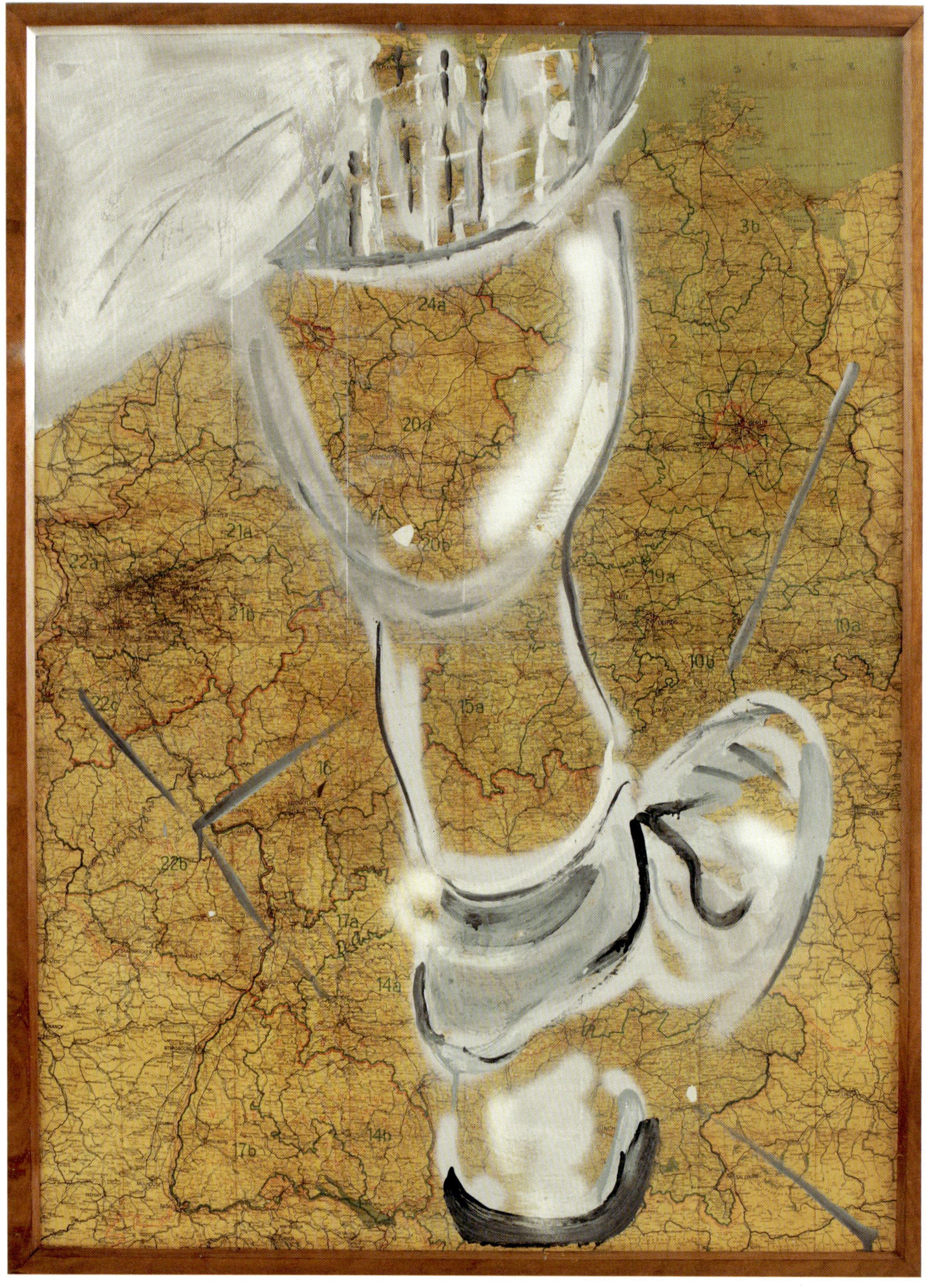

Martin Kippenberger, *Untitled*, 1979, 129.5 × 96 cm, acrylic, enamel and spray print on map on board in the artist's frame.

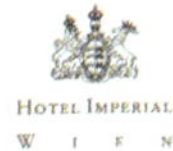

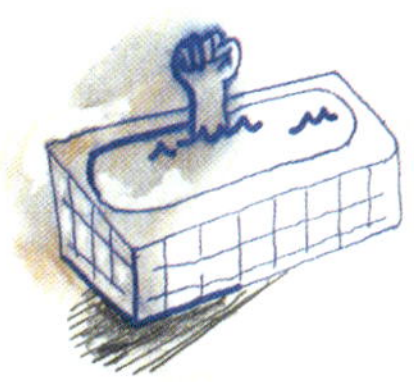

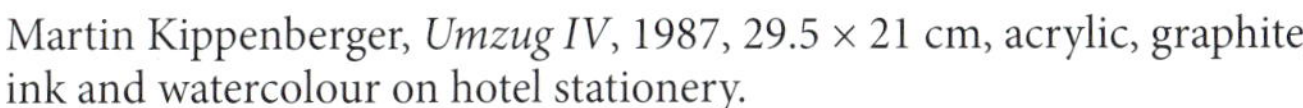

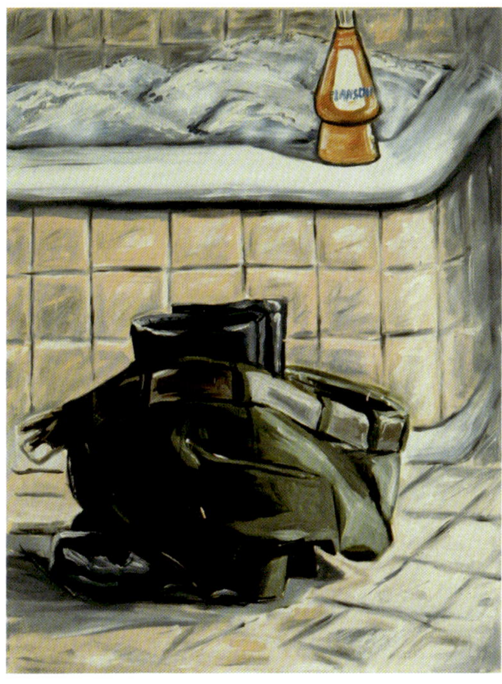

Martin Kippenberger, *Umzug IV*, 1987, 29.5 × 21 cm, acrylic, graphite, ink and watercolour on hotel stationery.

Martin Kippenberger, *Badender Russe nach gelungener Flucht*, 1984, 150 × 120 cm, oil on canvas.

Martin Kippenberger

The work of German artist Martin Kippenberger (Dortmund 1953–1997 Vienna) – which includes paintings, objects, performances, publications and music, as well as polymorphic projects – is often described, for lack of a better word, as *Selbstdarstellung* (self-representation): constantly impersonating oneself, promoting oneself and ultimately also, almost exhibitionistically, posing as oneself. The work rarely emerged in the isolation of the studio; his impatience and energy translated into an artistic-communicative practice with rapid results and dynamic social relations. As a result, Kippenberger cannot be placed among the New Painters who gave shape to their rejection of society and established structures in spontaneous, direct paintings. His performative attitude is comparable to what was customary on the rock-music scene at the time and also in new German film. Kippenberger's art is closely related to the alternative counterculture environments of West Berlin, Hamburg, Cologne/Düsseldorf and later also New York and Los Angeles. This manifests itself in countless collaborations, housing communities with other artists,

work relations with assistants and art students, and also in projects with friends and specialists, which defined a new connection between product, process, documentation and the persistent substratum of a bourgeois ideology regarding art and artist.

Kippenberger's self-promotion often starts out from his family name, resulting in recognisability and visibility, but also bringing up for discussion the subjectivity of the artist. He pushes his name forward like a brand, a substitute for the person, an alter ego that can be be combined and connected with all sorts of other names and references. This leads to endless cross-references, a sort of applied intertextuality that no longer refers to other authors or texts, but cites everything that the artist has seen or heard, in utterances, inscriptions, titles, jokes and lists. His fondness for naivety, simplification and sentimentality is striking, but also is the fact that authenticity has no value or meaning for him: 'Aside from himself, in Kippenberger's work there is no primary object of experience […]. The objects in his work derive instead from the already treated second or third

nature of medially transmitted images and concepts. This is not only a typical, often described response by the entire punk generation reacting against the cult of self-discovery […] and reacting against the pathos of true sensitivity, a belief in a first nature and its authentic expression by cultural means.'[1]

On a large map of West Germany a shod leg with rolled-up trouser-leg is painted in white and black. The burlesque representation does not refer to the national mythology, but to Kippenberger's habit of dancing at parties with his artist friends with one trouser-leg rolled up. The motif dominates the background: the map of the terrain of the country that he has toured many times, Germany with its middle-class conception of art and with its work ethic tied to the economic miracle.

A clenched fist in a bath with Deutschmark coins stuck on underneath, shown on an expressively painted foundation. Kippenberger uses the motif of the clenched fist, traditionally a symbol of protest or resistance, with the necessary irony: in the bath, declarations of war and strategy do not count for much.

The theme of the Cold War and the fear of the Red Army is also present in earlier, similar works, such as *Badender Russe nach gelungener Flucht* (Bathing Russian after a Successful Flight) (1984), which was inspired by a painting by Werner Büttner.

DS

1
Diedrich Diederichsen, '"Selbstdarsteller": Martin Kippenberger between 1977 and 1983' in *After Kippenberger*, eds Eva Meyer-Hermann and Susanne Neuburger, exh. cat., Eindhoven and Vienna 2003, p. 46.

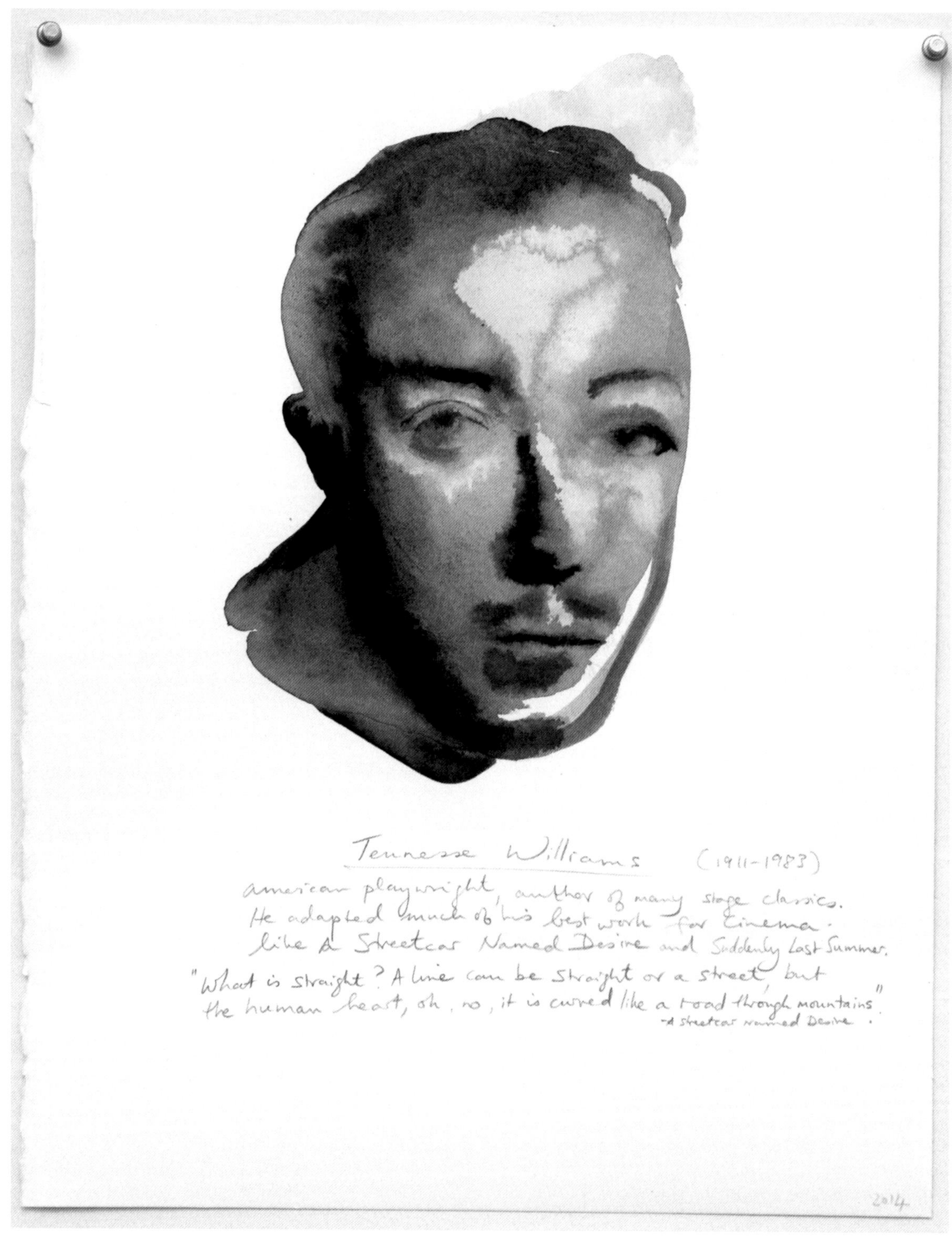

Marlene Dumas, *Great Men*, 2014, 44 × 35 cm, ink, pencil and metallic acrylic on paper. Tennessee Williams.

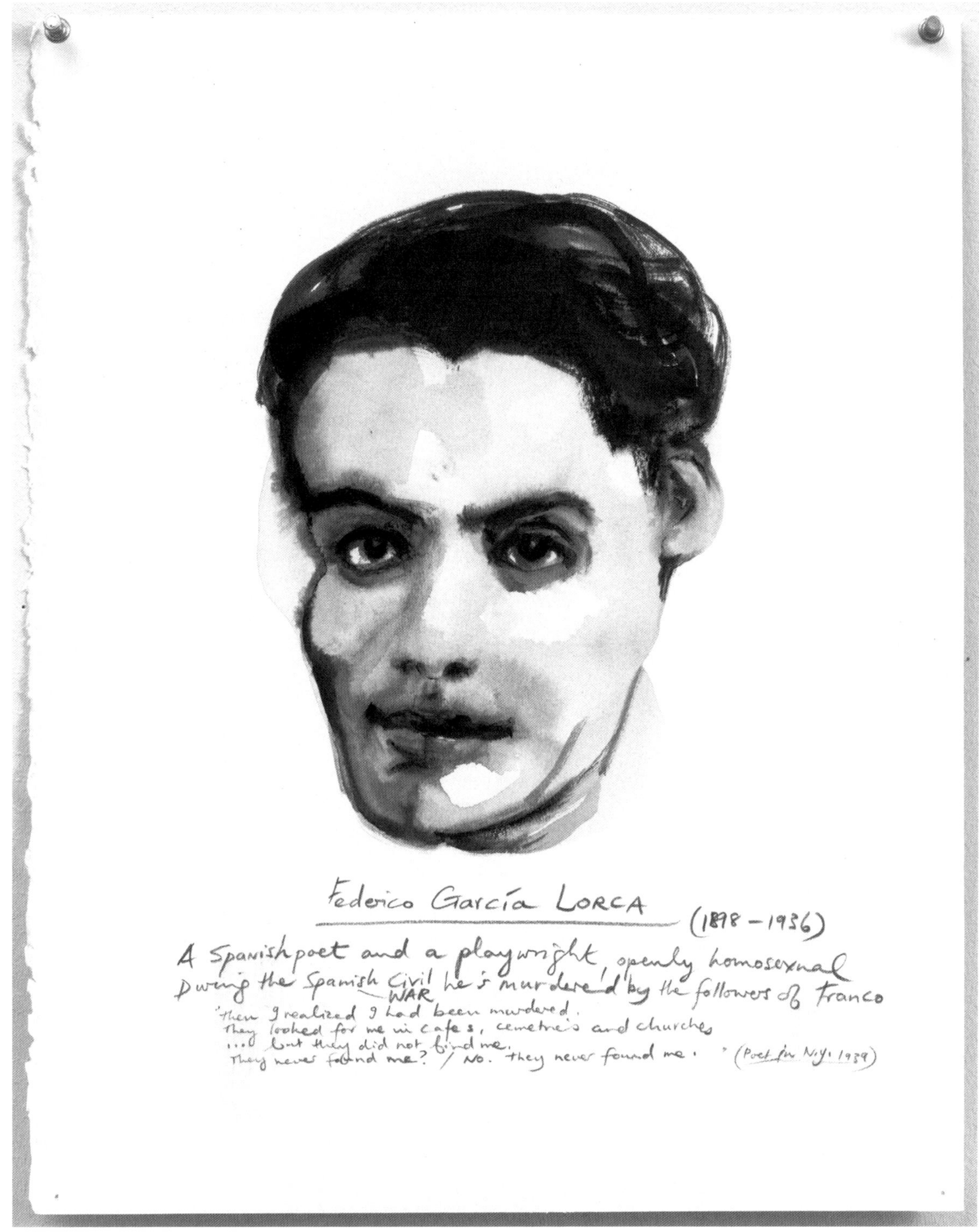

Marlene Dumas, *Great Men*, 2014, 44 × 35 cm, ink, pencil and metallic acrylic on paper. Federico García Lorca.

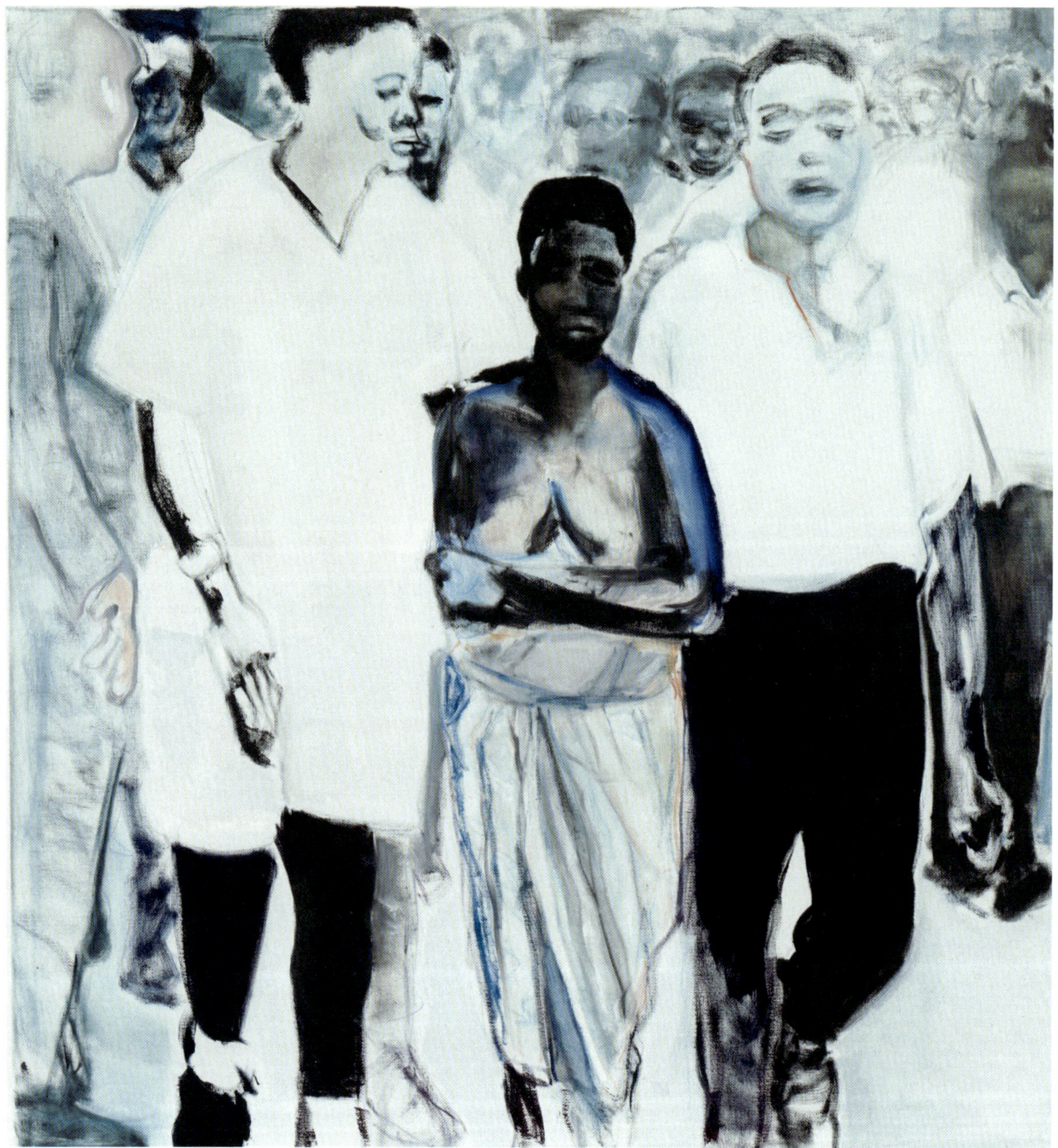

Marlene Dumas, *The Widow*, 2013, 150 × 140 cm, oil on canvas.

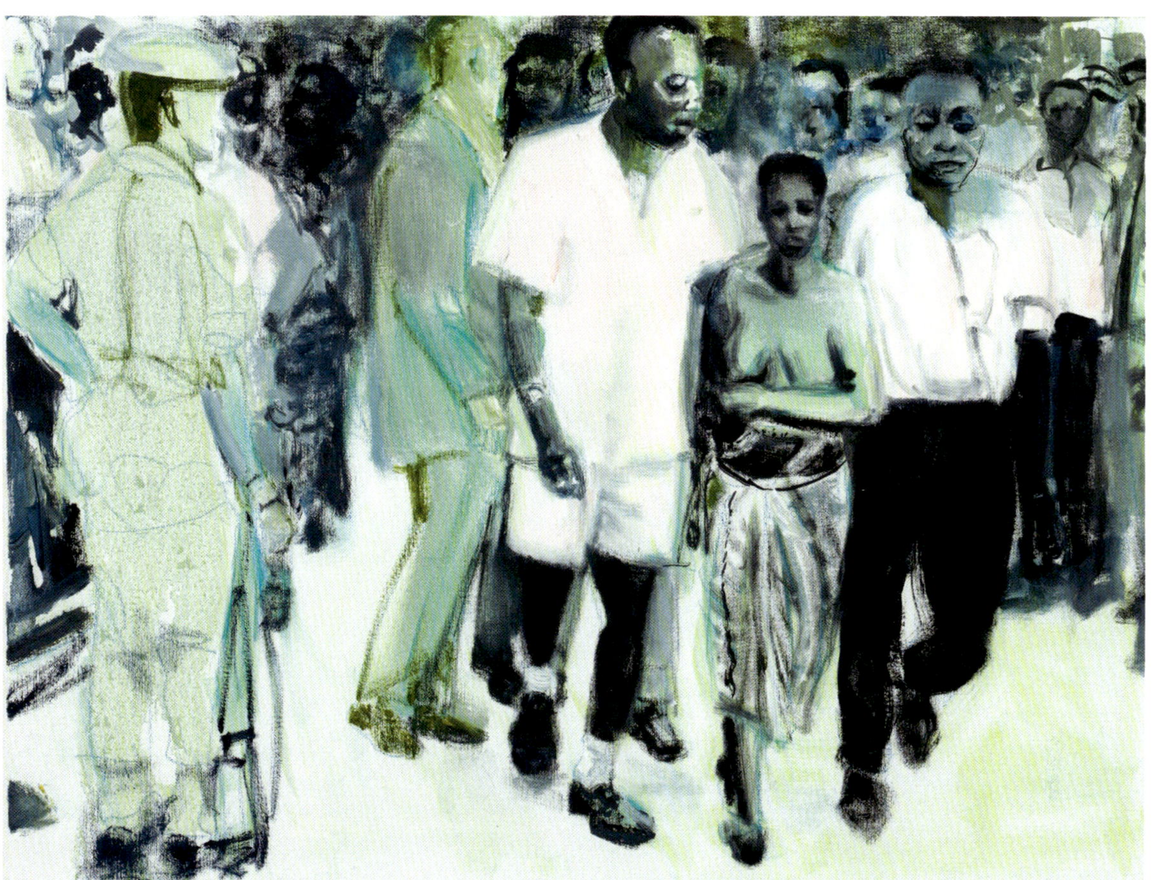

Marlene Dumas, *The Widow*, 2013, 60 × 80 cm, oil on canvas.

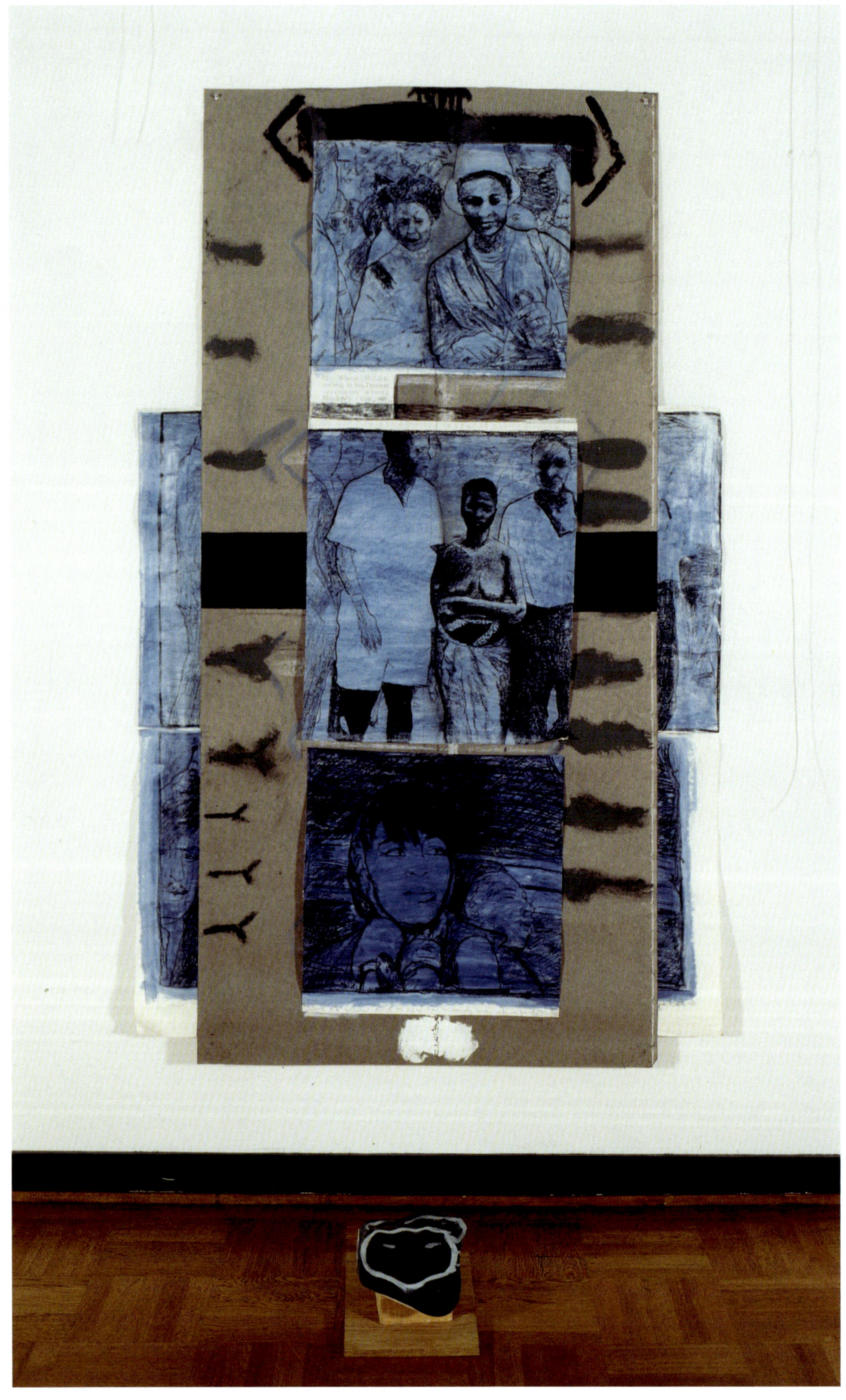

Marlene Dumas, *Drie vroue en ek*, 1982, 210 × 135 cm, acrylic, wood, chalk and felt paper.

al meddlers such as Nasser and Ghana's Nkrumah trying to take a hand in the Congo's internal affairs. Most of all, there seemed to be no end in sight under the present ground rules. For too long, U.N. troops, operating under fuzzy, limited orders, had stood listlessly by as the Congolese shot and stabbed one another; often the U.N.'s uncertain policy had prolonged more arguments than it settled.

But unlike the Soviet Union, the West wanted to strengthen, not weaken, the U.N. Since he took over the U.S. delegation three weeks ago, Stevenson has been energetically conferring with Hammarskjold, as well as with the Africans and Asians, in search of a "consensus" for a new formula that could break the long Congo stalemate. Hammarskjold wanted wider powers, enabling him to block money transfers from abroad to Congo banks and to search all incoming planes for

peat that about India and Nigeria." He knew Moscow could not come out flatly against any scheme with wide support among the Asians and Africans.

Common Ground. With the news of Lumumba's death, and in the thunder of Moscow's political drums, hopes of agreement suddenly faded in a welter of confusion. But it soon became clear that although several African nations (Ghana, Guinea, the U.A.R., Mali, Morocco) quickly joined the Russians in recognizing Gizenga's "government," that was where Moscow's success stopped. Mali and Guinea spoke up halfheartedly for Hammarskjold's resignation (but not his ouster); most shared the view of one Asian who admitted, "We're all at fault for not giving Hammarskjold a stronger mandate."

Faced with the prospect of U.N. withdrawal from the Congo, almost all were suddenly sobered. A major factor was the

ing about the shipment of foreign arms and equipment into the Congo, and did not give Hammarskjold's men the right to intercept such contraband. This was, after all, the key to peace. But when the U.S. proposed amendments to close these loopholes, some of the resolution's backers were strangely reluctant to agree; one of them was Nasser's U.A.R., which had been trafficking in arms for Gizenga for some weeks and perhaps wanted to continue doing so.

The Lunge. What induced Moscow to embark on this disruptive lunge? One answer is that Russia wants nothing, nobody, no agreement, no group of nations capable of hampering any adventure or pursuit the Kremlin might have in mind. Though the Russians value the U.N. as a propaganda forum, they have no interest in a U.N. with power to act (Zorin was quick to point out that he had nothing against the U.N. itself, only against its executive officer). Even if the present attack is beaten back, it has served the Russians' purpose in intimidating Hammarskjold. After Khrushchev's attack last fall, Hammarskjold became notably more cautious in the Congo, shied away from involvement in the Laos squabble, on the ground that the Russians were waiting for just such an opportunity to bring him down.

In Africa, the Zorin attack alarmed governments who look to the U.N. for protection and as a forum where they can make their voices heard. But even here, the Russians had scored by their own reckoning. For the Communists look over the heads of governments to Africa's impassioned students and wild-eyed nationalists. If sufficiently encouraged in their anti-colonial hatred for white men, they can be depended on, in the Communists' view, ultimately to rule the future of Africa. The 10,000 students who rioted last week in Nigeria were a warning of how effective this tactic could be; Nigeria's moderate government was frankly frightened by the outburst, at week's end privately warned the U.S. that it would be forced to be somewhat more anti-colonial in its future policies if it were to keep its influence in African councils.

Planes over the Sudan. But Western experts doubt that Khrushchev is prepared for really serious intervention in the Congo. If the Russians tried to move into the Congo, they would face as many difficulties as the U.N.—or Patrice Lumumba —and they know it. Even providing major aid to Gizenga would be enormously difficult. In the deep Sudan interior, the overland roads are perilous, and planes can bring in only a trickle of supplies, even if the Sudan permitted overflights (which it has so far refused to do). If the Congo ever became a theater for a clash between East and West on the model of the Spanish Civil War, the West would have all the advantages of supply lines. As it is, the Russians will have all they can do just sneaking planes through or around the Sudan to feed Gizenga enough supplies to keep him going as a troublemaker.

Cold Shock. Basically, Lumumba's death was too good an opportunity for Khrushchev to miss and a chance to prove to comrades the world over that he could

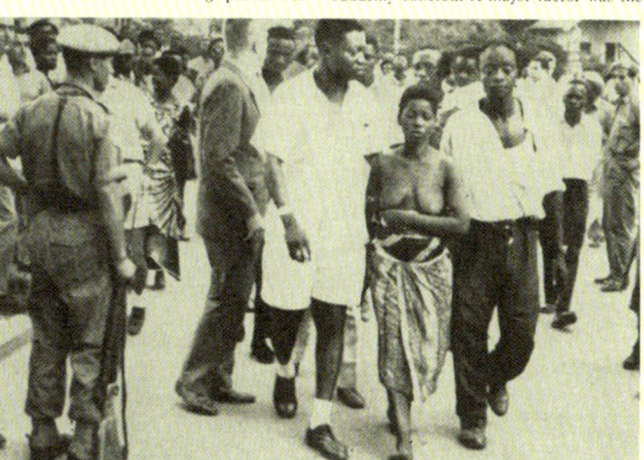

LUMUMBA'S MOURNING WIDOW IN LÉOPOLDVILLE
Gone were the Paris frocks.

arms. But many sensitive African nations were wary of too much power for the U.N. For its part, the U.S. was urging Belgium to cease its arms buildup in Katanga—aid that, in African eyes, was just as "unilateral" and disruptive as the Communists' support for Gizenga. (With extraordinarily bad timing, a chartered Stratocruiser arrived in Katanga last week carrying three crated jet fighters, doubtless procured with Belgian assistance.)

At one point, there was broad agreement among the Afro-Asians on a plan that would neutralize the competing Congolese army forces, oust all foreign military or paramilitary "advisers" and soldiers of fortune, bring back Parliament and a broadened central government. When Adlai Stevenson told Soviet Delegate Zorin about the plan, mentioning lightly that India and Nigeria—two conspicuous Afro-Asian names—might introduce it as a resolution, the Russian seemed startled: "What's that, what's that?" he barked at the interpreter. "Re-

conversion of India's Prime Minister Nehru, who had refused to send a single soldier to fight in Korea; since then Nehru has seen the Red Chinese in action in Tibet and elbowing at his own frontiers. "The future can be saved only by action —strong action!" he cried last week amid the ugly echoes of Moscow's threats, and announced that he was ready to contribute Indian combat troops to beef up Hammarskjold's Congo force.

Hastily, the Afro-Asians reached agreement at last on a resolution that most could support. Its main provisions: 1) the U.N. is to stop the Congo's civil war, using force if necessary to prevent clashes; 2) the opposing Congolese army units (Gizenga's, Mobutu's, Tshombe's) should be disarmed under U.N. control and taken out of politics; 3) all Belgians and other foreign military and political personnel should be forced out of the country; 4) Parliament is to be reconvened.

But the U.S. detected a couple of dangerous loopholes. The resolution said noth-

18

TIME, FEBRUARY 24, 1961

'The Congo: Death of Lumumba – & After', *Time Magazine*, 24 February 1961, page 20.

Marlene Dumas

Marlene Dumas (b. 1953 in Cape Town) grew up in South Africa but lives and works in Amsterdam. She is considered one of the most important and influential artists of our time. Over the past decades, her empathic paintings and drawings have impressed both the art world and the public, not only because of their sensitive, colouristic and deliquescent contours, but also because of their directness and expressiveness, and because of her choice of subjects. Dumas pays attention to marginal people, to discrimination and isolation, to nonconformity and the impossibility of meeting society's expectations. She approaches these subjects not in a confrontational manner, but, rather, indirectly, with quasi-realistic depictions and images from memory.

The Widow (2013) was inspired by a photo of Pauline Lumumba, the widow of the murdered prime minister of the Republic of Congo, taken during his funeral in 1961. The scene – which depicts her bare-breasted, with shorn hair, surrounded by fully-dressed men – possesses great dramatic force and import. Years before making this painting, while reading Simone de Beauvoir's autobiographical *Force of Circumstance*, Dumas had underlined the passage about Lumumba's funeral and also that exceptional moment when his widow was photographed. Already in 1982 she had included a drawing after that same photograph in a collage called *Drie vroue en ek* (Three women and I).

Great Men (2014–) is the title of a series of portraits of famous gay men rendered in Indian ink, in the halls of fame tradition of exhibiting images of geniuses and important personalities. These are people who are famous for their talents, but whose homosexuality has often been hushed up or obscured in their official biographies.

DS

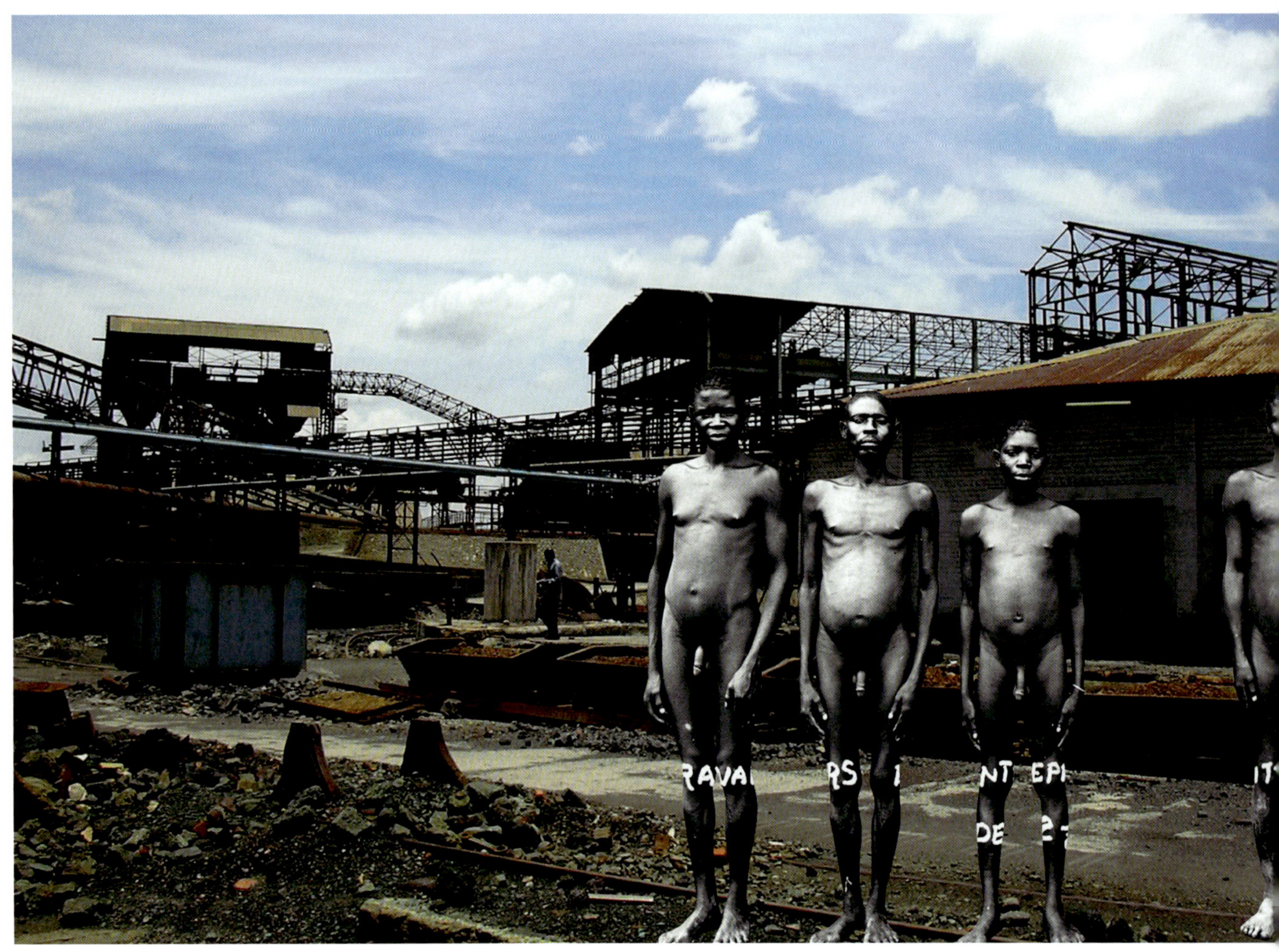

Sammy Baloji, *Untitled*, from the series *Mémoire*, 2006, 60 × 193.75 cm, digital print on matt satin paper.

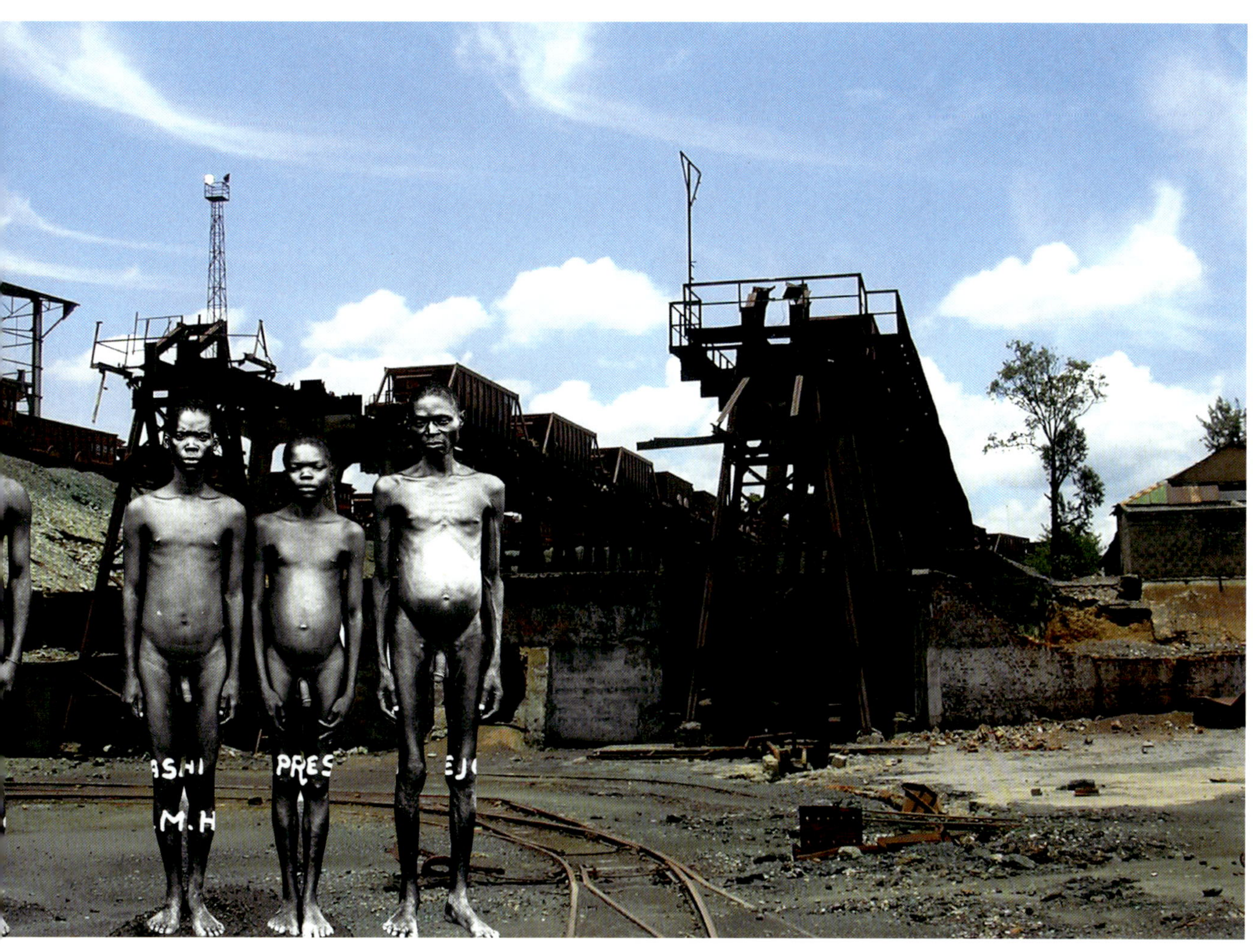
SHI   PRES   EJ
M.H

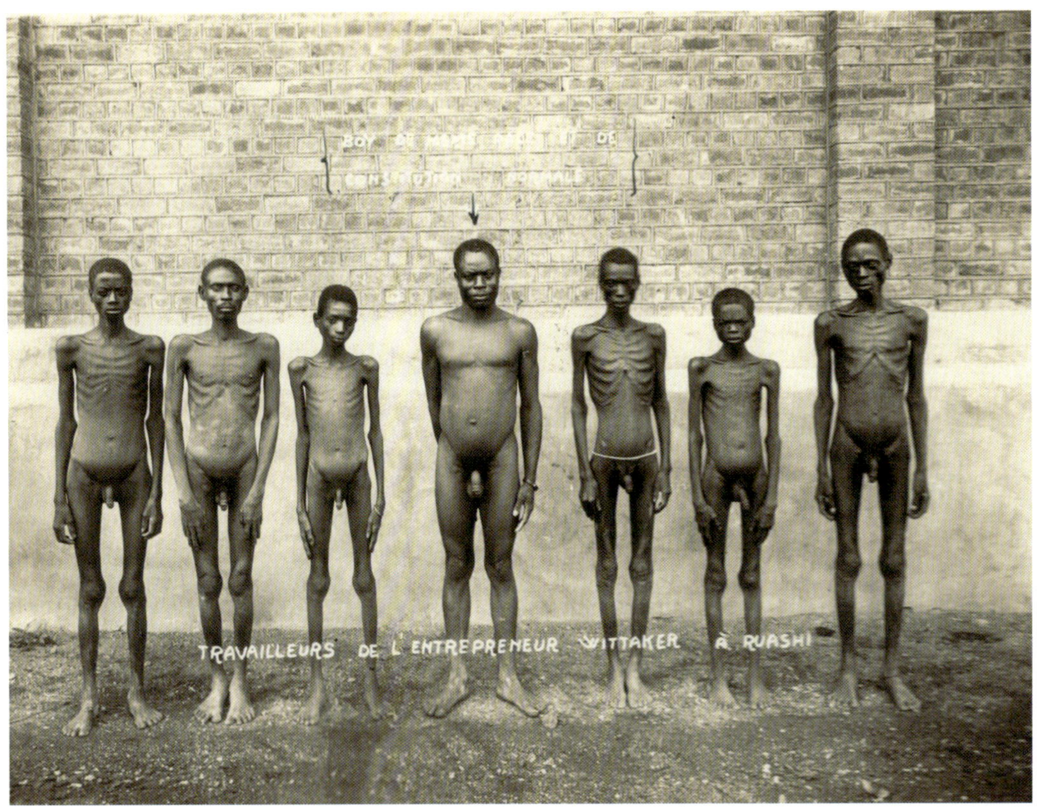

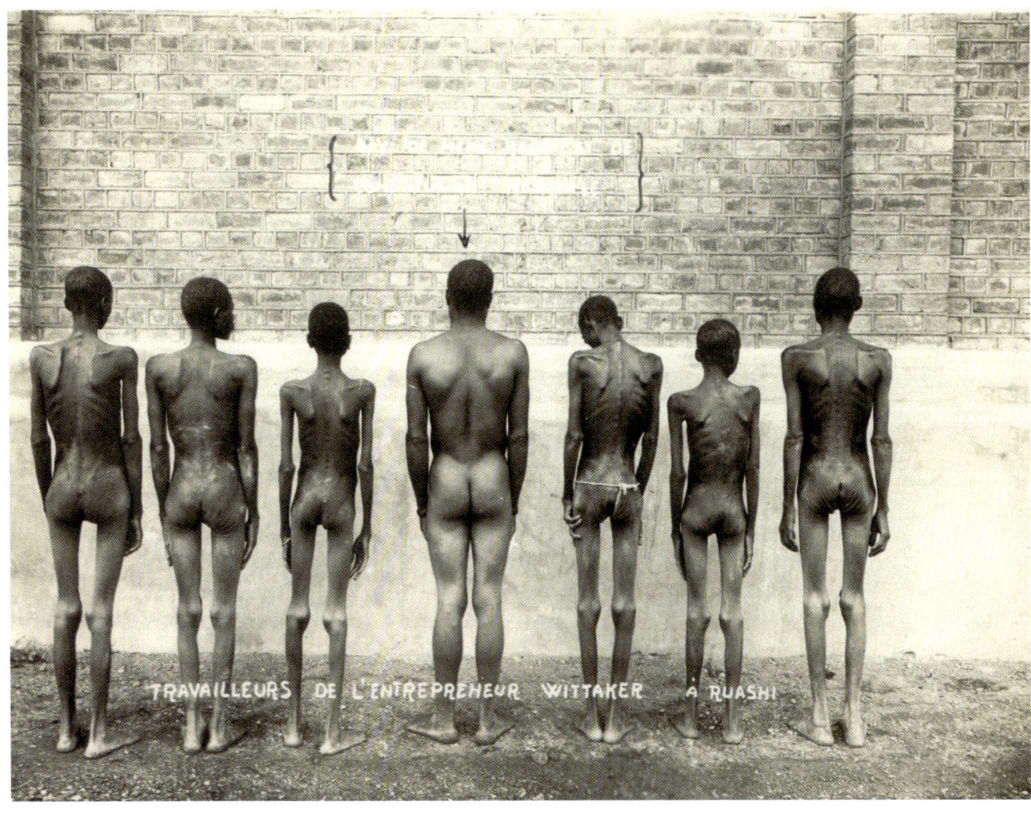

Photographs from the Archives of the Union Minière du Haut-Katanga (UMHK), Lubumbashi, former Belgian Congo, 1920s–30s.

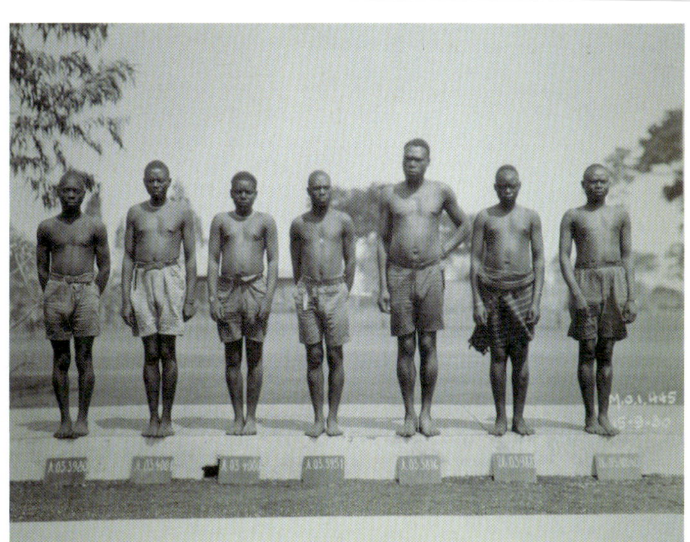 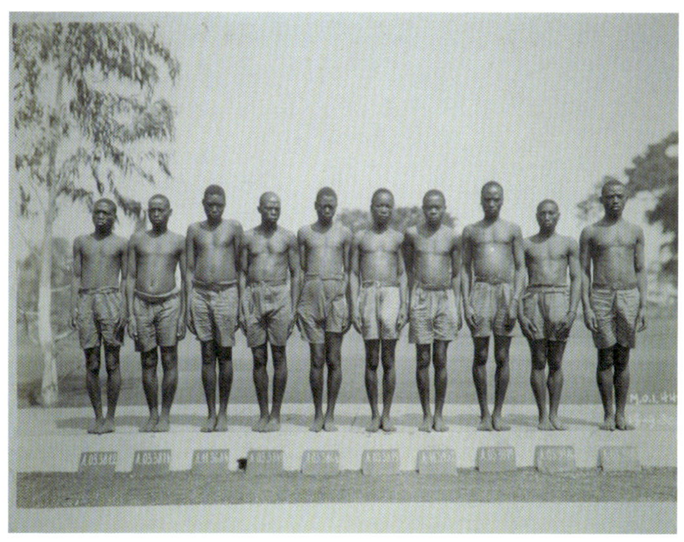

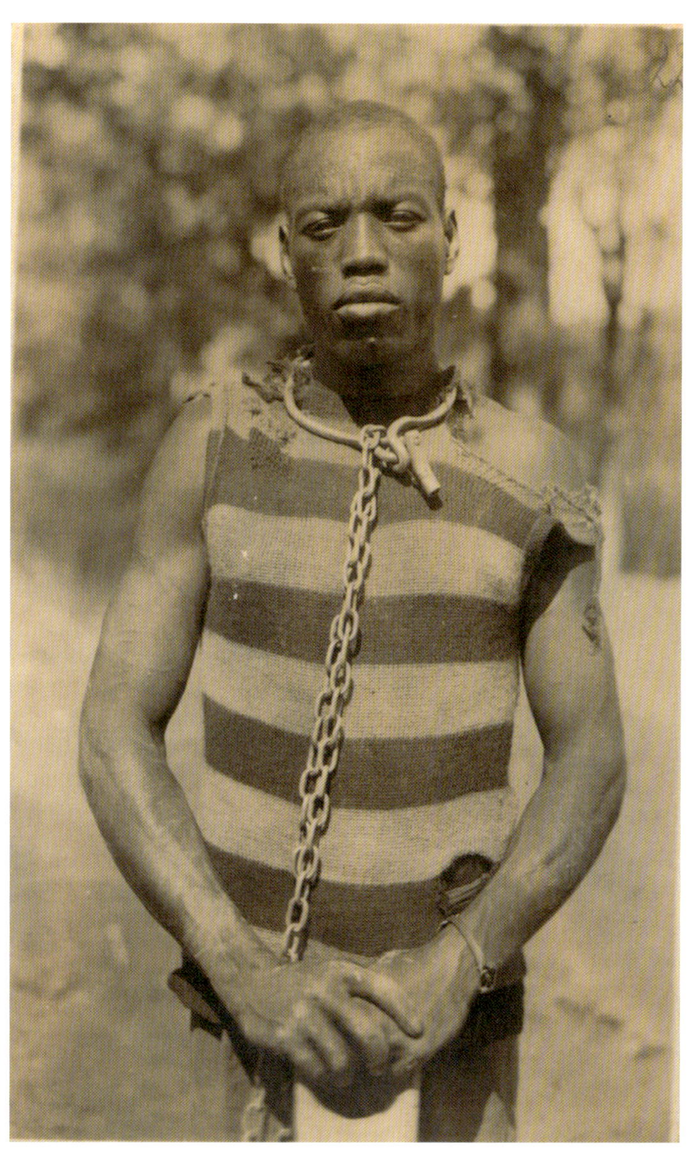

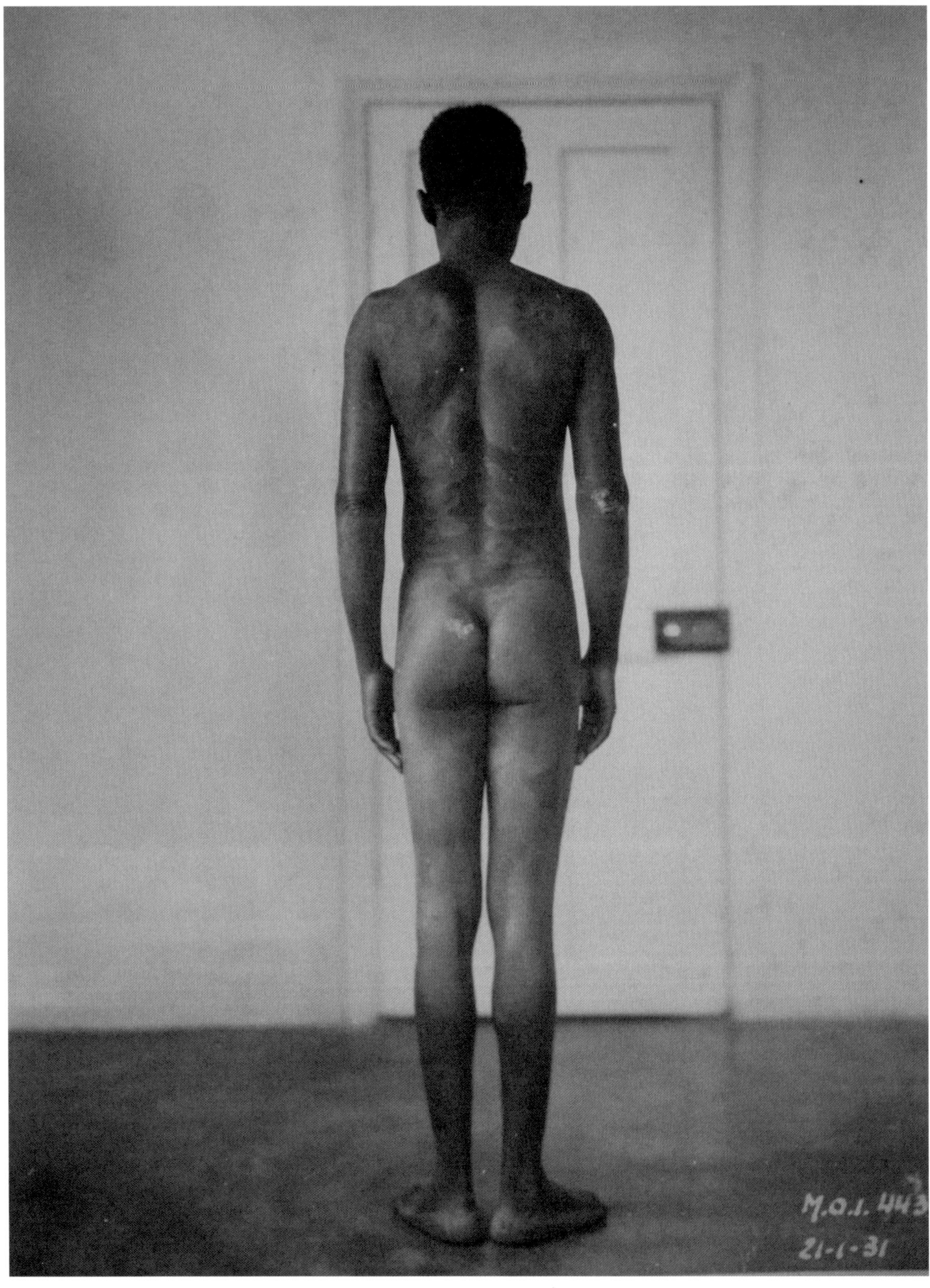

Photographs from the Archives of the Union Minière du Haut-Katanga (UMHK), Lubumbashi, former Belgian Congo, 1920s–30s.

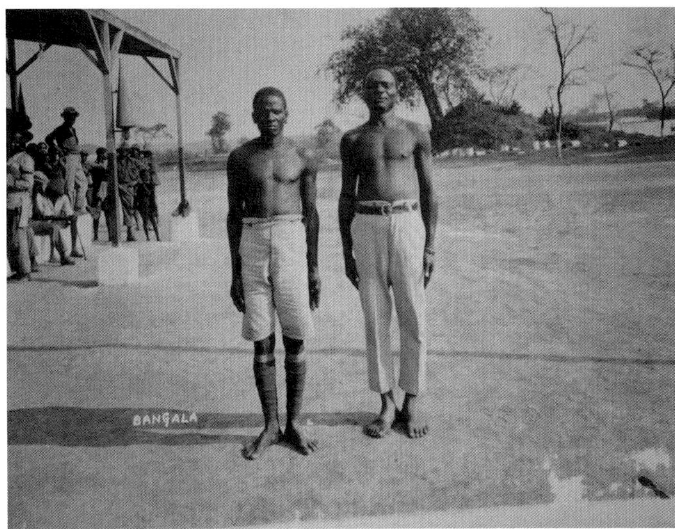

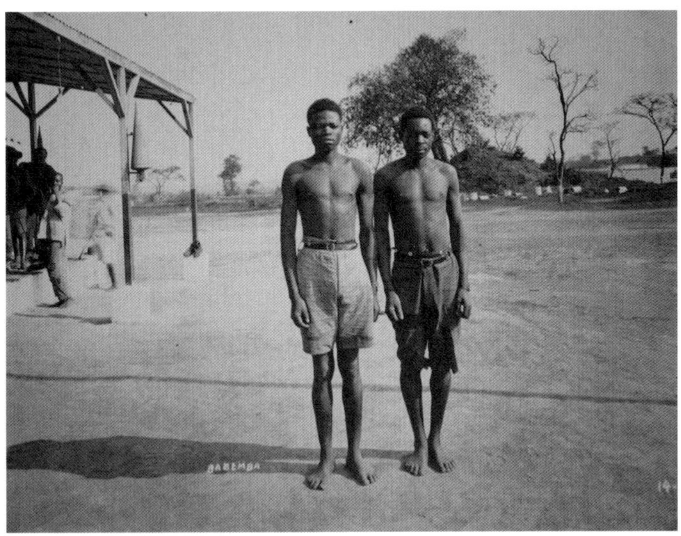

Sammy Baloji

Over the course of the past decade, Sammy Baloji (b. 1978 in Lubumbashi) has become one of the most astute observers of the social and cultural development of sub-Saharan Africa.
His probing work bears witness to the traumas and hopes, the tensions and contradictions of postcolonial reality. Before turning to photography, Baloji studied literature and social asciences at the University of Lubumbashi. This background undoubtedly influenced the way in which he approaches both the past and the present, and how in his approach he looks for patterns and structures rather than focusing on incidents and conflicts.

Lubumbashi is the capital of Haut-Katanga province and the second largest city in the Democratic Republic of the Congo. During the colonial era, Katanga was one of the wealthiest and most industrialised provinces of the Belgian Congo thanks to the copper industry. That industry has largely collapsed, but its traces are ubiquitous in the country and in the city. Baloji combines his photographs of that technological, architectural and cultural heritage with images from the colonial past, assembled from the archives of companies, government offices and organisations: photos of labourers, soldiers, village communities, and 'ethnographic' and

'medical' shots of individual men and women. These are often the only documents that bear witness to the existence and fate of these people. Baloji integrates them into his contemporary photos of post-industrial landscapes, abandoned mining sites and factory ruins. In doing so he composes series that confront the viewer with a colonial past and with the traces of decolonisation and of the republic, traces that will always remain in the life of the country and its inhabitants. Dating from 2006, *Mémoire* is a series that is representative of Baloji's artistic method. These are montages in which the various stages of a process

in full evolution are rendered visible simultaneously: the colonial era with white rule and the exploitation of the local populations, the decline since independence, and the current industrial revival under foreign, neocolonial control.

DS

stanley brouwn

Universal Embassy

66 av. Franklin Roosevelt
1050 Bruxelles
email: info@universal-embassy.be
site: www.universal-embassy.be

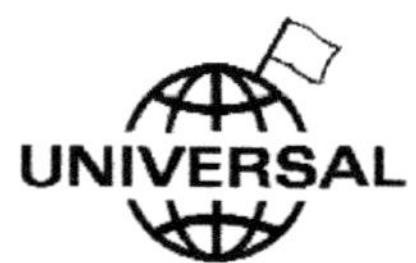

Universal Embassy

Franklin Rooseveltlaan 66
1050 Brussel
email: info@universal-embassy.be
site: www.universal-embassy.be

DECLARATION DE L'AMBASSADE UNIVERSELLE
12 décembre 2001

VERKLARING VAN DE UNI'
12. 12

Universal Embassy a été fondée par un réseau constitué autour de la lutte des sans-papiers. Elle veut réunir au-delà des frontières des disciplines, des citoyens concernés par une pensée universelle. A court terme, c'est une habitation d'urgence.

Universal Embassy s'est installée dans le bâtiment déserté de l'ancienne ambassade de Somalie qui ne tient plus sa fonction suite à la déchirure de l'état somalien. Nous citoyens du monde, avec ou sans-papiers, avons créé une ambassade hors du territoire pour reconstituer nos droits.

Le sans-papiers est un paria, il n'est chez lui nulle part. Il pose très clairement l'inanité de notre conception de la citoyenneté où les routes de l'inclusion croisent celles de l'exclusion. Les usagers de ce passage créent un monde commun. Universal Embassy propose de tracer l'expression politique de ce monde commun.

Production souterraine

Nous ne pouvons admettre un système qui entraîne des centaines de milliers d'êtres humains à vivre et travailler en Europe dans la clandestinité. C'est accepter la reproduction de tous les schémas d'exploitation. Le clandestin comme figure inversée, est un travailleur délocalisé du tiers-monde dans nos quartiers. L'économie informelle n'est pas à la marge, elle est la base de nombreuses branches de l'économie formelle. La démultiplication de la sous-traitance crée cette atomisation et ethnicisation de la production et de l'offre de services.

Les autorités belges mettent un point final au processus de régularisation exceptionnel qu'elles ont initié voici maintenant deux ans. Une trentaine de milliers de sans-papiers seront désormais libres de vivre ici. Générosité accordée du bout des lèvres. Pour tous les autres, seules la répression et l'expulsion sont à attendre. Hypocrisie. Chacun sait que quotidiennement, des migrants, hommes et femmes et enfants, tombent dans la clandestinité. Toutes les politiques de traitement des migrations mènent à cette impasse. La régularisation opérée n'y apporte aucune solution, elle n'est qu'un nettoyage temporaire de la clandestinité apparente..

Limites de la mondialisation

La mondialisation bouscule les échelles. Historiquement, les droits ont été lié à la nationalité et la nationalité à un territoire. La nation exprime une communauté de destin, celle à venir est planétaire. Le territoire, la frontière, sont l'apanage de la police. La répression est la seule potentialité politique à s'y réaliser. Une lame de fond traverse notre monde, elle est technique, financière, idéologique. La vie quotidienne de la myriade humaine est bouleversée. Le travail, le logement, la nourriture, les déplacement, le temps... ont changé de dimensions.

La figure du travailleur était intimement liée à l'émergence de la citoyenneté. Considérer le travailleur comme citoyen a permis d'abolir l'esclavage. Mais, le marché ne dépend plus des demandes exprimées par les territoires. Le travail s'organise de même. Nous percevons la réouverture sélective des frontières comme une scission fondamentale. L'ébauche d'un statut de travailleur immigré, intérimaire international (un employeur spécifique pour une période déterminée), discuté à Laeken, ouvre une tolérance à toute une série de sous-statuts inacceptables. Cette politique migratoire unilatérale déploie une logique strictement instrumentale... en sélectionnant soigneusement les compétences et les profils. Le travail impose une norme d'inclusion hors du droit. Une telle politique n'évitera pas la reproduction de la clandestinité et renforcera la criminalisation des étrangers dans leur ensemble.

Déconstruction

Schengen applique une politique d'exception. Nous subissons cette crispation autoritaire qui aujourd'hui réduit la liberté de circuler au sein de l'espace européen. Nous entendons ces appels à la suspension de cette même liberté pour les futurs citoyens européens de l'est. Cette proclamation formelle d'une citoyenneté européenne sans sa concrétisation est une résurgence inquiétante d'un esprit impérialiste (à l'instar de ces colonisés traités en frères et en sujets).

D'autres signes de régression sont perceptibles. Pourquoi rédiger de nouveaux textes comme la charte européenne des droits fondamentaux, alors que l'application d'autres textes plus précis et plus contraignants n'est pas pleine et entière? Il s'agit d'une déconstruction systématique des droits fondamentaux et leur substitution par des leurres démocratiques.

Constitution

Nous exigeons que l'Union Européenne ouvre les espaces qui nous permettent de concrétiser notre citoyenneté. Les habitants peuvent constituer leur citoyenneté dans un processus permanent de recomposition politique.

Le citoyen, sera l'habitant. Le domicile devrait transcender la question nationale: droit de se déplacer, de s'établir... choix de demeurer dans son lieu de naissance quels que soient les chahuts géopolitiques. Le lieu ancre le politique. Un hypothétique statut de citoyen du monde est une abstraction inutile. L'appartenance planétaire n'est pas un statut, c'est une réalité factuelle.

Le local, c'est le global à petite échelle. Paradoxalement, une expression politique possible germe dans le local. C'est l'espace habité. Les villes se recomposent perpétuellement, elles évoluent vers une inter-communauté sans origine majoritaire. L'urbain métissé est un monde à vivre. La reprise politique de l'espace de vie est une constitution de soi et de la collectivité. La citoyenneté n'est pas l'établissement de règles indépendantes des pratiques établies par la participation. Cette pratique est une recherche du commun dans la diversité. Elle se place avant le gouvernement.

Il faut défendre cette société potentielle entravée par les nationalités.

Universal Embassy is opgericht door een netwerk dat actief is in de strijd voor daklozen en immigranten. Het wil, uitstijgend boven de grenzen van de verschillende disciplines, burgers samenbrengen die zich aangesproken voelen door een universeel gedachtegoed. Op korte termijn is dat onderdak.

Universal Embassy is gevestigd in het verlaten gebouw van de voormalige ambassade van Somalië, die geen dienst meer doet als gevolg van de barsting van de Somalische staat. Wij, wereldburgers, met of zonder papieren, hebben een ambassade zonder land opgericht om onze rechten in ere te herstellen.

De migrant is een paria, hij is nergens thuis. Hij stelt heel duidelijk de zinloosheid van onze opvatting van burgerschap aan de kaak. De wegen van de insluiting kruisen die van de uitsluiting. De gebruikers van deze doorgang scheppen een gemeenschappelijke wereld. Universal Embassy een politieke uitdrukking geven aan deze gemeenschappelijke wereld.

Ondergrondse productie

We kunnen niet leven met een systeem dat honderdduizenden mensen tot het leven en werken in de illegaliteit in Europa aanzet. Dat zou neerkomen op het accepteren van de verbreiding van alle vormen van uitbuiting. Als de perceptie van de illegaal wordt omgekeerd, krijg je een werknemer die vanuit de Derde Wereld naar onze streek is gekomen. De informele economie draait niet in de marge, maar is de basis van een groot aantal officiële economiesectoren. De cascade van de onderaanneming verdeelt de productie en de dienstverlening in afzonderlijke atomen en etnieën.

De Belgische overheid rondt op dit moment de uitzonderlijke regularisatieprocedure af die twee jaar geleden werd opgestart. Zo'n dertigduizend migranten mogen hier blijven. Een gastvrijheid die met mondjesmaat wordt verleend. Voor alle anderen resten alleen repressie en uitwijzing. Dit is hypocriet, iedereen weet dat dagelijks migranten, mannen, vrouwen en kinderen, in de illegaliteit terechtkomen. Elk migratiebeleid leidt tot deze impasse. De uitgevoerde regularisatie biedt geen enkele oplossing, het is slechts een tijdelijke opruimactie van de zichtbare illegaliteit.

Grenzen aan de mondialisering

De mondialisering werpt schaalindelingen omver. Historisch waren rechten verbonden met een nationaliteit, en een nationaliteit met een territorium. De natie is de uitdrukking van een gemeenschappelijke bestemming; onze toekomstige bestemming is planetair. Territoria en grenzen zijn het terrein van de politie. Repressie is de enige politieke mogelijkheid die verwezenlijkt kan worden. Onze wereld wordt gescheiden door een diepe zee van technische, financiële en ideologische wateren. Het dagelijkse leven van de menselijke mierenhoop wordt omvergegooid. Werk, huisvesting, eten, transport, tijd... alles heeft een andere dimensie gekregen.

De figuur van de werknemer is nauw verbonden met de opkomst van het burgerschap. Door de werknemer te zien als een burger kon de slavernij worden

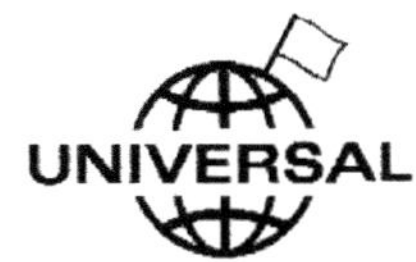

SELE AMBASSADE

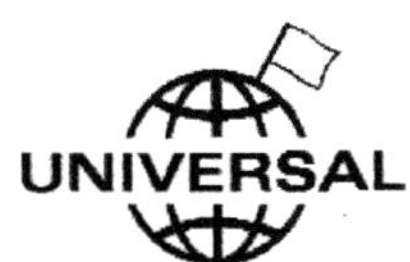

Universal Embassy
66 av. Franklin Roosevelt
1050 Bruxelles
email: info@universal-embassy.be
site: www.universal-embassy.be

DECLARATION OF THE UNIVERSAL EMBASSY
12 December 2001

chaft. Maar de markt is niet meer afhankelijk van de vraag van het ter-
Het werk organiseert zichzelf. Wij zien de selectieve heropening van de
en als een fundamentele kloof. De plannen voor een statuut van geïm-
erde werknemer of internationale uitzendkracht (een specifieke werkge-
oor een bepaalde periode) die in Laken werden besproken, openen de
aar een hele reeks onaanvaardbare onderstatuten. Dit unilaterale migra-
eid hanteert een strikt instrumentele logica… door zorgvuldig de vaardi-
n en profielen te selecteren. Arbeid legt een buitenwettelijke insluiting-
op. Zo'n soort beleid zal nooit de verbreiding van de illegaliteit tegen-
en leiden tot de criminalisering van buitenlanders in hun geheel.

aak

gen past een uitzonderingsbeleid toe. Wij ondergaan die autoritaire grip
genwoordig de bewegingsvrijheid binnen de Europese zone belemmert.
ren die oproepen tot de opheffing van diezelfde vrijheid voor de toekom-
burgers uit het oosten. Die formele proclamatie van een Europees bur-
hap zonder concrete invulling is een verontrustende wedergeboorte van
nperialistische mentaliteit (naar het voorbeeld van de gekoloniseerden
onderworpen broeders en zusters worden behandeld).

andere tekens van regressie zijn waarneembaar. Waarom zouden we
e teksten opstellen, zoals het Europees handvest voor de fundamentele
en, als andere, concretere en dwingendere teksten niet volledig worden
oerd? Dit komt neer op een systematische afbraak van de fundamente-
hten en de vervanging door democratische drogbeelden.

ouw

sen dat de Europese Unie ruimte biedt waarin wij ons burgerschap
d kunnen geven. De inwoners kunnen hun burgerschap vormgeven in
ermanent proces van politieke wedersamenstelling. De burger, dat is de
er. De woonplaats moet de kwestie van nationaliteit overstijgen: het
op verplaatsing, op vestiging… de keuze om in de geboorteplaats te bli-
ongeacht de geopolitieke woelingen. De plaats verankert de politiek. Een
hetisch statuut van wereldburger is een nutteloze abstractie. Het beho-
t de wereld is geen statuut, maar een feitelijke realiteit.

aatselijke is het mondiale op kleine schaal. Paradoxaal genoeg ontstaat
nogelijke politieke uitdrukking in het plaatselijke. Dat is de bewoonde
e. Steden stellen zich voortdurend opnieuw samen en evolueren naar
nderlinge gemeenschap zonder overheersende oorsprong. De stedelijke
kroes is de levende wereld. In de politieke overname van de levensruim-
irden den eigen persoon en de collectiviteit opgebouwd. Burgerschap is
et vaststellen van regels, onafhankelijk van de praktijk die de burgerlijke
iipatie in het leven roept. Die praktijk is een gemeenschappelijk onder-
binnen diversiteit. Die praktijk komt vóór de staat.

eten deze potentiële samenleving, gekluisterd door nationaliteiten, verdedigen.

Universal Embassy has been established by a network constituted around the
struggle of people without papers. It wants to bring together, beyond the borders of disciplines, citizens concerned with a universal thinking. On a short
term, the Embassy is an emergency housing.

Universal Embassy occupied the deserted building of the former Somali
embassy disused since the tearing apart of the Somali State. We citizen of the
world, with or without papers, have created an embassy out of the territory to
reconstitute our rights.

The man without paper is a pariah, he has nowhere to feel at home. He reveals
clearly the inanity of our conception of citizenship where the inclusion roads
are crossing the one's of exclusion. The users of this passage are creating a
common world. Universal Embassy intends to trace the political expression of
this common world.

Underground production

We cannot admit a system which trains hundreds of thousands of human
beings to live and work in Europe in clandestine. This is to admit the reproduction of all schemes of exploitation. The clandestine, as an inverted figure
is a delocalised worker from the third world in our neighbourhoods. The informal economy is not at the margin, it is the base of many branches of the formal economy. The multiplication of subcontracting is creating this atomisation
and ethnicisation of the production and services offer.

The Belgian authorities are finalising the exceptional regularization process
they initiated now two years ago. About thirty thousand people without
papers will be hereafter free to live here. Faint generosity. All the others have
only to expect repression and expulsion. Hypocrisy. Everyone knows foreigners are falling into illegality every day. All politics addressed to foreigners
are leading to this blind alley. The performed regularization brings no solution,
it is only a temporary cleansing of the prominent clandestineness.

Limits of the globalisation

Globalisation jostles the scales. Historically, rights have been linked to nationality, and nationality to a territory. Nation expresses a community of destiny.
The one to come is planetary. Territory, border are the prerogative of police.
Repression is the only political potentiality to realize itself. An undercurrent
runs through our world, it is technical, financial, ideological. The everyday life
of the human myriad is subverted. Work, housing, food, displacements, time…
changed their dimensions.

The figure of the worker is intimately tied with the emergence of citizenship.
To consider the worker as citizen permitted to abolish slavery. But the market

---

doesn't rely anymore on the demands of territories. The same for the organi-
zing of work. We perceive the selective reopening of borders as a fundamental shift. The outline of a migrant worker status, international interim worker
(a specific employer for a fix period), discussed in Laeken, opens a tolerance
for an all range of unacceptable under statuses. This unilateral migrant policy
displays a strictly instrumental logic… by selecting carefully competences and
profiles. Work is imposing inclusion norms out of the law. Such a policy will not
avoid the reproduction of clandestineness and will reinforce the criminaliza-
tion of foreigners in their globality.

Deconstruction

Shengen is applying an exception regime. We suffer this authoritarian shrivel-
ling which today reduces the movement freedom within the European space.
We are hearing these calls to the suspension of this same liberty for the future East European citizens. This formal proclamation of a European citizenship
without its concretisation is an alarming resurgence of an imperialist spirit
(like those colonized treated as brothers and as subjects).

Other signs of regression are perceptible. Why drawing up new texts like the
European Charter on fundamental rights, when the application of existing
more precise and more legally binding texts is not fulfilled? It is about a systematic deconstruction of fundamental rights and its substitution with democratic lures.

Constitution

We are demanding that the European Union opens the spaces which permit us
to concretise our citizenship in a permanent process of political reconstruction.

The citizen will be the inhabitant. The domicile should transcend the national
question: the right to move, to settle… choice to stay in ones birth place whatever the geopolitical rows. The place anchors the politic. Hypothetical world
citizen status is a useless abstraction. The planetary belonging is not a status,
it is a factual reality.

The local is the global on a small scale. Paradoxically, a possible political
expression germinates in the local. This is the inhabited space. Cities are per-
petually recomposing themselves, they are evolving into an inter community
without majority group origin. The urban diversity is a world to live. The political reclaiming of living space is a constitution of the self and of the collecti-
vity. Citizenship is not the establishment of rules independent of practices
made by participation. This practice is a searching of the common within the
diversity. It situates itself before governorship.

We have to defend this potential society hindered by nationality.

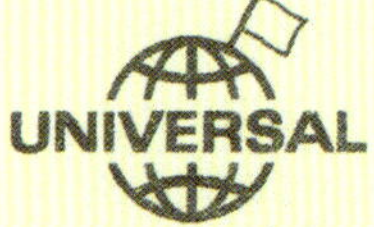

décembre 2001   Nº 1

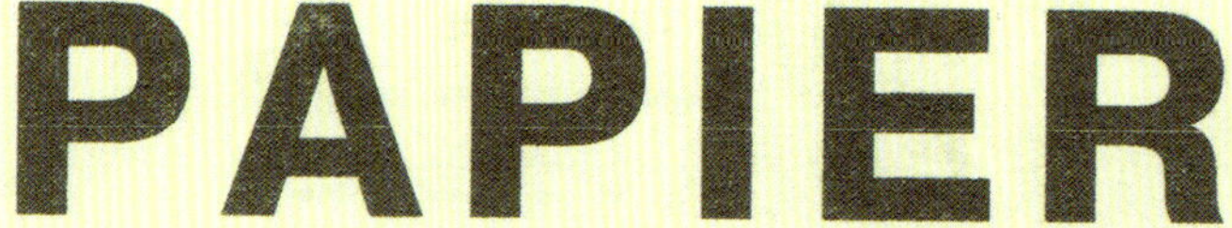

PAPIER

Carnet de bord - Universal Embassy - Bruxelles

SANS-PAPIERS
UNE PROBLEMATIQUE EPUISEE?

On pourrait croire que suite à la campagne de régularisation initiée en 1999, la problématique des sans-papiers est résolue ou sur le point de l'être. Il n'en est cependant rien.

Si de nombreux sans-papiers ont déjà pu bénéficier de la loi de régularisation du 22 décembre 1999, un grand nombre d'entre eux attend toujours, deux ans après, une réponse à la demande introduite dans le cadre de cette loi, et ce alors que le délai fixé pour le traitement des dossiers a été fixé à trois mois. Outre la question du respect de la loi que cela soulève, cet enlisement de la procédure a des effets plus que néfastes sur la vie des individus concernés. Pour ces personnes, la vie quotidienne conserve son aspect précaire et reste une lutte permanente pour une certaine reconnaissance sociale. Cette fragilité au quotidien induit également des souffrances psychologiques considérables liées notamment à l'absence de perspectives d'avenir.

Rappelons qu'à l'époque nombreux sont ceux qui n'ont pas rentré de dossier de régularisation en raison du manque de confiance envers la bonne foi des autorités belges. Et à juste titre d'ailleurs puisqu'à l'époque on a pu assister à de nombreuses tentatives en vue d'étouffer le mouvement des sans-papiers dans un contexte de surenchères électorales. Il était en outre, très difficile de porter un jugement cohérent sur les événements, notamment en raison des pressions constantes de divers milieux parties prenantes au débat sur cette campagne. Ce sentiment s'est également justifié par la suite du fait même que les délais prévus par la loi n'ont pas été respectés et qu'aucune disposition légale ultérieure n'y a apporté de solution.

INEGALITES

La loi du 22 décembre 1999 ayant été adoptée pour apporter une solution ponctuelle à une situation de crise n'a pas résolu le problème de ceux qui n'ont pas osé rentrer de dossier ou qui ne remplissaient pas tous les critères fixés par la loi. On voit donc que la problématique est loin d'être épuisée.

Aujourd'hui quelques sans-papiers introduisent une demande de régularisation sur base de l'article 9, alinéa 3 de la loi du 15 décembre 1980. Néanmoins les critères prévus par cette loi, de même que ses conditions d'application, sont tellement limités que cette possibilité ne laisse que de faibles espoirs de voir les dossiers aboutir.

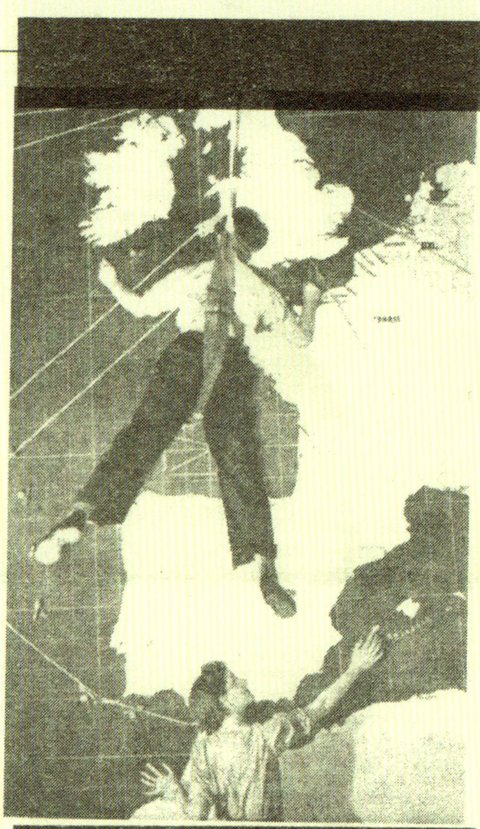

De plus, l'application pour une même situation de deux lois différentes (celle de 1980 et celle de 1999) suscite des inégalités entre les individus qui tombent sous leur application. Alors que la loi de régularisation de 1999 prévoit le droit au travail et parfois à l'aide sociale pendant la période d'attente, la législation de 1980, elle, ne permet de bénéficier d'aucun droit.

Il paraît indispensable, au vu de ces éléments, de revoir aujourd'hui la loi du 15 décembre 1980 en vue de mettre fin aux exploitations multiples des personnes sans papiers. Ainsi, ces individus doivent pouvoir compter sur le respect de leurs droits fondamentaux.

D'une manière plus générale, apparaît la nécessité d'adapter la loi à l'évolution d'une société de plus en plus inexorablement cosmopolite.

Mohamed Benzaouia

Mohamed Benzaouia, 'Sans-papiers: une problématique épuisée?', *Papier*, No. 1 (December 2001).

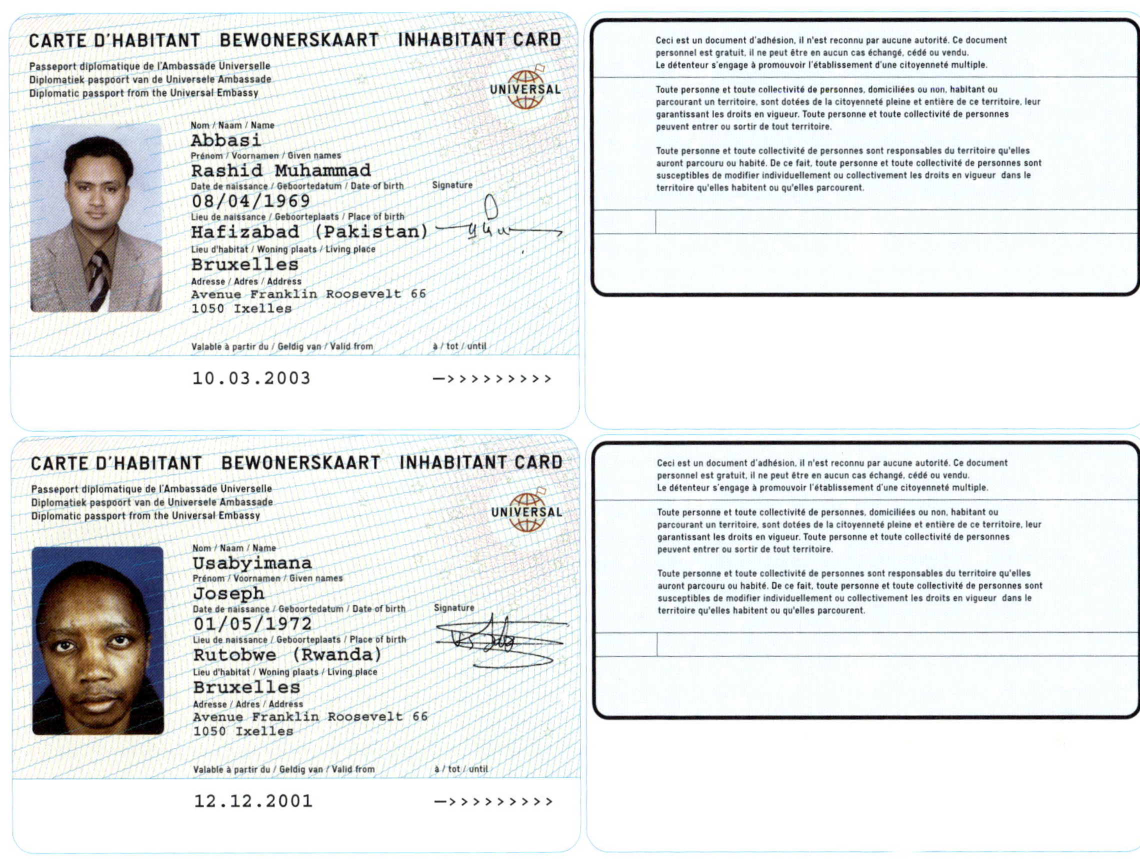

Universal Embassy
Inhabitant Cards.

The Universal Embassy Archives Inventory

Between 2000 and 2006 the Universal Embassy designated a building in Brussels whose main function was to accommodate people with no identity documents undergoing the regularisation process. It took its name from the building's previous occupant, the Embassy of Somalia, who had abandoned it due to the tragic civil war that had torn the country apart and brought all diplomatic activity to a halt. The property became universal as it gathered together individuals affected by problems of discrimination linked to their nationality. From 2001 to 2005, migrants with no identity papers continuously inhabited the building.

This political action was a direct continuation of the occupation in 1998/99 of the Saint John the Baptist at the Béguinage, a church in the centre of Brussels. The Universal Embassy brought together its inhabitants – undocumented migrants from numerous countries (Morocco, Algeria, Ecuador, Bangladesh, Albania, former Yugoslavia, Ukraine, Rwanda, Congo, Somalia, Iran, Afghanistan, Pakistan, Syria, Aruba…) and a network of individuals aware of the importance of their struggle, developing their own methods of resistance and expression through participation in various actions on a local, national and European level.

One archive document describes the significance of the action: 'Just as any embassy, it is a representation, but not of any one state. What is represented here is yet to come. Its inhabitants, the *sans-papiers*, the new pariahs of the free world, are actively challenging citizenship as related to a nation. By interfering in the contours of a state's representations, the embassy locally abolishes the limits of the border. Its inhabitants embody the "already-there" of a place present in the world.'

For the inhabitants and individuals supporting the action, this embassy-cum-dwelling place opened up new horizons with regards to new rights. It became a place of exchange and debate where migrants, *sans-papiers*, social actors, artists, cultural workers and inhabitants of the city together contemplated the notion of free movement and developed a new necessary solidarity.

This process of reflection translated into a declaration, into numerous texts and multiple actions. The Universal Embassy led to the struggle of the *sans-papiers* being evaluated in a forward-looking and sustained manner and to a move away from the one-dimensional vision of immigration as a matter solely for the Ministry of Interior and the Immigration Office.

In 2016, wishing to make the archives of the Universal Embassy accessible, members of the former support group made contact with the Etopia centre for private archives. Throughout 'The Absent Museum' exhibition, documents will re-emerge so that they can be described, organised and prepared, so as to make them accessible, usable and durable. Etopia will slowly analyse the many papers, photographs, films and digital files, some of which will be showcased during the archiving process.

Above and beyond its preservation, the preparation of these archives aims to provide a readable rendition of the history of a dwelling place that also functioned as a meeting ground for action and expression, an absolutely unique example of urban struggle, linking everyday practices with political imagination. As archivists, the focus of our endeavours is the widest possible dissemination of the content of these documents.

Szymon Zareba
Archivist, Etopia centre
for private archives, Namur

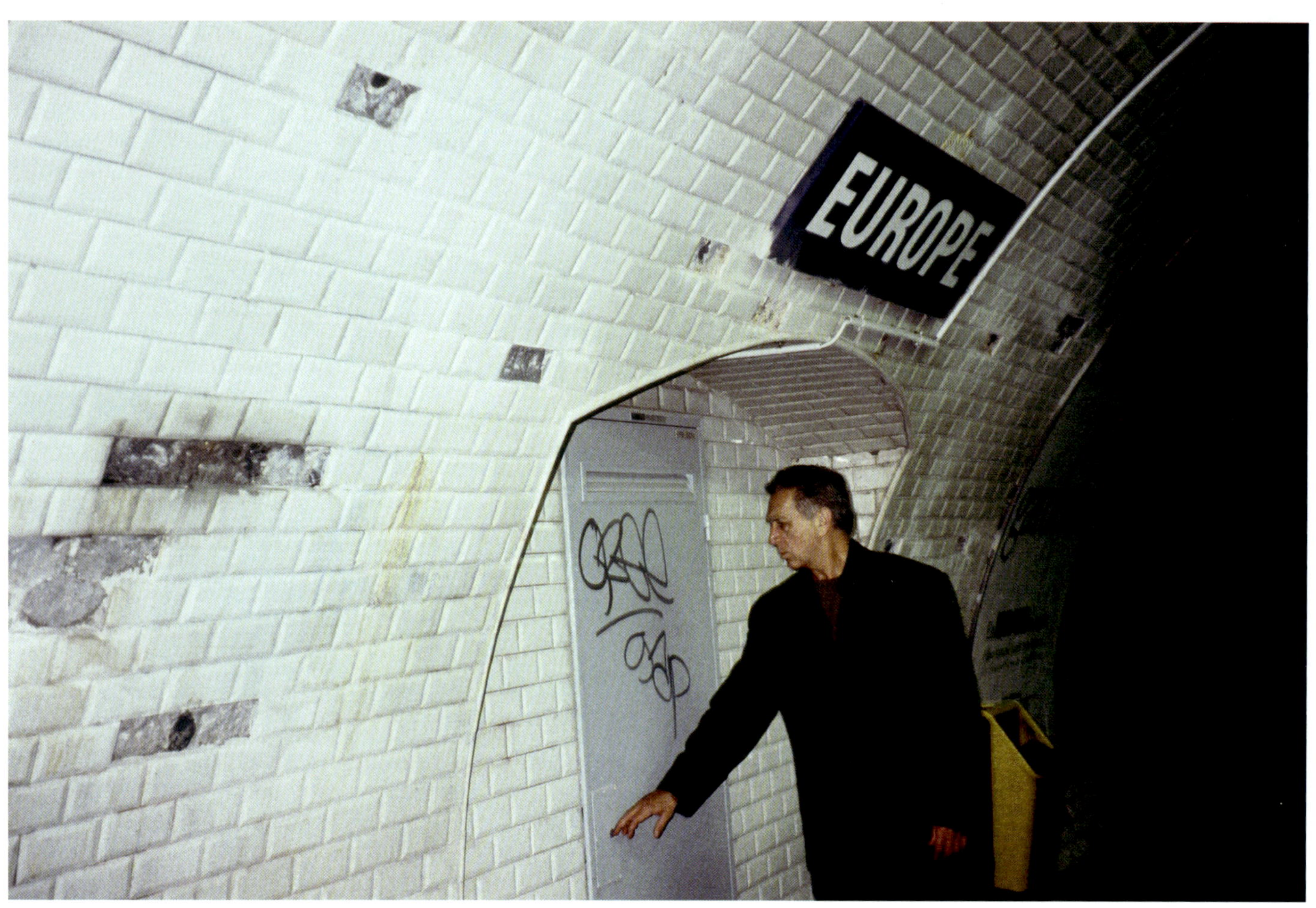

Jimmie Durham, *In Europe*, 1994–2011, variable dimensions, series of digitised photographs.

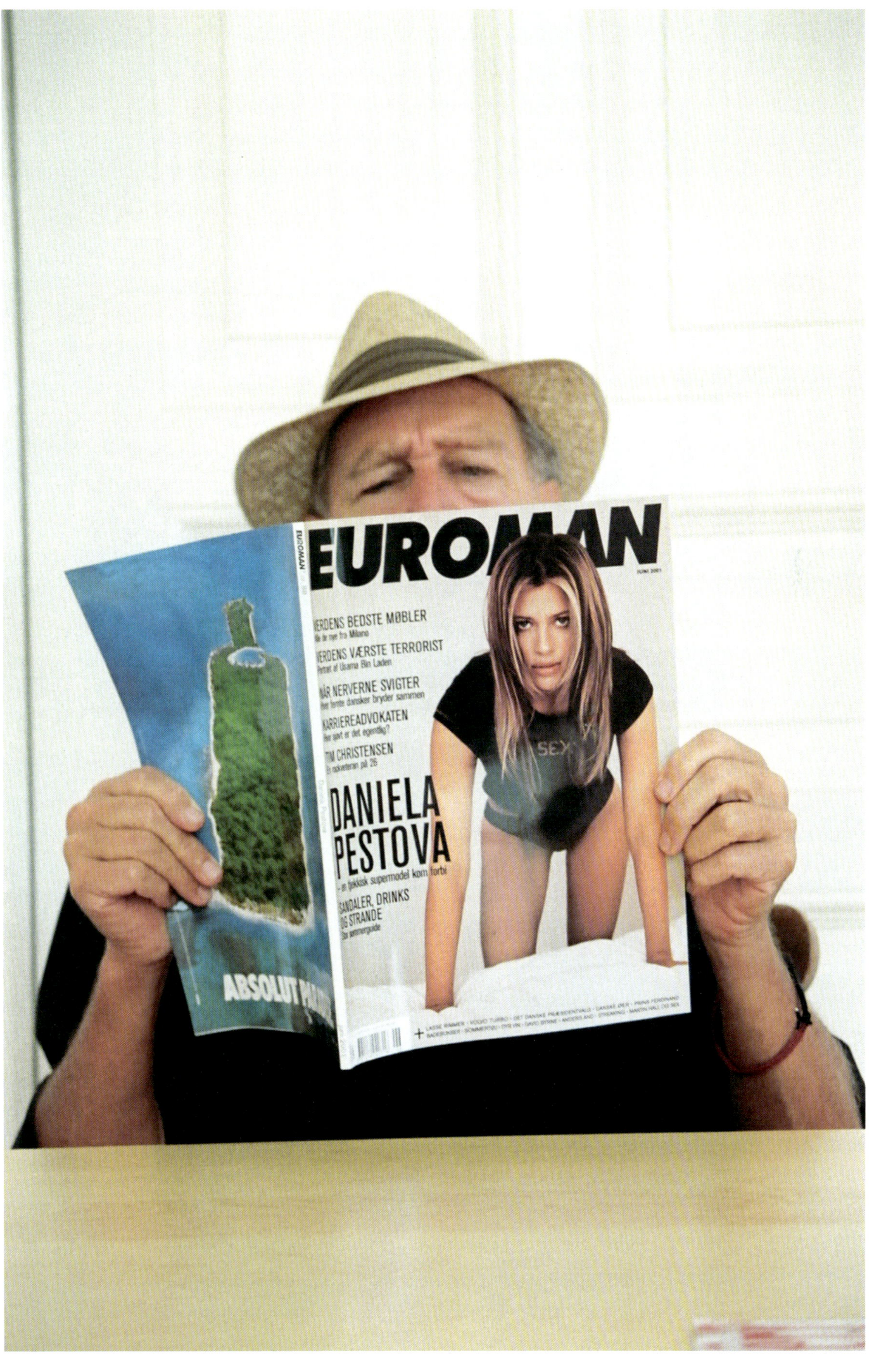
EUROMAN
VERDENS BEDSTE MØBLER
VERDENS VÆRSTE TERRORIST
NÅR NERVERNE SVIGTER
KARRIEREADVOKATEN
TIM CHRISTENSEN
DANIELA PESTOVA
SANDALER, DRINKS OG STRANDE
ABSOLUT

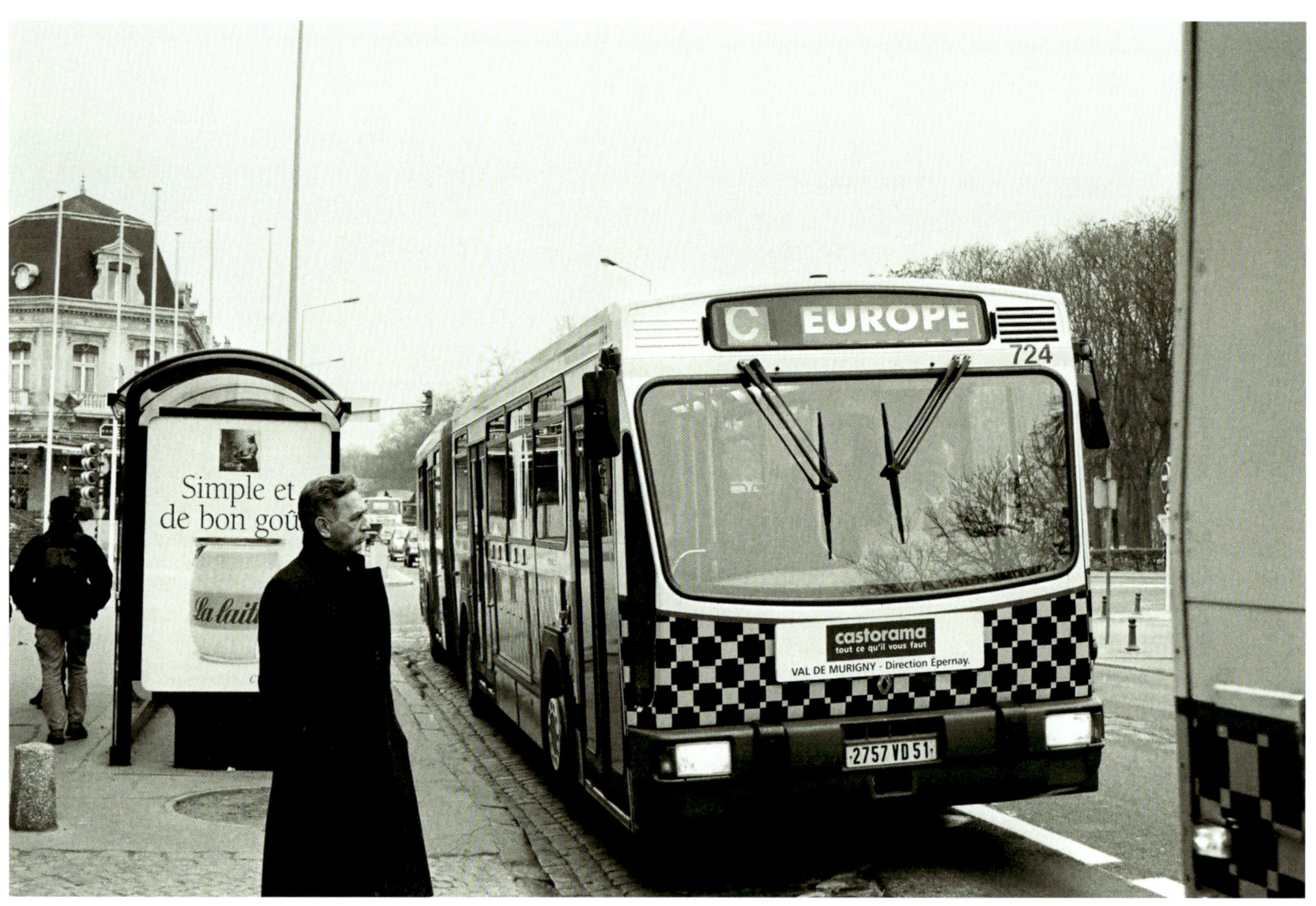

Jimmie Durham, *In Europe*, 1994–2011, variable dimensions, series of digitised photographs.

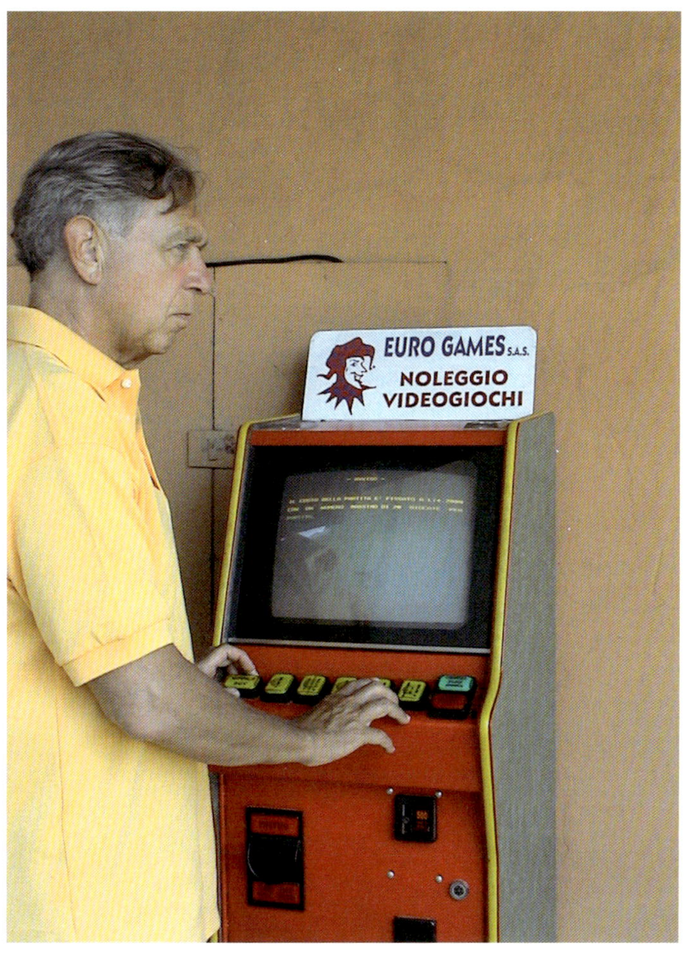

Jimmie Durham

Jimmie Durham (b. 1940 in Washington, AR) has been working as a visual artist, poet and essayist for over five decades. In the 1970s and 80s he was politically active in the US, defending the rights of Native Americans and for several years he was a representative of the American Indian Movement at the United Nations. Since then he has continued to campaign for the rights of indigenous minorities. In 1994, Durham moved permanently to Europe; he currently lives and works in Berlin and in Naples.

In his poetry, sculpture, assemblages, performances and films, Durham exposes and deconstructs the mechanisms and patterns that underlie the stereotypical conceptions in western culture about 'the other' and 'the foreign'. His work is characterised by ingenious investigations of materials, forms, substances and concepts. His experimental montages of diverse objects and signs question both deep-rooted philosophical concepts and political power structures, often with visual humour. He embraces ambivalence, excess, opacity and confusion as antidotes to iconic or univocal representation and communication.

In Europe is a photo series that Durham began for 'La Porte de l'Europe (Les Bourgeois de Calais)', an exhibition project that took place in Calais in 1996, and that was published as a book for the Neuer Berliner Kunstverein in 2015. The photographs were taken by Maria Thereza Alves and by friends in the various cities where Durham has made projects or has lived (Paris, Lille, Brussels, Berlin, Marseille, Rome, Murcia, etc.). He appears in them as a performance artist in poses that recall souvenir photos; in each case, the word 'Europe' appears next to the artist, whether as a sign, logo, name, concept, cliché or caption. Durham's physical appearance and his emphatic poses in the souvenir photos reveal 'the pipe dream', the longing for a destination, Europe.

Durham's photographic sequence can also be read as a humorous visual riddle in which the viewer must discover the subject common to all the images. With the work's title and his postures, Durham is also alluding to *Eurasia*, a famous 'action' performed by Joseph Beuys in Berlin in 1966, in which he symbolically united Europe and Asia, West and East, into the pre- or post-Cold War continent called 'Eurasia'. During the course of his photo series, Durham increasingly takes on the role of the travelling artist who, like a sort of shaman or messiah, perfects reality and restores it to its magical dimension, of which it has been deprived by technology and science. As a drifter or itinerant visionary, he is looking for his romantic ideal, an ideal Europe. More pragmatically, and stripped of this idealistic symbolism, it seems as though he is looking for a way into Europe, as though he were trying to open the notion, the concept of Europe; or, seen from a contemporary perspective, as though he were looking for a door as a refugee and migrant into Fortress Europe.

DS

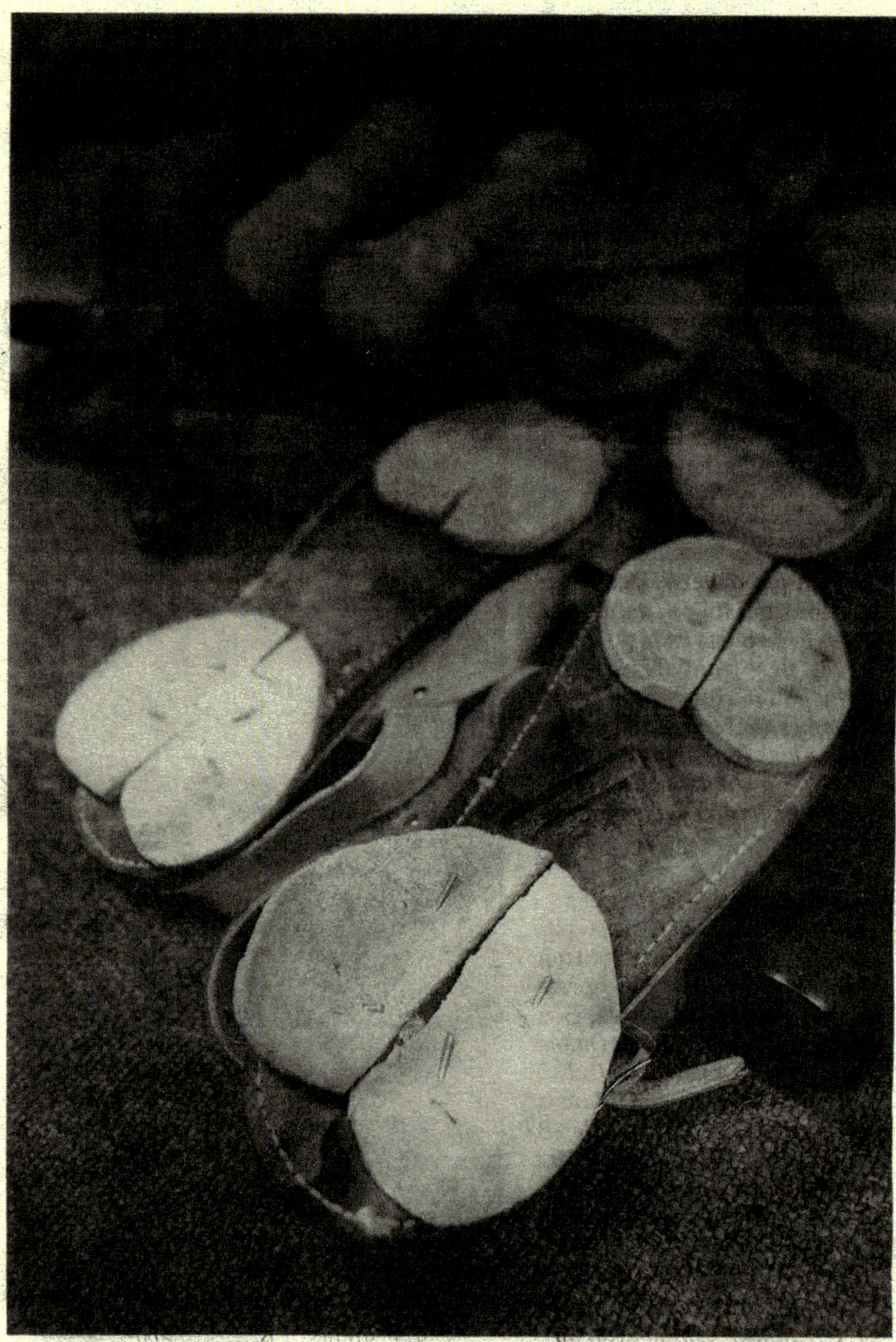

Michel François, *Fac-similé (Sandales vache)*, 2008, 21 × 14.5 cm, print on newspaper.

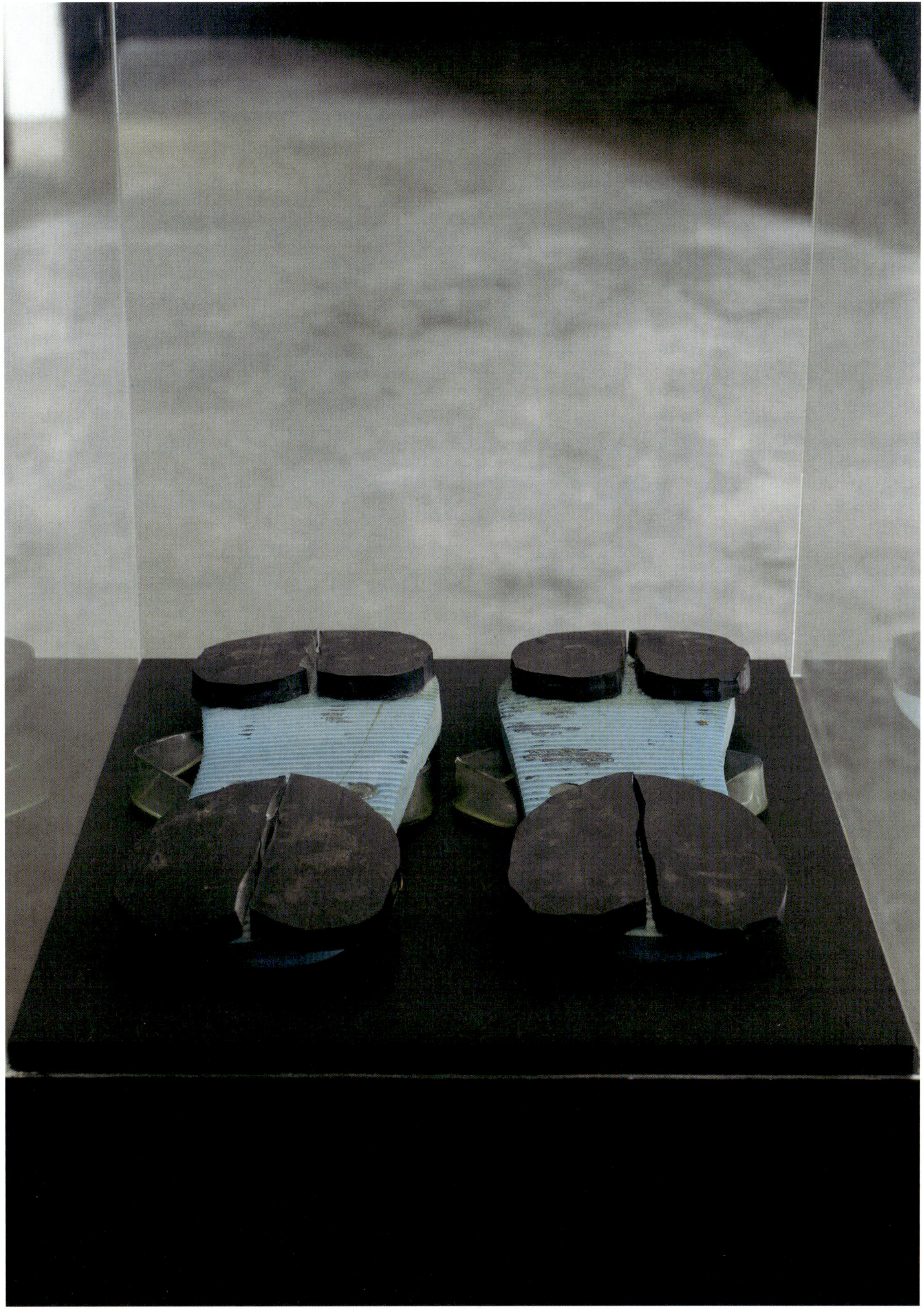

Michel François, *Pièces à conviction (Sandales vache)*, 2008, 27 × 11 × 1 cm, rubber, sandals.

Michel François, *Eco-system*, 2014, variable dimensions, asphalt, ice, cacti, bronze.

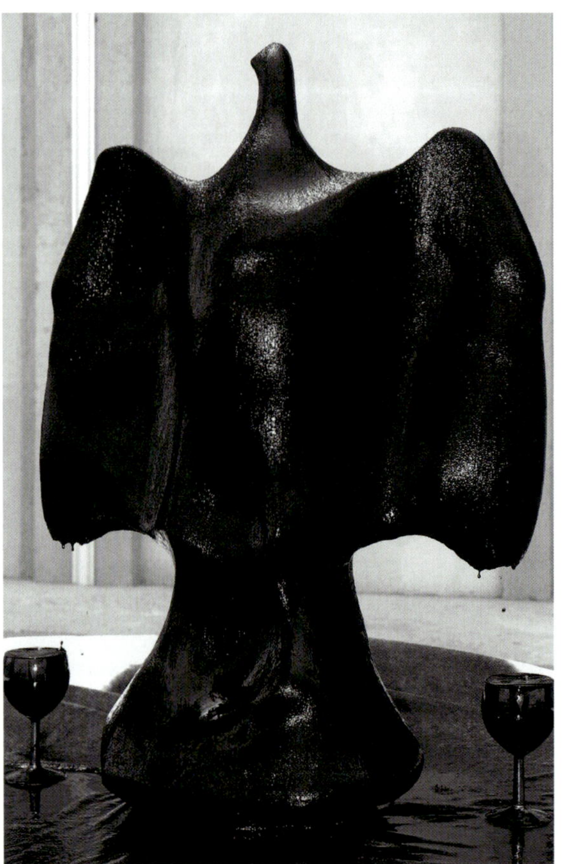

Michel François, *A Frozen Eagle Melting on the Theatre of Operations*, 2005, 80 × 65 × 30 cm, ice, black ink.

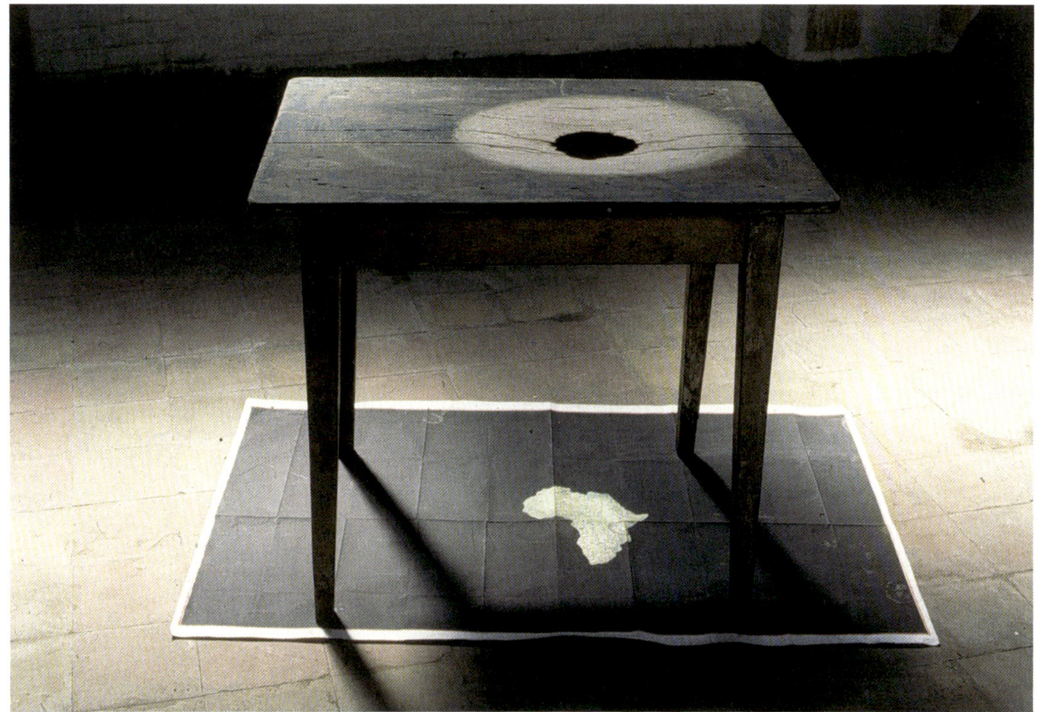

Michel François, *Afrique*, 1988, 63 × 86 × 74 cm, wooden table, world map, black paint.

Michel François

I am interested in corrupting things that appear very formal, by shifting them into the semantic field of the *pièce à conviction* (piece of incriminating evidence). This legal term gives an extraordinary status to an object that is otherwise banal or inoffensive. Out of the shapeless mass of objects, it suddenly becomes a precious thing, because it was implicated in a crime and testifies to something that took place. This nominal definition strongly determines our reading of the object, even if only provisionally, until it returns once again to anonymity.

Given the convention that an artwork is referred to as a 'piece', the *pièce à conviction* also relates to the desire to convince someone that an object is indeed art. The artist's signature functions as an authentication of provenance. In legal matters, DNA often adopts the role of a signature, used to identify a victim or perpetrator. A parallel can therefore be drawn between the two spheres. A 'piece', both by naming it so and through the signature it carries, promptly receives a unique status, as if by magic.

In the basement of the Palace of Justice in Brussels, over a million pieces of evidence from past crimes are stored, awaiting trial or the moment they are deemed obsolete. When its case is closed, the object loses its function and ends up once again amid the chaos of general things. In this sense, the notion of the piece of evidence is related to the question of the limit or border. I want to test the possibility of transgressing the outer limits of a given subject. If a material form refers to a geopolitical or social action, such as crossing a national frontier, the challenge is to transform this action into a work that offers an alternative reading. In *Fac-similé (Sandales vache)* (2008), cow-hoof sandals have become such exhibits. Based on a photograph published in the French newspaper *Le Monde*, the work documents the creative invention of a Mexican migrant, made in order to cross the US border without leaving identifiable tracks. Instead of footprints, the sandals leave animal tracks in the sand, in the hope of misleading the police.

The photographic reproduction is intended to distribute this semi-tragic image beyond the sphere in which it served to incriminate its maker. In an exhibition context, the stack of posters becomes a sculpture. By inviting each visitor to take one away, the image is returned to society.

I seek to present objects in a condition of instability, of disappearance, indicative of the fragile moment in which we find ourselves today. The material is meant to reflect this condition and introduce a form of resistance. The figure of the imperial eagle, for example, is considered to be a representation of stability, authority and fortitude. In *A Frozen Eagle Melting on the Theatre of Operations* (2005–), the eagle takes the form of a frozen, standardised mould, filled with ink. As time passes, it begins to thaw and disintegrate, while the black oily substance leaks away. The extreme fragility of this piece slowly annihilates its initial formal and symbolic qualities. Depending on its state when the viewers enter the room, they may witness an event that testifies to the collapse of an idea or ideology. This inner tension contained by the material thereby becomes transformative and opens up a parallel, more poetic reality.

Michel François, 2017

The words *Brot* and *pain*

Humans are linguistic beings. 'It is the linguistic being of man to name things,' argues Walter Benjamin.[1] Human language is the only 'naming' language that we know of. There is a necessity, an importance and also an alchemy of naming. '*Alchimie de la nomination, où je suis seule avec le français. Nommer l'être me fait être : corps et âme, je vis en français,*' recognises Julia Kristeva.[2] When we live in a language, we are in it body and soul.

In 'The Task of the Translator', Benjamin wrote: 'The words *Brot* and *pain* "intend" the same object, but the modes of this intention are not the same. It is owing to these modes that the word *Brot* means something different to a German than the word *pain* to a Frenchman, that these words are not interchangeable for them, that, in fact, they strive to exclude each other.'[3] Each language not only communicates information, but also conveys a particular social unconscious, different cultural attachments and emotional connotations. 'Sense in its poetic significance is not limited to meaning, but derives from the connotations conveyed by the word chosen to express it. We say of words that they have emotional connotations.'[4] Speakers of a certain language are not just linked in an obvious, external way, but also with an internal, mental code.

Jacques Derrida grew up in Algeria, as a Jew who spoke French and no longer had any connection with his language of origin. In an interview between Derrida and the free jazz musician Ornette Coleman, the latter asked him: 'Can a language of origin influence your thoughts? Do you ever ask yourself if the language that you speak now interferes with your actual thoughts?'[5]

1   Walter Benjamin, 'On Language as Such and On the Language of Man' in *Reflections: Essays, Aphorisms, Autobiographical Writings*, ed. Peter Demetz, trans. Edmund Jephcott, New York 2007, p. 317.
2   Julia Kristeva, *L'avenir d'une révolte*, Paris 2012, p. 67. 'In this alchemy of naming I am alone with French. To name being allows me to be: I live in French, body and soul.' Julia Kristeva, *Intimate Revolt: The Powers and Limits of Psychoanalysis*, trans. Jeanine Herman, New York 2002, p. 243.
3   Walter Benjamin, 'The Task of the Translator' in *Illuminations: Essays and Reflections*, ed. Hannah Arendt, trans. Harry Zohn, London 1999, p. 75.
4   Ibid., p. 78.
5   Ornette Coleman, 'The Other's Language: Jacques Derrida Interviews Ornette Coleman, 23 June 1997', trans. Timothy S. Murphy, in 'Blue Notes: Toward a New Jazz Discourse', a special issue of *Genre: Forms of Discourse and Culture*, ed. Mark Osteen, vol. 37, no. 2 (Summer 2004), p. 326.

Armenian	Armenian		
ա	Ա	AYP	AYP
բ	Բ	PEN	PEN
գ	Գ	KEEM	KEEM
դ	Դ	TA	TA
ե	Ե	YECH	YECH
զ	Զ	ZA	ZA
է	Է	AI	AI
ը	Ը	UT	UT
թ	Թ	TO	TO
ժ	Ժ	JE	JE
ի	Ի	EENEE	EENEE
լ	Լ	LEWN	LEWN
խ	Խ	KHAI	KAI
ծ	Ծ	DZA	DZA
կ	Կ	GVEN	GVEN
հ	Հ	HO	HO
ձ	Ձ	TZA	TZA
ղ	Ղ	GHAT	GHAT
ճ	Ճ	GEAI	GEAI
մ	Մ	MEN	MEN
յ	Յ	HEE	HEE
ն	Ն	NOO	NOO
շ	Շ	SHA	SHA
ո	Ո	VO	VO
չ	Չ	CHA	CHA
պ	Պ	BAI	BAI
ջ	Ջ	CHAI	CHAI
ռ	Ռ	RRA	RRA
ս	Ս	SAI	SAI
վ	Վ	VAIV	VAIV
տ	Տ	DEWN	DEWN
ր	Ր	RAI	RAI
ց	Ց	TZO	TZO

Armenian	Armenian		
ւ	Ւ	HEWN	HEWN
փ	Փ	PURE	PURE
ք	Ք	KAI	KAI
օ	Օ	O	O
ֆ	Ֆ	FAI	FAI

Marshall McLuhan argued that every language (every mother tongue and every one of our personal languages) entails a different representation of reality: 'Each mother tongue teaches its users a way of seeing and feeling the world, and of acting in the world, which is quite unique.'[6] In the nineteenth century, linguist William Whitney asserted that: 'Every single language has its own logic, its particular framework of established distinctions, its shapes and forms of thought.'[7] Our experience and knowledge of the world is structured by the particular framework of our mother tongue. Your personal use of language structures the world (*your world*) in a different way than mine does, or, as Ludwig Wittgenstein phrased it, '*Die Grenzen meiner Sprache bedeuten die Grenzen meiner Welt.*'[8] Language structures the world and creates a certain reality. By living in a different language, we create a different and unique world.

Through his studies of foreign languages and 'primitive' tongues, Wilhelm von Humboldt argued that 'the difference between languages is not only in sounds and signs but in world-view'.[9] Since language is the forming organ of thought, there must be an intimate relation between the laws of grammar and the laws of thinking. 'Thinking is dependent not just on language in general but to a certain extent on each individual language,' von Humboldt concluded. 'The real differences between languages,' he argued, 'are not in what a language is *able* to express but rather in "what it encourages and stimulates its speakers to do from its own inner force."'[10] Humboldt's concept of the inner form of language implies that a specific form of saying something is expressed in a particular language and, at the same time, a particular cultural significance is generated through this linguistic form.

The subtleties and differences in the language we speak can unite as well as distinguish us. As Edward Sapir notes: '"He talks like us" is equivalent to saying "He is one of us."'[11]

Language nurtures and alienates; it is at the same time a homecoming and alien, or even enemy territory. How do we come to terms with the foreignness of language? Walter Benjamin suggested that 'an instant and final […] solution of this foreignness remains out of the reach of mankind', arguing that a 'temporary and provisional solution' is revealed, only, through translation.[12] Translation expresses the central reciprocal relationship between languages, which rests in the intention underlying each language as a whole, in what they want to express. Benjamin saw the task of a translator as revealing the untranslatability of language and as a coming to terms with the foreignness of language – advancing the idea of exile as the first metaphor for language and the human condition. Similarly, Kristeva professes that 'speaking an "other language", in other words, is quite simply the minimum and primary condition for being alive'.[13] Our human condition is marked by exile. We all speak a foreign language.

Mekhitar Garabedian

6   Marshall McLuhan, 'The Spoken Word: Flower of Evil?' in *Understanding Media: The Extensions of Man*, Cambridge MA and London 1994, p. 80.
7   William Whitney, cited in Guy Deutscher, *Through the Language Glass: Why The World Looks Different in Other Languages*, London 2011, p. 137.
8   '*The limits of my language* mean the limits of my world.' Ludwig Wittgenstein, *Tractatus Logico-Philosophicus: German and English*, trans. C.K. Ogden, New York 2005, p. 74.
9   Wilhelm von Humboldt, cited in Guy Deutscher, *Through the Language Glass: Why The World Looks Different in Other Languages*, London 2011, p. 135.
10   Ibid., p. 136.
11   Edward Sapir, *Selected Writings in Language, Culture, and Personality*, ed. David G. Mandelbaum, Berkeley, Los Angeles and London 1985, p. 16.
12   Benjamin, 'The Task of the Translator' in *Illuminations*, op. cit., p. 75.
13   Kristeva, *Intimate Revolt*, op. cit., p. 254. '*Parler une autre langue est tout simplement la condition minimale et première pour être en vie.*' Kristeva, *L'avenir d'une révolte*, op. cit., p. 87.

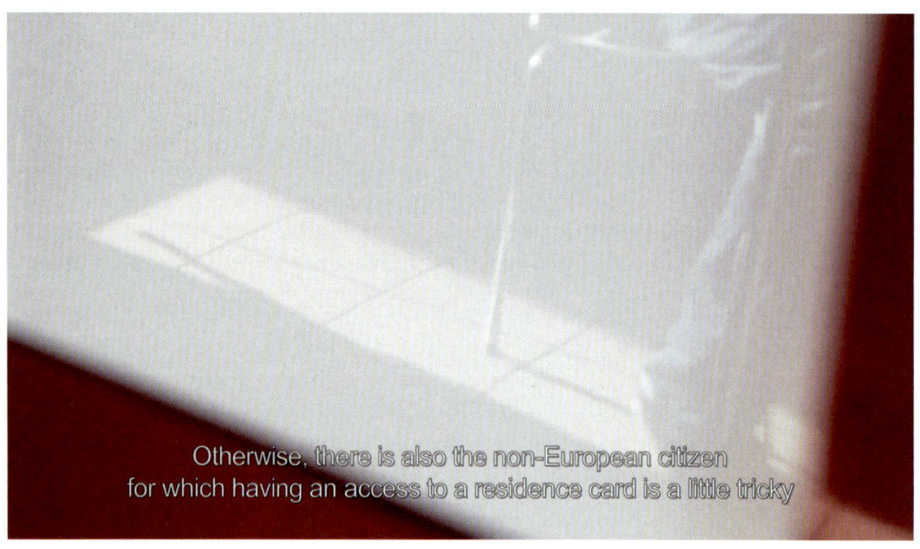

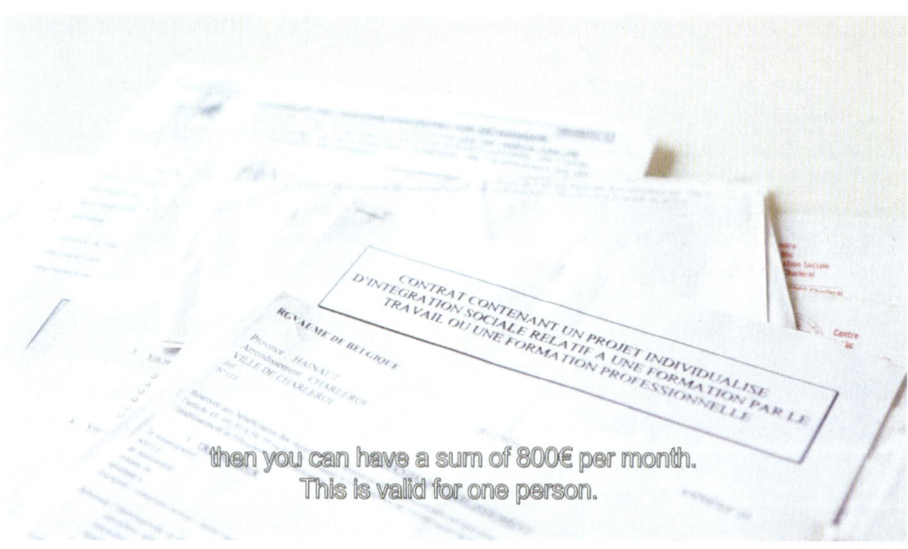

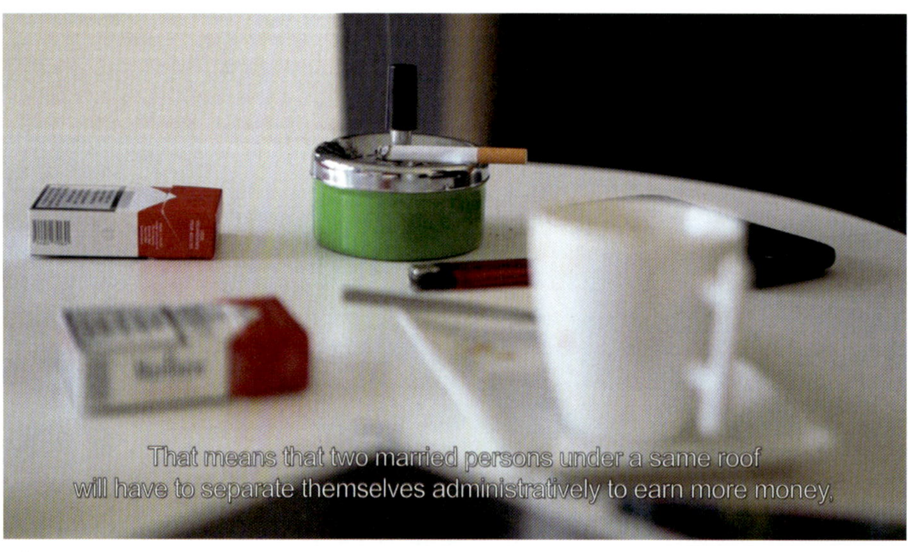

Younes Baba-Ali, stills from *Être et ne pas avoir*, 2014, HD video, 16:9, colour, sound, 5' 54".

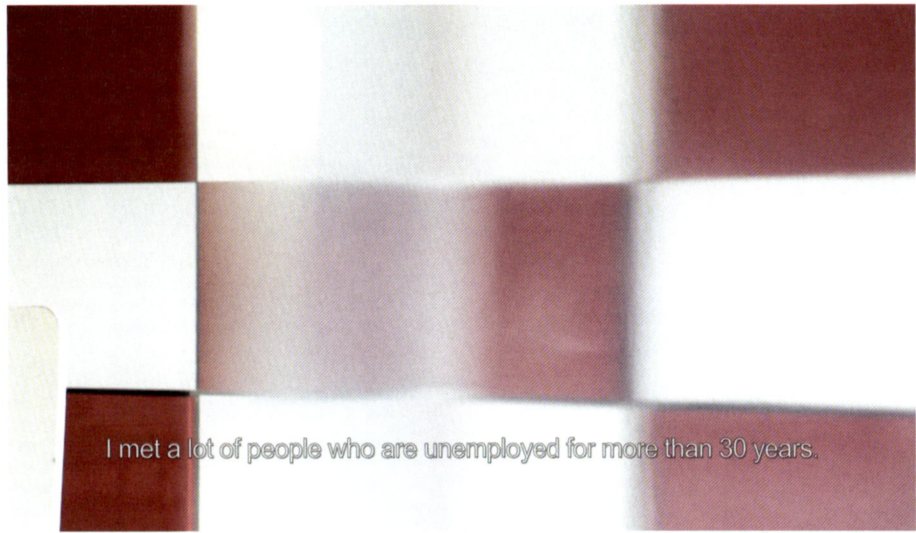

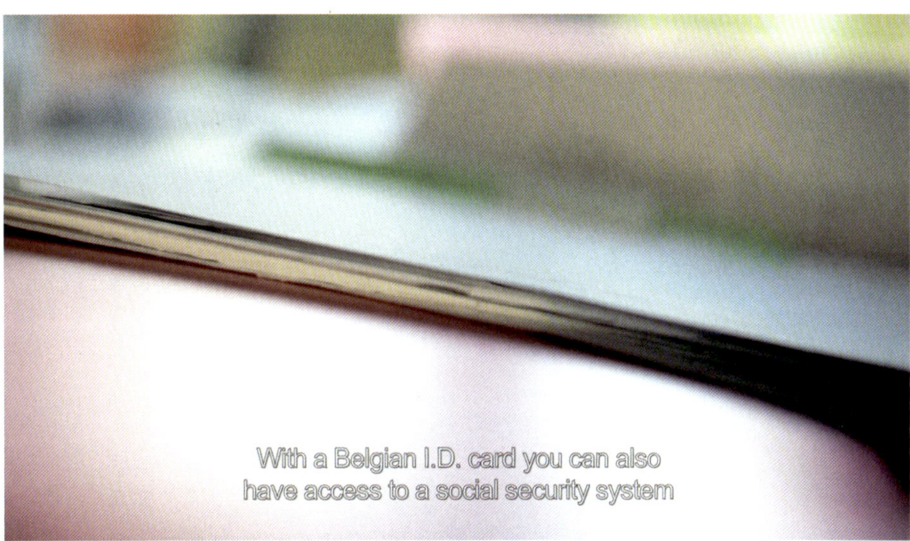

Younes Baba-Ali

Younes Baba-Ali (b. 1986 in Oujda) was born in Morocco, grew up in France and has been living in Brussels for six years. Taking his own personal relationship with the Moroccan diaspora as his point of departure, he raises questions that go well beyond the specifics of this community: how do we experience multiculturalism and its implications? *Être et ne pas avoir* (To be and not to have, 2014) is a video in which a Belgian resident explains the different strategies of access linked to the local social welfare system. This work refers to the flaws of a social system and the money it can generate, as well as the phenomenon of a new form of immigration familiarly called 'social tourism'. The project's title refers to how these individuals advertise themselves as people in need.

HK

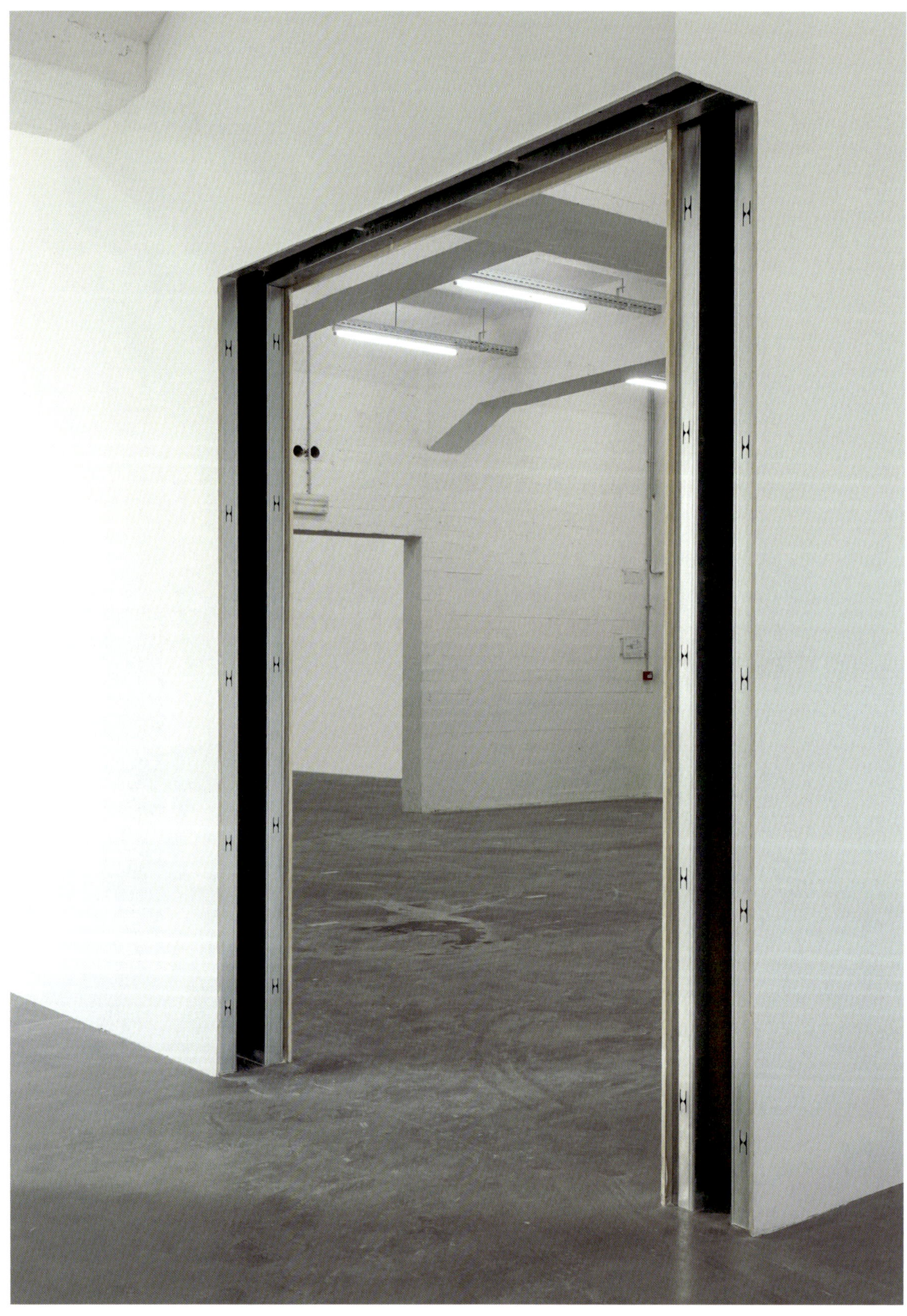

Richard Venlet, *The Absent Museum*, WIELS, 2017. Exhibition architecture.

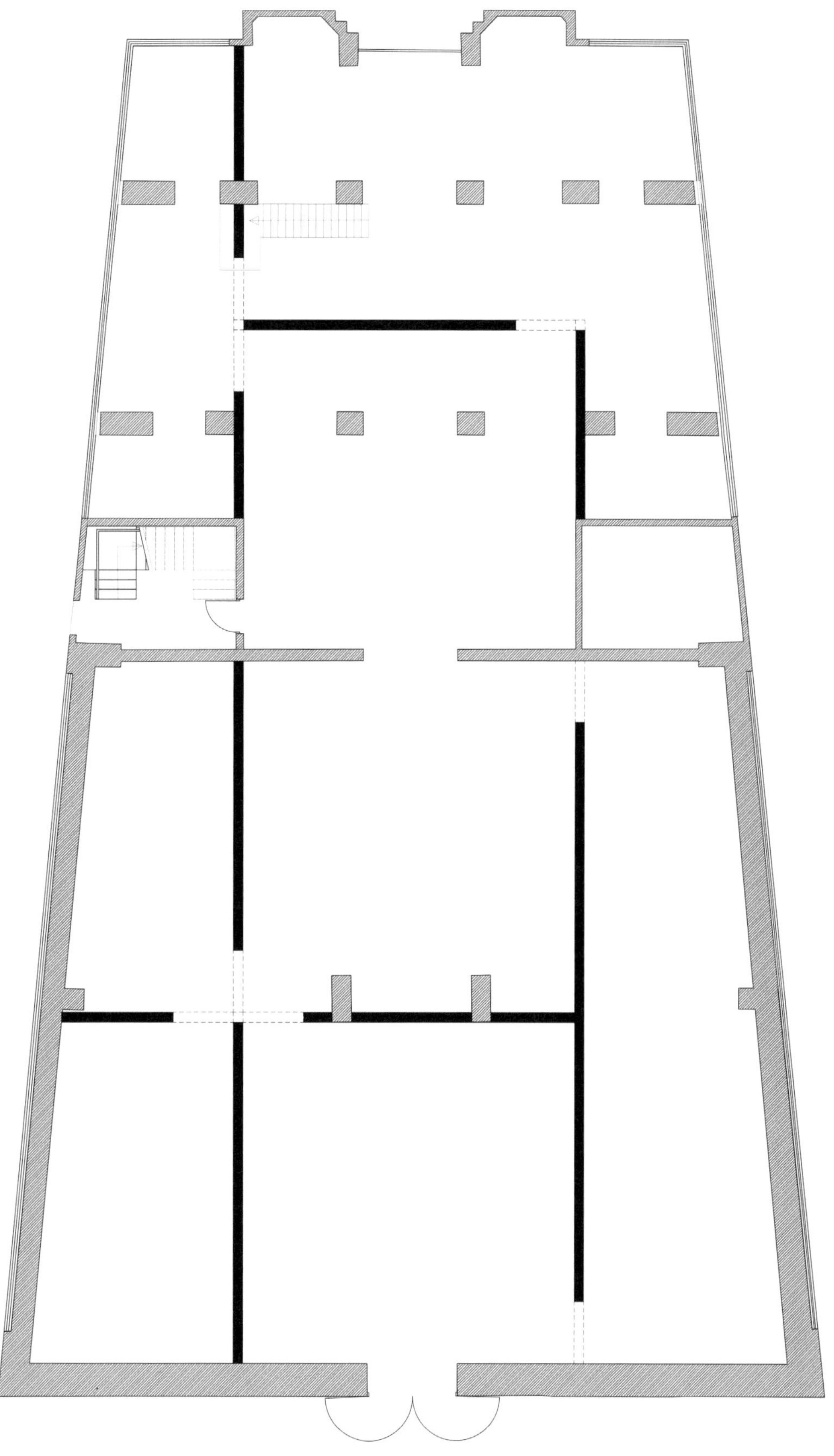

Richard Venlet, *Floorplan: First Floor of The Absent Museum*, WIELS, 2017. Drawing in collaboration with Carlo Siegfried.

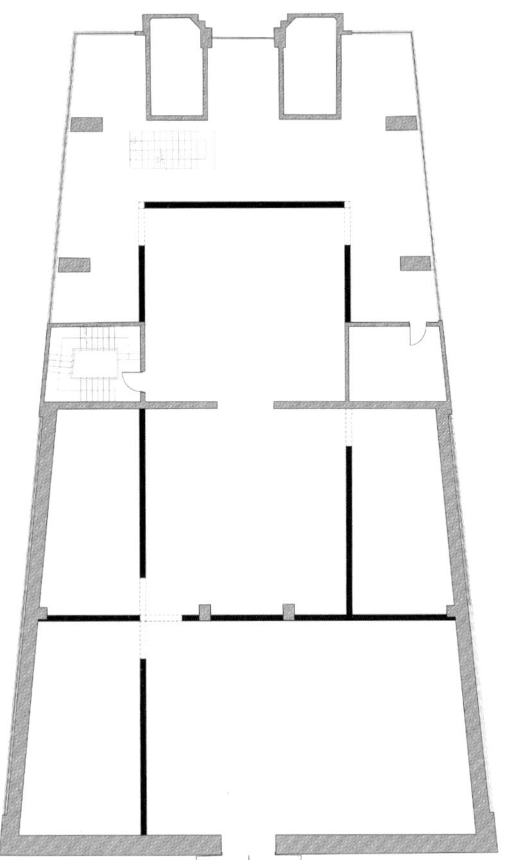

Richard Venlet, *Floorplan: Second Floor of The Absent Museum*, WIELS, 2017. Drawing in collaboration with Carlo Siegfried.

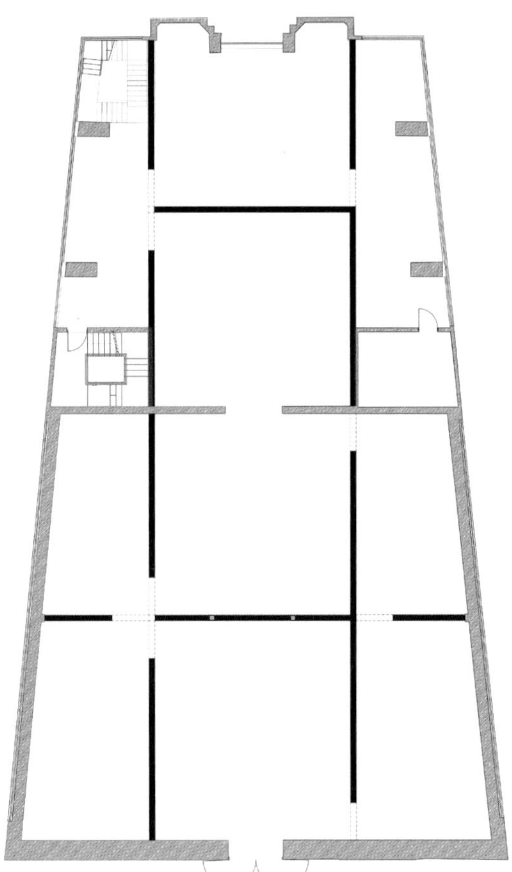

Richard Venlet, *Floorplan: Third Floor of The Absent Museum*, WIELS, 2017. Drawing in collaboration with Carlo Siegfried.

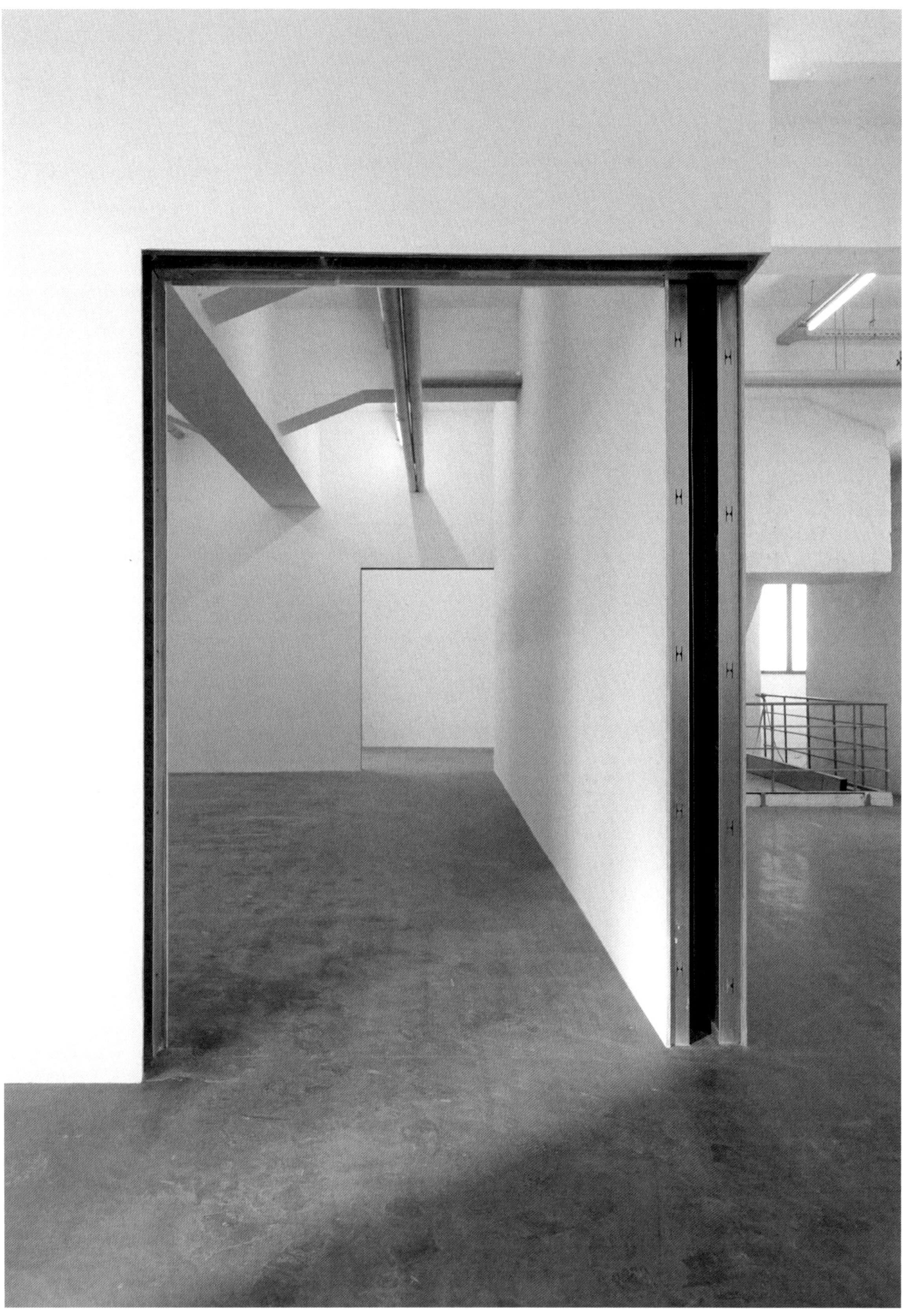

Richard Venlet, *The Absent Museum*, WIELS, 2017. Exhibition architecture.

THE [ABSENT] MUSEUM

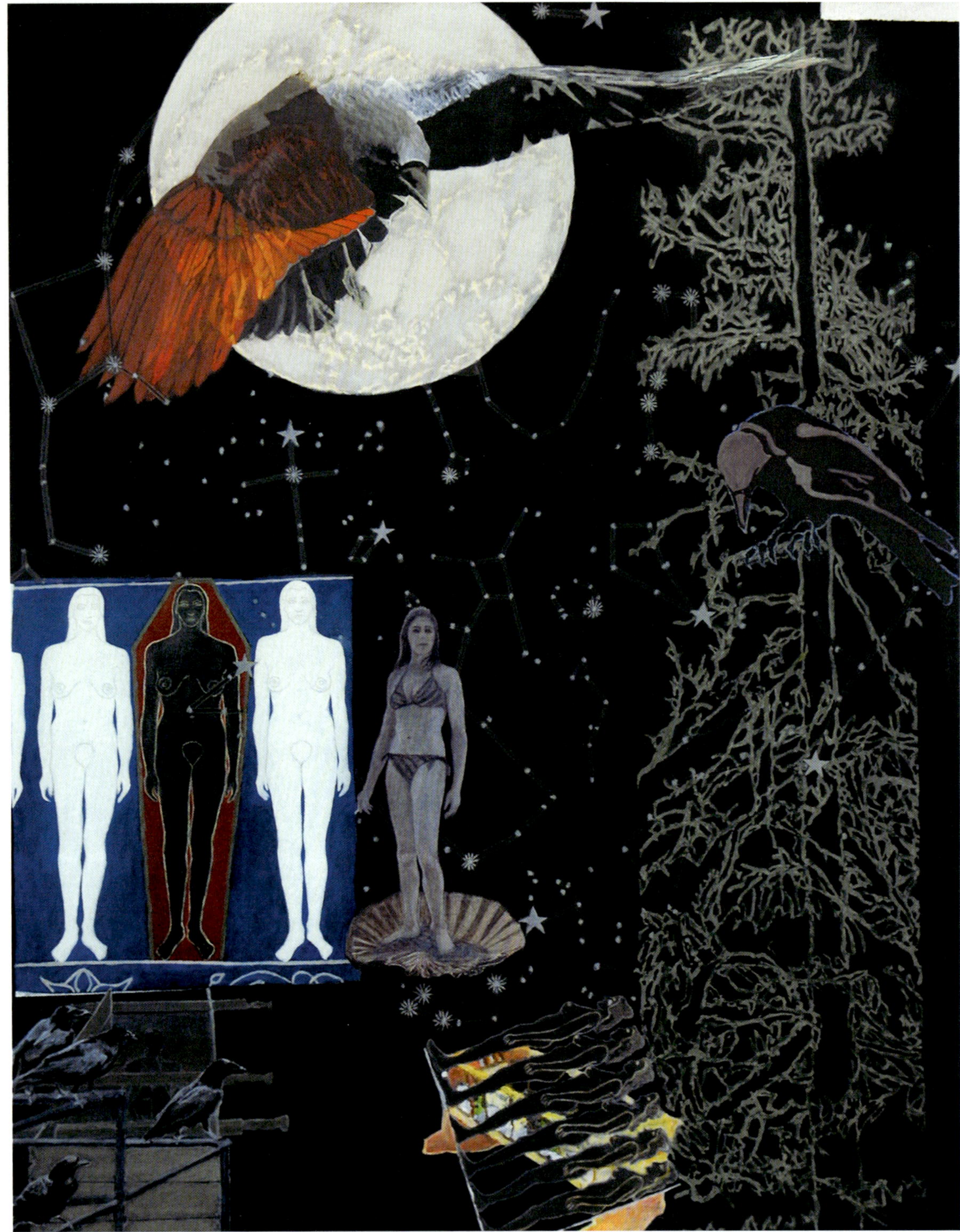

Jo Baer, *Memorial for an Art World Body (Nevermore)*, 2009, 183 × 160 cm, oil on canvas.

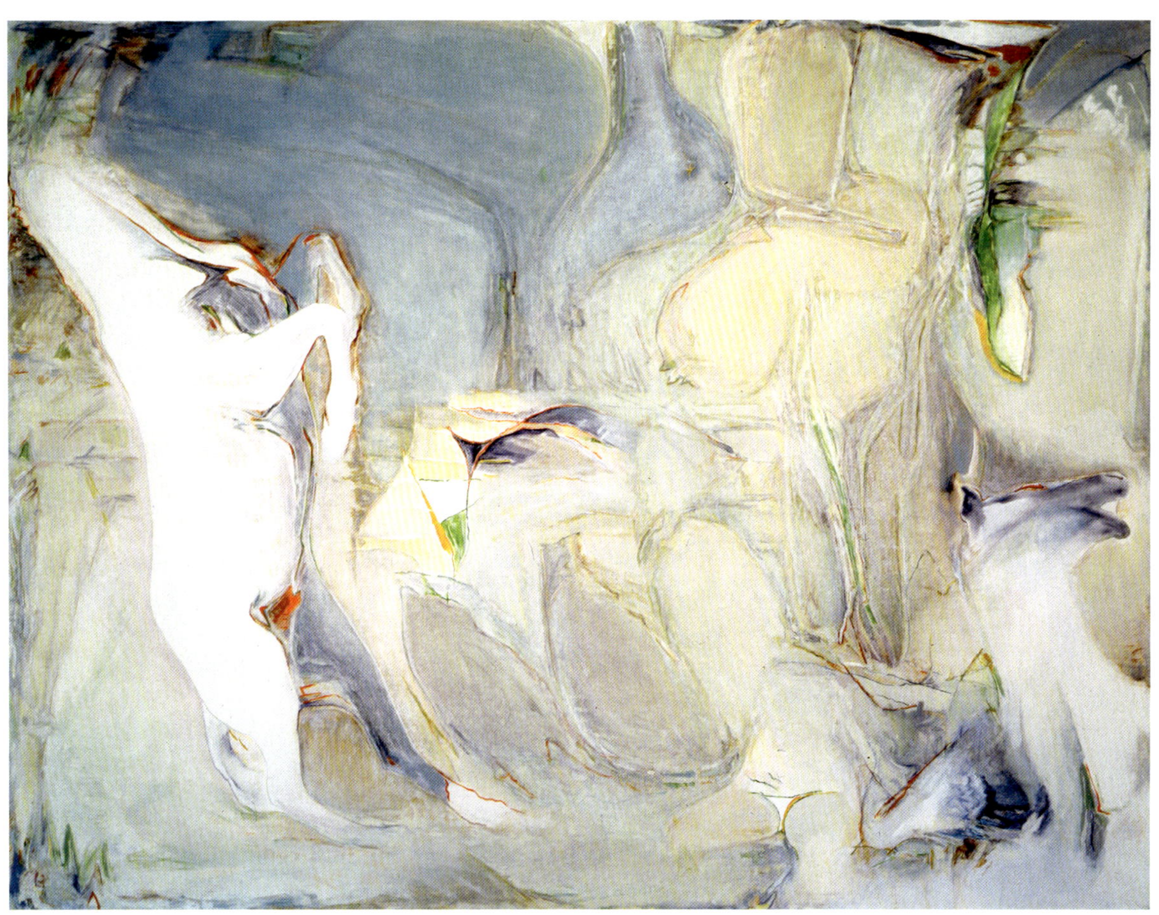

Jo Baer, *Red, White and Blue Gelding Falling to its Right (Double-Cross Britannicus/Tricolor Hibernicus)*, 1984–86, 243.8 × 314.9 cm, oil on canvas.

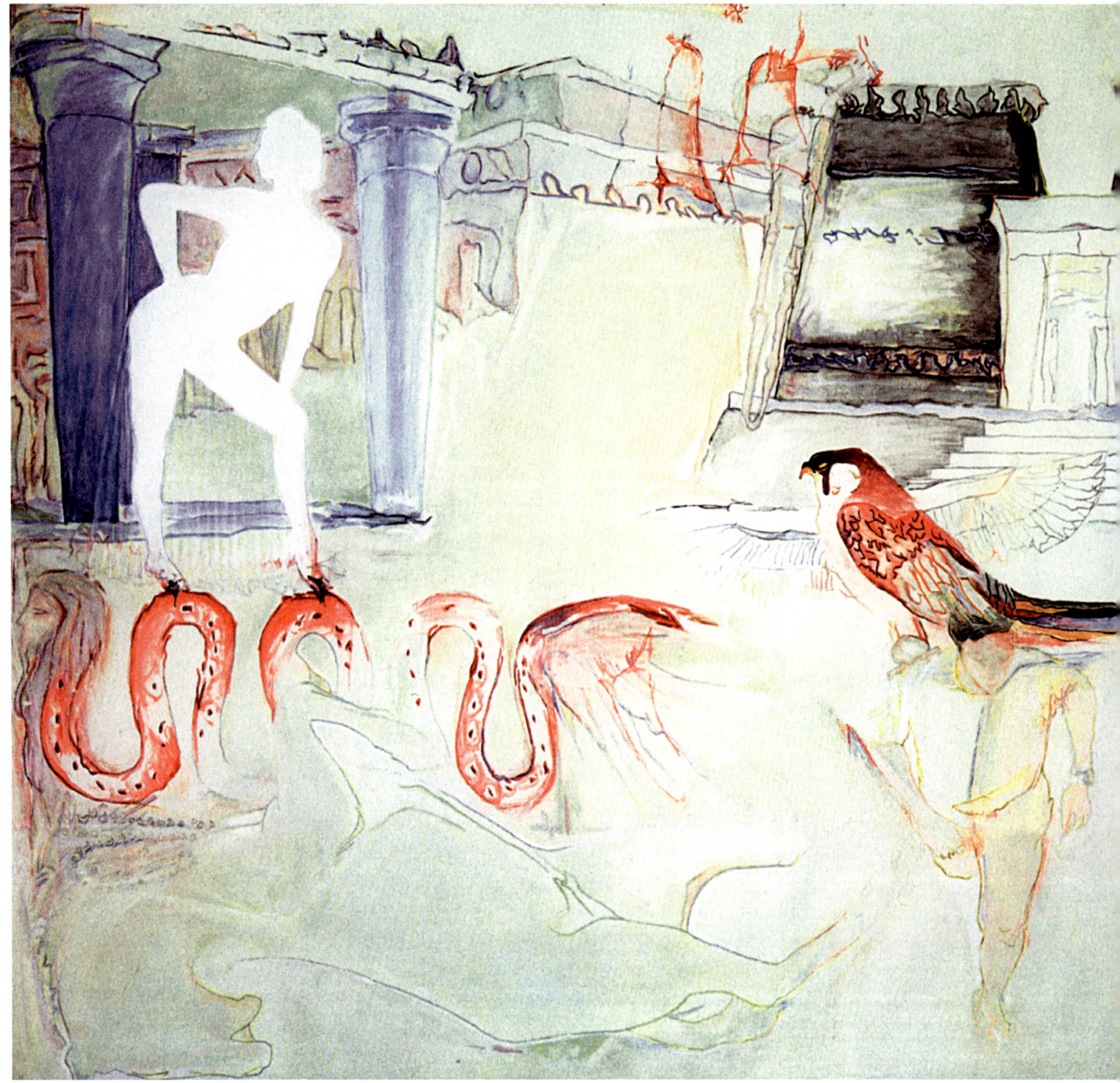

Jo Baer, *Tis Ill Pudling in the Cockatrice Den (Là-Bas)*, 1987, 244 × 244 cm, oil on canvas.

Paintings will sometimes confound time. When images chosen from a mix across the centuries are gathered onto a single surface, new dialogues occur which were – in other forms and at other times – denied. Assembled in this way with a view towards useful contemporary comment, and though, as a poet has said: '"Nowadays" is a civilisation in which serpent, lion and eagle belong to the circus-tent; ox, salmon and boar to the cannery; racehorse and greyhound to the betting-ring', we may still – via painting's unique perspectives – revive our trite and ravaged icons (if only in the space of a picture's breadth). For time's lost beasts and clichéd images will gain modern and valuable, commutative meanings when re-deployed to opposition and context in configured plans… non-narratives from which – out of scattered histories and cultures – we might yet shape new and timely scenarios.

Jo Baer, 1989

Jo Baer

In the mid-1970s Jo Baer traded her sophisticated, abstract-geometric reduction aesthetics for a pronounced figurative and metaphorical style. It was a rupture such as is rarely seen in post-war art. She turned her back on the radical minimalism that had made her famous; her visual idiom had to regain 'more subject and more meaning'. How deeply founded her transformation was is also evident from her article 'I am no longer an abstract artist', published in 1983 in *Art in America*. She developed a new style that she described as 'radical figuration', with paintings and drawings in which she incorporated mythological, topographical and historical elements into complex visual narratives, in a collage-like fashion.

Baer's reorientation coincided with her departure from the United States and her move to Europe. At various places across the continent she studied the correspondences between iconographies and spiritual, mythological and historical contexts, in a series of paintings that stand out thanks to their vast, epic compositions. Baer's self-conscious standpoints and convictions, which manifest themselves in her work as well as in her writings and interviews, place her pictorial research in a feminist perspective. Her epic, narrative and collage-like visual idiom, in which female themes and archetypes are emphatically present, defines her idiosyncratic position in the painting revivals since the 1970s, in which the 'heroic' male painters claimed the male privilege over the medium time and again.

DS

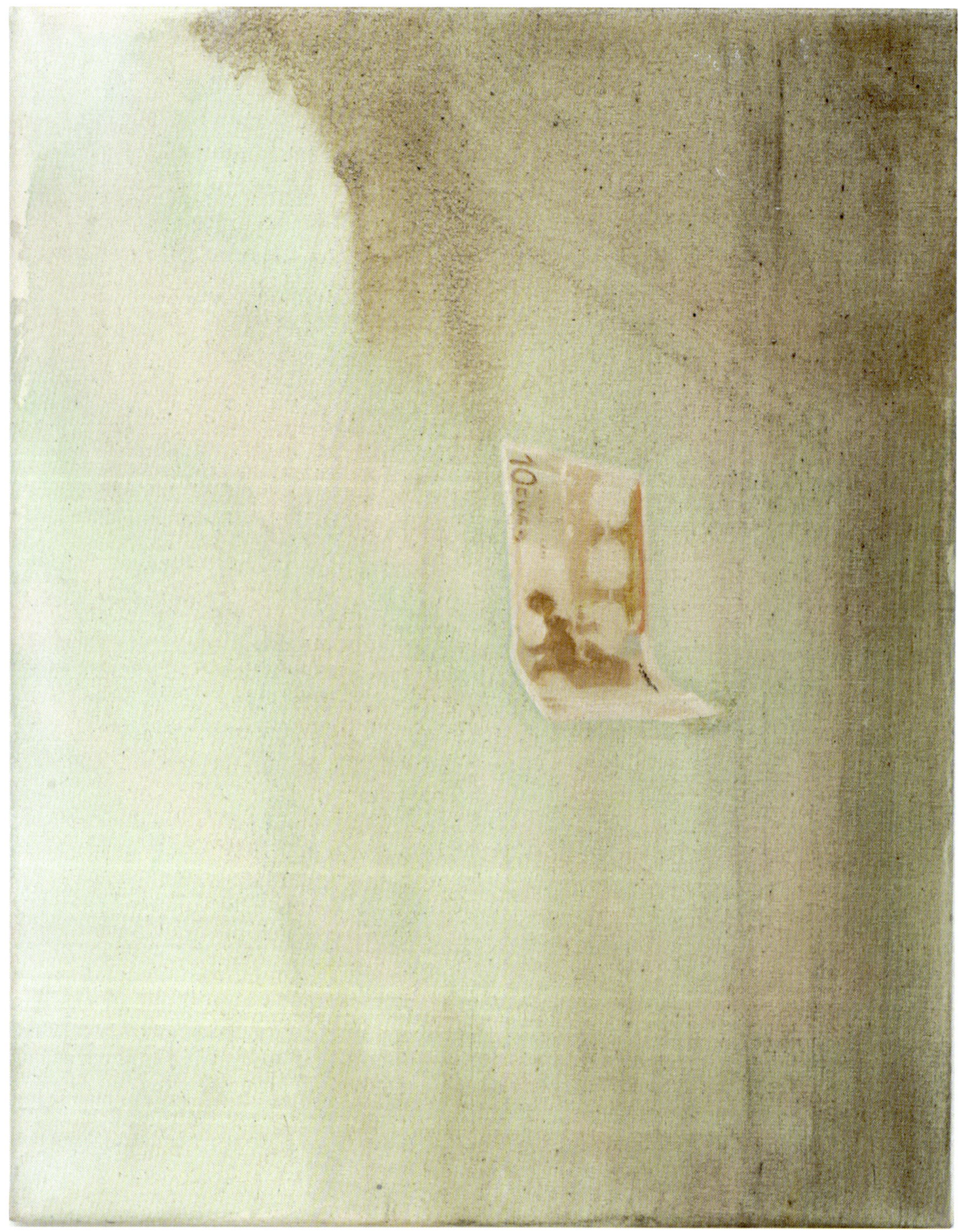

Monika Baer, *Untitled*, 2005, 50 × 40 cm, ink, ashes, oil on canvas.

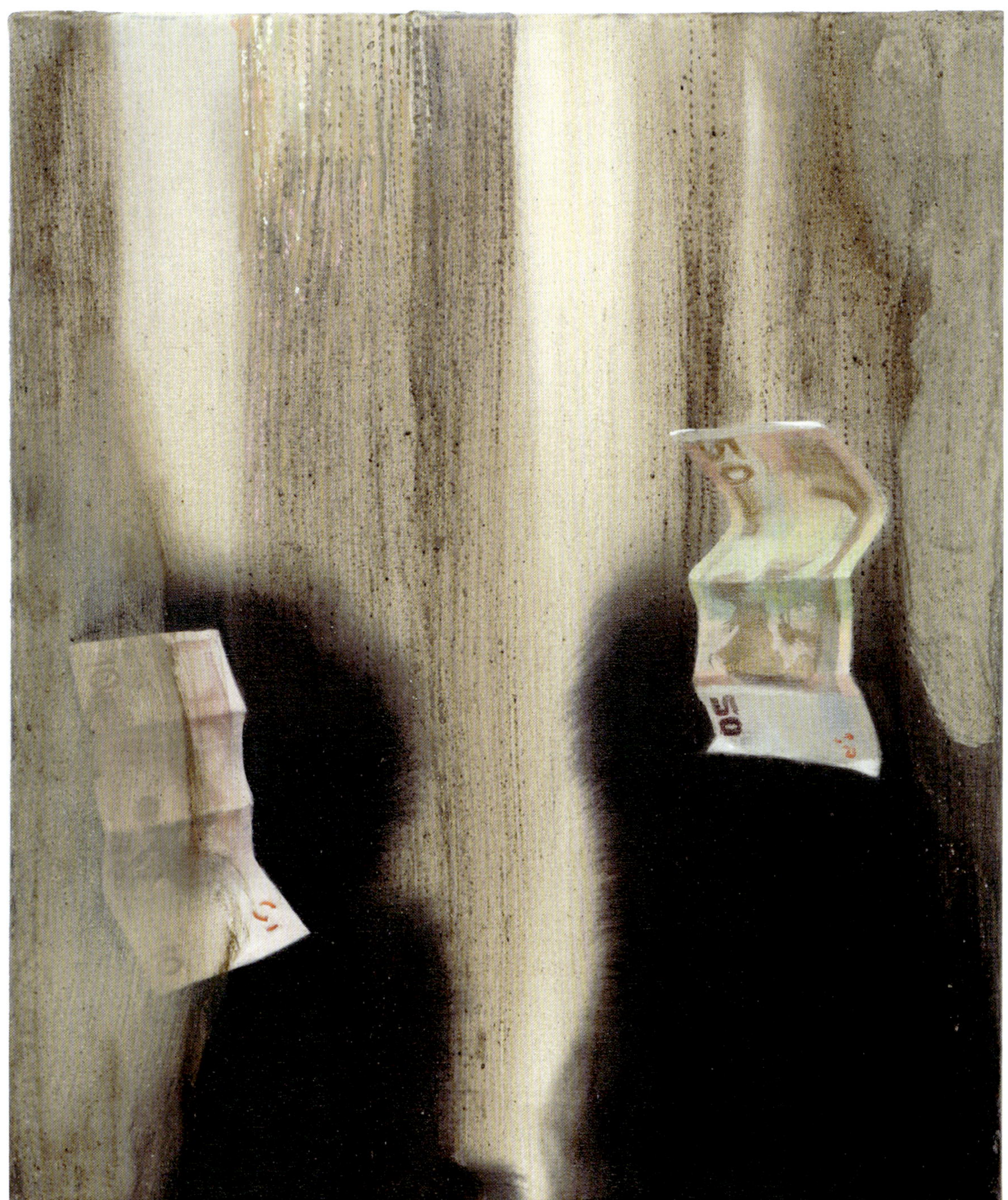

Monika Baer, *Untitled*, 2005, 47 × 40.5 cm, watercolour, ashes, oil on canvas.

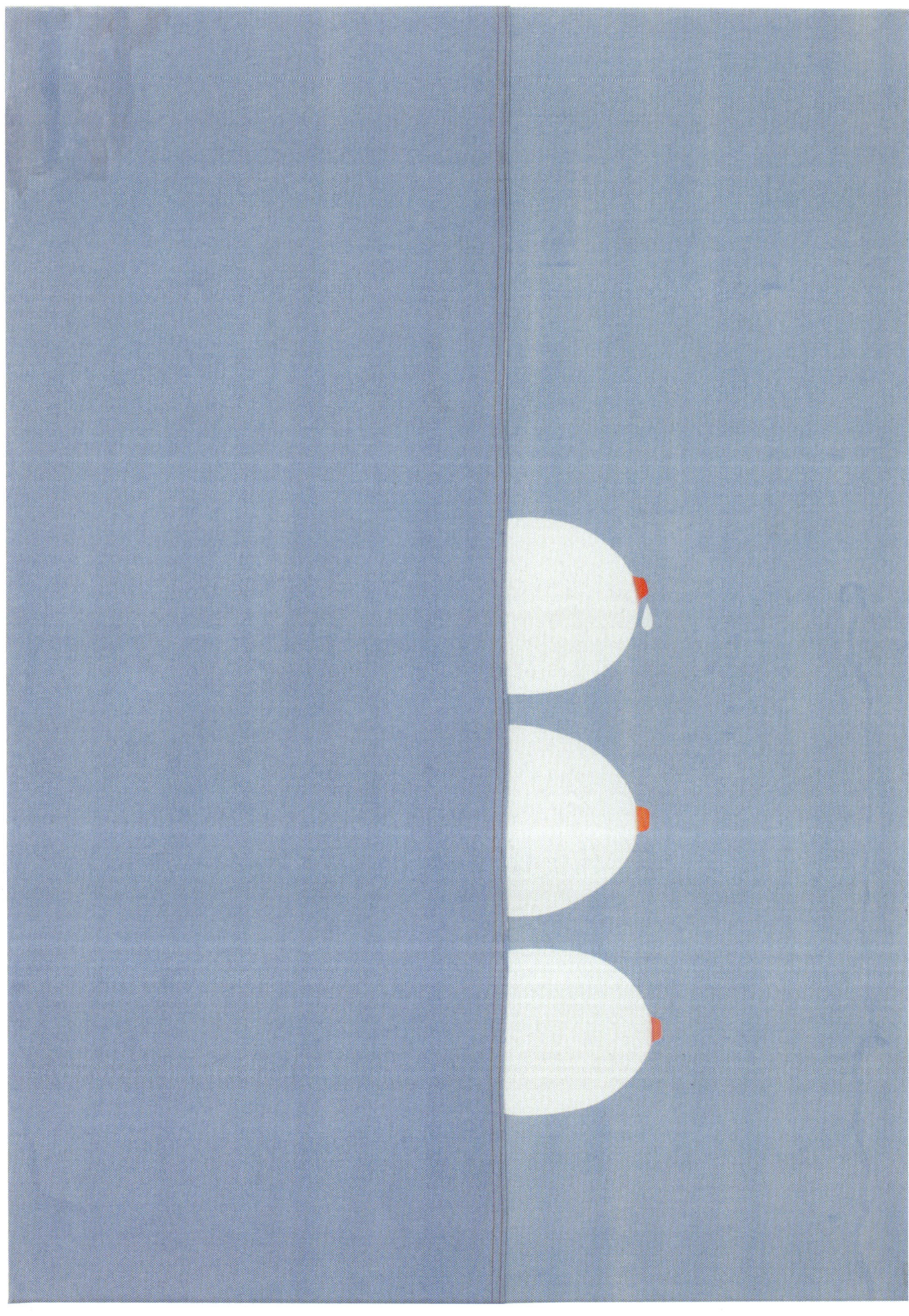

Monika Baer, *Untitled*, 2008, 119 × 86 cm, watercolour, acrylic, oil on canvas, thread.

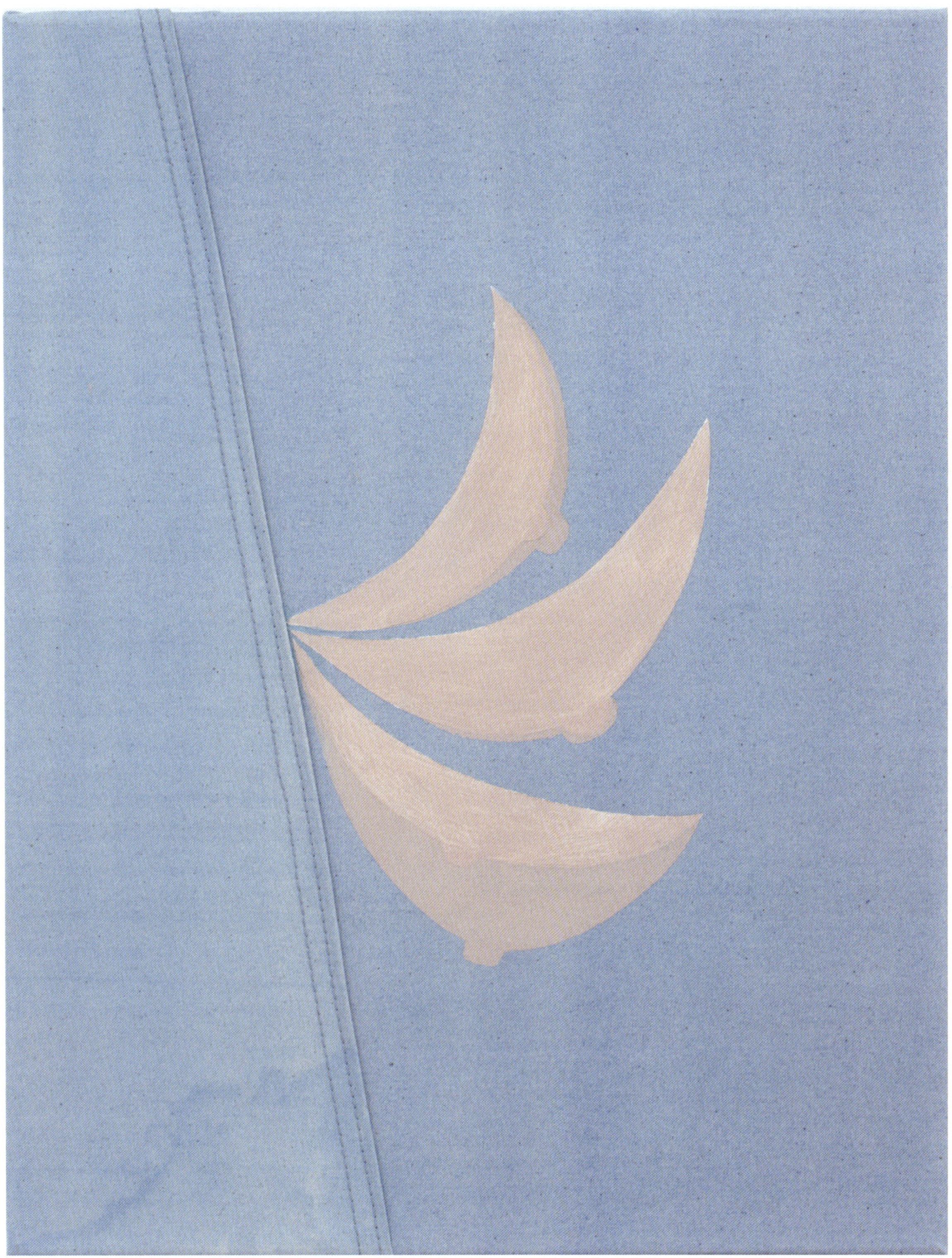

Monika Baer, *Untitled (Stocking)*, 2008, 50 × 39 cm, watercolour, acrylic, oil on canvas, thread.

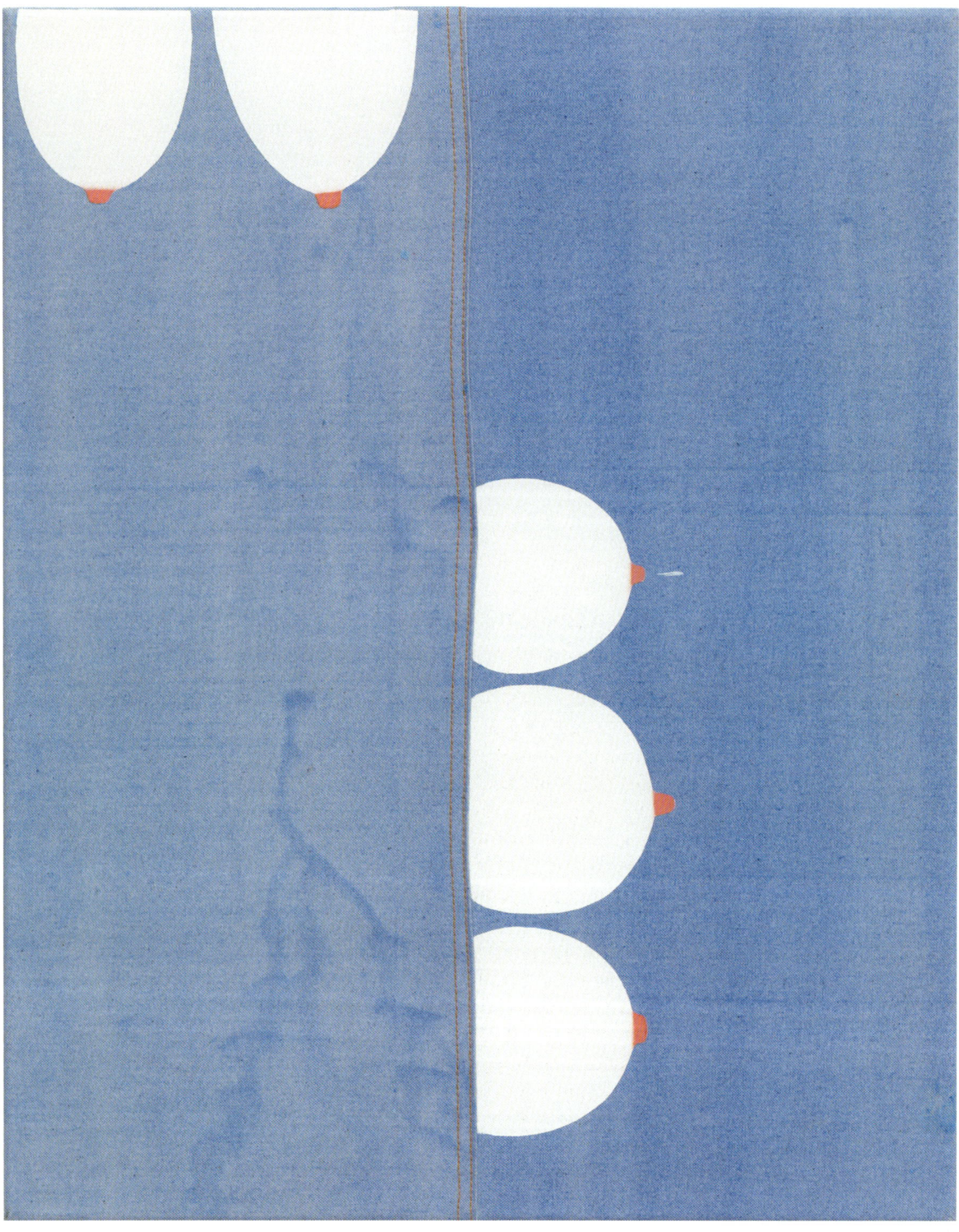

Monika Baer, *Untitled*, 2008, 70 × 56.5 cm, watercolour, acrylic, oil on canvas, thread.

Monika Baer

Monika Baer's media are painting and drawing, the first being the one with most public exposure – a catalyst of expectations, mythology and politics. Unlike many other artists, Baer does not appropriate from the vast expanse of tradition, technique and convention that constitute the legacy of painting. She *works* the conventions and reinvents painting as a topos for deep poetic action. Material, reference, surface and illusion are simultaneously set in a dynamic of association, in which the canvas functions as the intersection between practice and discourse.

Baer has created several series of paintings where everyday motifs, such as paper money, metal coins, sausage slices, alcohol bottles and metal chains, both attract and obstruct the gaze, interrupting 'the desire for painting, the desire to see'.[1] The paper money represents economic value; the anal or scatological aspect of a painting as economic value. Baer represents the bills as floating, flying or hanging in a dense, visceral and experimental painterly surface: a space where transparent colours are mixed with ashes, punctuated by drippings, unformed spots, splashes and streaks. In this ambiguous space, intense painterly relationships reign, while they are perforated by the illusionistic depiction of concrete objects that seem to be present as much for their

shape and obstruction as for their iconographical meaning. These things and objects also have different shapes and surfaces from the canvas. The bill and the meat slice seem to be situated outside the painting, their surfaces protruding from the painterly space. If their meaning is self-evident, in the sense of convention and habit linked to the trading of paintings, their realistic representation activates different experiential dimensions, related to physical and tactile qualities of paint. 'Painting can be a preferred venue for this performance of contact due […] to painting, especially since modernity, being subject to the paradigm of embodiment and thus providing the possibility of a tactile, affective, somatic reception.'[2]

In an earlier series, the marking of painting as an incarnation or an embodiment is double. On a watercolour surface suggesting a textile pattern of blue denim jeans, an illusion is made tangible by the division of the space by a seam that affirms the canvas's objecthood. Here, Baer represents a single set or a series of 'magazine illustration-style' breasts. Their alignment on the edges of the canvas, or along the seams, not only triggers but also frames the gaze. With it, the whole complex of discourses from psychoanalysis to phenomenology, which have been mobilised by feminist critique to articulate an alternative

to the bond between an actively objectifying foreign gaze and a passive female body, the double tactile and bodily association of denim and breasts oppose the mechanisms of perception and objectification. Baer's stylised, funny but strangely unbodily and noncarnal figurations of the breast, represent and act like agents to provoke discourses about the gaze and desire that correspond to and are associated with most idealised feminine representations – to which Baer responds with a depiction of tactile, gendered, bodily, visual interruption in a figure – ground constellation that is impossible to disentangle.

DS

1
Susanne Leeb,
'Liquid Gazes
(On Contemporary
Painting)' in
Aesthetics of the Flesh,
eds Felix Ensslin
and Charlotte Klink,
Berlin and New York
2014, p. 20.

2
Ibid., p. 17.

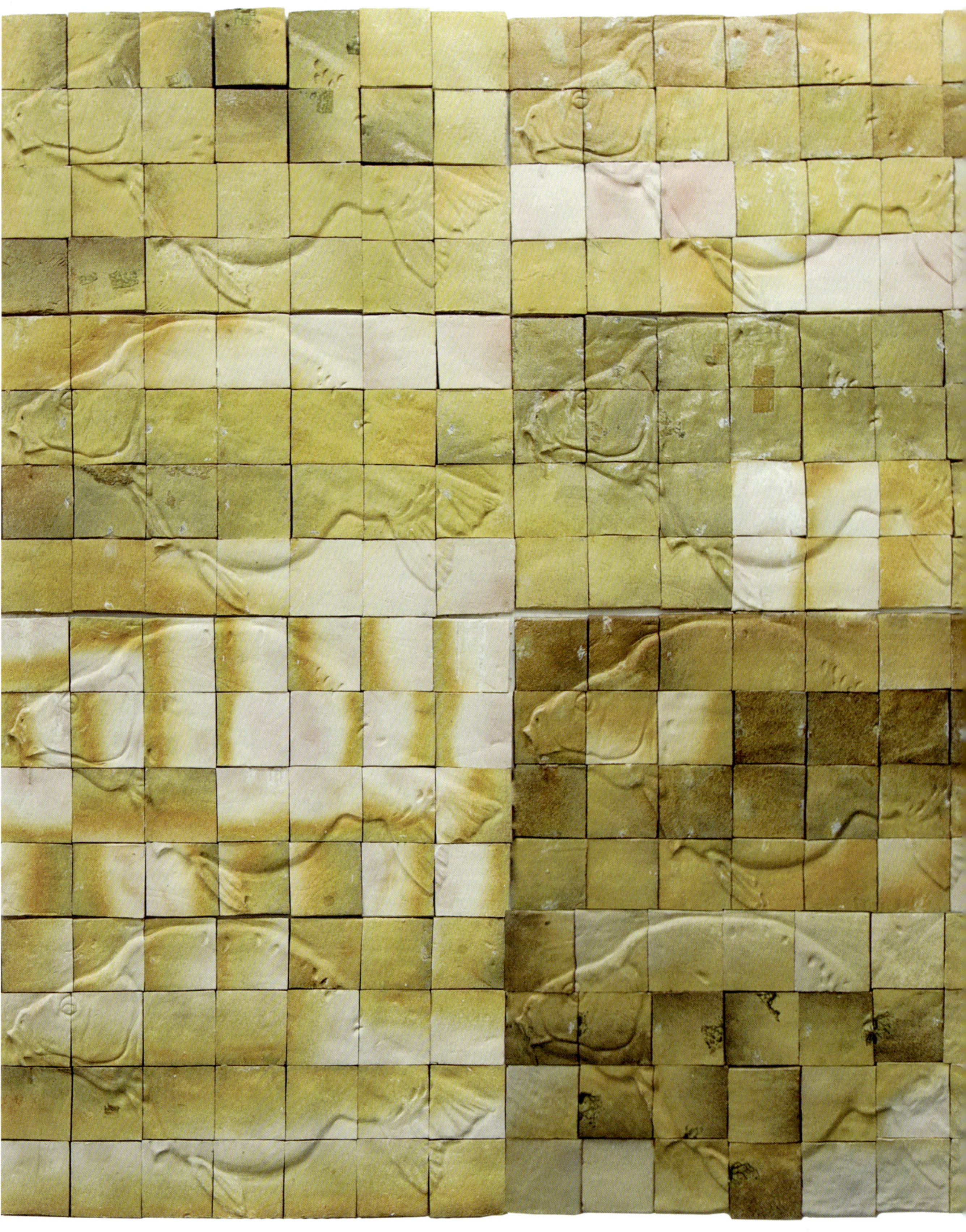

Daniel Dewar & Grégory Gicquel, digital simulation of *Stoneware Mural with Carp*, 2017, 224 × 784 × 2 cm, high-fired stoneware mounted on aluminium.

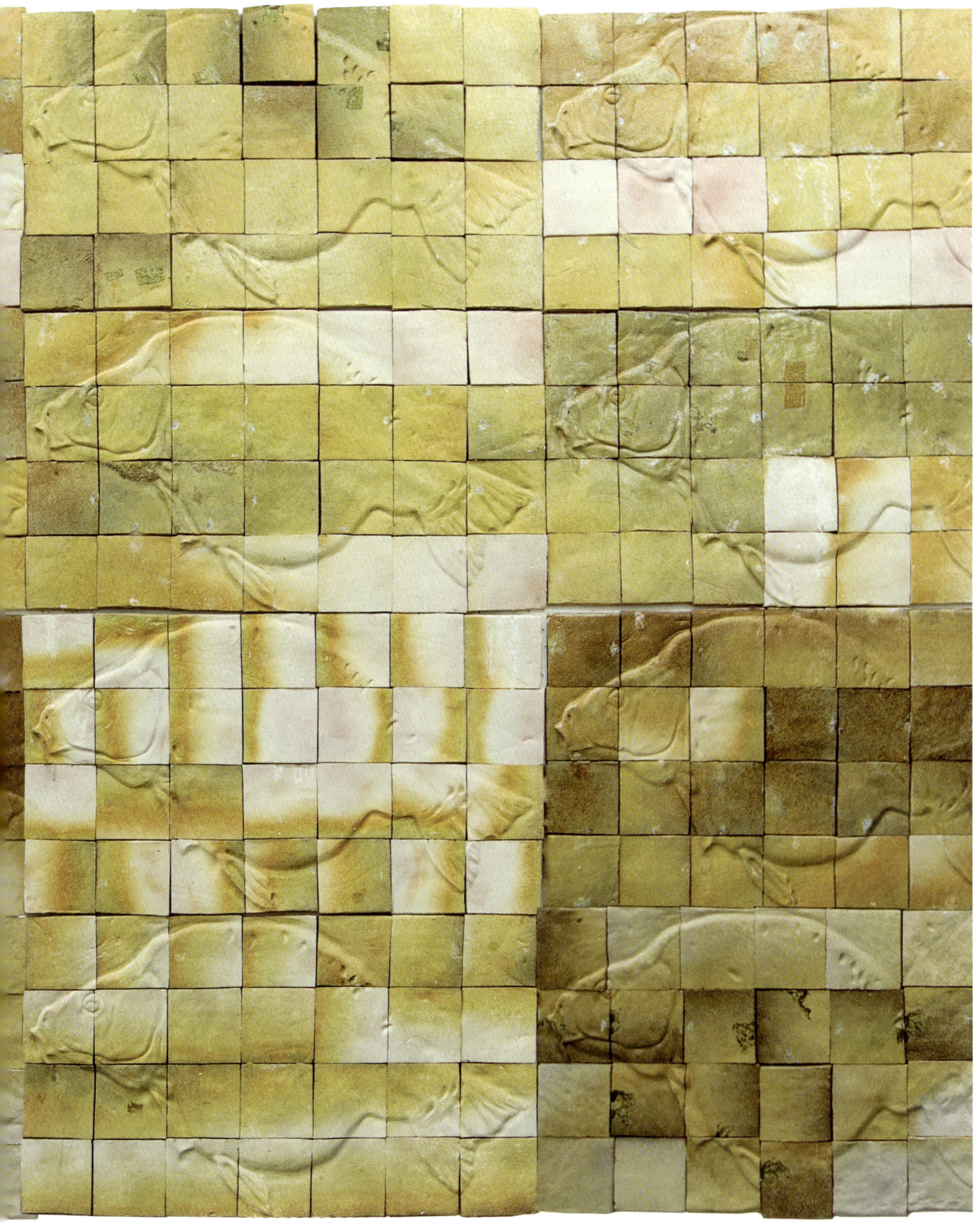

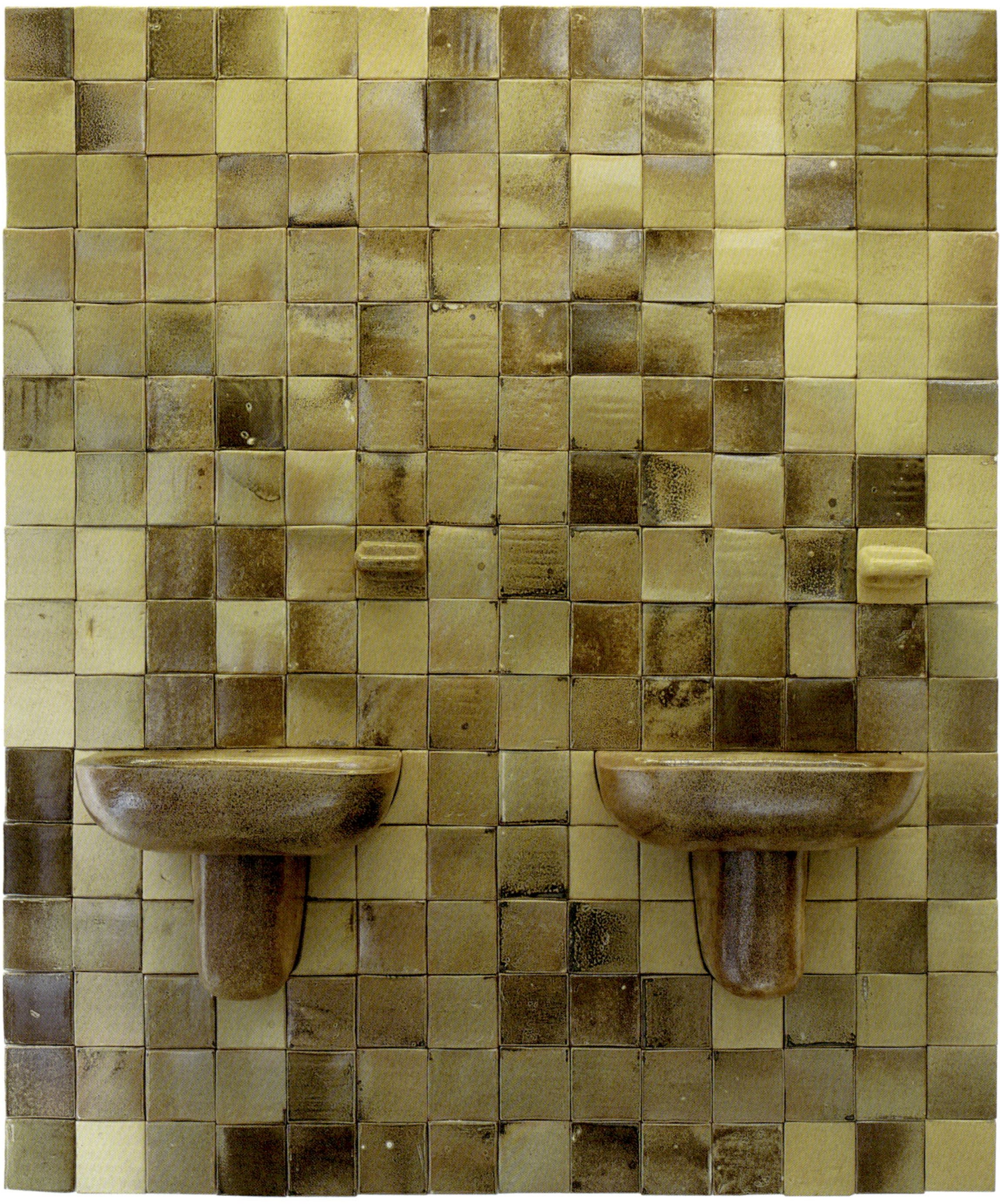

Daniel Dewar & Grégory Gicquel, *Stoneware Mural with Two Sinks and Two Soapdishes*, 2016, 240 × 210 × 52 cm, high-fired stoneware mounted on aluminium.

Daniel Dewar & Grégory Gicquel

For the past twenty years, Dewar & Gicquel have worked together on an ambitious sculptural practice that ranges from stone-carving to weaving and woodworking to ceramics. Whatever they are making, their chosen material is central to their conceptual approach, as they explore its possibilities and push the limitations of the techniques usually associated with it.

In 2012 the duo photographed their process of making a series of monumental (yet ephemeral) clay sculptures in the open air (depicting a recumbent cow, a psychedelic pattern of rams' horns, a pair of disembodied legs dancing a minuet…). The resulting images were transformed into simple animations – resembling GIF files – and projected full-scale as video loops. This way of working changed how the artists considered repetition: having projected the same few, repeated movements, they rethought their approach to ceramics, a medium often marked by the repetition of unique gestures (a potter throwing the 'same' pot again and again, or the manufacture of porcelain plates, cups, bowls). Collaborating with Dewar's father – a ceramicist – they started making the series *Stoneware Vessels* (2014–),

vases of differing sizes that combine the cast shape of a human foot with the thrown shape of a jug. These ambiguous, somewhat disconcerting forms are hard to define or to date, as they seem to combine elements from ancient statuary with the modest and rustic aesthetic of traditional pottery.

Keen to be completely engaged – physically and conceptually – with the ceramics medium, the artists built a large wood-fired kiln in their studio in Brittany, for the single purpose of producing high-fired stoneware. They started creating toilet bowls, sinks, bidets, soap dishes and smoking pipes, hand-making forms that are usually mass-produced. While the formal references to Duchamp's *Fountain* (1917) or Magritte's *The Treachery of Images* (1928–29) might seem inevitable, for the artists the desire was not to once again stir up the debate about ready-mades or the question of artistic mimesis. The point was to see how the function of these forms changed through their repeated serial production and decorative presentation, shifting from a pragmatic to an imaginative or psychological function.

Dewar & Gicquel's newly produced piece, *Stoneware Mural with Carp* (2017), is also shaped by repetition. It comprises thirty-two panels made up of twenty-eight tiles, each panel depicting the same motif of a mirror carp in bas-relief. Carps rummage for food in the muddy clay of the riverbed, so the artists have in a certain way returned the animal to its natural habitat. Like their vases and sinks, they see the carp as a container, a semi-solid form that contains liquid. Their piece also taps into the tradition of the carp as an ornamental image, notable in Japanese art. And the fact that they have chosen a mirror carp means that the glaze, evoking the fish's shimmering scales, is of great importance. It is another example of their interest in animal forms, here presented as if fossilised in the clay or fragmented like pixels of a digital photograph.

ZG

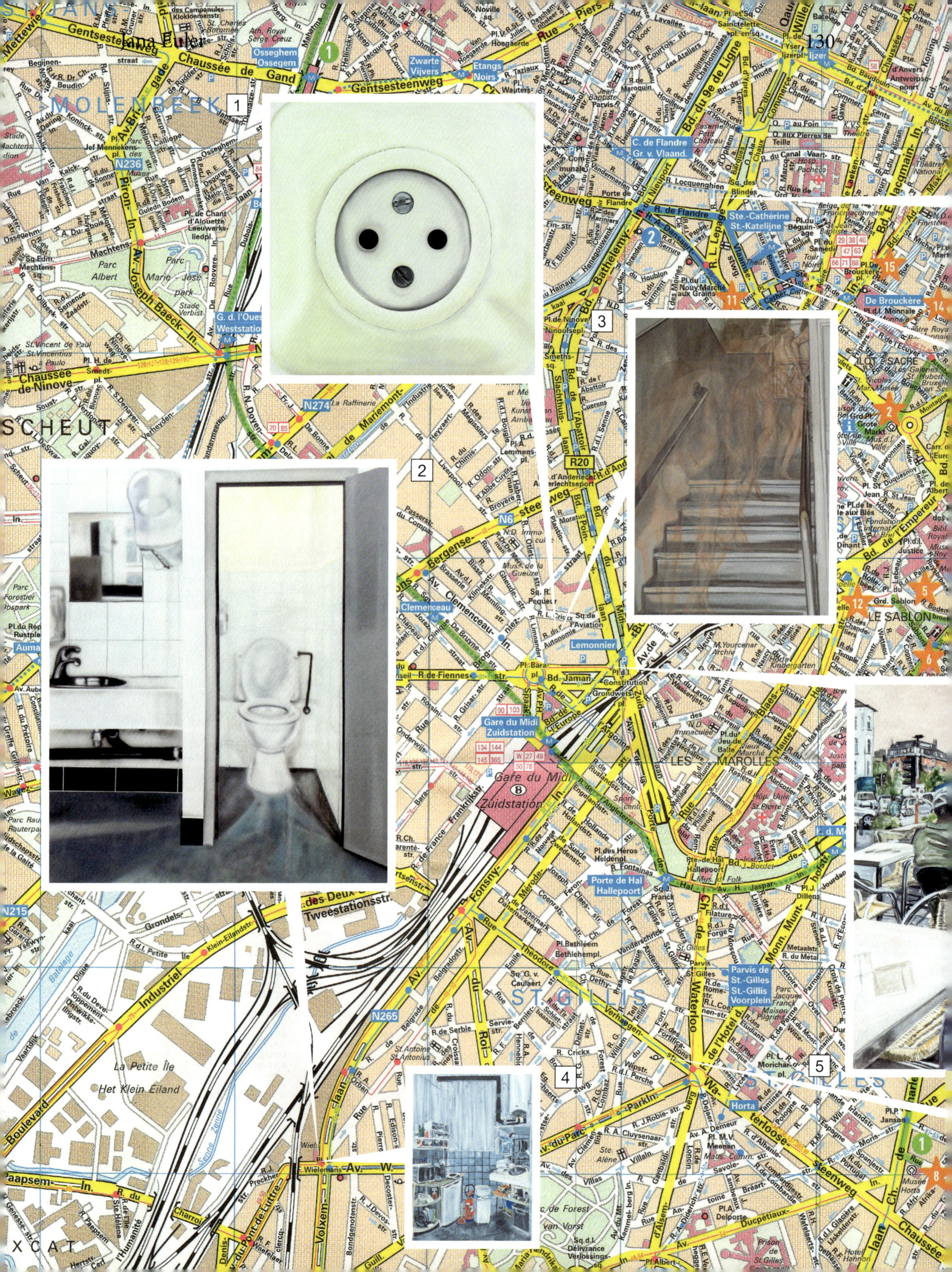
130

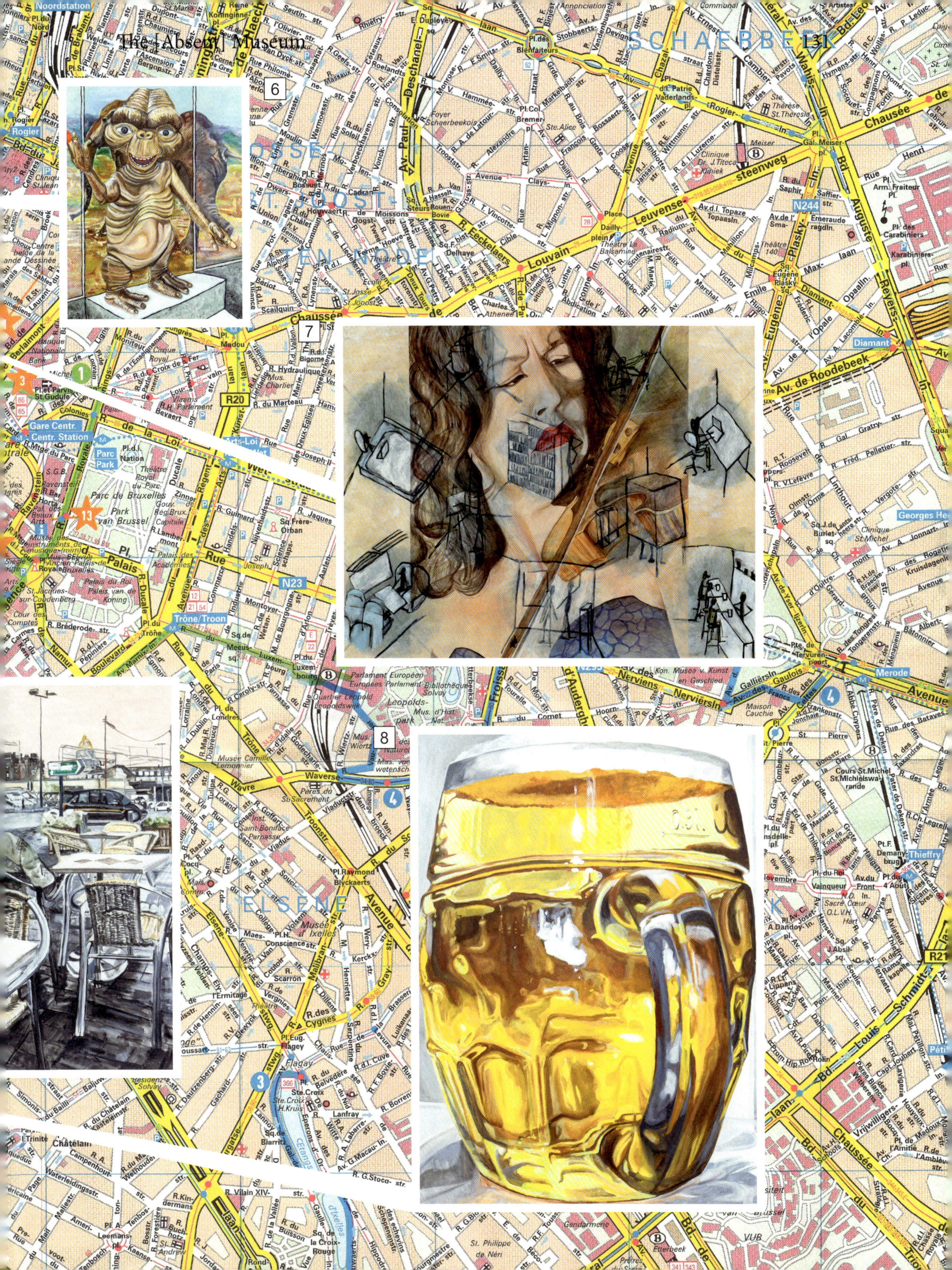
The Absent Museum
6
7
8

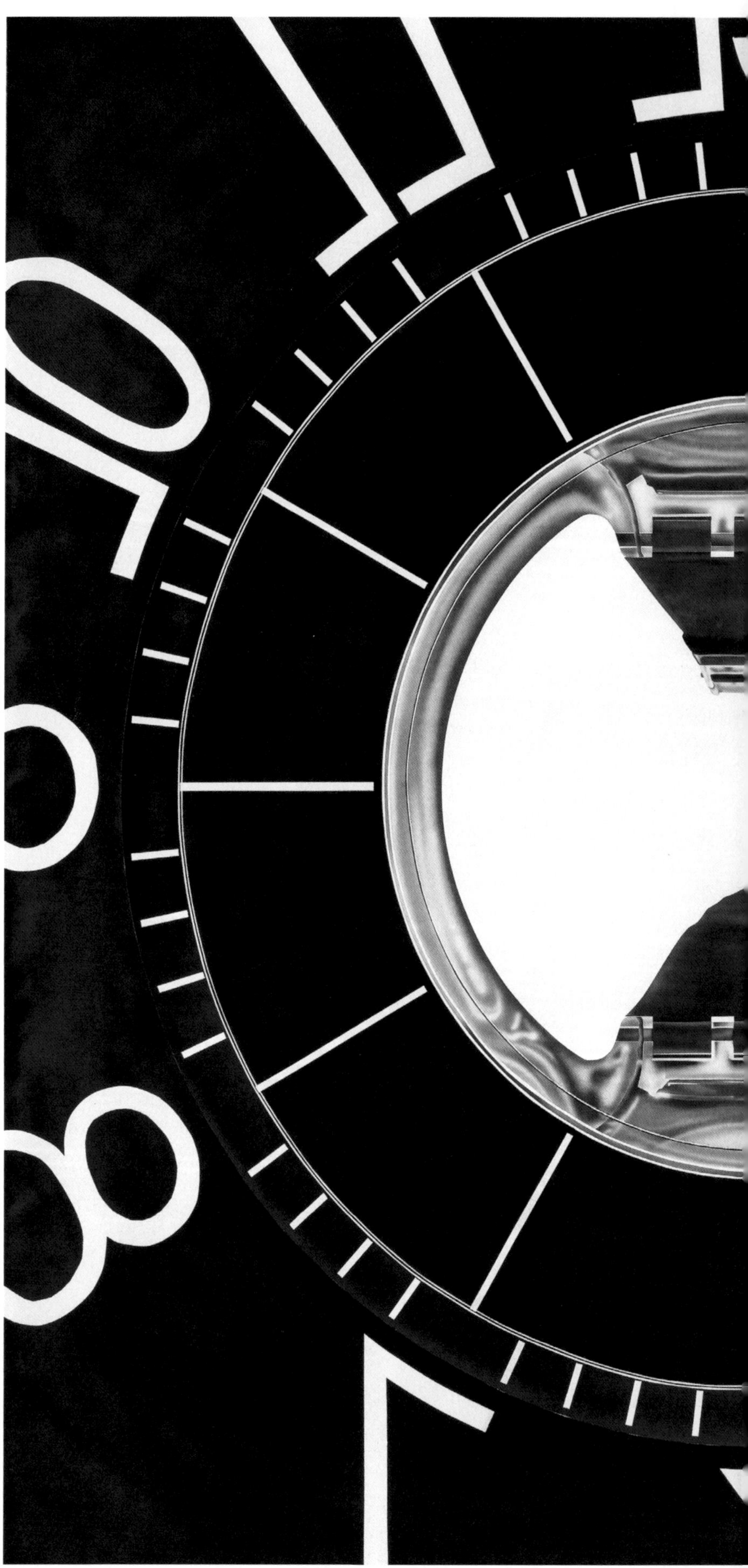

Jana Euler, „ “, 2016, 210 × 210 cm, acrylic on canvas.

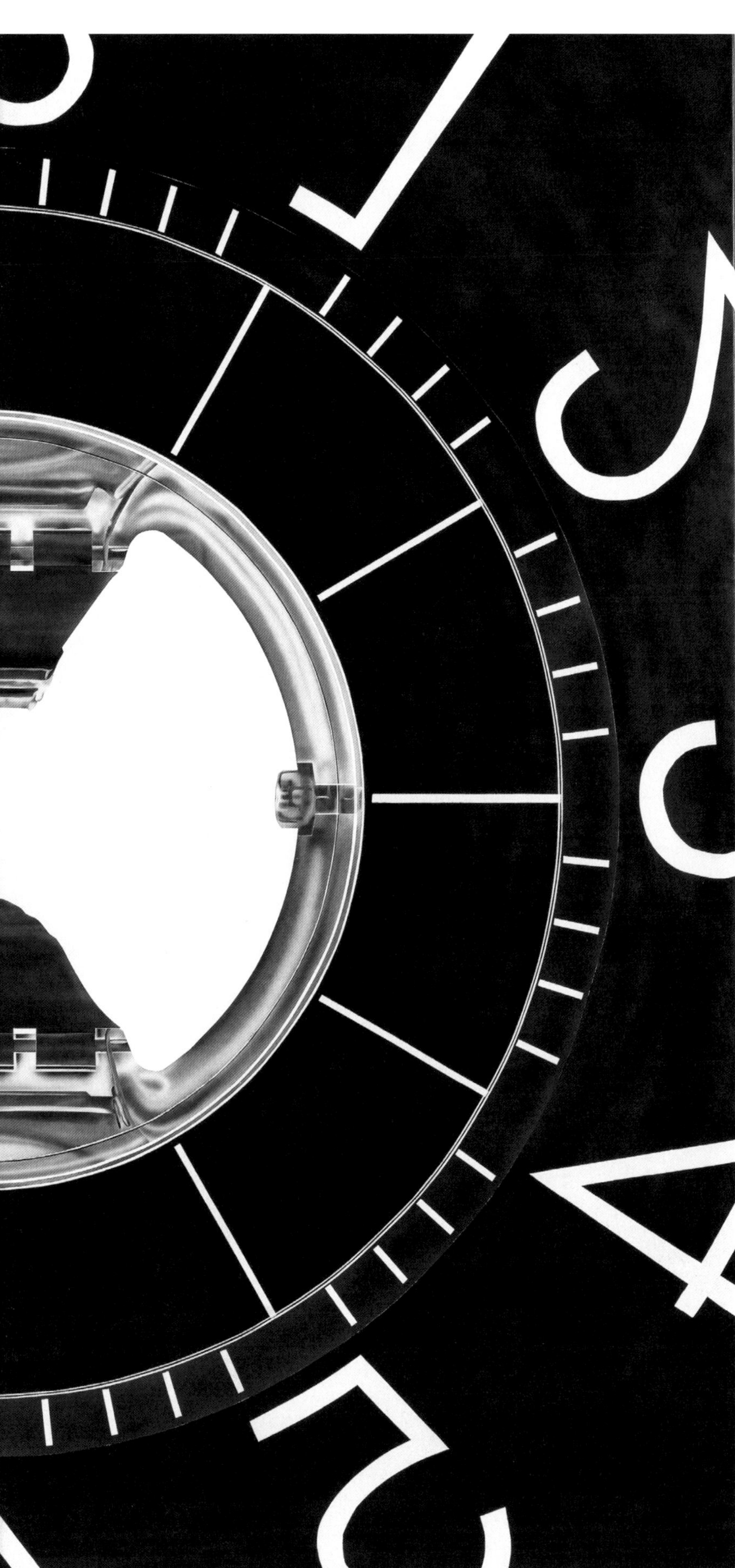

1
Jana Euler, *Where the Energy Comes From 2*, 2014, 210 × 210 cm, acrylic on canvas.

2
Jana Euler, *Female Toilets*, 2013, 240 × 210 cm, acrylic on canvas.

3
Jana Euler, *Nude Climbing up the Stairs*, 2014, 180 × 120 cm, oil on canvas.

4
Jana Euler, *School Politics*, 2013, 130 × 110 cm, acrylic on canvas.

5
Jana Euler, *In Brussels*, 2013, 180 × 140 cm, oil on canvas.

6
Jana Euler, *Self-Portrait as E.T. Re-entering the Gallery*, 2013, 140 × 110 cm, oil on canvas.

7
Jana Euler, *Untitled*, 2009, 120 × 160 cm, oil on canvas.

8
Jana Euler, *Beer without Glass*, 2013, 240 × 180 cm, oil on canvas.

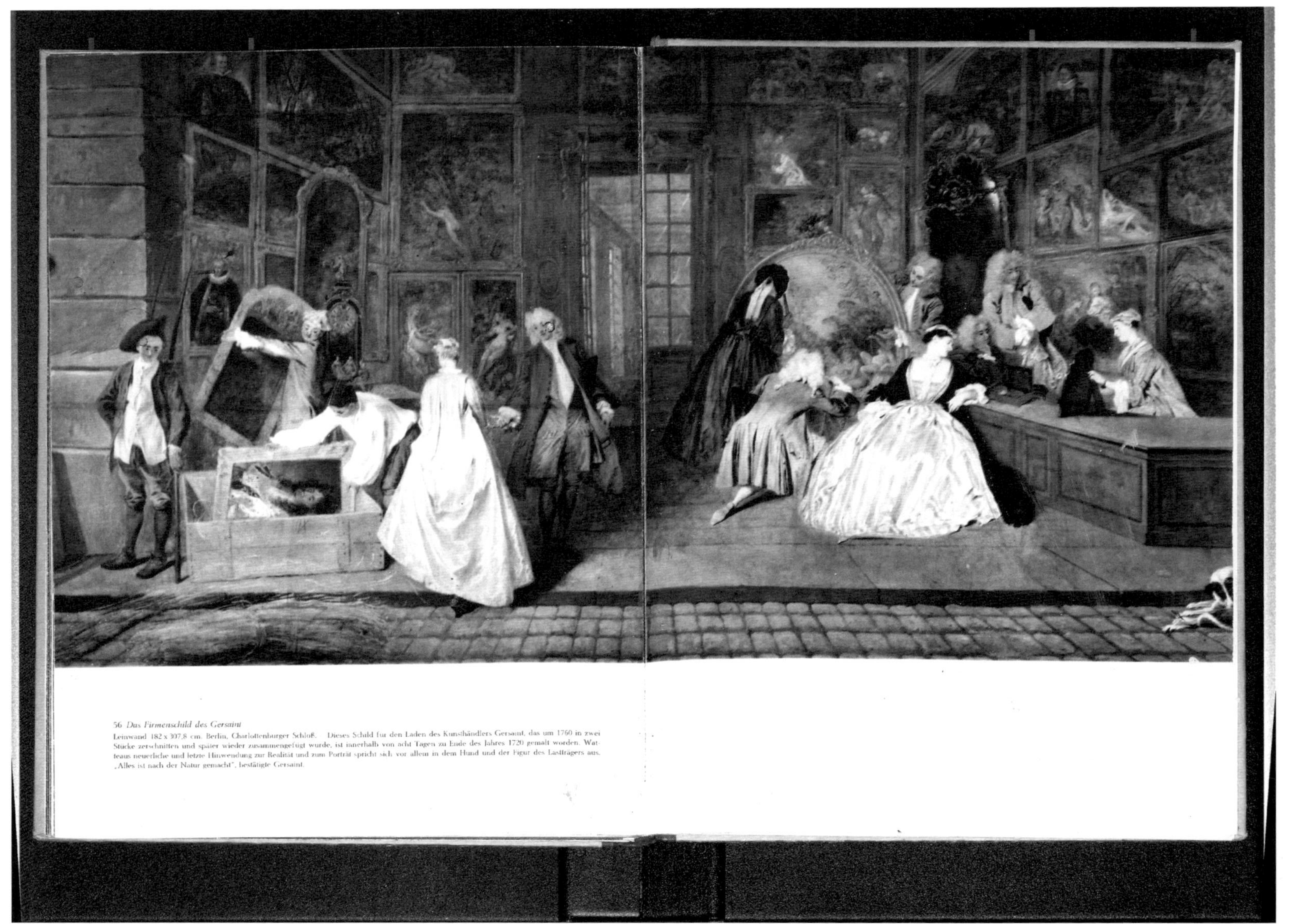

56 *Das Firmenschild des Gersaint*
Leinwand 182 x 307,8 cm. Berlin, Charlottenburger Schloß.   Dieses Schild für den Laden des Kunsthändlers Gersaint, das um 1760 in zwei Stücke zerschnitten und später wieder zusammengefügt wurde, ist innerhalb von acht Tagen zu Ende des Jahres 1720 gemalt worden. Watteaus neuerliche und letzte Hinwendung zur Realität und zum Porträt spricht sich vor allem in dem Hund und der Figur des Lastträgers aus. „Alles ist nach der Natur gemacht", bestätigte Gersaint.

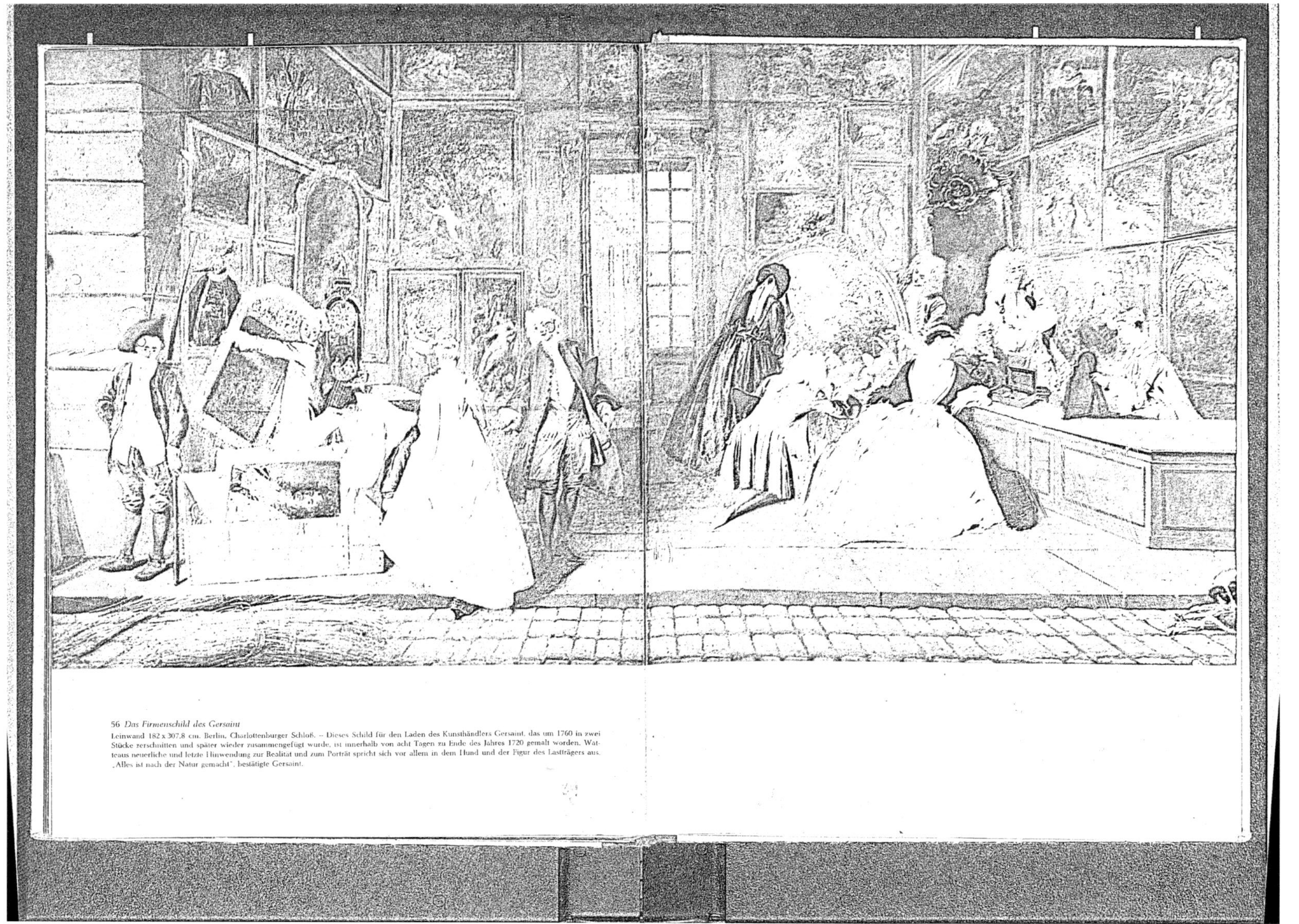

56 *Das Firmenschild des Gersaint*

Leinwand 182 x 307,8 cm. Berlin, Charlottenburger Schloß. – Dieses Schild für den Laden des Kunsthändlers Gersaint, das um 1760 in zwei Stücke zerschnitten und später wieder zusammengefügt wurde, ist innerhalb von acht Tagen zu Ende des Jahres 1720 gemalt worden. Watteaus neuerliche und letzte Hinwendung zur Realität und zum Porträt spricht sich vor allem in dem Hund und der Figur des Lastträgers aus. „Alles ist nach der Natur gemacht", bestätigte Gersaint.

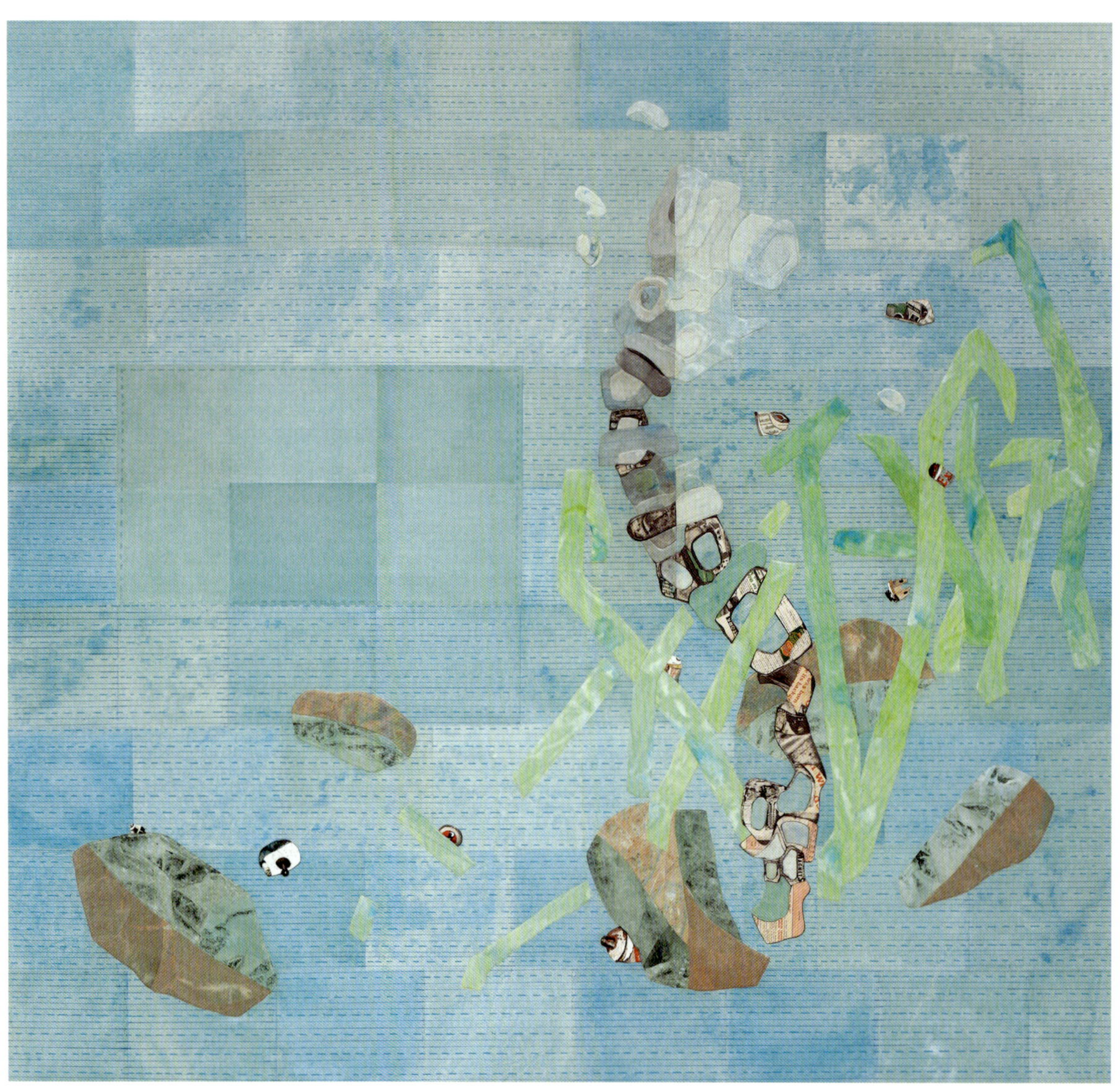

Ellen Gallagher, *Dew Breaker*, 2015, 188.2 × 202.9 cm, pigment, ink, oil, graphite and paper on canvas.

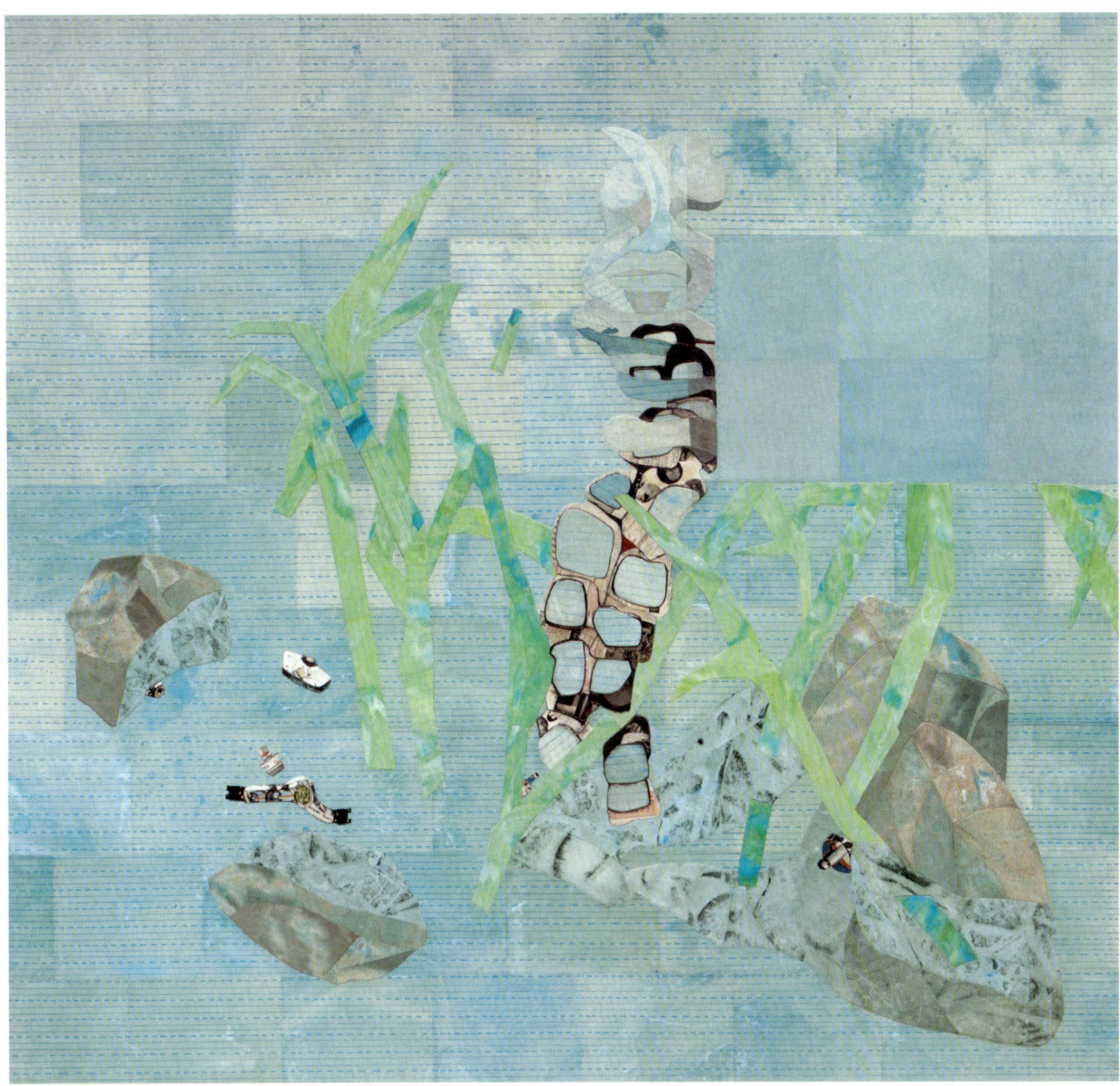

Ellen Gallagher, *Dew Breaker*, 2015, 188.2 × 202.9 cm, pigment, ink, oil, graphite and paper on canvas.

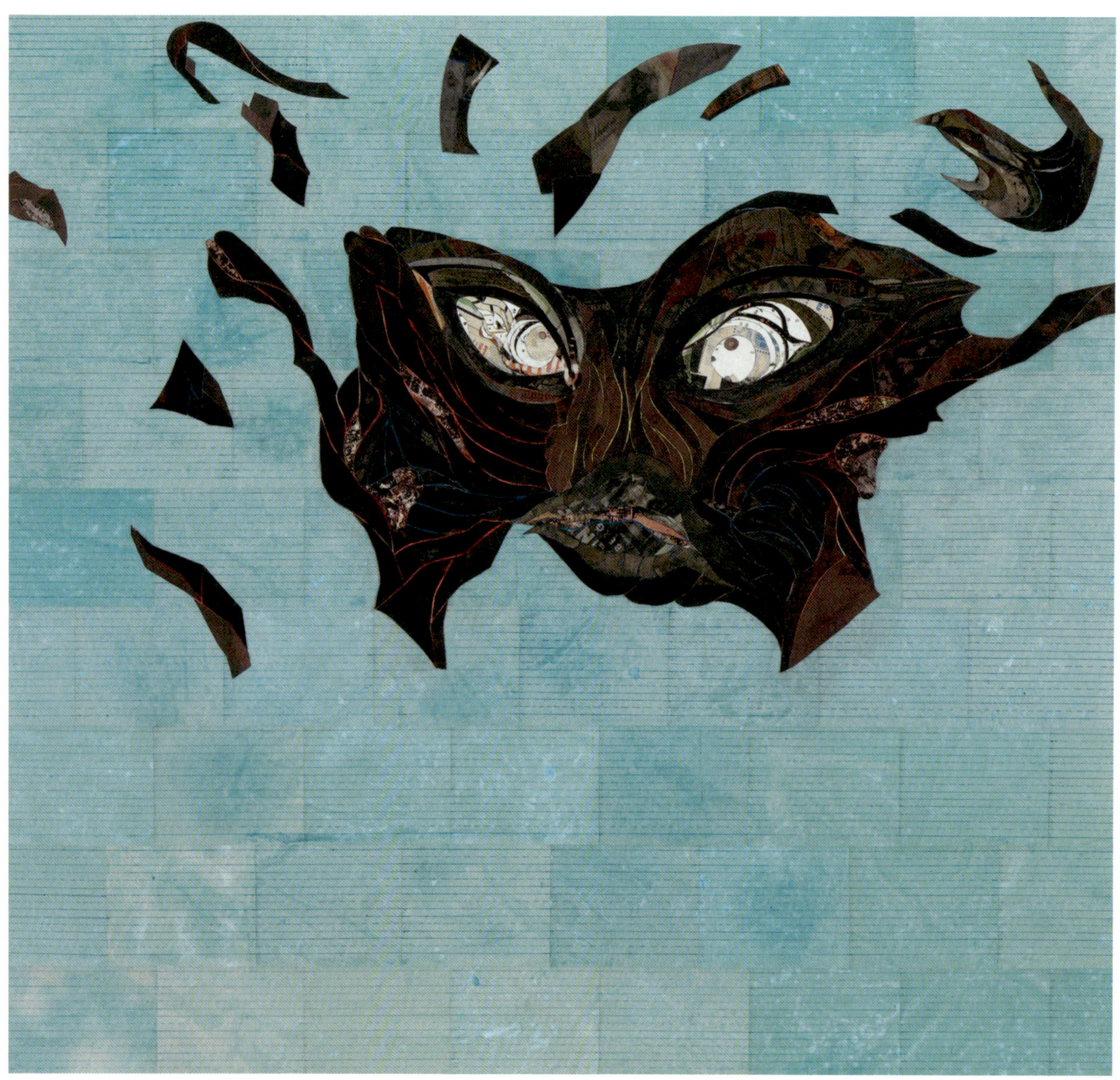

Ellen Gallagher, *Dr. Blowfins*, 2014, 188.2 × 202.9 cm, ink, graphite and paper on canvas.

Ellen Gallagher,
Abu Simbel,
2005, 62 × 90 cm,
photogravure,
watercolour, colour
pencil, varnish,
pomade, plasticine,
fake fur, gold leaf and
crystals.

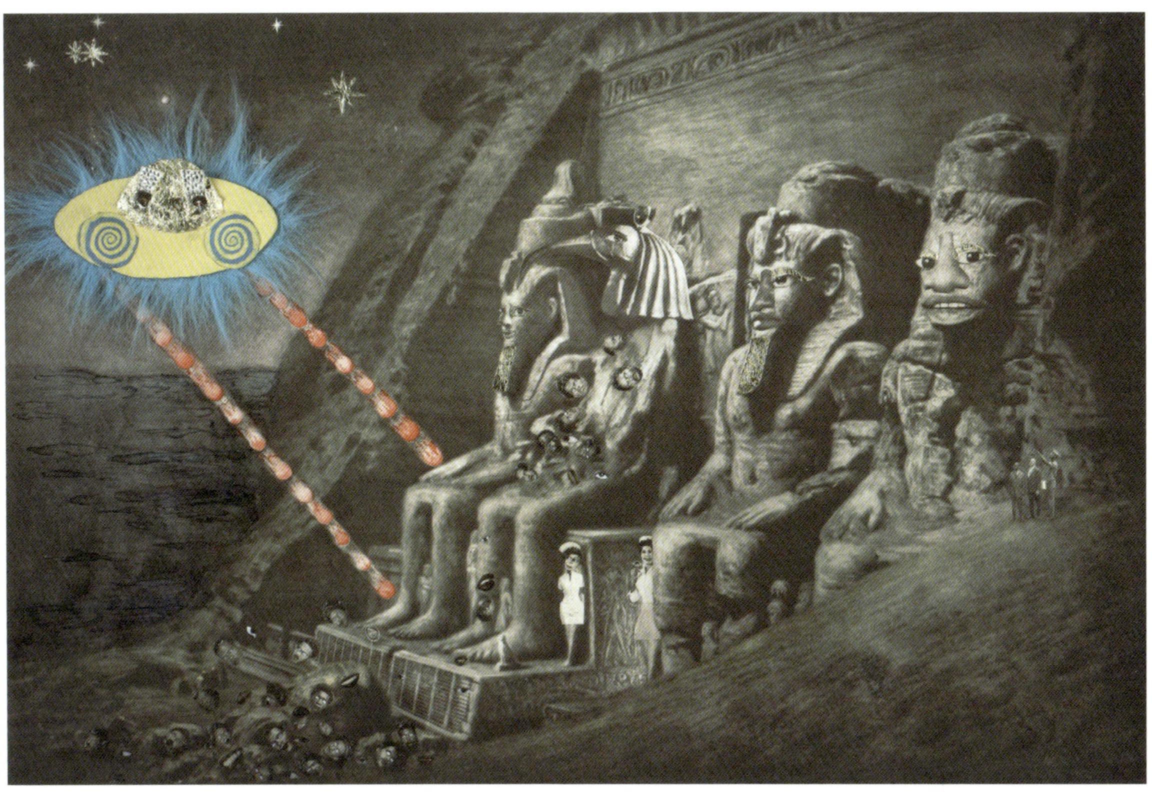

Dew Breaker

Named for the time of day under the blanket of night while the grass was still wet they arrived for their victims. The Dew Breaker were henchmen, the violent secret controlling force of Haiti's Papa Doc Duvalier. In my *Watery Ecstatic* realm, the Dew Breaker are made up of living tatters which come forward like maggots out of our living past and the promise of advertisements:

tombstones
war helmets
radios
spark plugs and speakers
wigs and hairpieces
hamsters
medicinal remedies and pills

Unpicked from their magazine spines and woven into a zombie blue breath the Dew Breaker become coffin bearers.

Inseparable, hinged to the weight of the corpse, forced into a throbbing vertebrae dance.

This corpse represents the people of the transatlantic slave trade, the route known as the Middle Passage where the sick and dying abducted passengers were thrown overboard or took their own lives by leaping into the sea.

With this violent history in mind a Detroit-based duo of electronic musicians began the project known as Drexciya. The band imagined Drexciyans as water breathing battalions waging a perpetual war 'against planetary control systems'.

My Drexciya is less about war and revenge than about ideas of regeneration and a transhistorical nation, with Dew Breaker as its carrier.

When image is added to image, the metaphor of the forces grow stronger. Steps of movement and fluidity, the Voyage as a way for creating a reality which is always more than the present.

This excess, a passage to symbolic and social potential.

Ellen Gallagher, 2017

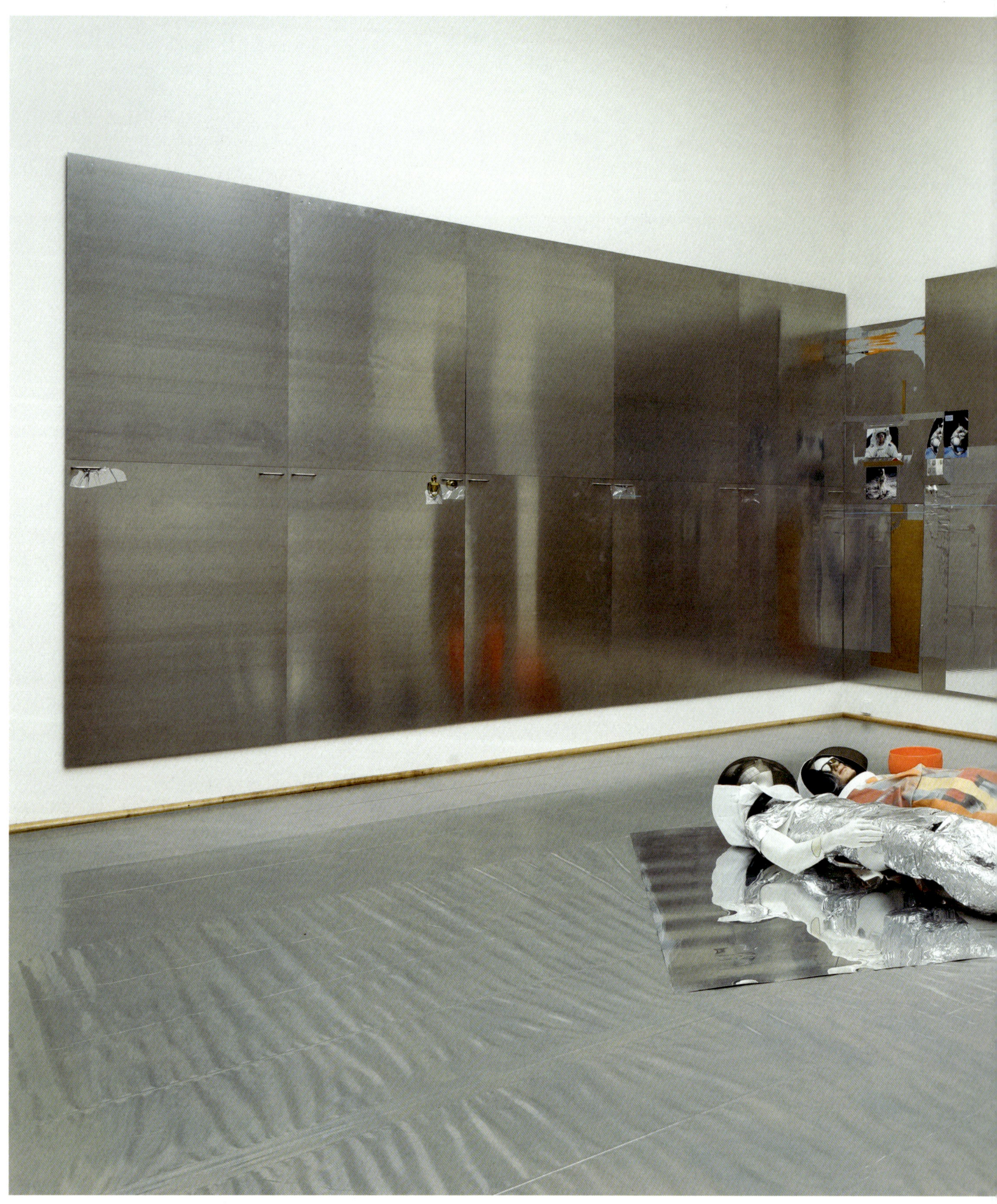

Isa Genzken, *OIL XV / OIL XVI*, 2007, variable dimensions, 2 mannequins, 3 plastic vessels, metal foil, plastic, cloth / 23-part wall installation: aluminium plates, metal foil, adhesive tape, metal, paper.

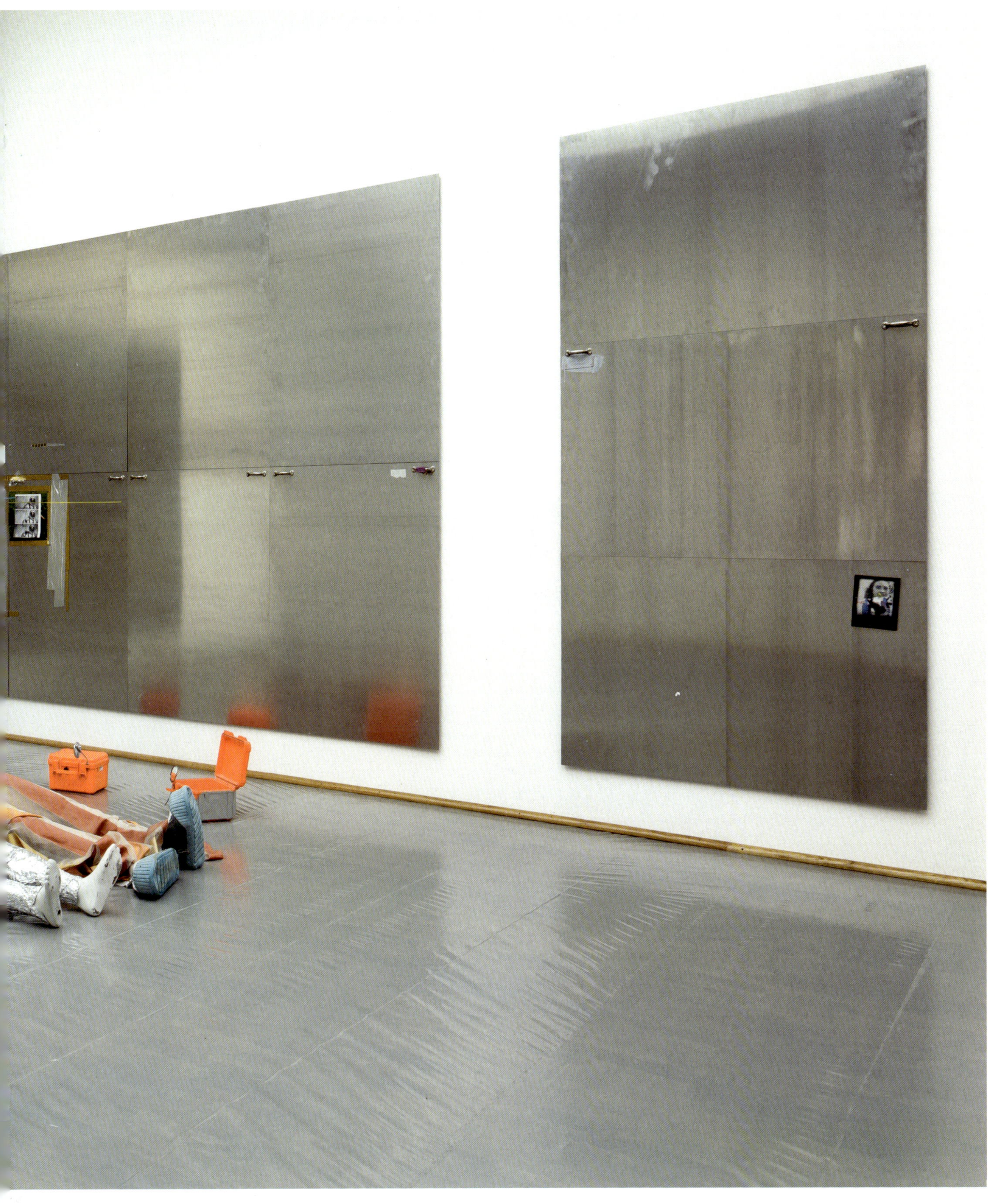

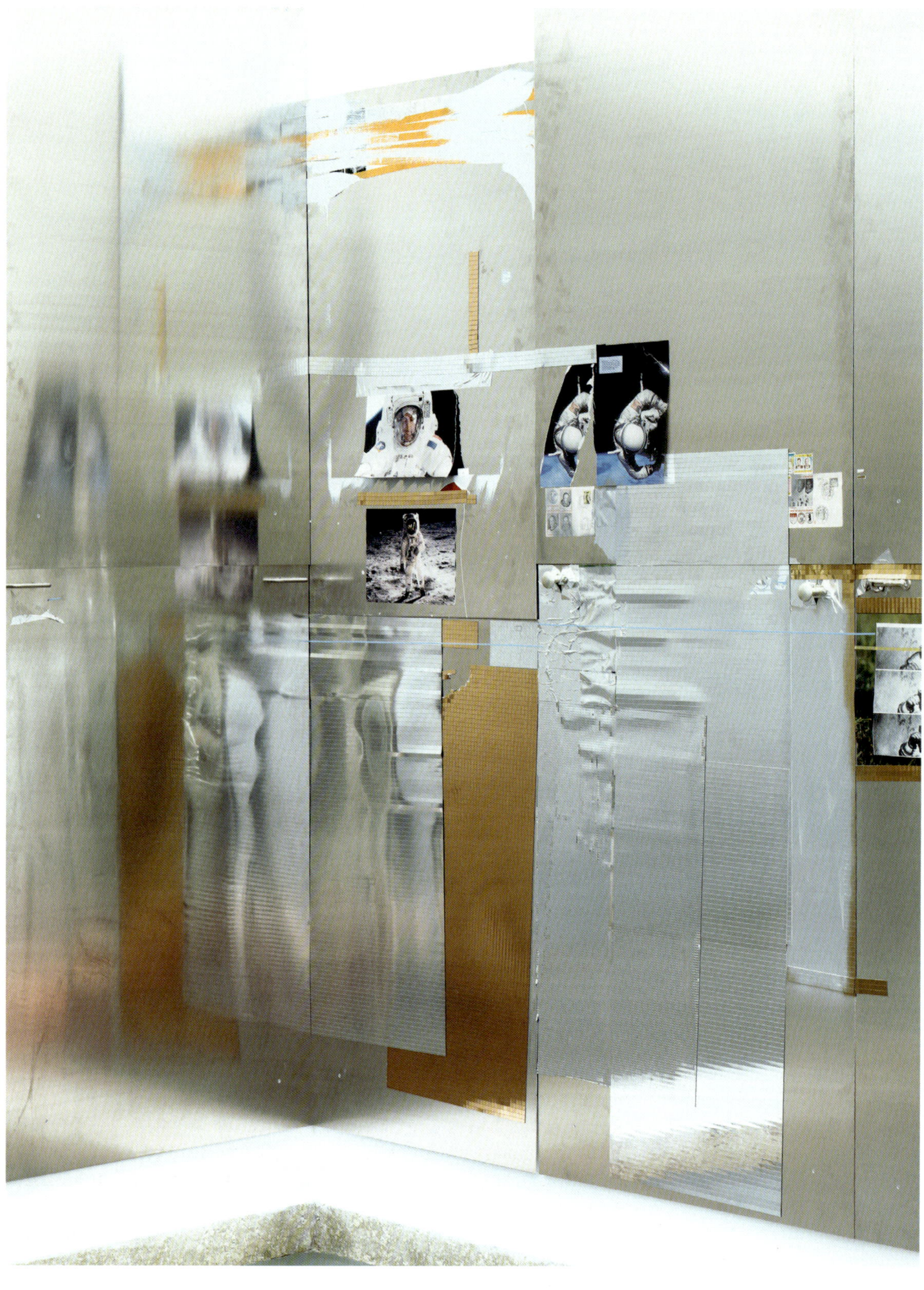

Isa Genzken, *OIL XVI*, 2007, variable dimensions, 23-part wall installation: aluminium plates, metal foil, adhesive tape, metal, paper.

Isa Genzken

The work of German artist Isa Genzken has been influenced since the 1970s by ideas about hybrid art forms. Today these are summed up by the term 'post-medium', a discipline in which painting, sculpture and photography exchange their characteristics. Over the past decade, Genzken has also developed an interest in collage and the *objet trouvé*. In these installations, for instance, slick design objects stand alongside cheap household appliances, banal souvenirs alongside artistic pictures. Genzken represented her country at the 2007 Venice Biennale with the exhibition 'OIL'. The title refers directly to the unlimited and uncontrolled use by humanity of natural energy resources.

The two-part work *OIL XV/OIL XVI* consists of a pair of life-size, androgynous dummies wearing space helmets. The dummies are lying on their backs, staring at the ceiling, against a background of reflective aluminium plates on which Genzken has attached door knockers and pictures of moonwalks. The dummies are in an unclear space. The door knockers refer to an 'inside' that is within reach, while the astronaut iconography insinuates an immeasurable outer space, the 'universe'. The relation between the two dummies is also ambiguous: although they are placed close to one another, there is no attempt at intimacy. For that the environment is too cold, the bodies too stiff. This sense of attraction and repulsion is heightened by their clothing: one is wrapped in soft colourful material, the other partly in tinfoil. Textile is a material that 'weaves' symbolically and technically, while the silver-coloured metallic wrapping reflects the artificial qualities. The different positions of the visors – open vs. closed – emphasise the various perspectives on the outside world.

The piece seems to be an allegorical representation of humanity after the expulsion from Paradise – into the present translated as the awakening from the utopian pipe dream of technoscientific progress. The desire to control the chaos of nature, with space travel as the sublime culmination, has not led to a new harmony between humanity and the world. Locked in their own individualities, the dummies contemplate the gaping void of the outside world that they wanted to discover. The most traumatic legacy of the twentieth century is perhaps the knowledge that humanity does not live in but on a sphere, that humanity is not the central point, but part of a limitless whole.

BVB

EMPEROR RO
REPORT OF A COUP
IN OUR REGIONS

THE COUP

12 December 1990: powerful jammers force all radio and TV stations off the air. Radio masts and some broadcasting stations are blown up. The population is left in silence until, after half an hour, some light is thrown on the situation. A message is broadcast on all radio and TV stations to the effect that the country is now under the authority of new rulers. Democracy is immediately suspended. The legislative, executive and judiciary as well as the military are in the hands of the newly crowned Emperor Ro. The population becomes terribly confused as to the veracity of this coup and initially undertakes nothing, but it soon appears that the new emperor is in earnest. Innocent people are chased out of their homes and shot dead or deported to an unknown destination. Others are picked up, questioned and tortured at length so as to extract absurd confessions. Eminent, universally respected politicians do not escape a similar fate. Airports and motorways are blocked and a series of absurd economic measures, such as declaring the national currency worthless, plunge the country into unprecedented chaos. But the new regime is not only characterised by negative and destructive policies. Other nationals are elevated for obscure or non-existent reasons into the nobility, while cripples and lunatics are appointed to high-ranking positions and animals are freed from meadows and parks. The reckless way in which Emperor Ro sets to work generates anarchy among the population. Pockets of resistance surface here and there, but the collapse of communication channels and the tremendous confusion that reigns mean they do not stand a chance. No one knows exactly who to resist since the imperial army is indistinguishable from the ordinary population. It is clear that international leaders see the global order begin to suffer after a few days. The speed and brutality with which Emperor Ro seized power characterise his downfall too. Tanks and aeroplanes of an international armed force take less than an hour to terminate the rule of Emperor Ro. The putschists see their end approach. Some break down and die. Emperor Ro and his last supporters retreat to a villa in the country. Heavy artillery fire forces them to surrender. A few days later, when peace has returned to the country, they are tried by a national court of law in Ledeberg. What remains are documents and pictures that can give us a vague idea of Emperor Ro's ideology and what the consequences would have been if the coup had succeeded.

Jos de Gruyter & Harald Thys, 1993

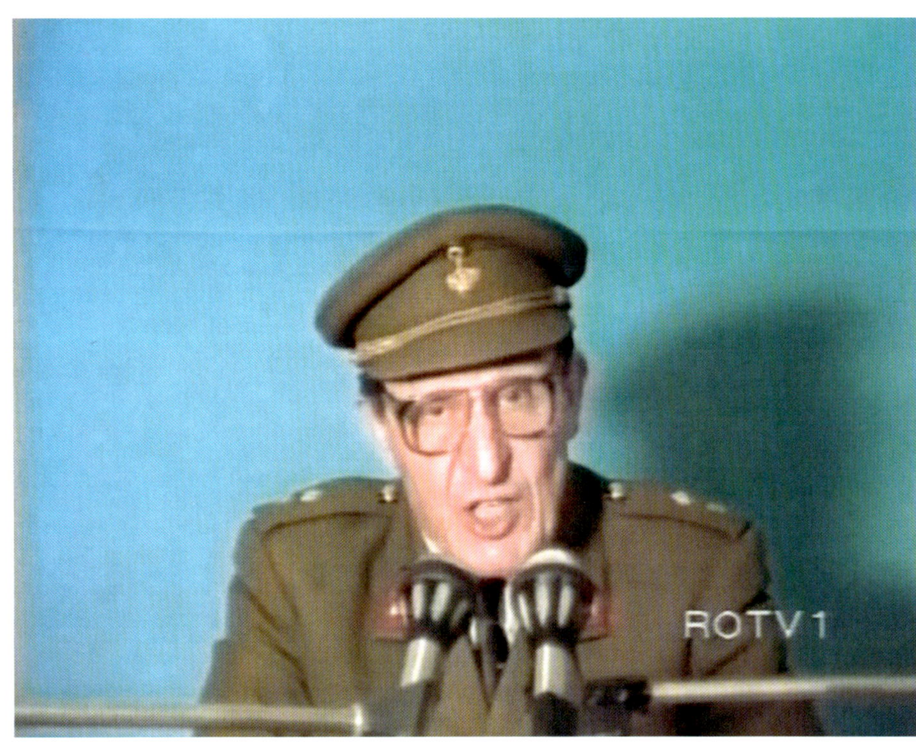

Newsreader Colonel Durant speaks to the people on ROTV1.

Execution file compiled by Commander Driessens.

Manuscript of Emperor Ro.

1 8 DEC. 1990   DRIESSENS
                                                      28e
                                              Anti-terreurraad
                                              Keizer Ro

betraft: executie GILBOS Wim

Wegens het zich in gebreke stellen van artikel 61 BIS aangaande
de wet betreffende het verdubbelen van voorwerpen van metaal met
dewelke deuren, schuiven, kasten, ramen en koffers kunnen
gesloten of geöpend worden

draag ik U overeenkomstig de orders van Zijne Majesteit
Keizer Ro het bevel over tot arrestatie en berechting
met de kogel van:

        naam: GILBOS Wim, Johan, Leopold
                geboren 9/2/'54 te Sterrebeek
                sinds 1988 zaakvoerder van het
                griekse restaurant "Knospos"
                te Machelen

        adres: Grimbergsesteenweg 32 of 34 te
                1800 VIlvoorde

        persoonsbeschrijving:

                - ± 1,70m
                - bruine ogen
                - kaal met zwaarte pruik
                - zwaarlijvig
                - verplaast zich in rode
                  NISSAN 100 NX

Deze persoon is ZEER GEVAARLIJK en dient zo snel mogelijk
opgezocht, gearresteerd en ter plaatse berecht te worden.
De persoonlijke bezittingen alsmede de inboedel dienen
overgebracht te worden naar SECTOR 11 GEBOUW A7 te Kortenberg

Verdere inlichtingen vindt U in bijgevoegde borst.

afgevaardigde tegen Zijne Majesteit
Berechtingsuitvoerder

Dhr. LACROIX Pierre

ik wil dat de steden aalst, lekkervoort, ronse
charleroi, dendermonde aangevallen word
en en alle huizen en mensen met
Rommeln vernietigd worden

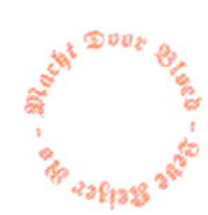

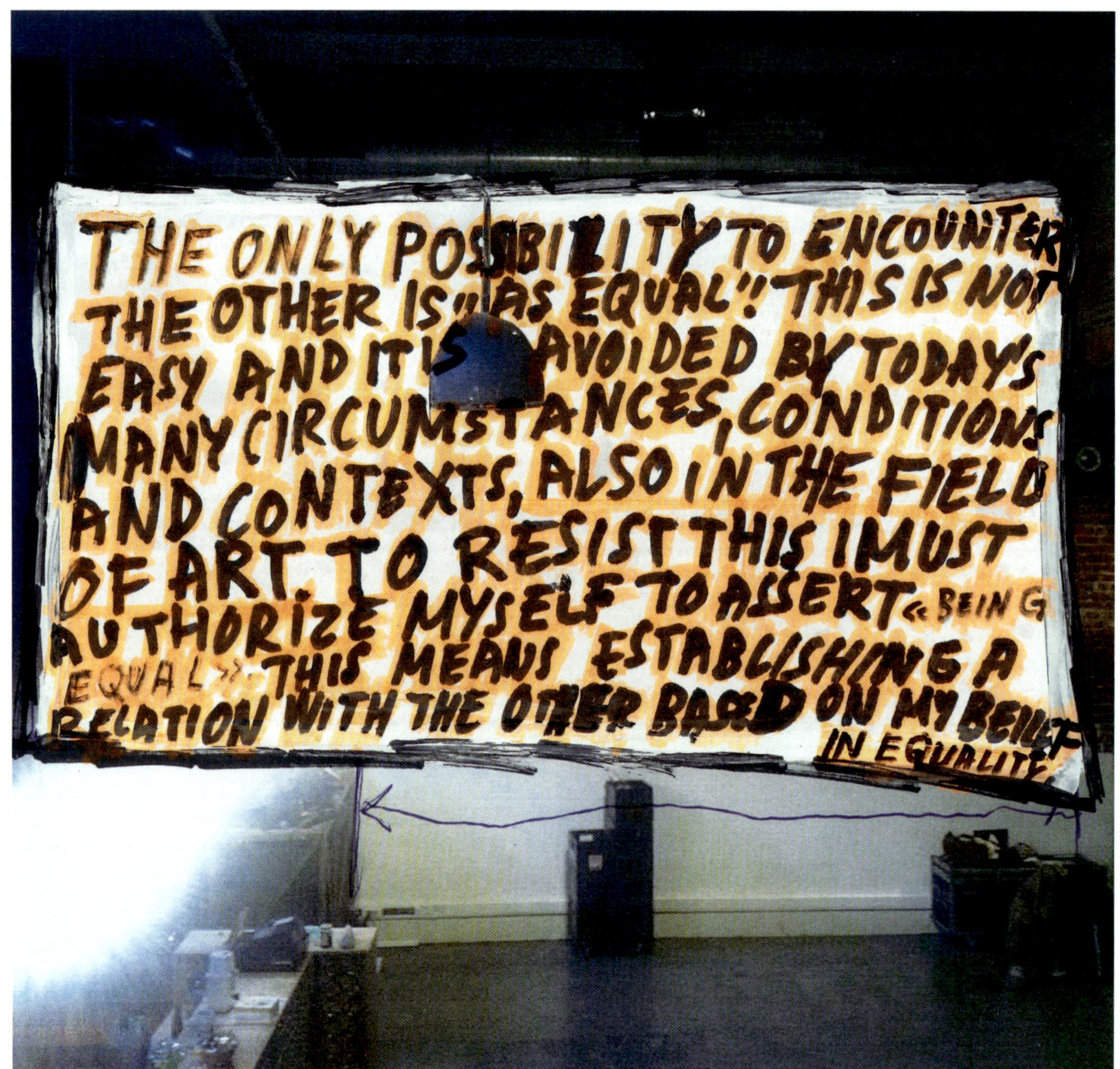

Thomas Hirschhorn, preparatory sketch for *Banner*, 2017, 450 × 820 cm, spray paint on cloth. Specific installation for BRASS.

Why is it Important – Today – to Show and Look at Images of Destroyed Human Bodies?

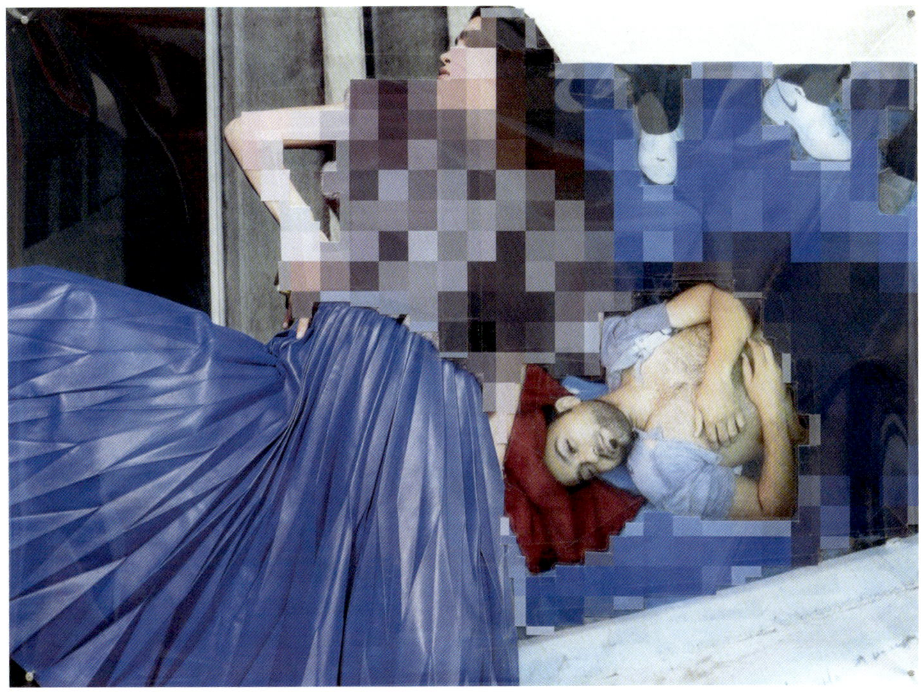

I will try to clarify, in eight points, why it's important – today – to look at images of mutilated human bodies like those I have used and incorporated in various works such as *Superficial Engagement* (2006), *Concretion* (2006), *The Incommensurable Banner* (2007), *Ur-Collage* (2008), *Das Auge* (2008), *Crystal of Resistance* (2011), *Touching Reality* (2012), *Collage-Truth* (2012), *Easycollage* (2014) and *Pixel-Collage* (2016).

1. Origin
The pictures of destroyed human bodies were taken by non-photographers. Most of them were taken by witnesses, passers-by, soldiers, security or police officers, rescuers or first-aid workers. The origin of the images is unclear and often unverifiable; there is no source, whatever we believe a source to be. This unclear provenance and this unverifiability reflect today's uncertainty. This is what I am interested in. Often the origin is not guaranteed – but what can be guaranteed in our world today, and how can 'under guarantee' still make sense? These images can be downloaded from the Internet; they have the status of testimony and were placed online by their authors for many different reasons. Furthermore, the origin of these images is not indicated; sometimes it is confused, with an unclear, perhaps even manipulated or stolen address, as is often true of many things on the Internet and in social media these days. This is something that confronts us every day. The uncertain provenance is one of the reasons why – nowadays – it's important to look at and display such images.

2. Redundancy
The images of destroyed human bodies are important in terms of their redundancy. What's redundant is that such a vast amount of images of destroyed human bodies exists today. Redundancy here isn't repetition of the same thing because it's always another human body that has been destroyed and as such appears to be redundant. But it's not about images – it's about human bodies, about the human, the picture of whom is a witness. The images are redundant because the fact that human beings are being destroyed is redundant. Redundancy is important here. I want to treat it as something important, and I want to see this redundancy as a form. We don't want to accept the redundancy of such images because we don't want to accept the redundancy of cruelty toward humans. This is why it's important to look at and display images of destroyed human bodies in their very redundancy.

3. Invisibility
In today's newspapers, magazines and TV news, we rarely see images of destroyed bodies because they are hardly ever shown. These pictures are non-visible and invisible: the assumption is that they will hurt the viewer's sensitivities or only satisfy voyeurism, and the justification is to protect us from this threat. But this invisibility isn't harmless. The invisibility is the strategy of supporting, or at least not discouraging, the war effort. It's about making war acceptable and its effects commensurable, as was expressed by, for example, Donald Rumsfeld, former US Secretary of Defense (2001–06): 'Death has the tendency to encourage a depressing view of war.' But are there really any views of war which aren't depressing? Looking at and showing images of mutilated human bodies is a way of campaigning against war and its justification and propaganda. Since 9/11, this phenomenon of invisibility has been reinforced in the West. Refusal to accept this invisibility as a given fact or as a 'precautionary measure' is why it's important to look at such images.

Thomas Hirschhorn, *Pixel-Collage n°14*, 2016, 33 × 45 cm, prints, tape, transparent sheet.

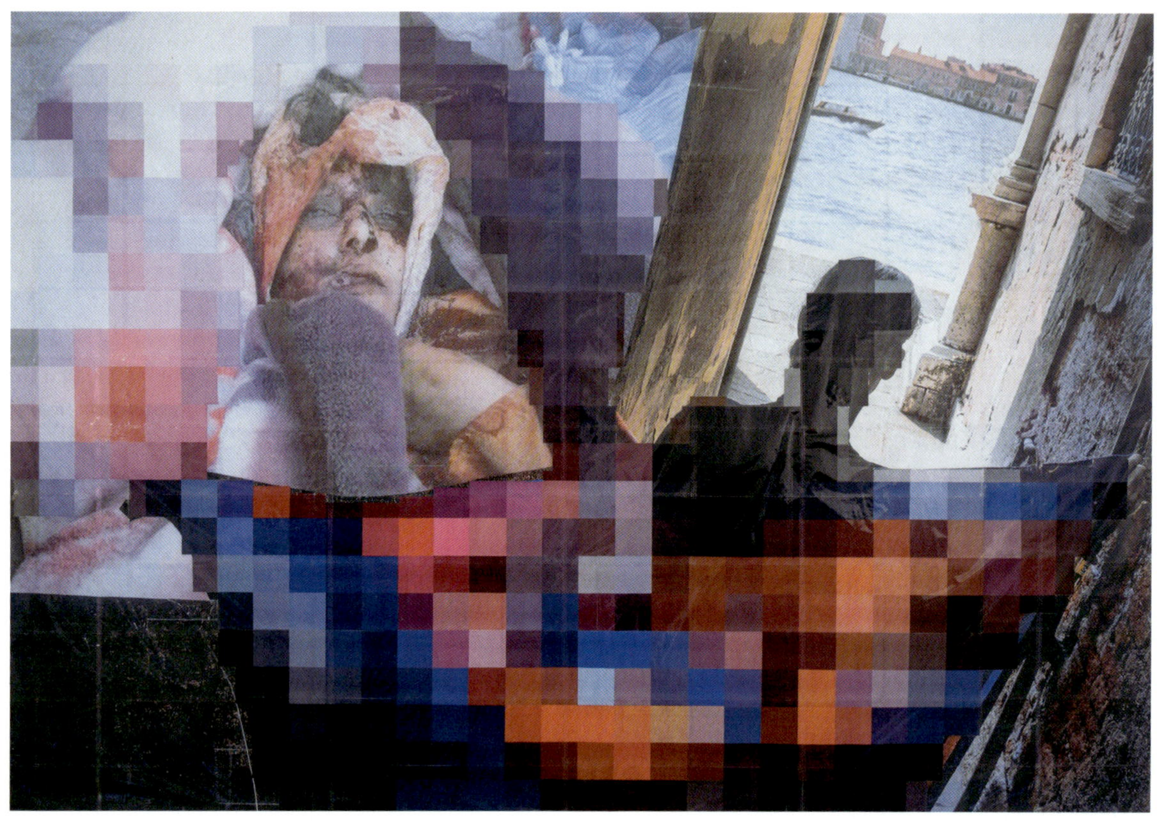

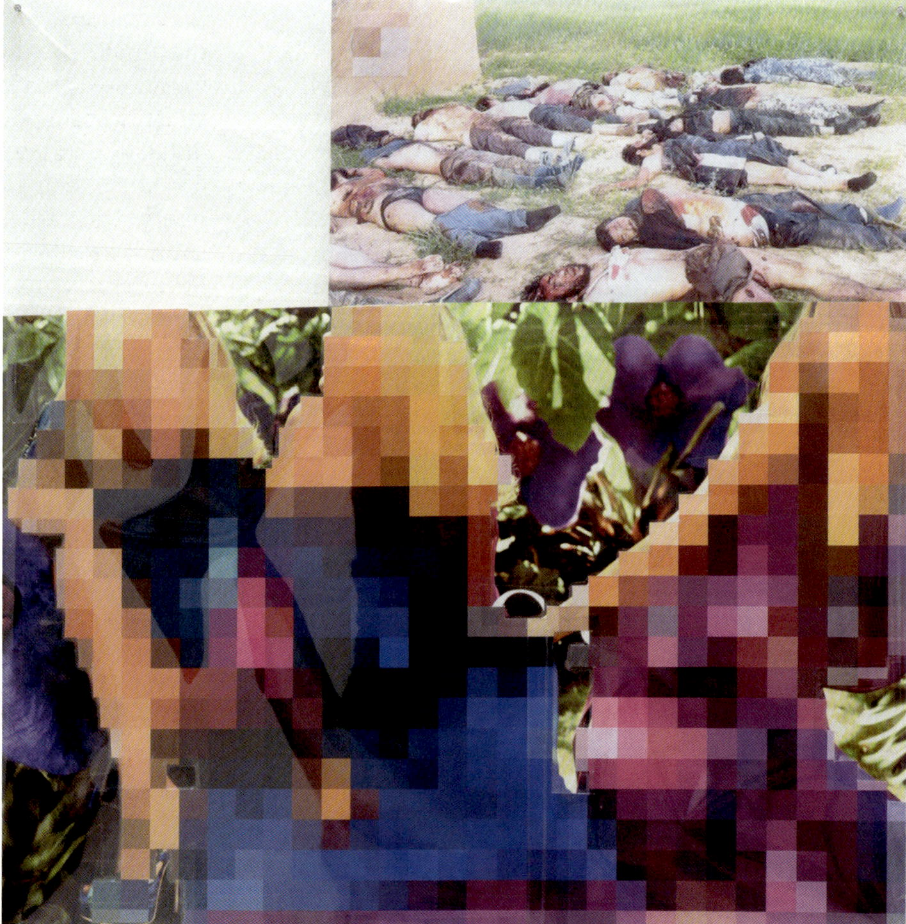

Thomas Hirschhorn,
Pixel-Collage n°7,
2016, 332 × 490 cm,
prints, tape,
transparent sheet.

Thomas Hirschhorn,
Pixel-Collage n°13,
2016, 43 × 44 cm,
prints, tape,
transparent sheet.

4. Tendency to iconism
The tendency to 'iconism' still exists to this day. 'Iconism' is the habit of 'selecting', 'choosing' or 'finding' the image that 'stands out', the image that is 'the big one', the image that 'says more', the image that 'counts more' than the others. In other words, the tendency towards 'iconism' is the tendency to 'highlight' something; it's the old, traditional procedure of favouring and imposing, in an authoritarian way, a hierarchy. This is not a declaration of importance towards something or somebody, but a declaration of importance towards others. The goal is to establish a common importance, a common weight, a common measure. But the 'iconism tendency' and 'highlighting' also have the effect of avoiding the existence of differences, the non-iconic and the non-highlighted. In the field of war and conflict images, this leads to choosing the 'acceptable' for others. It's the 'acceptable' image that stands for another image, for all other images, for something else, and perhaps even for a non-image.

This image or icon has to be, of course, correct, good, right, permitted, chosen – the consensual image. This is what makes it manipulation. One example is the much discussed image (even by art historians) of the Situation Room in Washington during the killing of Bin Laden by the Navy SEALs in 2011. I refuse to accept this image as an icon; I reject its 'iconism', and I reject the fact that this image (and this goes for all other 'icons') stands for anything other than itself. Struggling against the 'iconism tendency' is the reason why looking at images of destroyed bodies is important.

5. Reduction to facts
In today's world of facts, information, opinion and comments, much is reduced to being factual. Fact is the new 'golden calf' of journalism, and journalists want to give it the assurance and guarantee of veracity. But I'm not interested in the verification of a fact. I'm interested in truth, not a verified fact or the 'correct information' of a journalistic story. The truth I'm interested in resists facts, opinions, comments and journalism. Truth is irreducible; therefore the images of destroyed human bodies are irreducible and resist factuality. I don't deny facts and factuality, but I want to oppose the texture of facts today. The habit of reducing things to facts is a comfortable way to avoid touching truth, and resisting this tendency corresponds to the dynamics which lead to touching truth. Unconditional acceptance of facts is intended to impose on us factual information as 'the measure', instead of looking and seeing with our own eyes. I want to see with my own eyes. Resistance to today's world of facts is what makes it important to look at such images.

6. Victim syndrome
Looking at images of mutilated human bodies is important because it can contribute to an understanding that the incommensurable act is not the looking; what is incommensurable is that destruction has happened in the first place – that a human, a human body, has been destroyed, indeed, that an incommensurable number of human beings have been destroyed. It is important – more than anything else – to understand this. It's only by being capable of touching this incommensurable act that I can resist the suggestive question: Is this a victim or not? And whose victim? Or is this perhaps a killer, a torturer? Perhaps it's not a victim at all? Perhaps this mutilated human body shouldn't be regarded or counted as a victim? Classifying destroyed human bodies as victims or non-victims is an attempt to make them commensurable instead of thinking that all these bodies are the incommensurable. The victim syndrome wants me to give a response, an explanation, a reason to the incommensurable and finally to declare who 'the innocent' is. The only surviving terrorist in the Mumbai killings in 2008 declared to the court that sentenced him to death: 'I don't think I am innocent.' I think the incommensurable in this world has no reason, no explanation, and no response – beforehand or afterwards. In this incommensurable world, I have to reject the commensurability of accepting classification as victim or non-victim. I do not want to be neutralised by anything which wants to make the world commensurable. *I refuse to explain and to excuse everything because of its context. I do not want to be neutralised by 'the context'.* Looking at images of destroyed human bodies is important because I don't want to give up in response to the victim syndrome.

7. Irrelevance of quality
These pictures – because they were taken by witnesses – don't have any photographic quality. I am interested by this. It is the confirmation that, under conditions of urgency, 'quality' is not necessary. I have always believed in 'quality = no, energy = yes'. There is no aesthetic approach here beyond the objective to capture the image. Concerns of quality are irrelevant when facing the incommensurable. This is shown by images of destroyed bodies. No technical skill is needed. No photographer is needed. The argument of 'photographic quality' is the argument of those who stand apart, aren't present, and who, on behalf of the 'quality' argument, express their distance and their attempt to be the supervisor. But there is no supervising anymore; what is 'needed' is to be a witness, to be there, to be here and to be here now, to be present, to be present at the 'right time' at the 'right place'. Most images are taken with small cameras, smartphones or mobile phones. They match our way of witnessing 'today's everything' and 'today's nothing' in daily life and making it 'public'. The irrelevance of quality of these images is an implicit critique of 'embedded' journalism, including photo-journalism. This irrelevance of quality is what makes it important to look at such images.

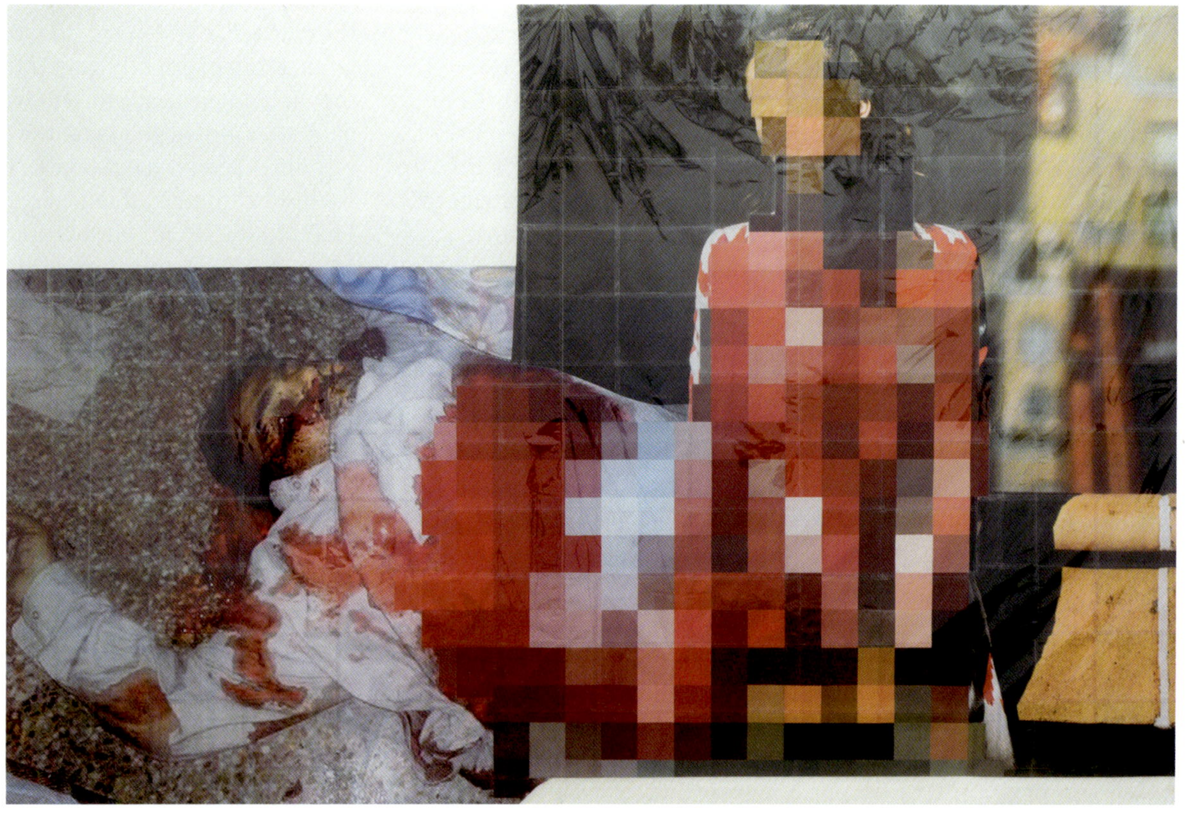

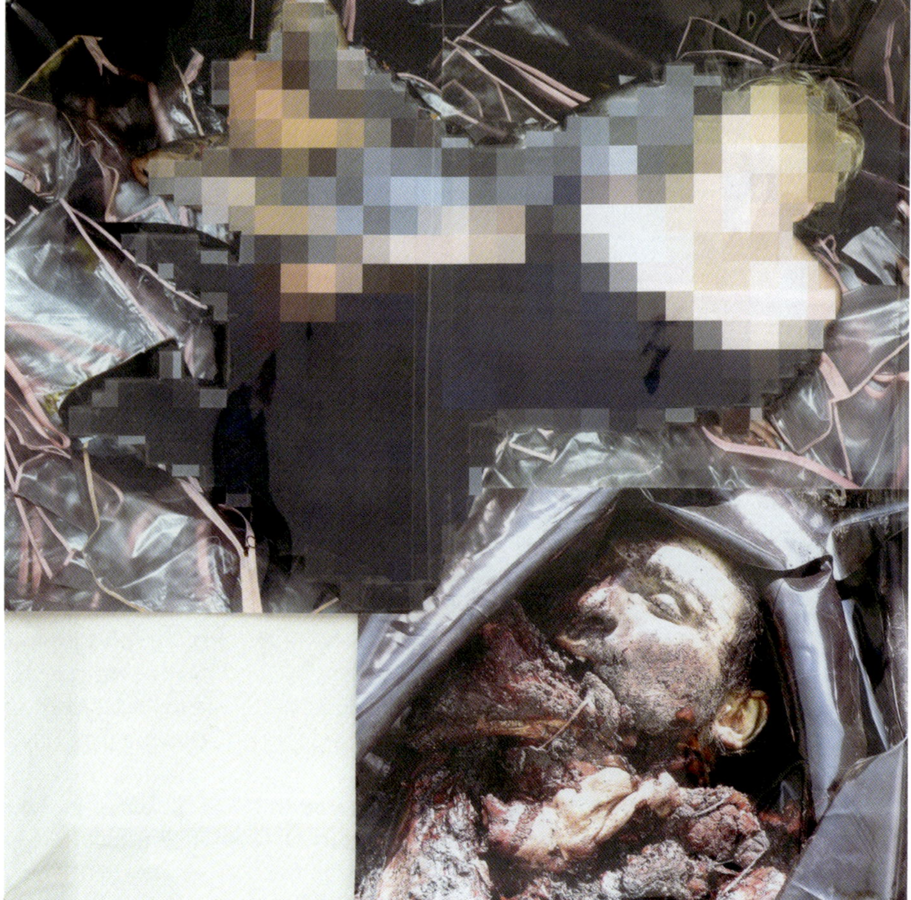

Thomas Hirschhorn, *Pixel-Collage n°5*, 2016, 330 × 507 cm, prints, tape, transparent sheet.

Thomas Hirschhorn, *Pixel-Collage n°16*, 2016, 45 × 47 cm, prints, tape, transparent sheet.

8. Detachment through 'hypersensitivity'

I am sensitive and I want to be sensitive, and at the same time I want to be alert. I don't want to stand aside; I don't want to look away. Sometimes when viewers are looking at images of destroyed human bodies, I hear them saying: 'I can't bear to look at this, I'm too sensitive.' This is a way of keeping a comfortable, narcissistic and exclusive distance from today's reality, from the world. From our world, the unique and only world. The discourse of sensitivity – which is actually 'hypersensitivity' – is about retaining one's comfort, calm and luxury. Distance is only taken by those who – with their own eyes – won't confront the incommensurable of reality. Distance is never a gift; it's something taken by a very few to keep their exclusivity intact. 'Hypersensitivity' is the opposite of the 'non-exclusive public'.

In order to confront the world, to struggle with its chaos, its incommensurability, in order to coexist and to cooperate in this world and with the other, I need to confront reality without distance. Therefore it's necessary to distinguish 'sensitivity', which means to me being 'awake' and 'attentive', from 'hypersensitivity', which means 'self-enclosure' and 'exclusion'. To resist 'hypersensitivity', it is important to look at those images of mutilated human bodies.

Thomas Hirschhorn, 2012

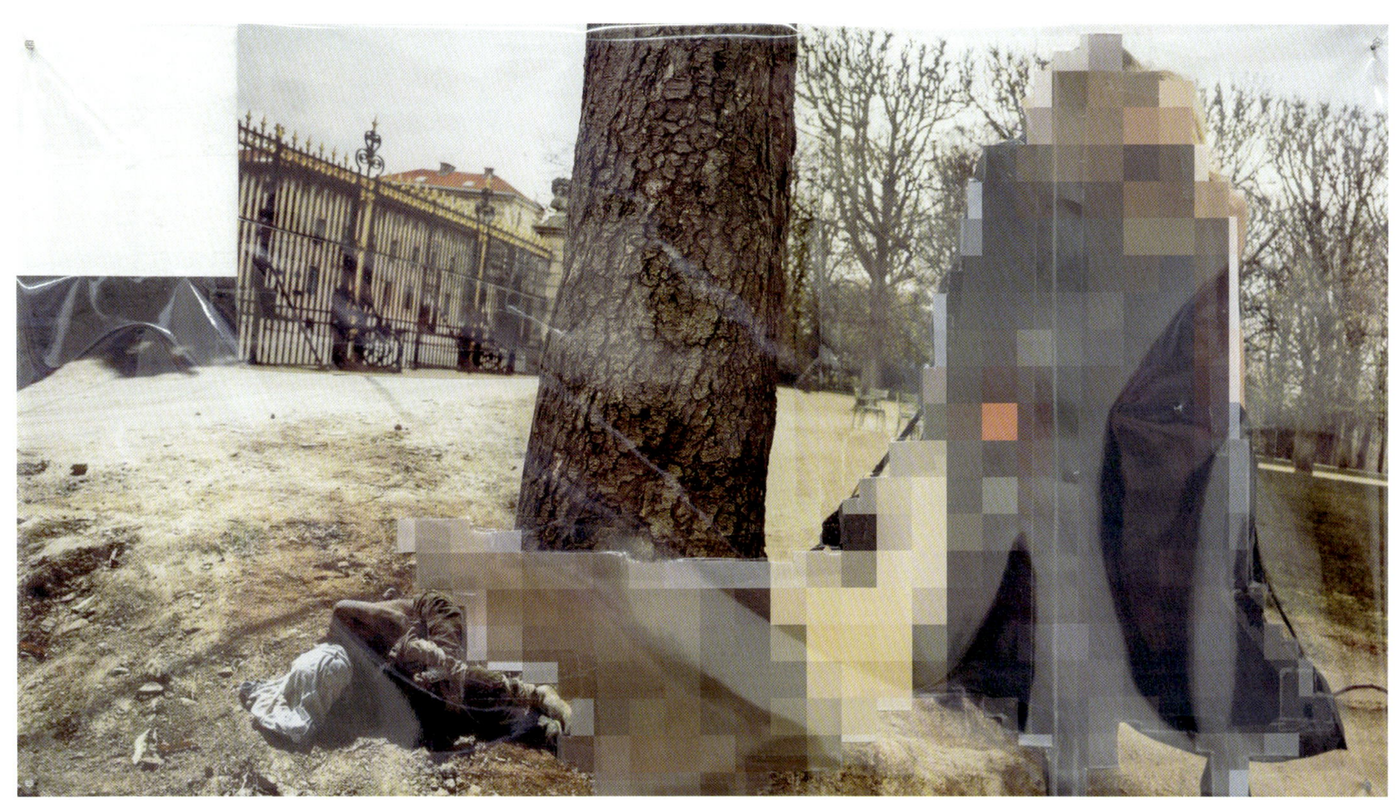

Thomas Hirschhorn, *Pixel-Collage n°15*, 2016, 30 × 55 cm, prints, tape, transparent sheet.

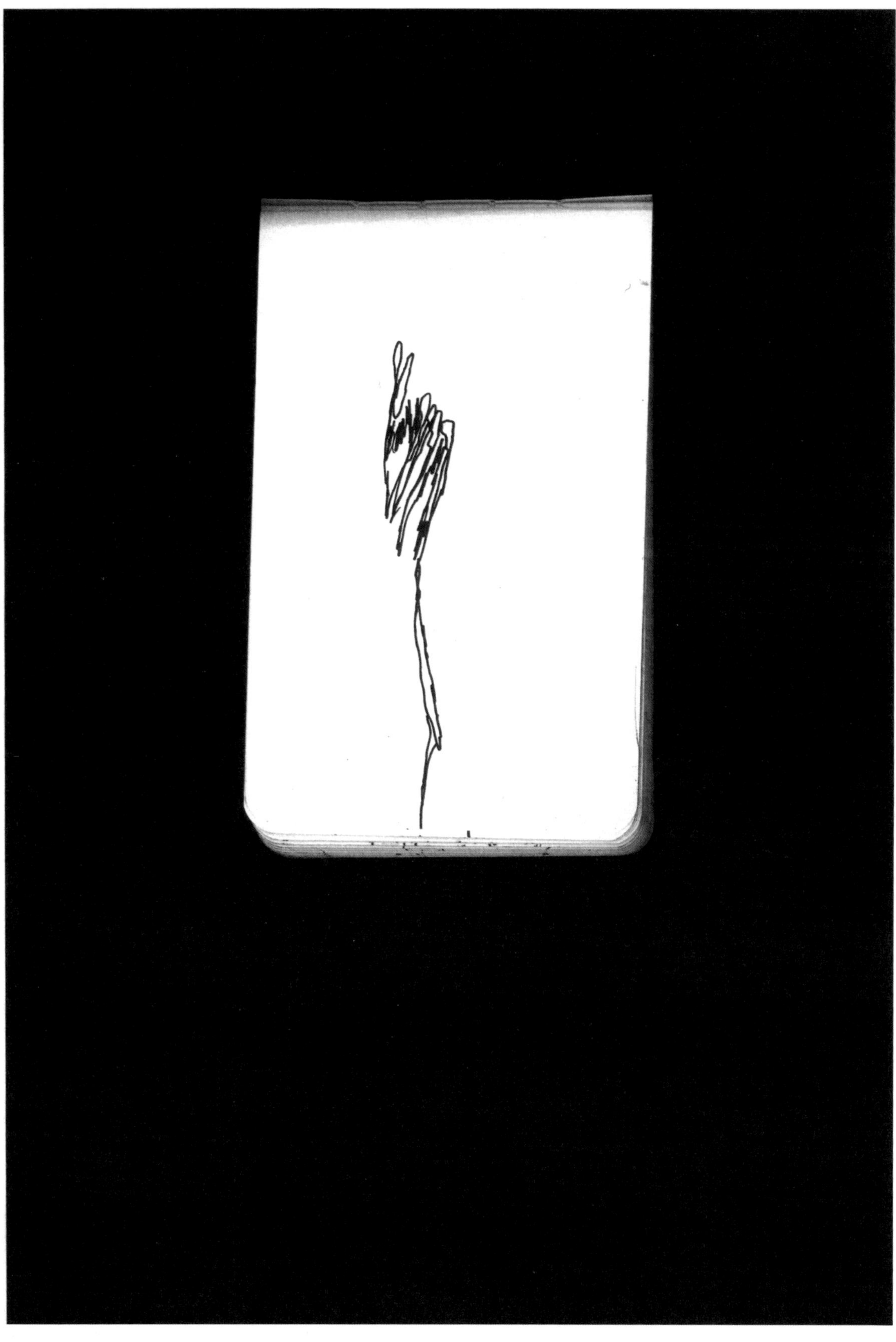

Cameron Jamie, *Untitled* (from *KOPBF* journal), 2016–17, ink on paper.

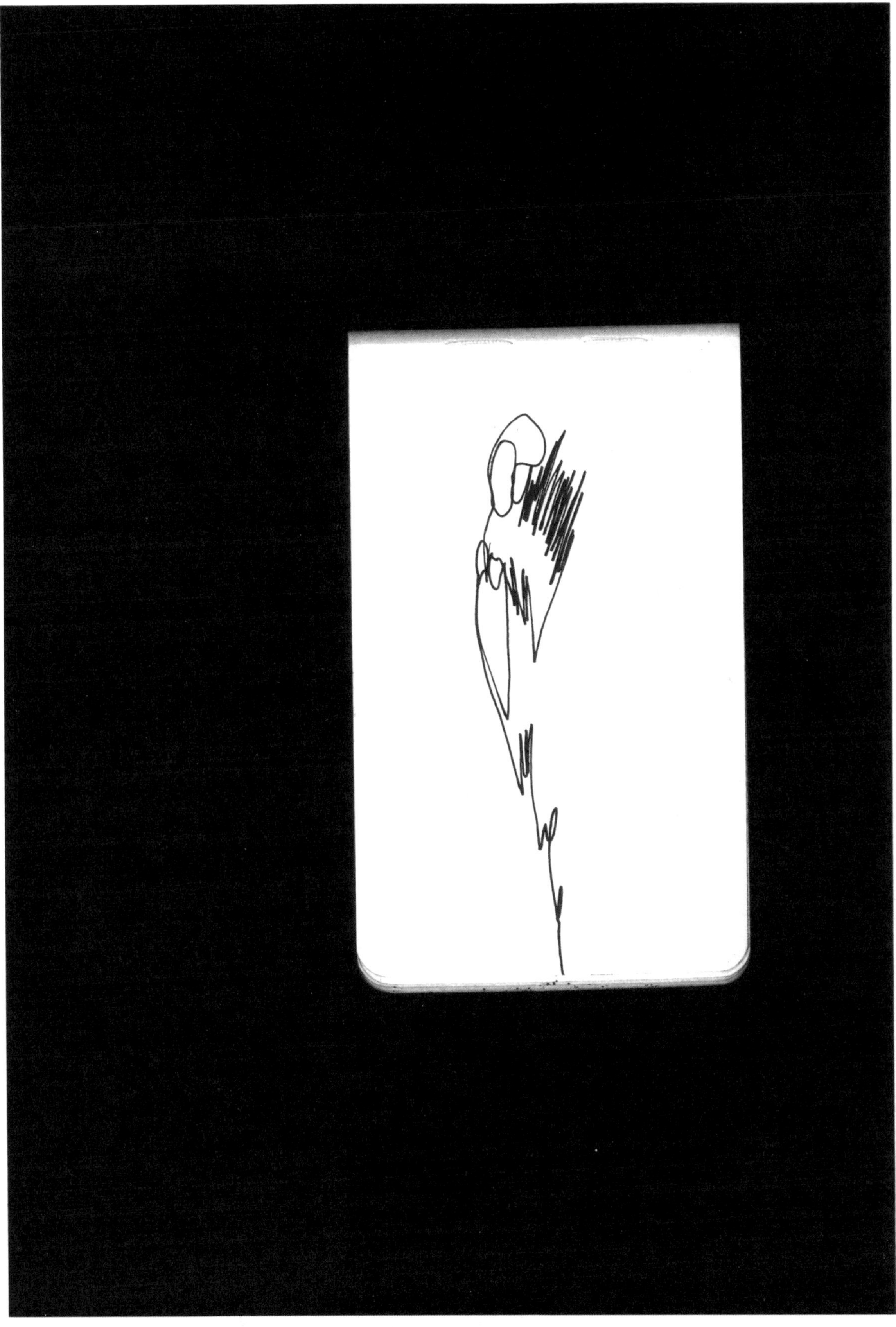

Cameron Jamie, *Untitled* (from *KOPBF* journal), 2016–17, ink on paper.

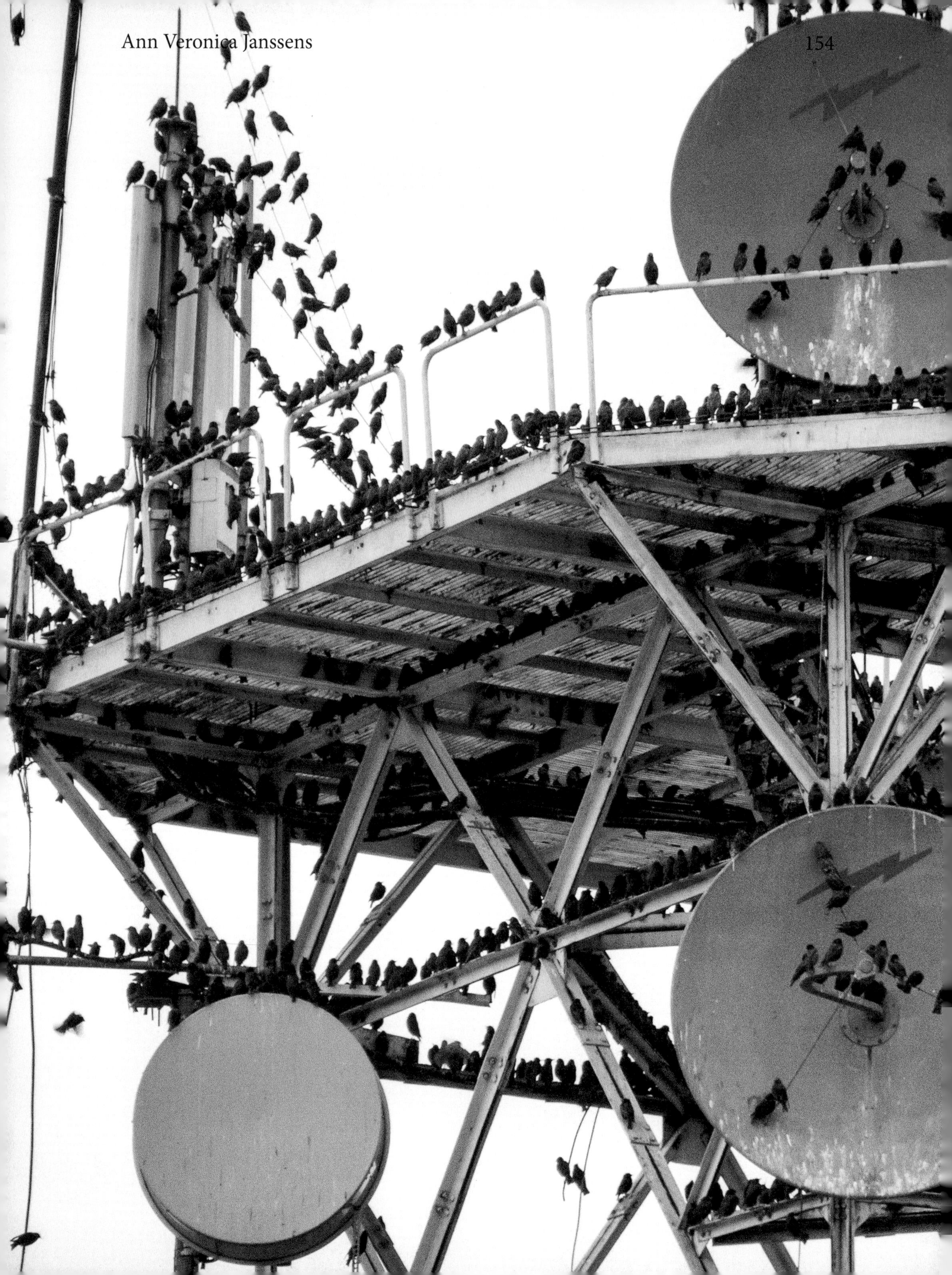

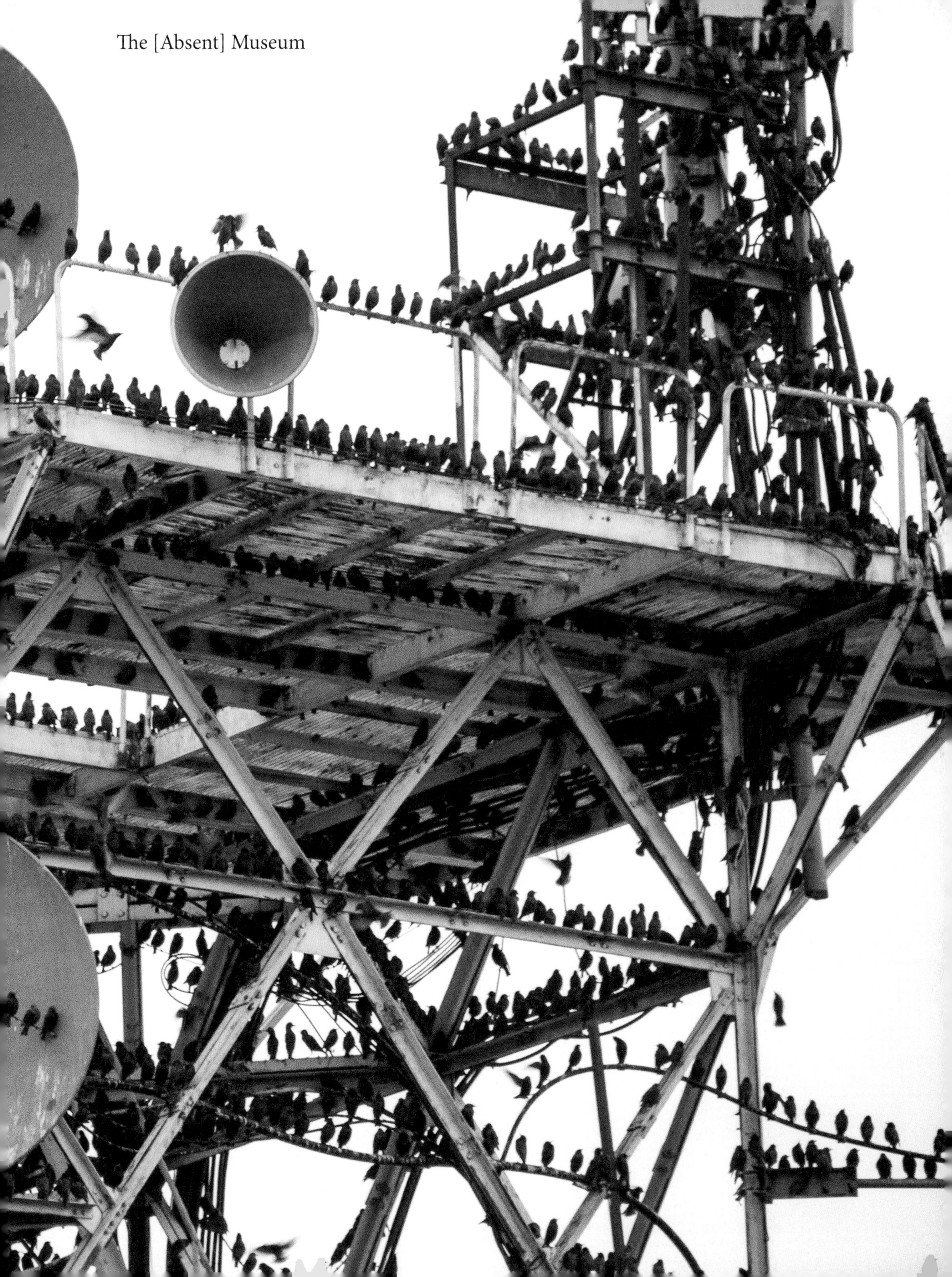
The [Absent] Museum

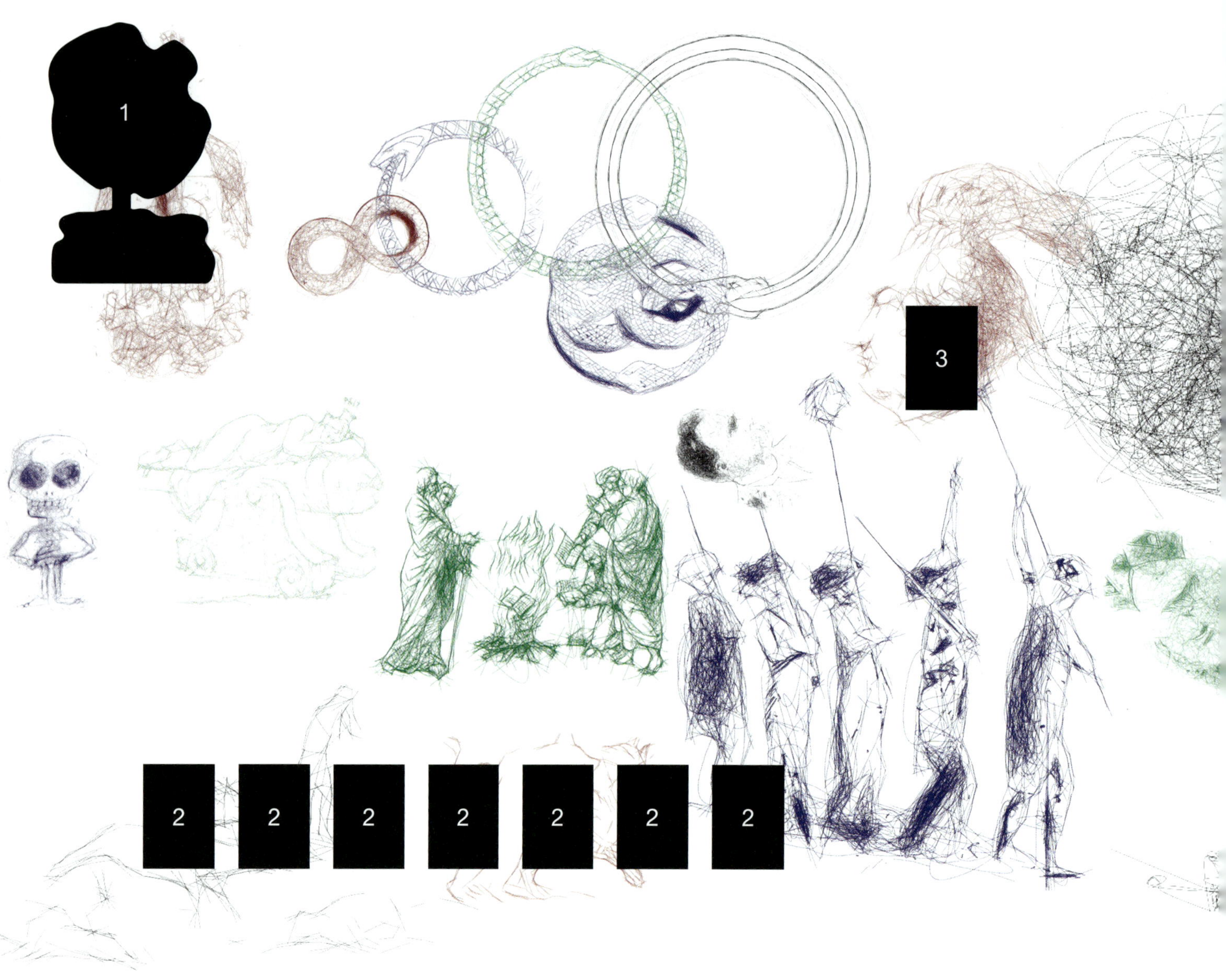

Goshka Macuga, *Before the Beginning and After the End: Transhumanism* features:

1. *Okimono of a Skull with Snake*, Japanese, Meiji period, late 19th century.
2. *Letter from Albert Einstein to Sigmund Freud*, 30 July 1932.
3. Albert Einstein and Sigmund Freud, *Why War?*, 1933.
4. Eadweard Muybridge, *Animal Locomotion (Plate 348)*, 1887.
5. Claudio Parmiggiani, *Che cosè la tradizione*, 1997.
6. Mary Shelley, *Frankenstein draft Manuscript, MS. Abinger c.56, fols. 60v, 61r, 61v*, c. 1816.

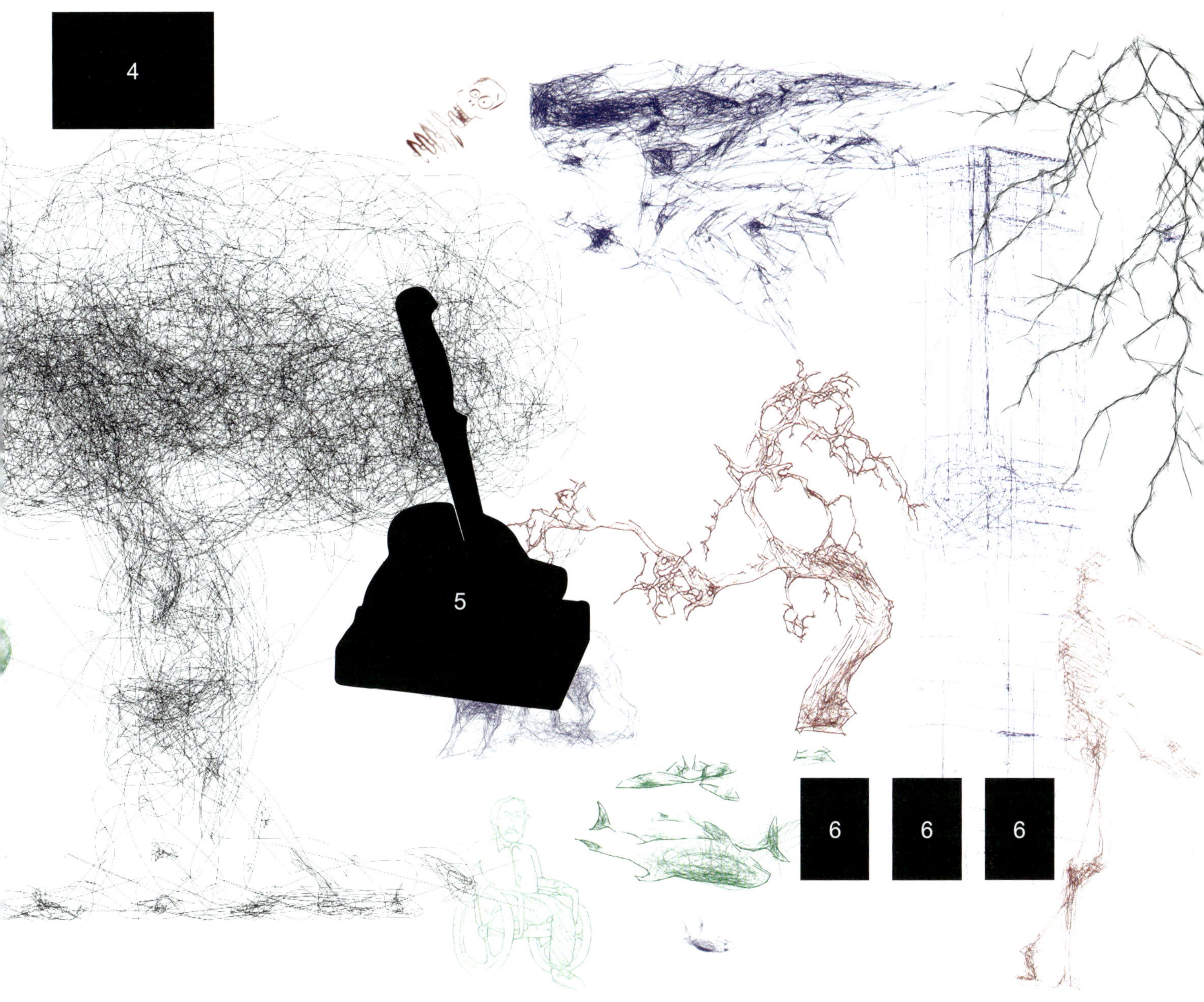

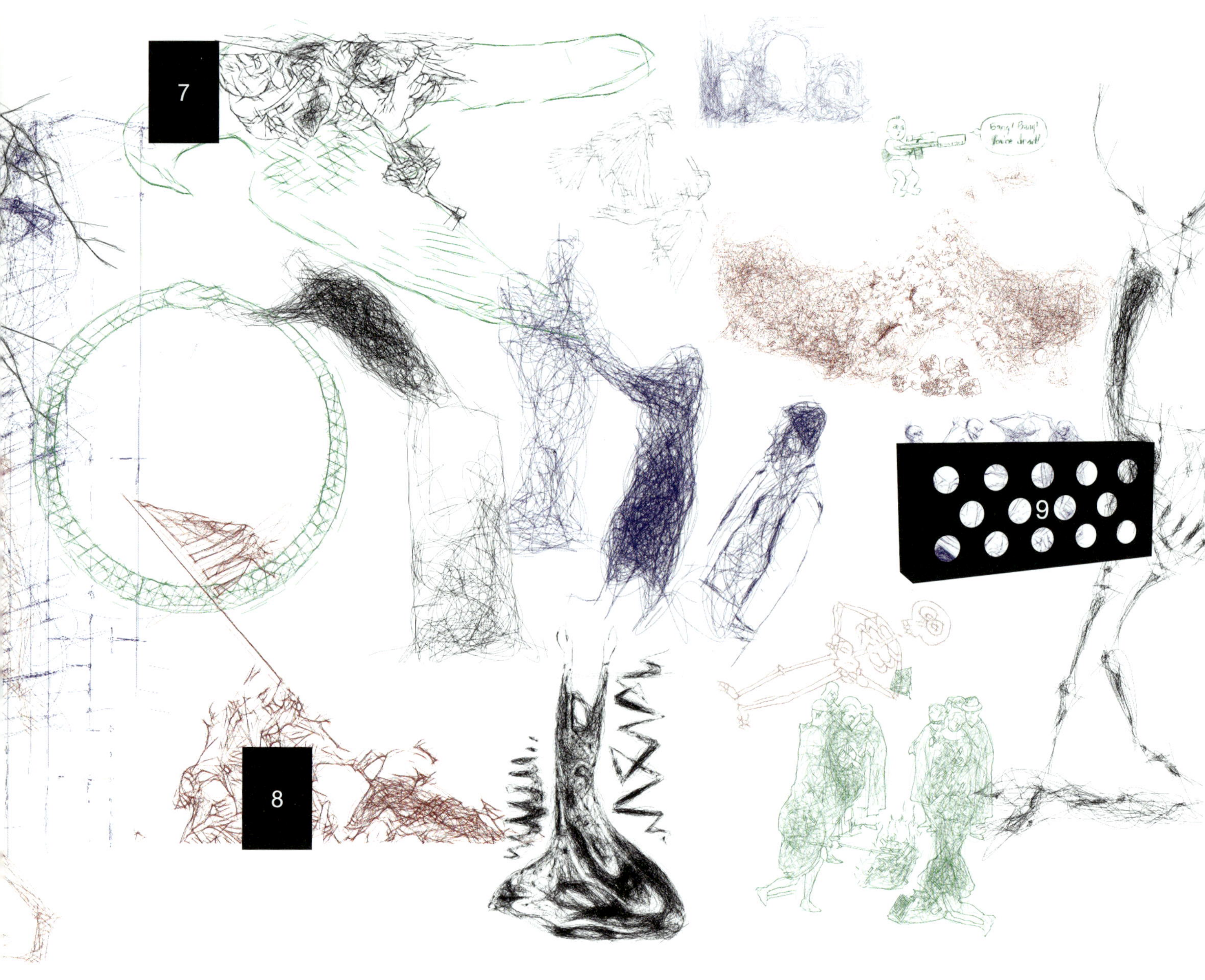

Goshka Macuga, *Before the Beginning and After the End: The Destructive Nature of Humankind* features:

7. Walter Benjamin, *Theses on the Philosophy of History*, c. 1940.
8. Ray Bradbury, *Fahrenheit 451*, 1953.
9. Peter Fischli & David Weiss, *Brick*, 2005.
10. John Latham, *Book in Processed Oil Shale from Bing*, 1976.
11. Friedrich Nietzsche, *Also Sprach Zarathustra*, 1883–85.
12. Panamarenko, *Puk Bot, Archaeopteryx III*, 1991.

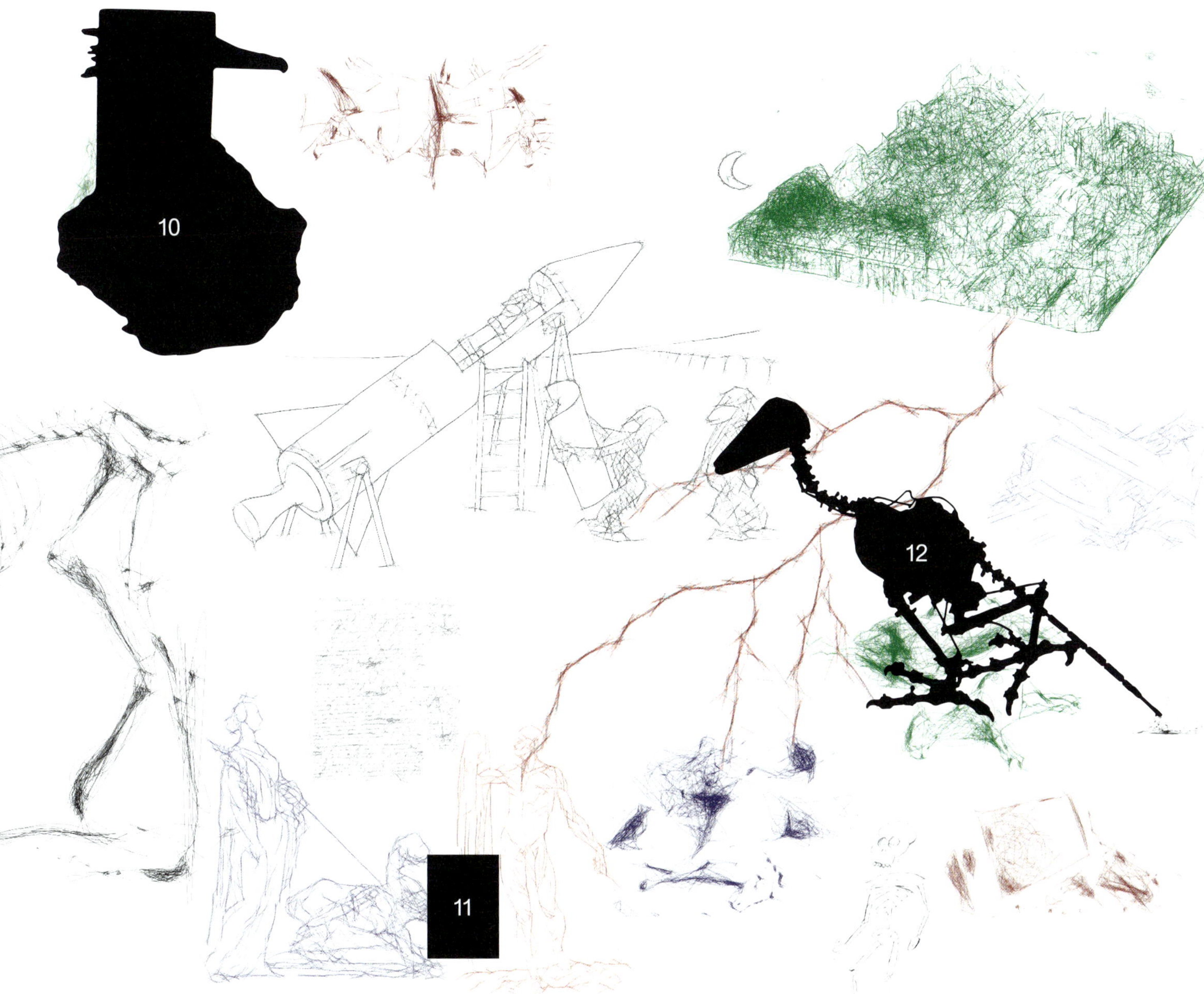

Goshka Macuga

Before the Beginning and After the End (2017) is the latest variant of the installation for which Goshka Macuga collaborated with the artist-scientist Patrick Tresset. Two 4.5-metre-long paper scrolls lie over a set of industrial tables containing biro sketches and writings, traces of an illustrated narrative of the progress of humanity.

The production of scrolls dates back to ancient Egypt, where some of the first forms of texts were composed. These parchments are traditionally associated with record-keeping and documentation, and as such embody the processes of categorisation and preservation of human knowledge familiar to Macuga's work. These implied historical references are juxtaposed with the futuristic technology of Tresset's 'Paul-n' system, represented by robots and autonomous computational systems that produced the drawings on the scrolls. Tresset developed these systems through research into human behaviour: more specifically, how artists make marks that depict how humans perceive artworks and how humans relate to robots.

The tables develop and display the themes 'Transhumanism' and 'The Destructive Nature of Human Kind', punctuated with objects and artworks. They offer contemplations of humans as finite beings, as if they were subjects of a scientific study leading to a different type of consciousness.

CF

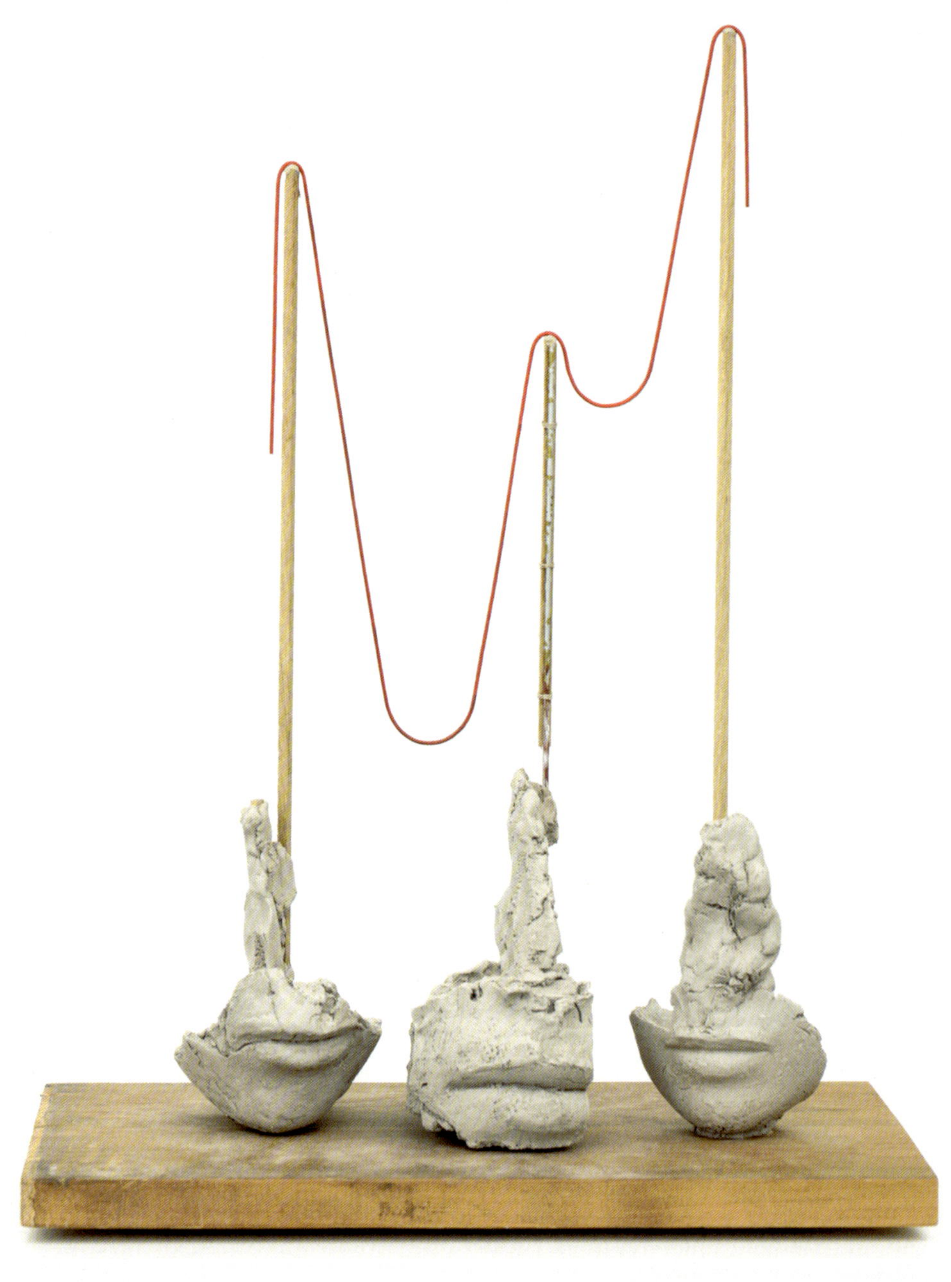

Mark Manders, *Still Life with Thin Red Rope*, 2015–16, 56 × 43 × 24 cm, painted epoxy, wood, painted iron.

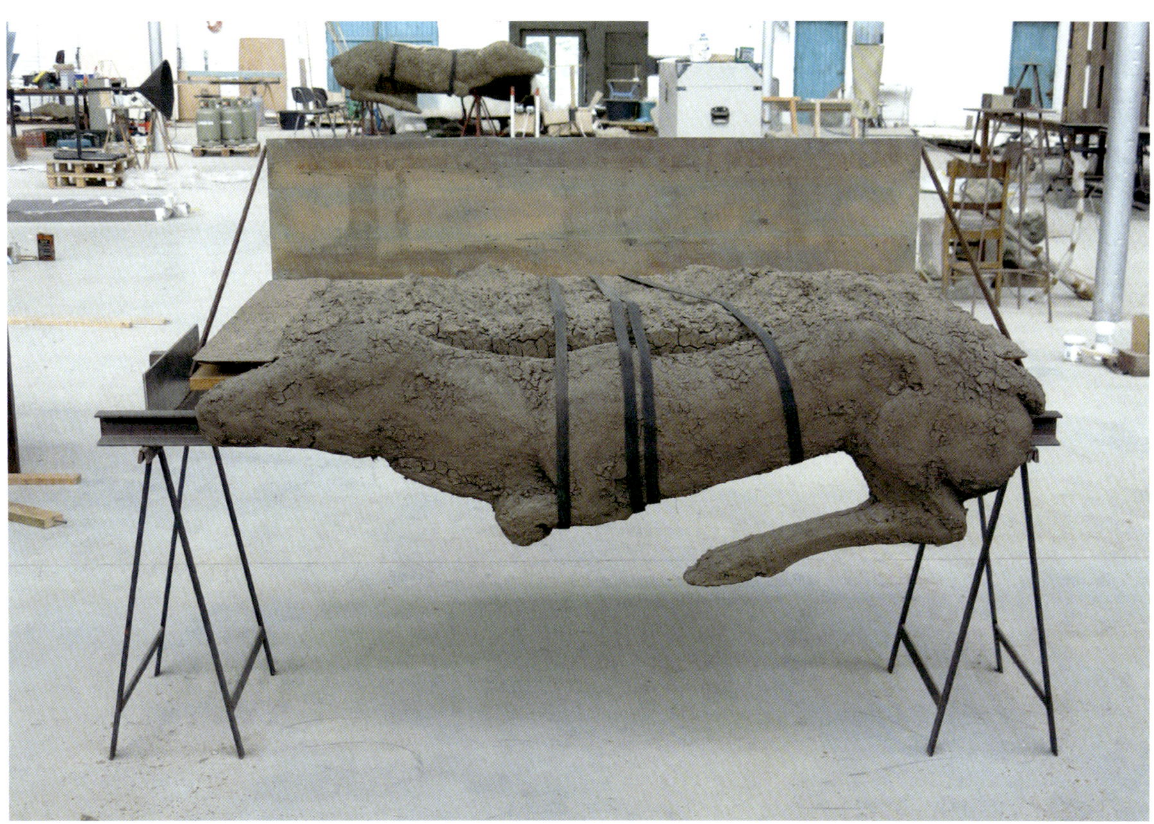

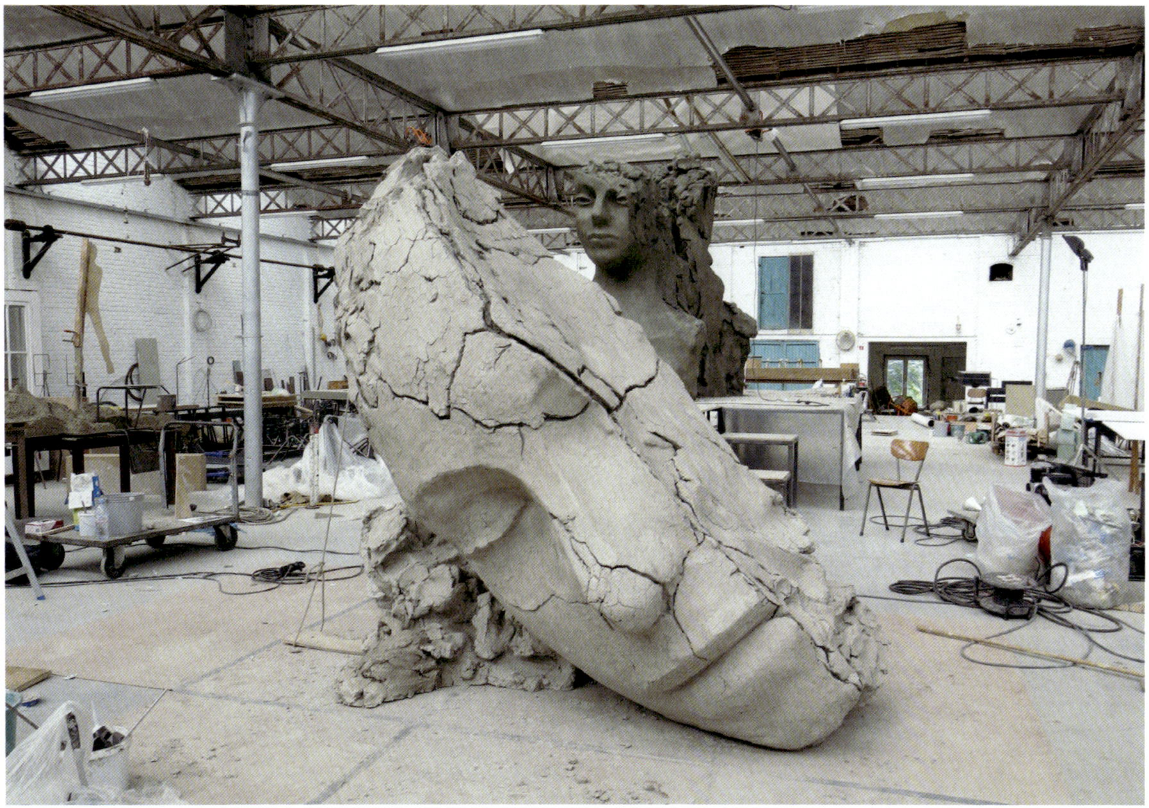

Mark Manders, *Landscape with Large Animal*, 2013–14, 203 × 118 × 129 cm, various materials.

Mark Manders, *Dry Clay Head*, 2015–16, 233 × 155 × 283 cm, painted bronze, rope, plywood, offset print on paper.

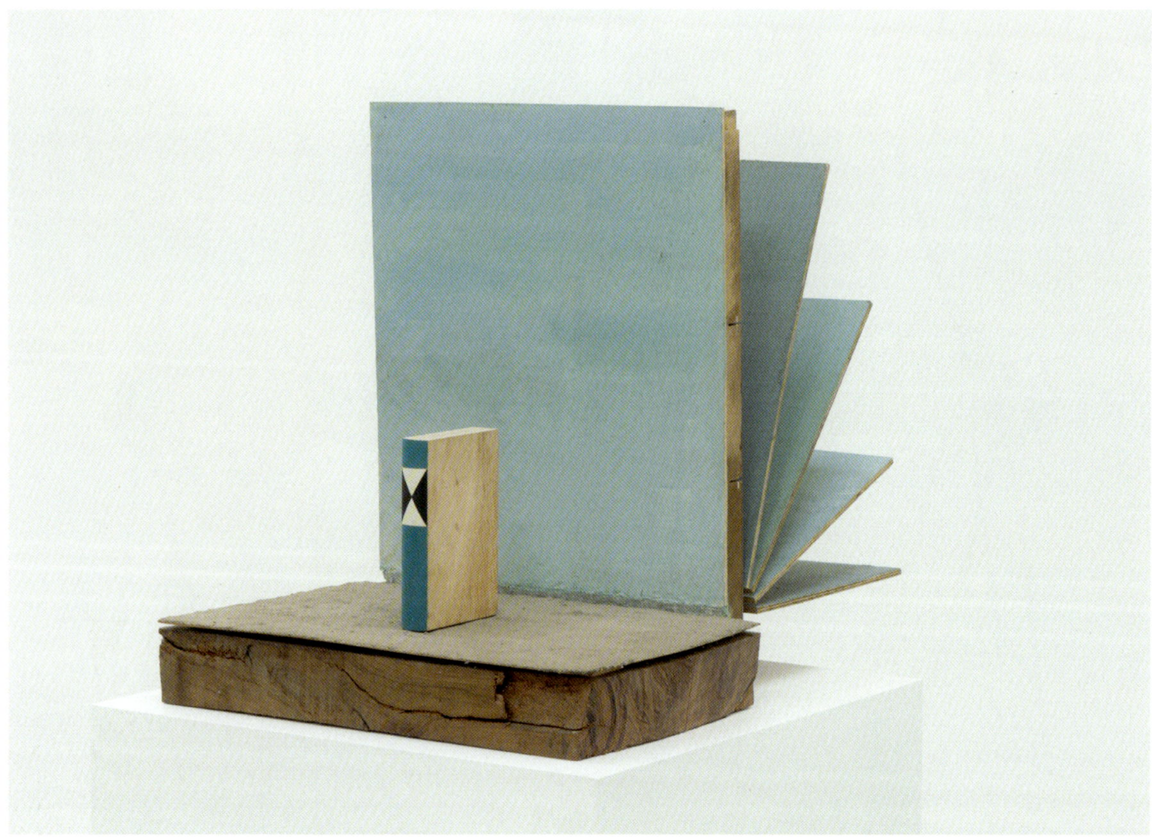

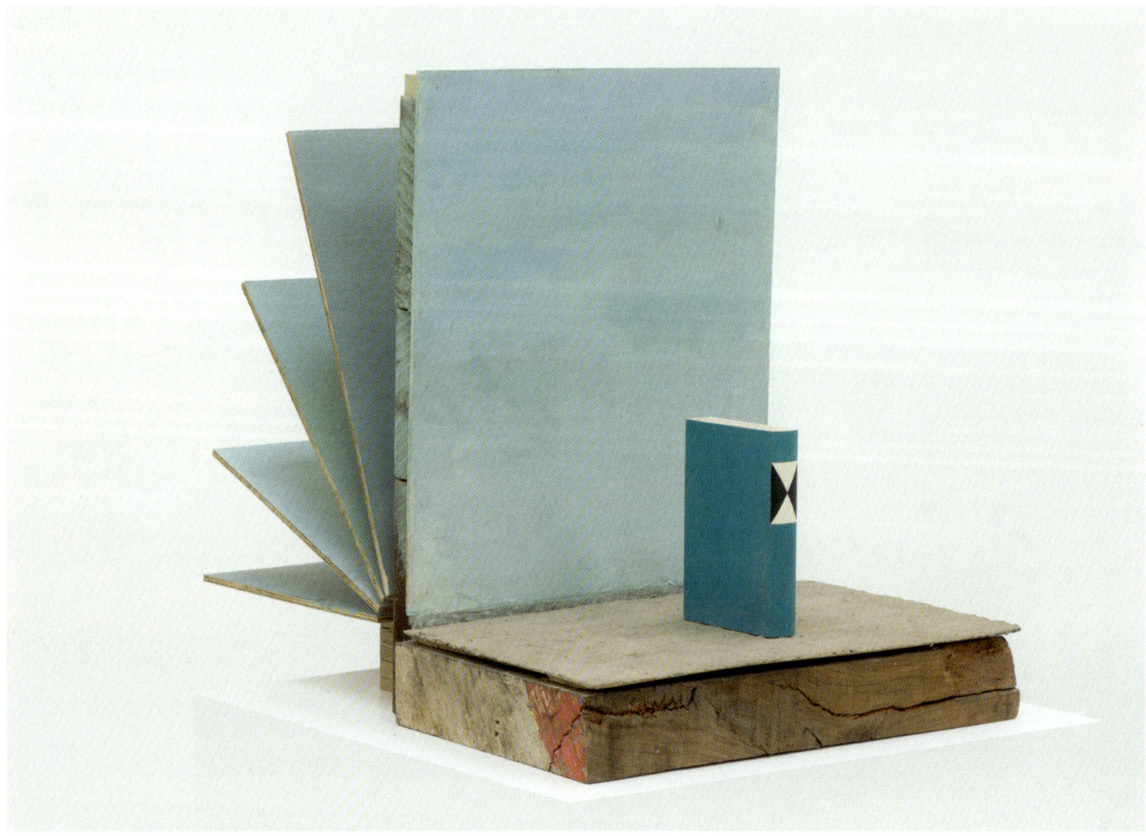

Mark Manders, *Landscape with Fake Dictionary*, 2012–14, 64.5 × 58 × 78 cm, painted wood.

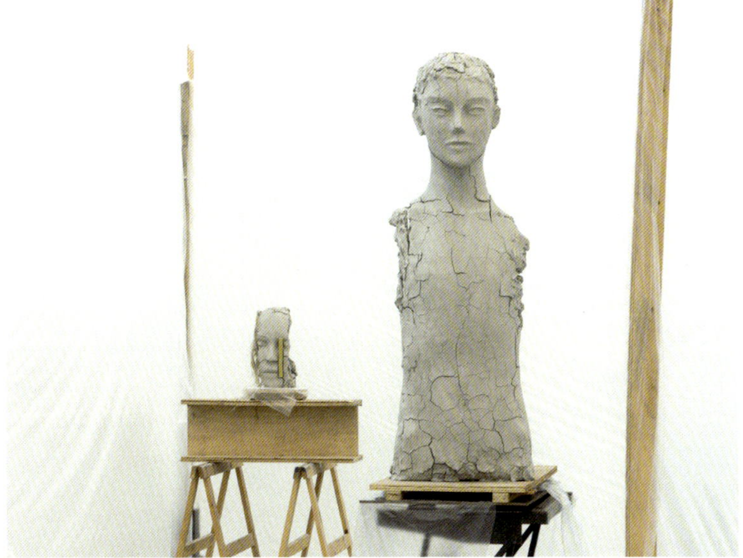

Mark Manders, *Room with Unfired Clay Figure*, 2014, 273 × 440 × 620 cm, painted bronze, wood, iron, plastic, painted ceramic, chair, painted epoxy.

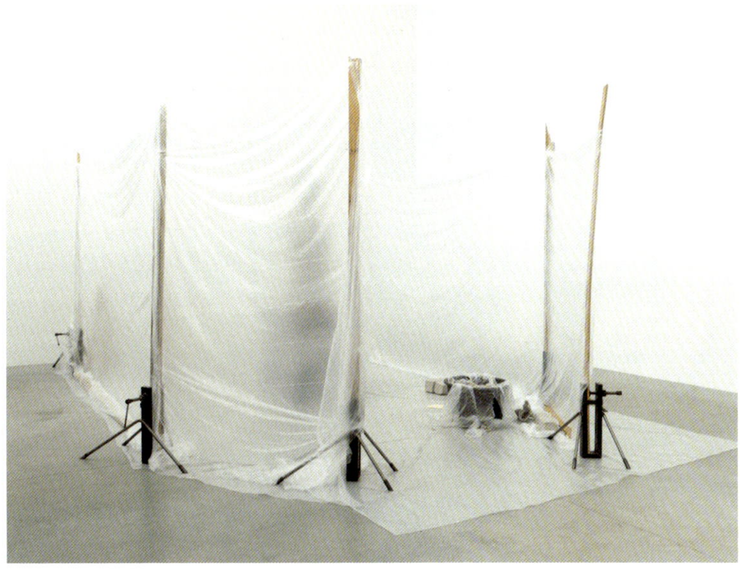

Mark Manders, *Room with Unfired Clay Figures*, 2011–15, 189.5 × 293.7 × 104.1 cm; 237.2 × 359.4 × 129.5 cm, painted bronze, iron, wood, offset print on paper.

Mark Manders, *Studio with Unfired Clay Animal*, 2014, 101.6 × 297.2 × 35.6 cm, painted bronze, iron, plastic and wood.

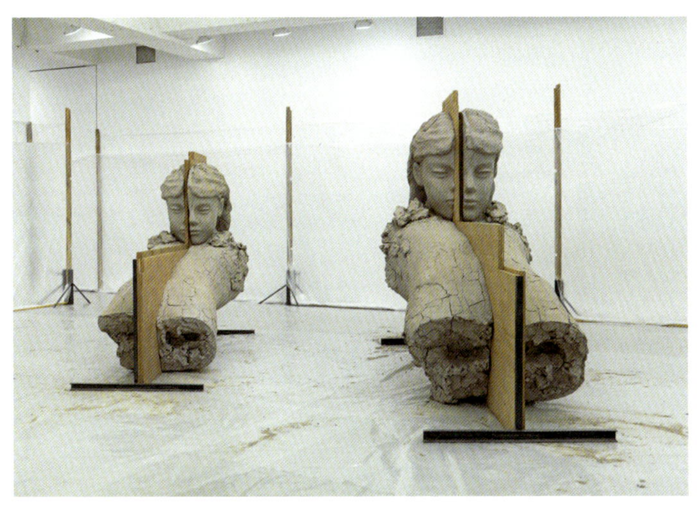

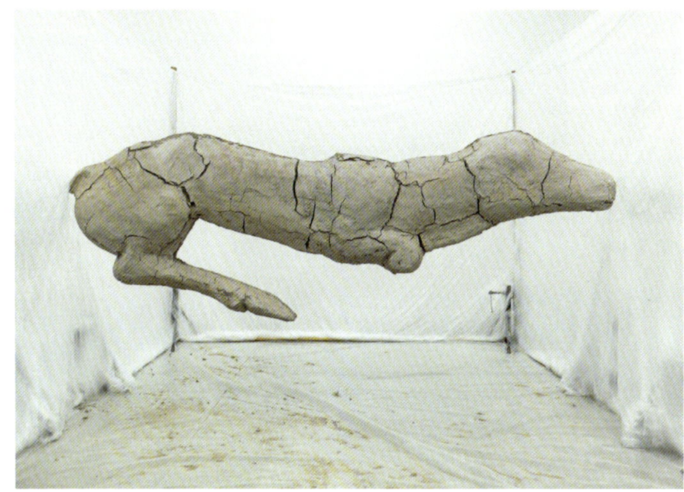

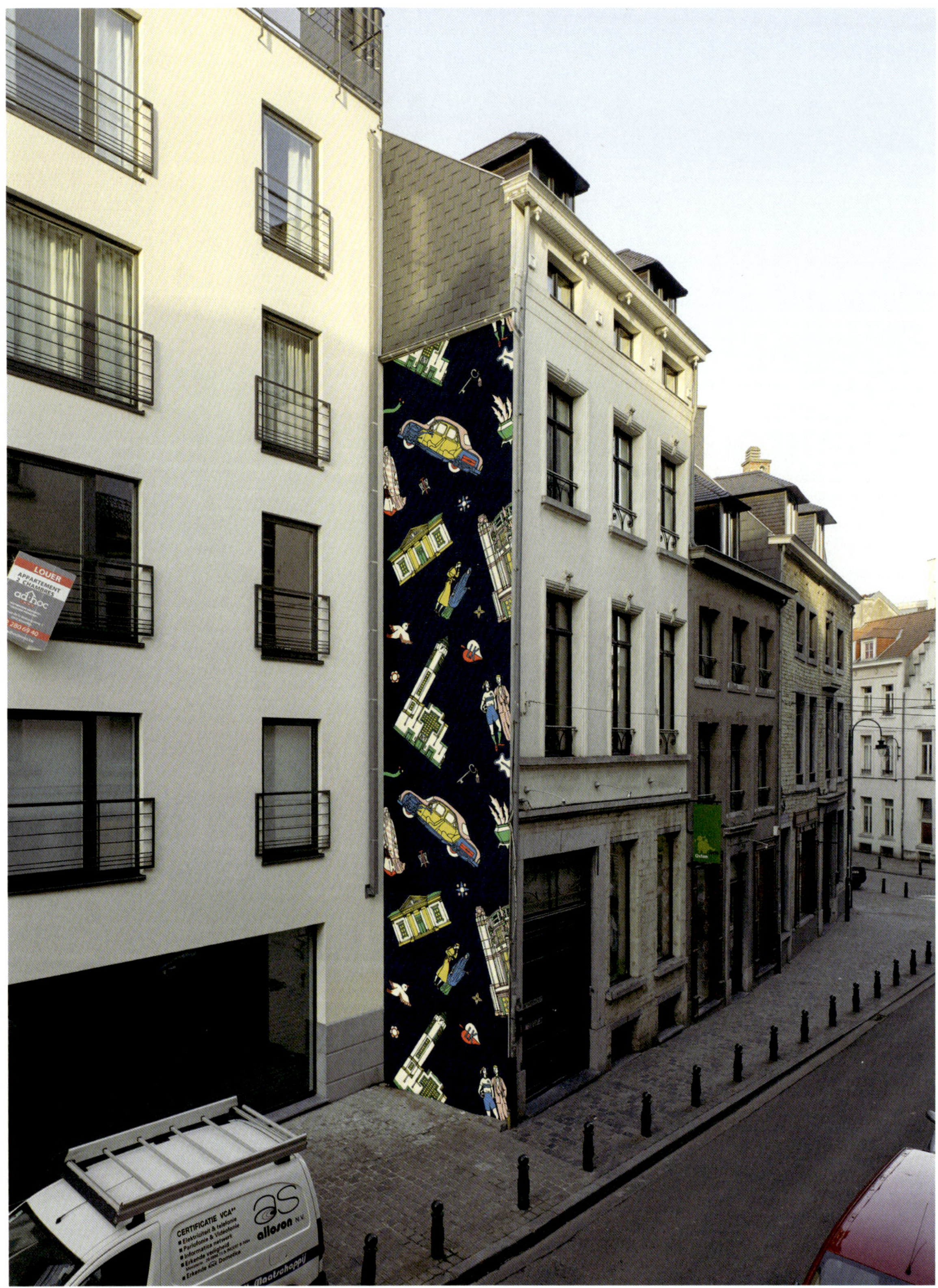

Lucy McKenzie, *In My Area (For Kato)*, 2017, 37.25 sq m, digital simulation of the mural at Rue des Chartreux/
Kartuizerstraat, Brussels.

Mural for Rue des Chartreux/ Kartuizerstraat

The evidence of Brussels' artistic and commercial past is inscribed on its streets. Art nouveau sgraffito above kebab shop signs, neon arrows for bars down cobbled passageways, faded murals advertising Solo margarine. This tradition of dressing public areas with images continues, but its motivation has shifted. Today the most visible public décor in the city centre comes from the civic-backed *parcours* of comic art murals and sanctioned spaces for graffiti art.

These two forms of public mural painting differ stylistically, but are both intended to add character to the most visible part of the city for inhabitants and visitors, and are means to the same end – that of signalling a vibrant and specific local culture in a cost-effective manner. The comic murals illustrate Belgium's celebrated *bande dessinée*, providing a platform for contemporary comic artists to promote their work, a kind of outdoor 'hall of fame'. Graffiti artists being given designated space or actually employed by the city to paint buildings has a more generic function, that of artificially altering the look of a quarter to make it appear more diverse, urban and youthful. In many cities it is used as a cosmetic way to obscure symbols of old power rather than tear them down, which is why it is so popular in the city centres of former Soviet Bloc countries. It gives imposing architecture a human face.

Both of these illustrative graphic forms express the individuality of their artists, and that this individuality has an almost exclusively male point of view is clear from the identities of the chosen artists and the content of their work. From a blonde being saved from a masked attacker to large arses in shorty-shorts, a kind of adolescent male subconscious prevails, and this has ended up dominating Brussels' public art unchallenged.

This means that Brussels' public space is gendered, and the message that public space is male space is reinforced. Though they may appear benign, these murals concur with other attitudes. I would argue that this is just as important an issue as that of gentrification, by which public art is inherently instrumentalised.

My mural on the Rue des Chartreux/Kartuizerstraat has no faux urban edge: it is festive, pleasant and anachronistic. Its femininity and antiquated feel are the tools at my disposal to antagonise the mentality it has to live within.

It uses the drawing style of Belgian *ligne claire* comics to render images of architecture, figures and motifs within the geometric order of wrapping paper. Because the image is a repeat pattern, it is differentiated from the comic-strip mural *parcours*, which mostly illustrates a scene or character literally. By contrast, the repeat suggests a fragment that mentally extends outside the boundaries of the thin strip of wall, creating an atmosphere rather than a narrative.

For those who take a closer look, they will find buildings such as Molenbeek's Church of Saint-Jean-Baptiste, the Pavillon de l'Octroi (Sewers Museum) at Porte d'Anderlecht, and the Institut des Arts et Métiers. The choice of buildings radiates from my home at the physical and cultural intersection of the city centre, Anderlecht and Molenbeek. The beauty of local architecture is usually obscured by daily life, but here, rendered in simple lines, we see the buildings as the elegant structures they are.

The other motifs are enigmatic and arbitrary – geometric shapes, nature, vague logos and a diagram of a car. The figures depicted are all women. In their chadors, football strips, suits and elegant skirts, they are the local types who will see the mural every day, and complete the work with their gaze.

Lucy McKenzie, 2017

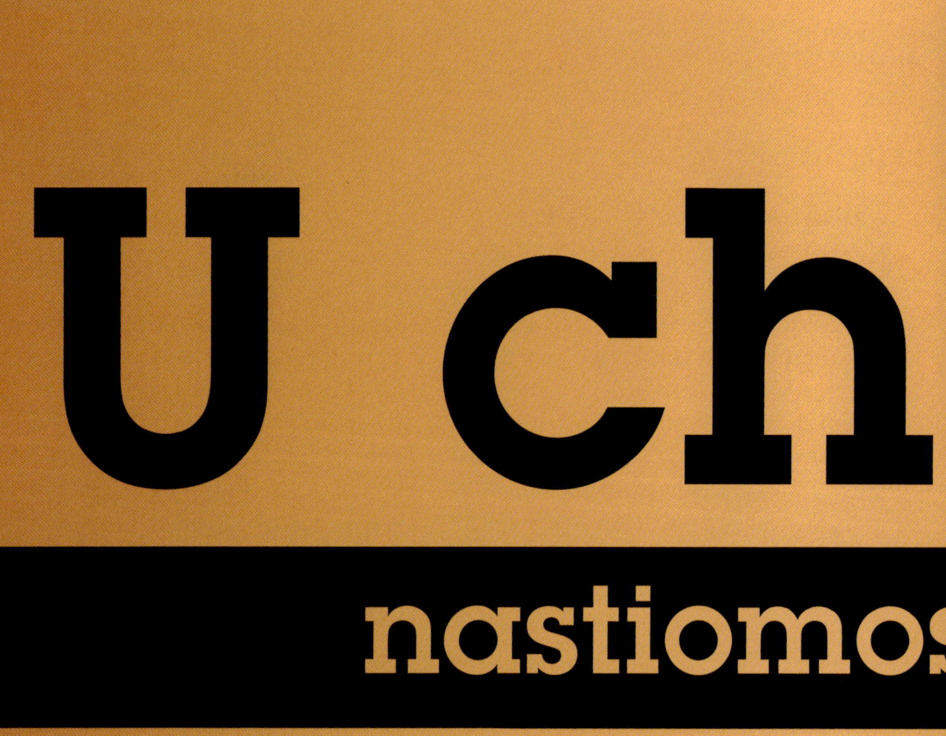
U ch
nastiomos

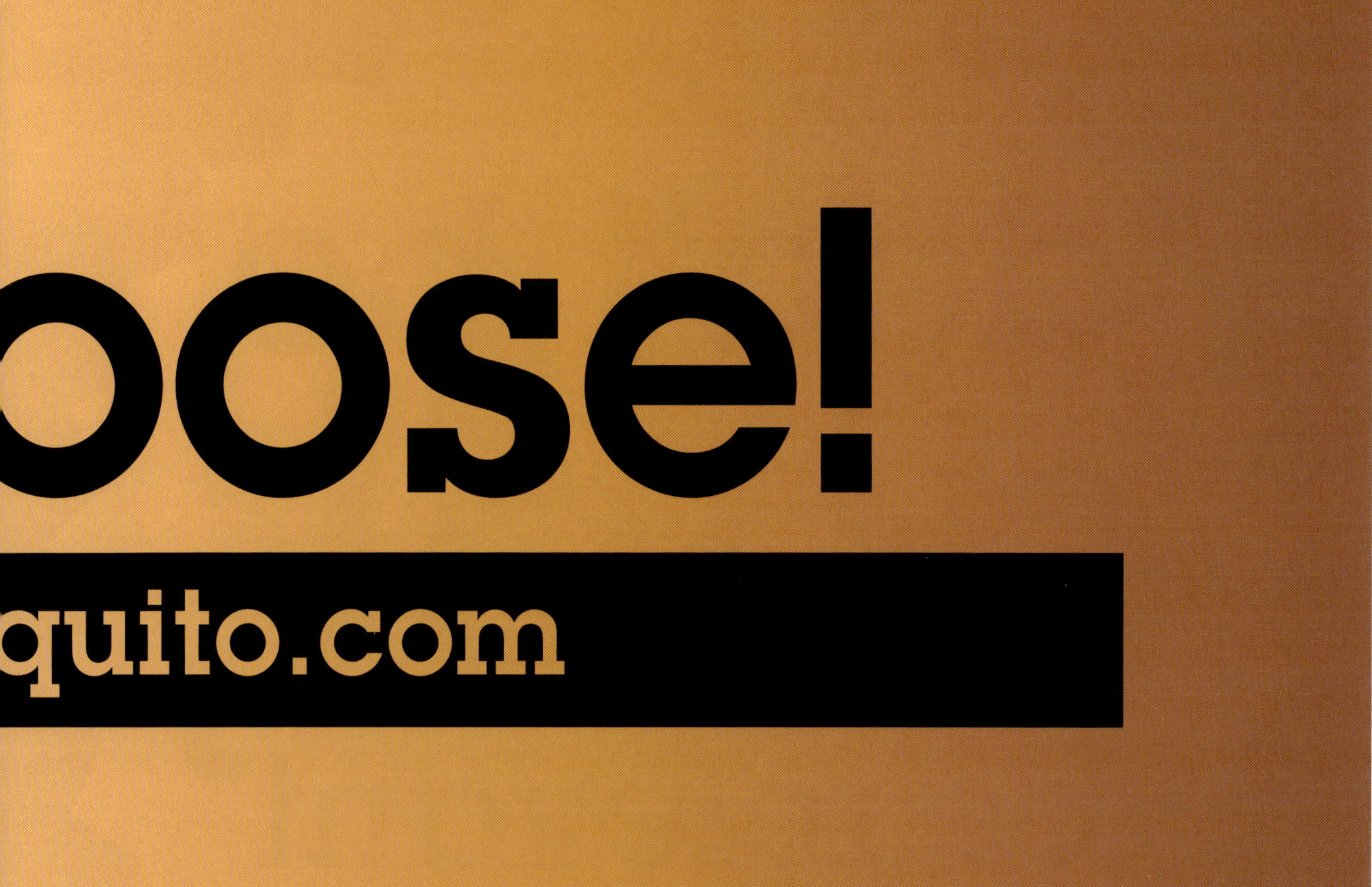
oose!
quito.com

don't be
cool,
be relevant
nastiomosquito.com

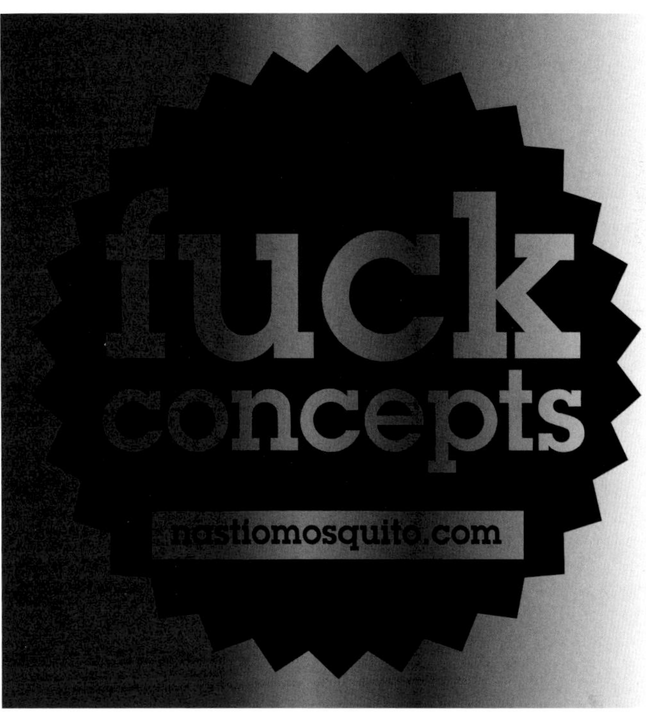

Nástio Mosquito

A video-maker, performer, poet and musician, Nástio Mosquito is an artist who moves freely between disciplines. He creates performances that see him play with roles and attitudes, shifting between host, storyteller, preacher and political orator. Adopting various personas – and thus placing himself centre stage while simultaneously sidestepping the limelight – he subverts the notion of a fixed cultural, social or political identity. For example, in his 2008 installation *Nástia's Manifesto*, he becomes the female character Nástia, who delivers a manifesto titled 'Hypocritical, Ironical and Do Not Give a Fuck'.

Humour, irony and satire are Mosquito's weapons of choice in his passionate, head-on engagement with the world. He is fascinated by the possibilities of language, both as a means of expression and as a tool of empowerment. There is an exhilarating immediacy to his work that stems from its live performance, but which also successfully translates into his works in other media. In his videos, Mosquito often draws upon the conventions and the aesthetics of a music clip or the direct address of infotainment television, formats which are ripe for *détournement*.

In 'The Absent Museum', Mosquito becomes Abdul RodeLaisse, a guide taking refugees, homeless people and other 'forgotten citizens' through the exhibition. The work is titled *The Guided Tour – Once We Shared Consequent Masturbation* (2017), and Mosquito describes it as 'a convulsion of love, indignation, hope, despair and the fight to have the path of faith, commitment, focus and trust under control. Failure is celebrated in this performance with scientific discipline.'

ZG

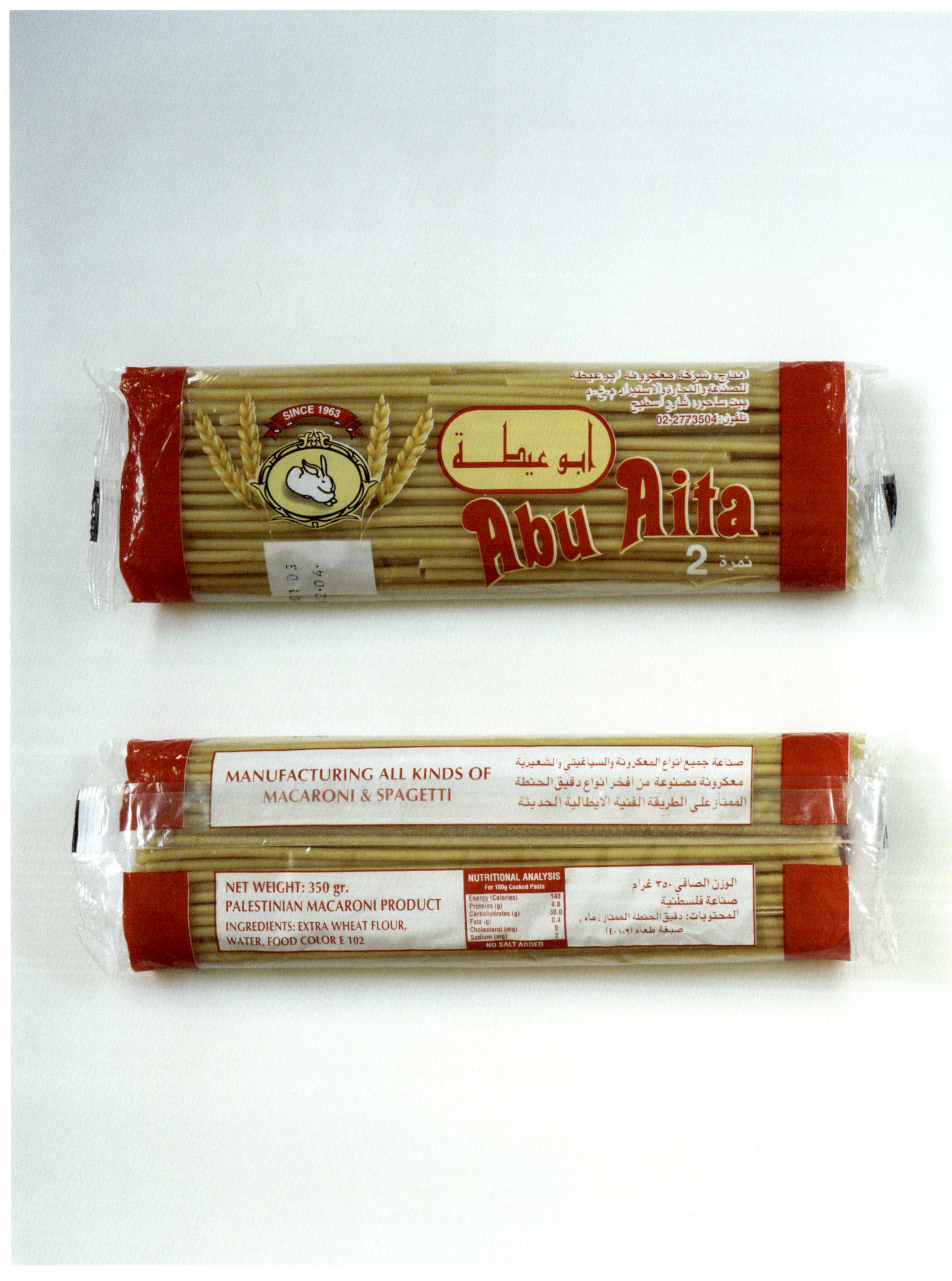

Jean-Luc Moulène, *Produits de Palestine / Pâtes alimentaires*, 2003, 50 × 40 cm, Cibachrome under Diasec.

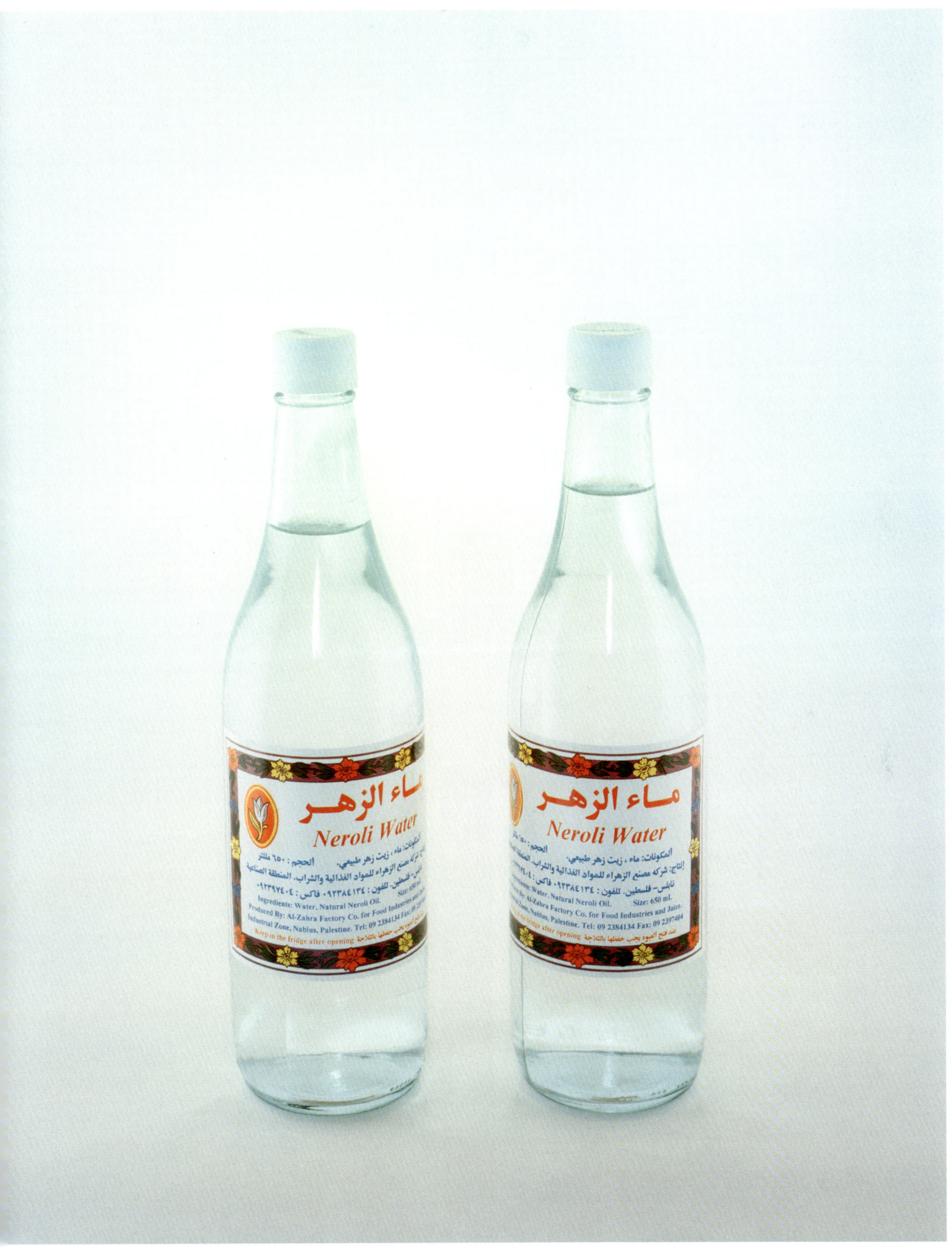

Jean-Luc Moulène, *Produits de Palestine / Eau de fleur d'oranger*, 2003, 50 × 40 cm, Cibachrome under Diasec.

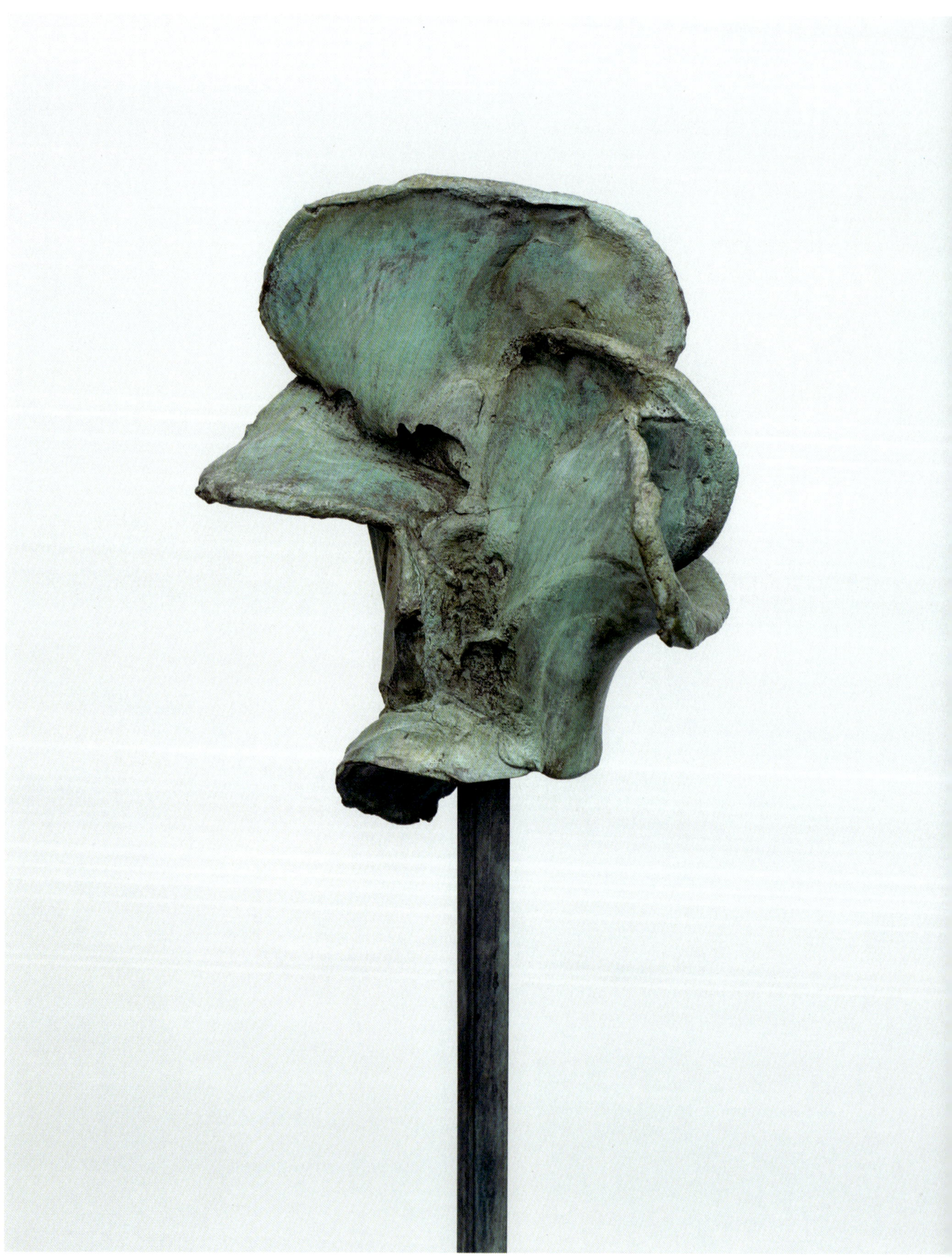

Jean-Luc Moulène, *Knot 5.1 Varia 02*, Paris 2012, 150 × 20 × 15 cm, bronze.

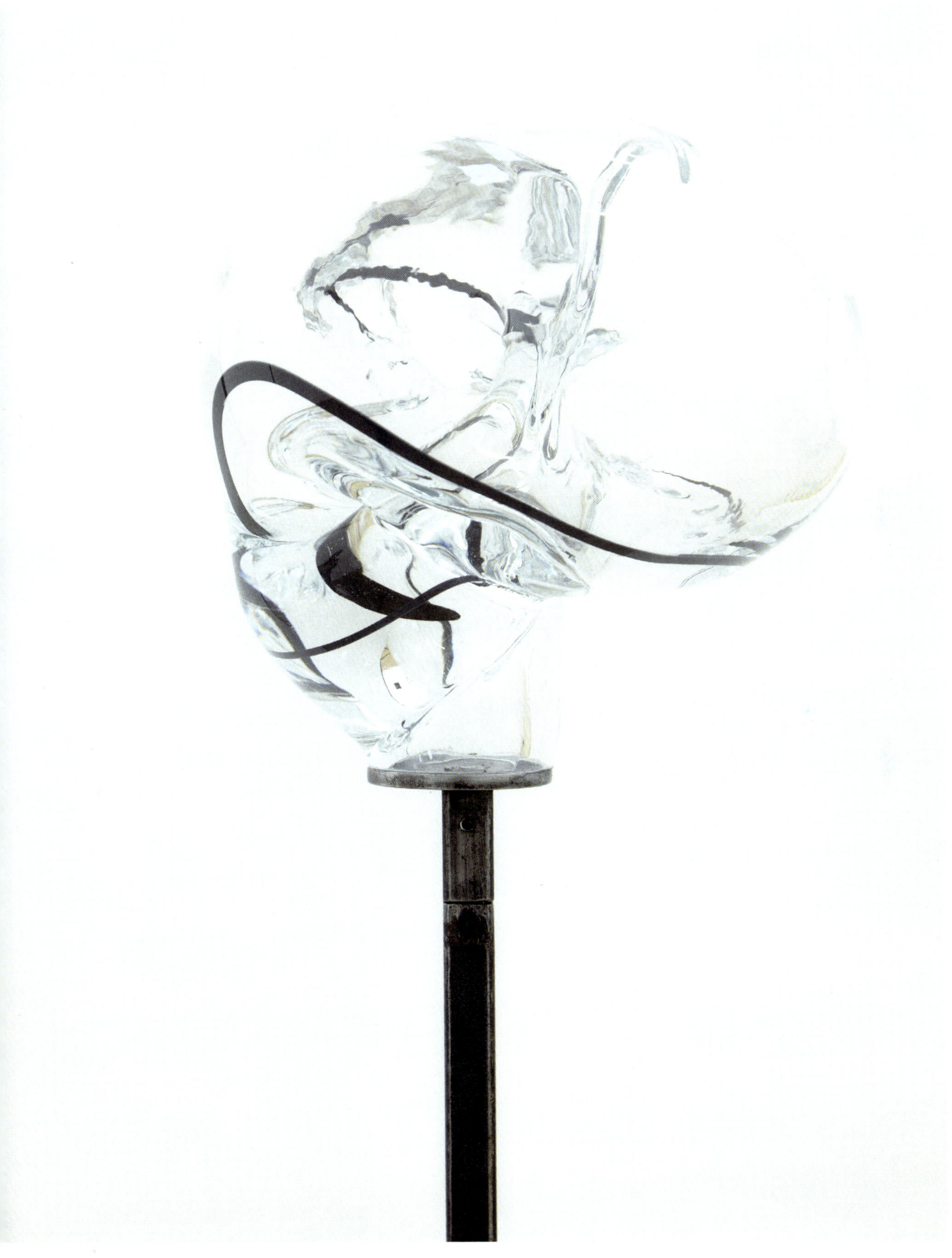

Jean-Luc Moulène, *Blown Knot 3.1 Varia 01*, Marseille 2012, 150 × 20 × 20 cm, glass, steel.

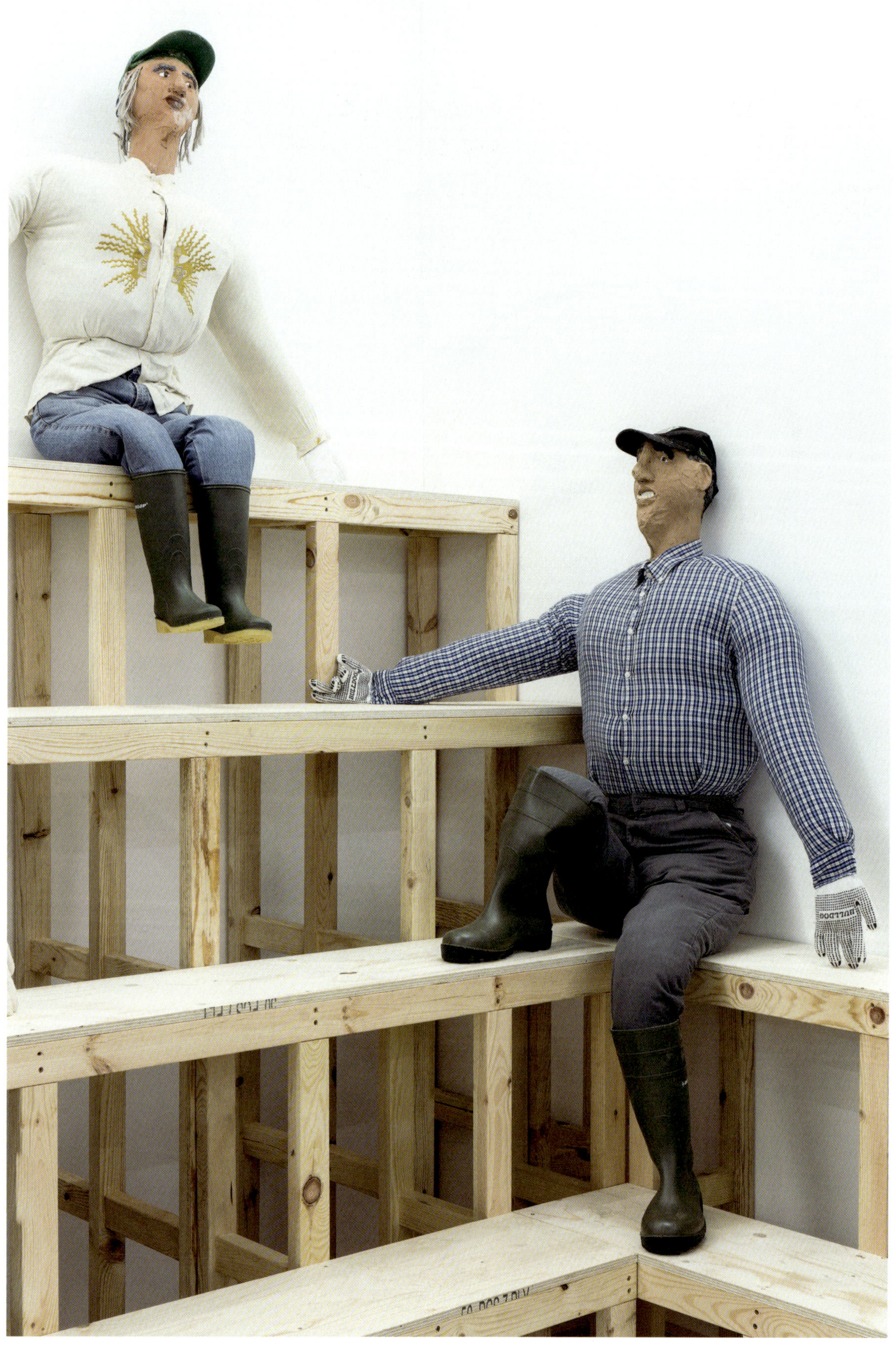

Oscar Murillo, *Human Resources*, 2016, variable dimensions, wood, fabric, papier mâché.

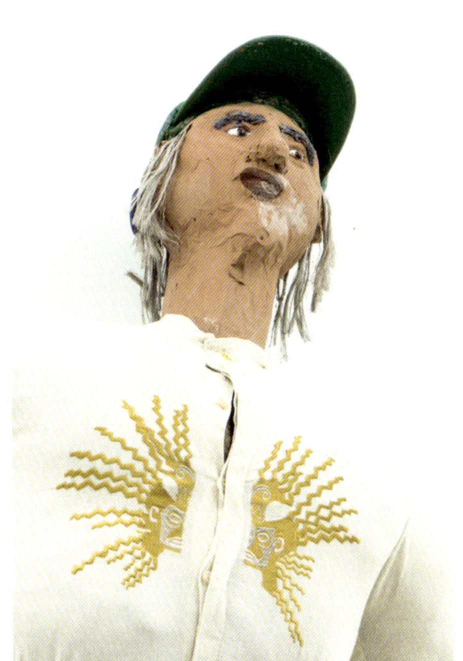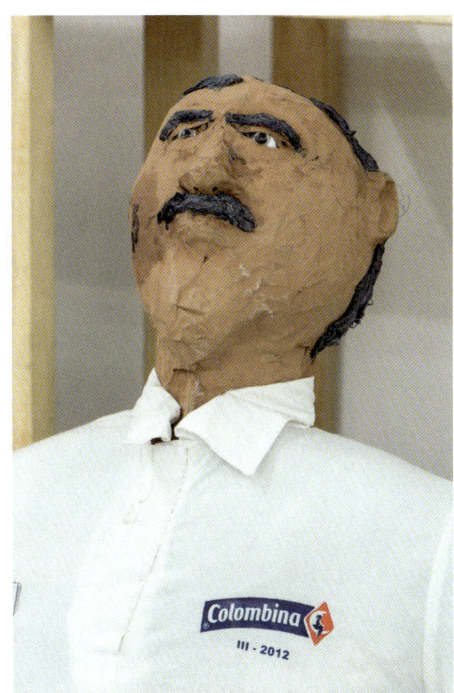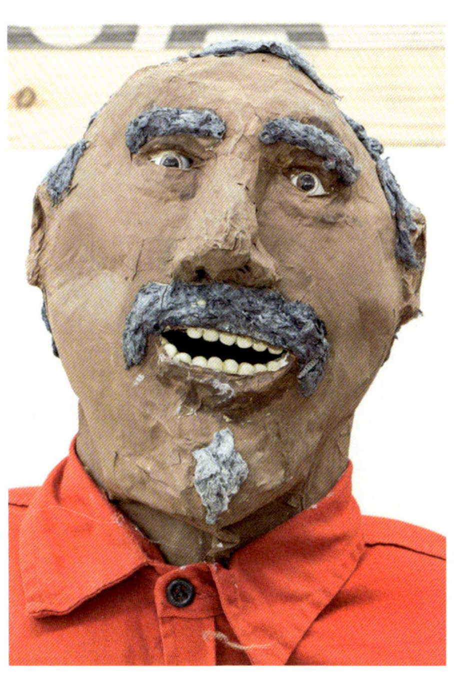

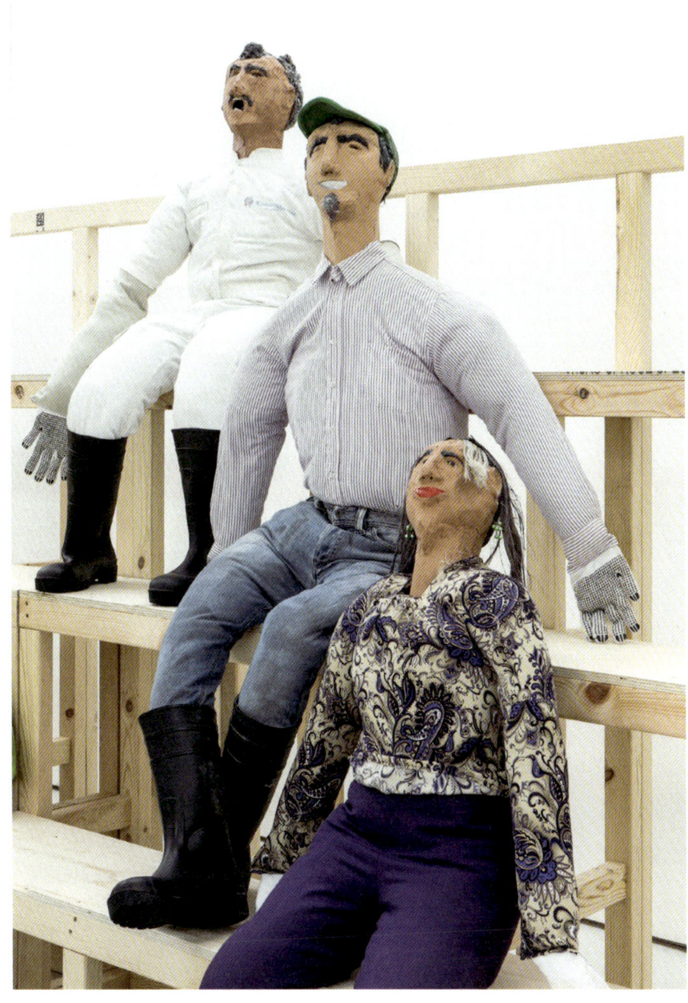

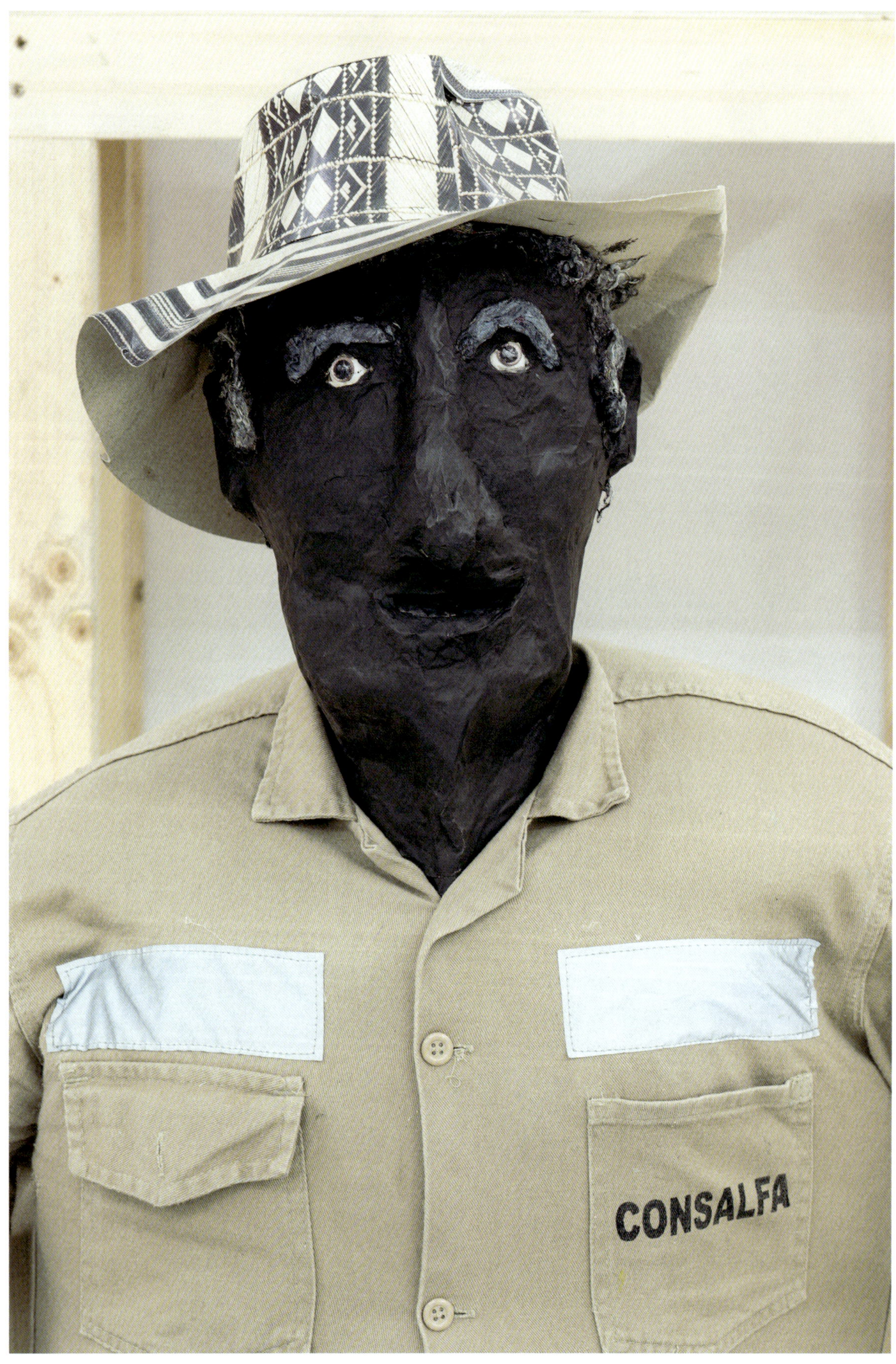

Oscar Murillo, *Human Resources*, 2016, variable dimensions, wood, fabric, papier mâché.

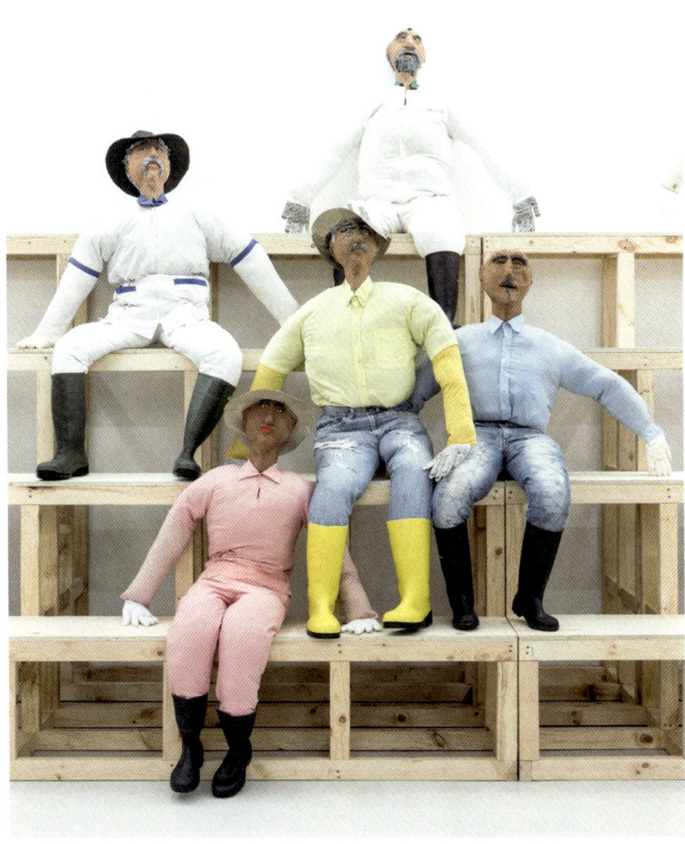

Oscar Murillo

In Oscar Murillo's dynamic work, ideas and materials often shift and evolve from one project to another. This has been the case since the early days of his practice, when he placed a canvas on the floor of his studio, held a party and then presented the resulting marks as a painting on canvas. Recently, this reuse of materials has become more complex: for example, in some paintings on canvas, he screen-prints over his marks, before collaging the results into new compositions. This is the organic result of his vital way of working, in which energies flow through different situations and media. In addition, Murillo's expansive approach allows other people to be included in his creative process; these are often members of his extended family but also people he encounters on his travels. His philosophy of hospitality is interwoven with his interest in the formation of social groups and the division of labour.

The work included in 'The Absent Museum' began as Murillo's 2015 exhibition at the Centro Cultural Daoíz y Velarde in Madrid. That spring, in the face of a growing anti-austerity movement, the Spanish Senate passed a law limiting the right to freedom of assembly, making the organisation of public protest an offence. Murillo proposed staging a demonstration as part of his exhibition, but the plan was vetoed by his hosts. In response he created 150 'placard' paintings, which were installed throughout the gallery space, and titled his show 'De marcha… Una rumba? No, solo un desfile con ética y estética' (To march… A rumba? No, just a fashion show with ethics and aesthetics). Aptly – although coincidentally – at the opening of his show the building was surrounded by protestors demonstrating about forthcoming elections. Murillo invited them in and incorporated their signs into his (unpublished) installation. As William Rees notes in his analysis of the work, 'Ironically,

censorship of Murillo's planned demonstration could not stop an actual one taking place.'

Murillo had also created a series of almost-life-sized figures with papier-mâché heads, their bodies made from stuffed clothes, resembling effigies made for folk festivals or carried (and sometimes burned) in protests. When in the Madrid space, they sat around on the floor as if awaiting an occupation, dressed as if ready for factory work. Later they travelled to Korea, where they became participants in a shamanic ritual. This was partly a way of keeping the artist company, providing a community to accompany him on his travels in an unknown context, but the figures also became witnesses to another stage of his practice.

Now the effigies have come to WIELS, where they sit on bleachers, facing one another and the audience. This evokes an agora or forum for discussion, in which the audience is invited to participate. Throughout the exhibition, a text is read at regular intervals by the WIELS invigilators and staff. These are the words of the artist's father, Belisario Caicedo-Florez, recounting his experience as a union representative in Colombia, a prisoner in Panama and an asylum seeker in London. The account is read in Spanish, English, French, Dutch, Arabic and Hebrew, in order to highlight the universality of the themes it explores.

ZG

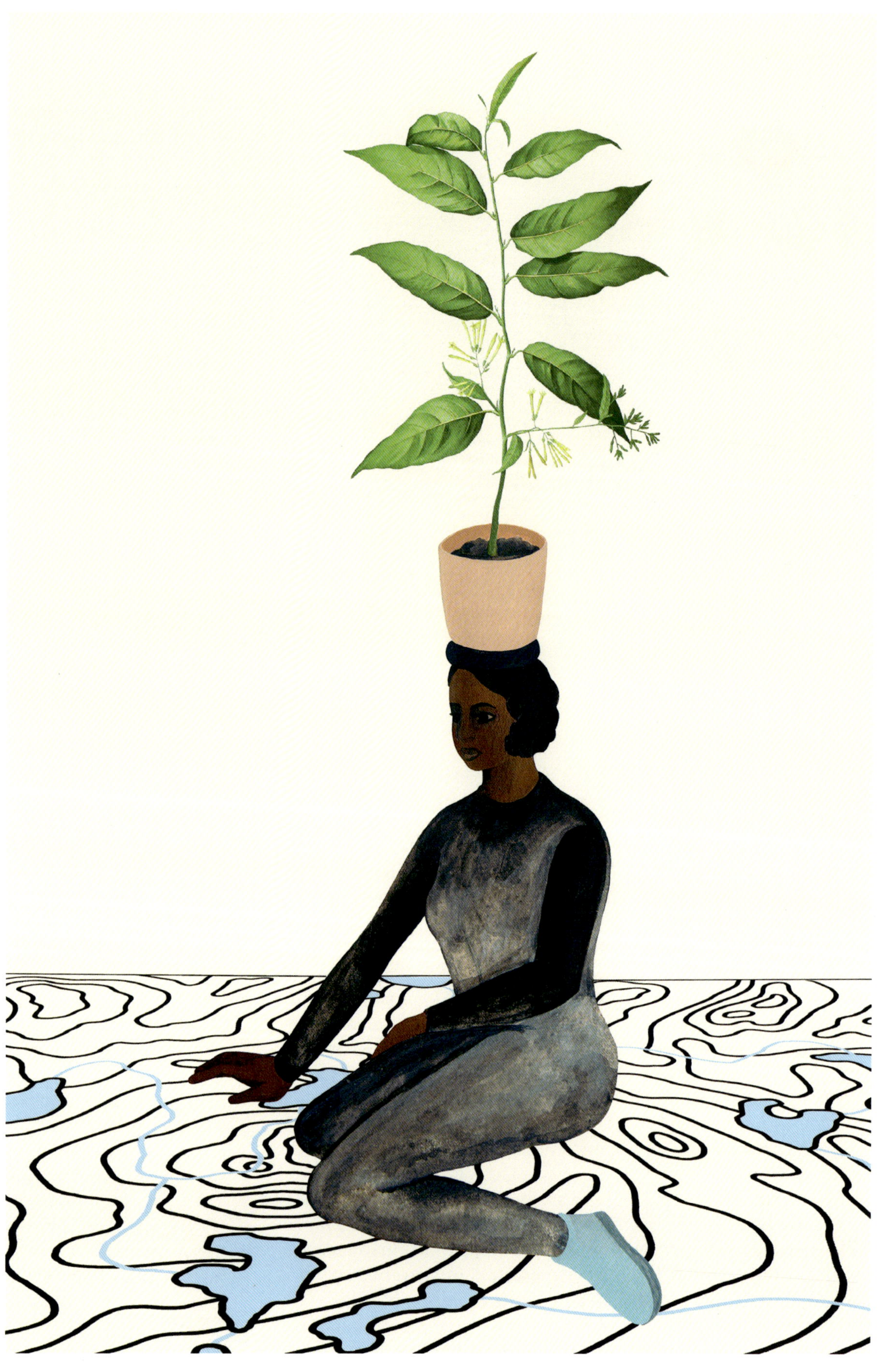

Otobong Nkanga, *Queen of the Night*, 2014, 36 × 27 cm, acrylic and collage on paper.

Forget All Not

One root was plucked
To see how they hurt
Deep in the core
Second root burned
To hear them scream
Loud, louder
Forget me not

Green leaves grew
Filled with pain
Slow to alter the DNA
Leaving its threads
Stretched, we hear
Loud, louder
Forget us not

Branches stayed firm
But lost its head
To the sip that stole
Its soul, the whole
A hole, to behold
Loud, louder
Forget we not

Stems raised high
To grab a ray
That shines no more
Faded leaving a mark
A stain, filled with memories
Loud, louder
Forget me not

Barks were cracked
To steal the juice
That feed the greed
Scarred each day
Blemished but alive
Loud, louder
Forget all not

Otobong Nkanga, 2016

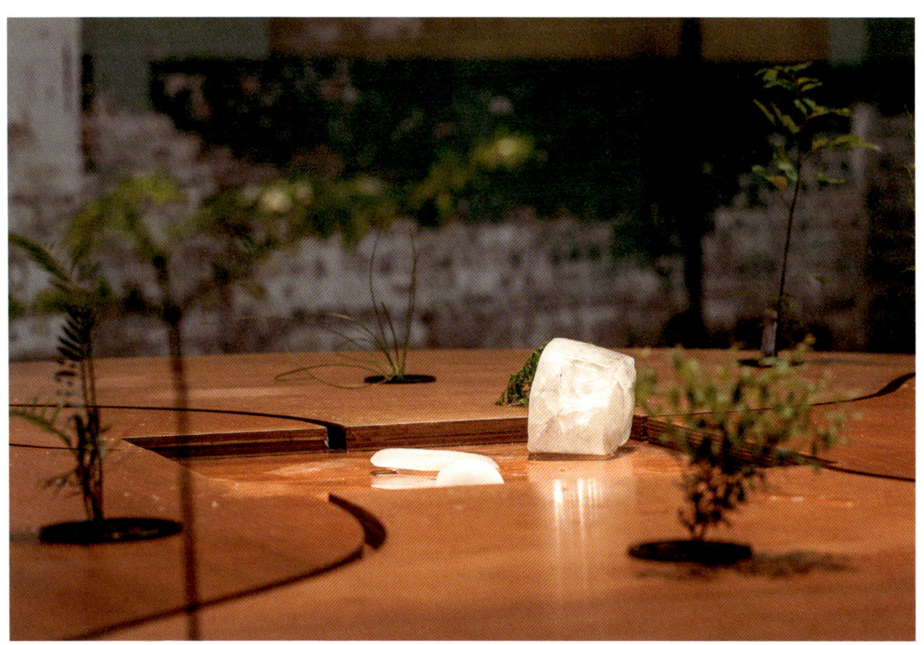

Otobong Nkanga, *Forget Me Not*, 2016, variable dimensions, wooden table, ice blocks, plants, glass vases, poetry readings.

Otobong Nkanga

Otobong Nkanga's installation *Forget Me Not* continues her work across different landscapes and contexts, questioning the dialectics of what is 'indigenous' and what is 'foreign'. At the centre of the installation is a block of melting ice, with a variety of plants placed on the surrounding surfaces. Among them is the *Myosotis*, a plant commonly known as the 'Forget Me Not'. In parallel to this native plant, Nkanga is also interested in 'invasive' species; different types of plants that have entered the country through colonialism and the movement of peoples. Carried not only on the body, but also in the air as seeds or by birds, these plants are a reference to migratory elements that cannot be contained. Each of these foreign plant varieties possesses its own history and has intermingled with the indigenous Belgian flora in diverse ways. Many varieties have not survived, as steps were taken to limit their spread by burning, cutting or other means of destruction. Nkanga is interested in the extraordinary resistance developed by many of these plants, which have adapted by growing deeper roots or exploding with seeds.

ZG

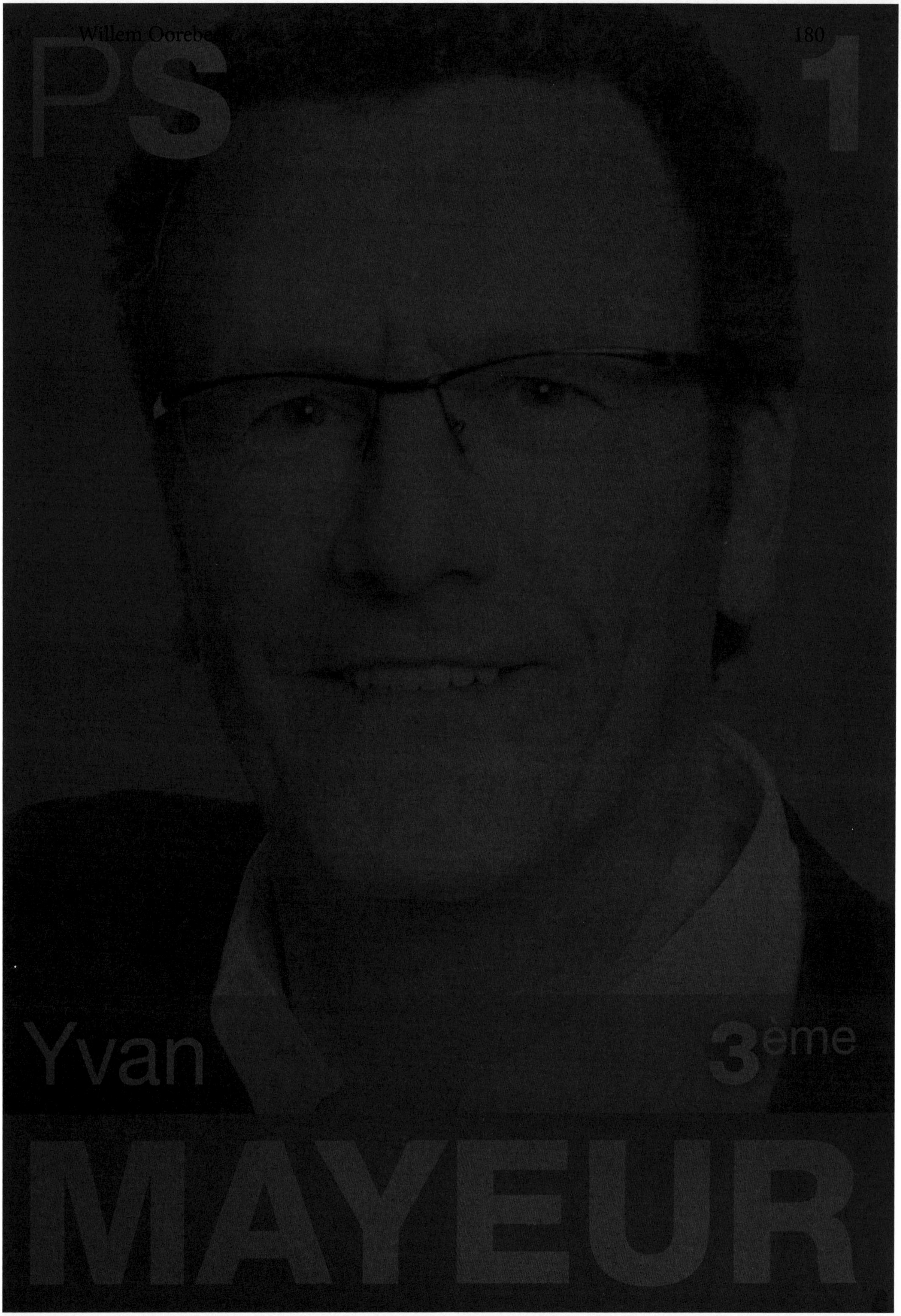

PS
1
Yvan
3ème
MAYEUR

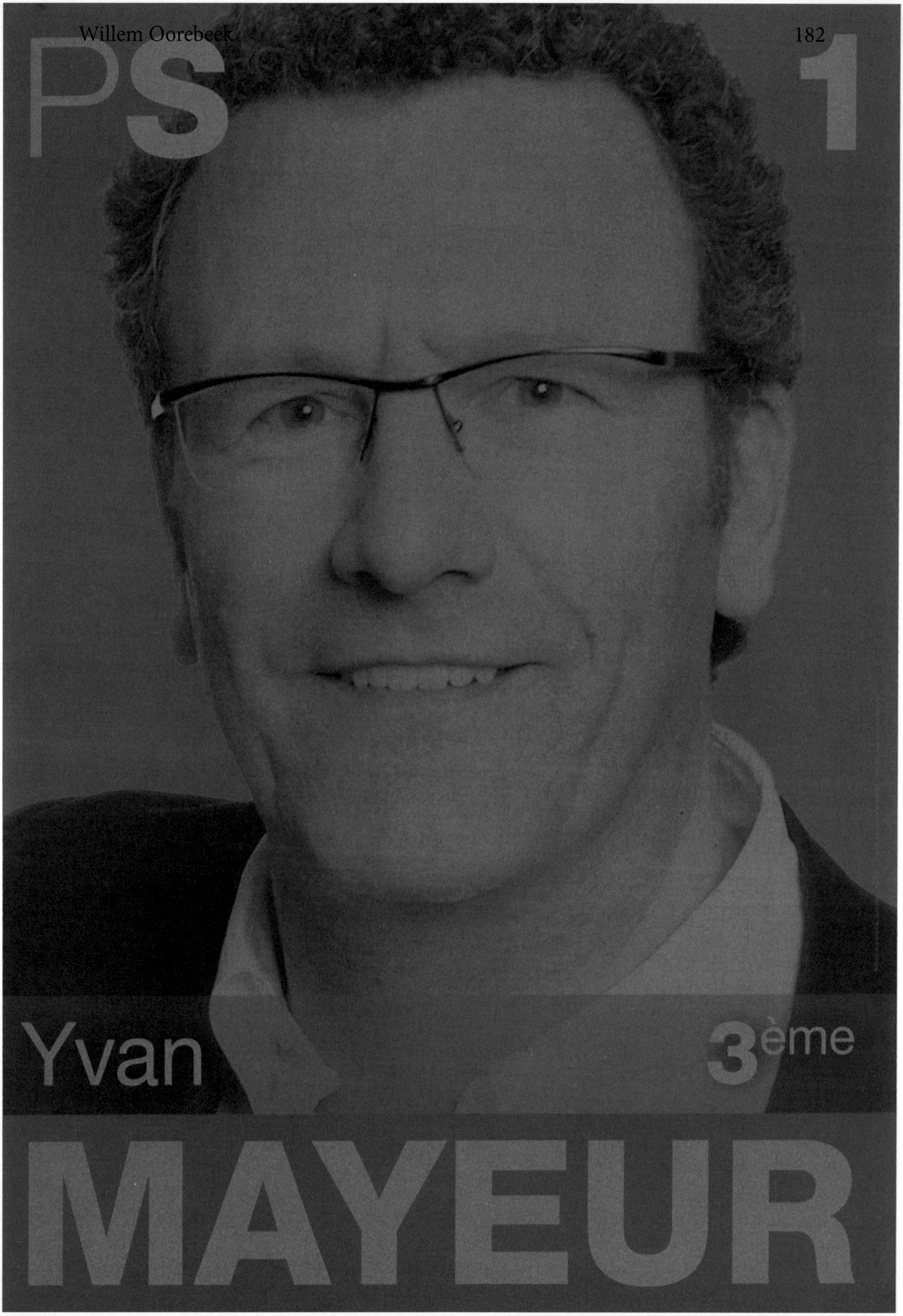

PS
1
Yvan
3ème
MAYEUR

PS 1
Yvan
MAYEUR
3ème

Willem Oorebeek, *Monogrammatic Studies 1999-2007-2016*, #5 (~~Pantone 1565C~~), #6 (~~Pantone 183C~~), #7.

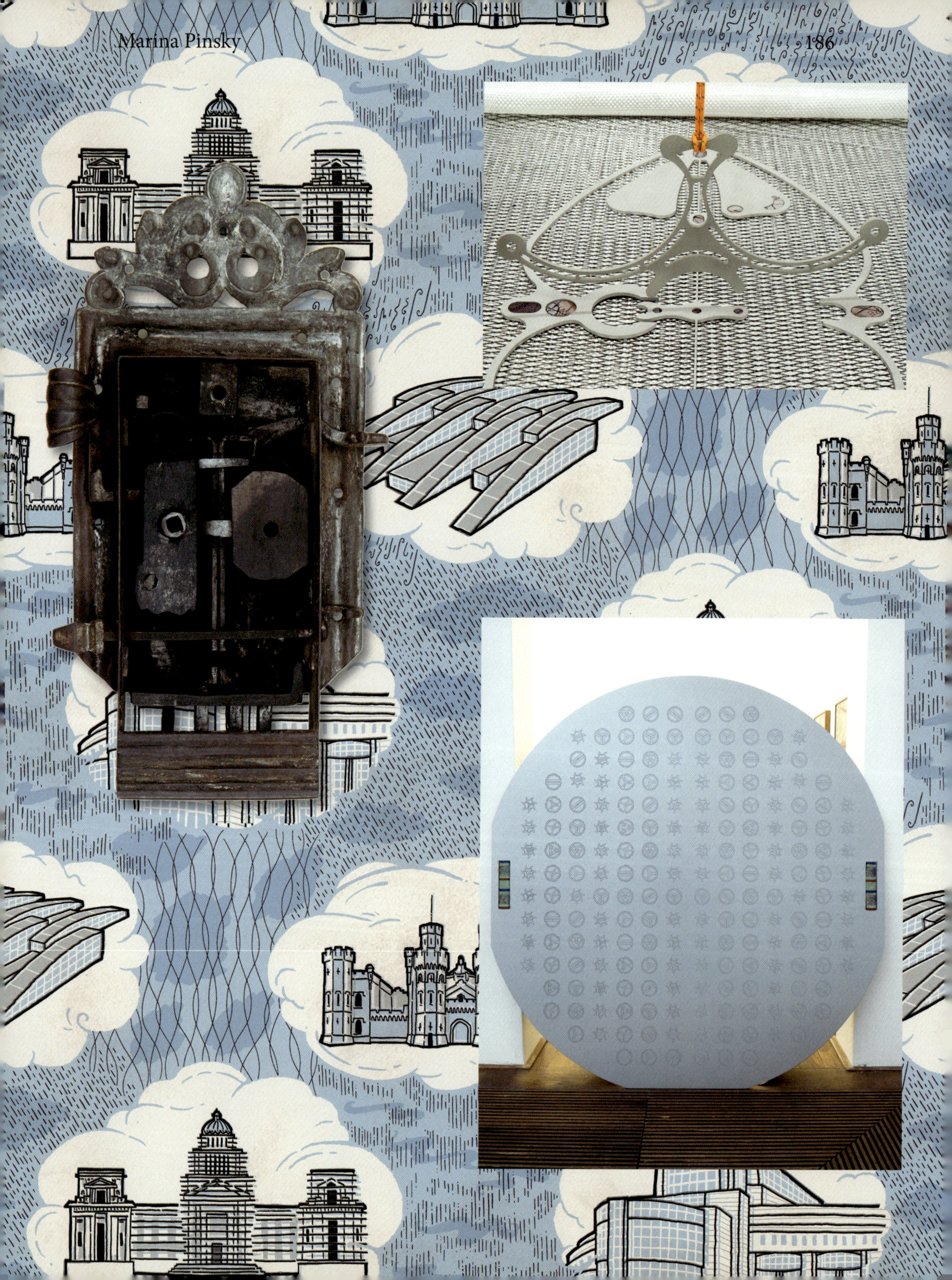

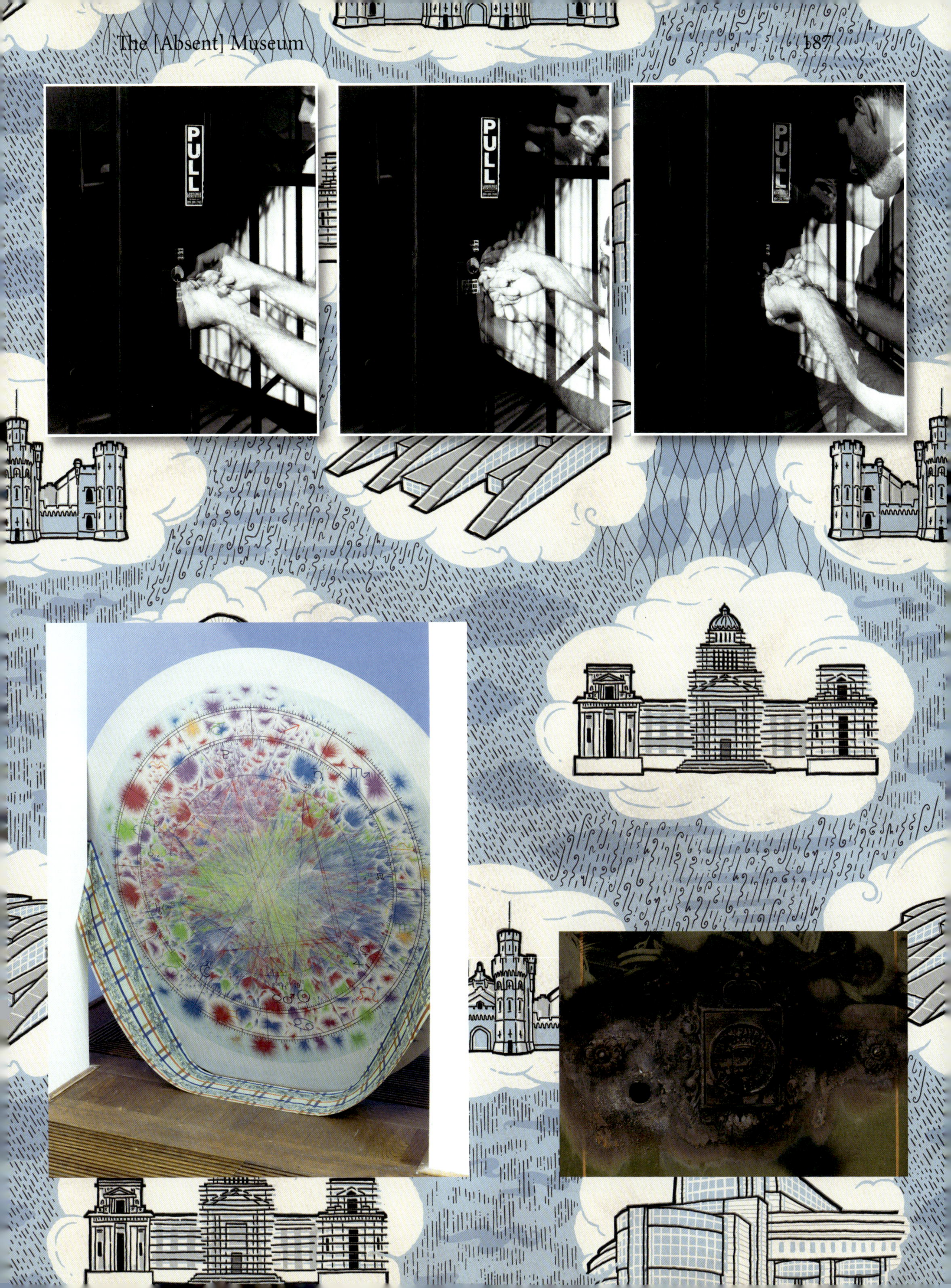

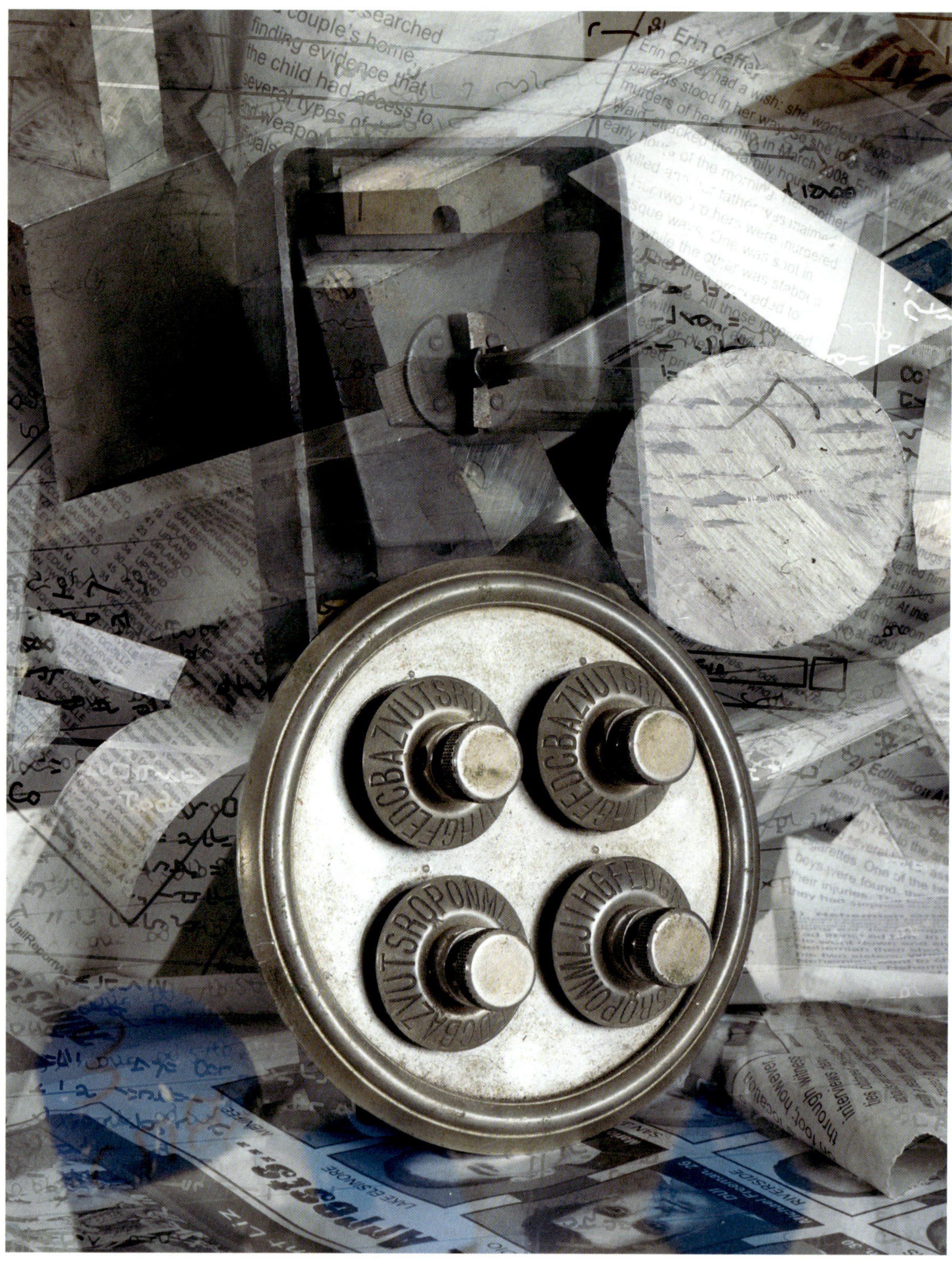

Previous page: Marina Pinsky, details and installation views of *Constant Escapement*, 2013; *Instruction Manual*, 2013; *July 15, 2015*, 2015; *Polar*, 2016.

Marina Pinsky, *Lake Elsinore*, 2013, 91.5 × 72.4 cm, UV-cured inkjet print on aluminium.

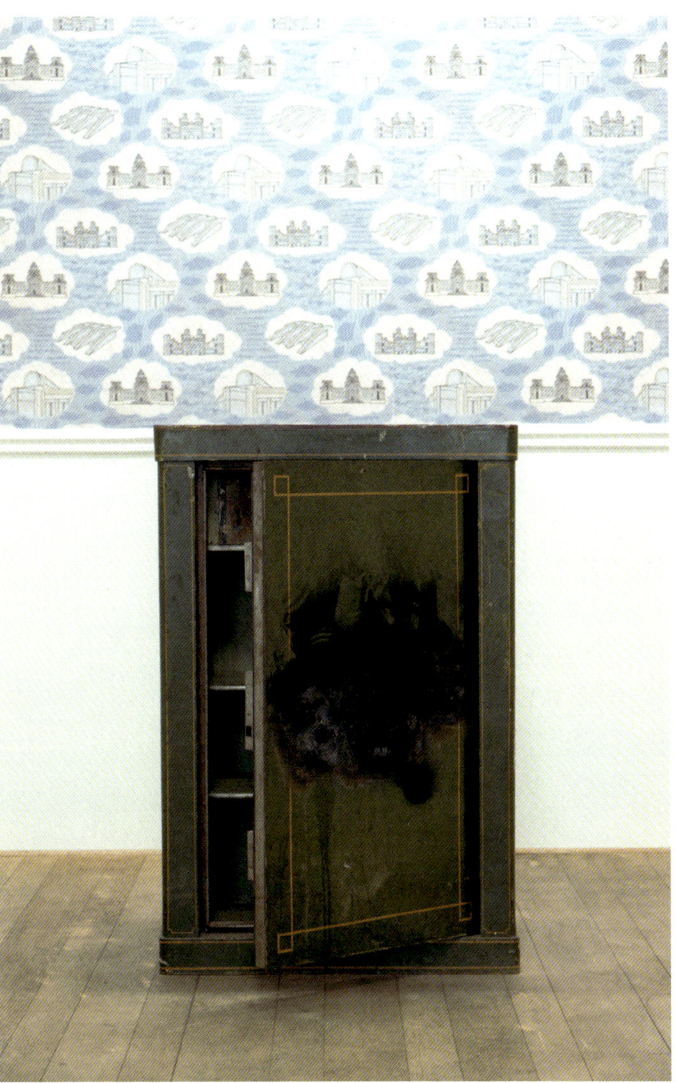

Marina Pinsky

At the crux of projects made by Marina Pinsky is a rich tension between photography and sculpture, in which the two media are intertwined, resulting in cryptic forms and narratives. The starting point for her work often lies in her fascination for an object or an anecdote, unearthed in unexpected corners of the city. For her new work made for 'The Absent Museum', she explored lesser-known aspects of well-known Brussels institutions: more specifically, the wallpaper library of La Cambre art school, the archives of the Royal Museums of Fine Arts, and the plaster-cast workshop of the Cinquantenaire Museum. She also delved into a private collection of keys and locks.

Like an unreliable detective, Pinsky creates rather than collects evidence. Carefully selected pieces of information are recorded, often by photography, and subsequently transferred into hybrid objects such as the wallpaper, double door, lock and moulds that make up her installation at WIELS. Her scenographic intervention suggests a typical bourgeois interior, quaint-looking yet loaded with enigma. Clues can be read in the wallpaper motifs – from humorous illustrations of Belgian types of rain, to depictions of Saint-Gilles Prison or the European Parliament, landmarks of Brussels and symbols of authority. Other clues can be found in the prominent lock on the double door,

with its antique mechanism but oddly new patina, luring the visitor to the other side, the outside, the bright space that can be guessed at behind. Finally, the contemporary casts of keyholes from three different centuries reveal an unsettling sense of anachronism and an elaborate construction of histories.

CF

MUSEUM STAFF

DID YOU NOTICE THESE IMAGES
PACKED IN THIS SHOW WE'RE INSTAL
ALL THESE BODIES, THESE HISTORIES
THEY STARE AT US, THEY MIRROR US
THEY QUESTION US, THEY BEG FOR U
BUT WHAT DO THEY SAY, WHAT DO TH

DID YOU NOTICE THESE MEMORIES
PACKED IN THIS SHOW WE'RE WORKI
THEY'RE NOT THE PAST, THEY'RE HER
AND THEY HURT US, AND THEY MOVE
THEY QUESTION US, THEY BEG FOR U
BUT WHAT DO THEY SAY, WHAT DO TH

HOW COME SOMEONE CAN COME TO
AND THROW THESE THINGS INTO OUR
AND THROW OUR PAST INTO OUR GAZ
WITHOUT CARING, WITHOUT KNOWIN
BUT WHAT DO YOU SAY, ARTIST ?
AND WHAT DO YOU SING, MUSEUM ?

HOW CAN WE GET OUR VOICES HEARD
AND GIVE OUR BODIES A REAL LIFE
HOW CAN WE GET OUR VOICES HEARD
AND GIVE OUR HISTORY A REAL PRICE
HOW CAN WE SING OUR DISCOMFORT
AND MAKE SILENCE IRRELEVANT ?

BUT WHAT DO YOU SAY, ARTIST ?
AND WHAT DO YOU SING, MUSEUM ?

CURATOR

SOMETIMES I LIKE TO GET OUTSIDE T
TO WALK AND THINK AND REMEMBE
WHEN IMAGES WERE FIXED IN BOOK
WERE FIXED IN TIME, WERE FIXED IN

SOMETIMES I LIKE TO GET OUTSIDE T
TO WALK AND THINK AND REMEMBE
WHAT IT FELT LIKE TO ENCOUNTER
ART HISTORY IN LIBRARIES, IN CATA
IN MONOGRAPHS, IN STORAGES, IN (

SOMETIMES I LIKE TO GET OUTSIDE T
TO WALK AND THINK AND REMEMBE
WHEN IMAGES WERE FIXED IN BOOK
WERE FIXED IN TIME, WERE FIXED IN

BUT WITH THIS SHOW I WANT TO SAY
THAT IMAGES OF THE PRESENT ARE
TO CIRCULATE, REVERBERATE AND (
THEY'RE NO MORE PURE, THEY'RE N
THEY DON'T BELONG TO ANYONE, TH

BUT WITH THIS SHOW I WANT TO THI
ABOUT CULTURE AND ABOUT US IN A
WE DON'T BELONG TO ANYTHING, WI
WE CIRCULATE AND WE CONSUME, V
WE ORCHESTRATE AND WE UNLEASH

BUT WITH THIS SHOW I'D LIKE TO PR
THAT WE ALL SHARE THIS NEW PRES
WE DON'T BELONG TO ANYTHING, WI
WE ARE ALL EXPOSED, WE'RE CONFF

YES WE ALL SHARE THESE IMAGES A

YES WE ALL SHARE THESE IMAGES A

YES WE ALL SHARE THESE IMAGES A

ART CRITIC

OH HOW MUCH I LOVE LOVING THIS W
I LIVED SO LONG NOT KNOWING IT
I LIVED SO LONG IGNORING WHY
NO ART WORK TALKED TO MY BODY

YOU SEE (OR MAYBE YOU DON'T ?)
I'M NOT THE MAN WHO SHIES AWAY
FROM SUCH PHYSICAL MATERIAL

YOU SEE (OR MAYBE YOU DON'T ?)
I'M NOT THE CRITIC WHO ASSUMES
THAT WORDS AND SYNTAX ARE THE K

YOU SEE (OR MAYBE YOU DON'T ?)
I TRUST DESIRE MORE THAN LANGUA
AND WHAT I SEE HERE IS PURE DESIR

YOU SEE (OR MAYBE YOU DON'T ?)
MOST OBSESSIONS ARE NOT OUR OW
BUT A THING WE BUILD WITH THE OTH

YOU SEE (OR MAYBE YOU DON'T ?)
WE KEEP SILENT ALL THESE STORIES
BECAUSE LANGUAGE WOULD UNDO T

THE ONLY PROBLEM WITH THIS WORK
IS OUR REFUSAL TO BE REAL,
TO NAME OUR VARIOUS BODY PARTS
AND TO SEE THE OTHER'S BODY

THE ONLY VIOLENCE IN THIS WORK
IS THAT IT FORCES US TO FEEL
BEYOND OUR VARIOUS BODY PARTS
AND TO FACE THE OTHER'S BODY

THE ONLY PRESENT IN THIS WORK
IS WHEN OUR PAST REPEATS ITSELF
BECAUSE WE'RE SO ASHAMED OF IT
WE CAN NOT TAKE A GLANCE AT IT

COMMUNITY

WE ARE DISCONCERTED
WE FEEL SO EXHAUSTED
WE FEEL VERY TIRED
WE FEEL NAUSEATED

WE'VE BEEN WORKING SO HARD
TO DISMANTLE THE PAST
TO TEAR VIOLENCE APART
HOW CAN IT STILL PERVADE ART ?
WE CAN'T MOVE IN THIS SPACE
WE CAN'T BREATHE IN THIS SPACE

WE ARE DISCONCERTED
WE FEEL SO EXHAUSTED
WE FEEL VERY TIRED
WE FEEL NAUSEATED

WE'VE BEEN WORKING SO HARD
TO APPEASE OUR PEOPLE
TO OVERCOME THE WORST
HOW CAN WE FACE THESE WORKS ?
AND EVEN MOVE IN THIS SPACE ?
AND EVEN BREATHE IN THIS SPACE ?

WE ARE DISCONCERTED
WE FEEL SO EXHAUSTED
WE FEEL VERY TIRED
WE FEEL NAUSEATED

WE'VE BEEN WORKING SO HARD
TO RECLAIM OUR LIVES
TO MAKE SENSE OF ALL THAT
HOW CAN THERE BE NO LIFE
IN THESE PICTURES OF US ?
IN THESE BODIES THAT ARE OURS

WE ARE DISCONCERTED
WE FEEL SO EXHAUSTED
WE FEEL VERY TIRED

ACTIVIST ARTIST

IT'S TIME TO ASK FOR ANSWERS
TIME TO RECLAIM WHAT'S OURS
WE WON'T BE TREATED AS OBJECTS
THERE'S SO MUCH WE CAN'T ACCEPT

IT'S TIME TO ASK MORE FROM ART
TO GIVE IT DIFFERENT STANDARDS
WE WON'T BE TREATED AS OBJECTS
THERE'S SO MUCH WE CAN'T ACCEPT

BECAUSE THIS CITY HAS SUFFERED
AND BECAUSE WE NEED TO BE HEARD
WE WON'T BE TREATED AS OBJECTS
THERE'S SO MUCH WE CAN'T ACCEPT

WE NEED TO ASK FOR ANSWERS
THIS MUSEUM SHOULD BE OURS
AND NOT A DISCONNECTED VOID
CUT FROM THE LIVES OF THE PEOPLE

I RESPECT ART THAT GIVES ANSWERS
ART AS A LANGUAGE SHOULD BE CLEAR
SO IT'S FOR EVERYONE TO SHARE
THIS MUSEUM SHOULD BE OURS

I AM AN ARTIST AND I CARE
ABOUT ALL THE PEOPLE WHO DARE
BEING RESTLESS ABOUT THEIR LIVES
BEING RESTLESS ABOUT THEIR PRIDE

ARTIST

I DON'T THINK THAT WORDS CAN RE
THE MOMENT I PRONOUNCE THEM,
ON MAYBE SOMETHING FALSE
ON MAYBE SOMETHING ELSE

MEANING IS LAYERED AND MEANING
OVER THE YEARS AND OVER THE LA
IT MIGHT BE SOMETHING FALSE
IT MIGHT BE SOMETHING ELSE

IN THE SAME WAY THAT I FEEL THIS
I FEEL THESE IMAGES AND THEIR OP
THEY MAY BELONG TO YOU
THEY MAY BELONG TO US

IMAGES OF VIOLENCE, IMAGES OF O
THEY PERFORM IN A WAY, THEY RES
AND I DO THINGS WITH THEM
I DO THINGS ONTO THEM

THERE'S SOMETHING SO FLAT IN TH
WHY WOULDN'T I GET THIS, WHY WO
I THINK I CAN SHOW THESE BODIES
I CAN SHOW THEIR RESILIENCE

WHAT INTERESTS ME IS HOW CAPITA
YES IT FLATTENS CONTENT AND MA
I DIDN'T MAKE THINGS LIKE THIS
I DIDN'T CHOOSE THAT

MEANING IS LAYERED AND MEANING
THERE'S MY OWN HISTORY, MY PRIV
AND THERE'S THE ONES WE SHARE
HOW DO WE DEAL WITH IT ?

IMAGES OF OUR PAST, IMAGES OF V
THEY RESURFACE, PERFORM IN A W
AND I DO THINGS WITH THEM
I DO THINGS ONTO THEM

COMMUNITY AND ACTIVIST ARTIST

BUT WHO DOES THIS SPEAK TO ?

WHO ARE THE PEOPLE ON YOUR IMAG

DON'T THEY HAVE A NAME ?

WHY ARE THEY STUCK IN SUCH SILEN

WHY THESE PICTURES, WHY NOT OTH

WHAT MAKES YOU FEEL YOU CAN US

WHO WILL PROFIT FROM THIS DISPLA

WHO IS IT YOU WANT TO ADDRESS ?

DO YOU SOMETIMES THINK OF WHO T

BUT WHO DOES THIS SPEAK TO ?

WHO ARE THE PEOPLE ON YOUR IMAG

WHAT MAKES YOU FEEL YOU CAN US

WHY ARE THEY STUCK IN SUCH SILEN

DON'T THEY HAVE A NAME ?

WHY THESE PICTURES, WHY NOT OTH

WHO WILL PROFIT FROM THIS DISPLA

DO YOU SOMETIMES THINK OF WHO T

WHO IS IT YOU WANT TO ADDRESS ?

WHO ARE THE PEOPLE ON YOUR IMAG

ACTIVIST ARTIST

PLEASE CLOSE THIS SHOW IT HAS TO
NONE OF OUR QUESTIONS HAVE BEE
NONE OF OUR VOICES WERE REALLY
NONE OF OUR CLAIMS WERE CONSID

I'VE BLOCKED MY SENSES AND MY SI
NOW THAT IT OCCURED TO MY MIND
THAT NONE OF US WAS CONSIDERED
AND OUR ANGER DIDN'T MATTER

PLEASE CLOSE THIS SHOW IT HAS TO
THERE'S NO MEANING BEHIND ALL TH
THERE'S NO REASON FOR SUCH VIOL
THERE'S NO DEFENSE FOR THIS SILE

MAYBE YOUR WORLD CAN SWALLOW
BUT IN MY VIEW THIS CAN'T EXIST
THERE'S NO REASON FOR SUCH
THERE'S NO DEFENSE FOR THIS SILE

PLEASE CLOSE THIS SHOW IT HAS TO
MAKE THIS MUSEUM A DECENT PLAC
OPEN IT TO ITS REAL AUDIENCE
PEOPLE WHO KNOW WHERE THEY BE

I WANT TO SEE ART THAT IS STRONG
ART THAT KNOWS WHY IT'S BEING MA
ART THAT KNOWS WHO IT EXISTS FO
ART THAT CAN STAND FOR ITS IDEALS

PLEASE CLOSE THIS SHOW IT HAS TO
NONE OF OUR QUESTIONS HAVE BEE
NONE OF OUR VOICES WERE REALLY
NONE OF OUR CLAIMS WERE CONSID

<u>Small Tragic Opera
of Images and Bodies
in the Museum</u>

Libretto by Lili Reynaud-Dewar,
music by Nicolas Murer

Somewhere in a city traumatized
and exhausted by the assassination
of a young black man by the police,
a museum hosts an exhibition by
an artist whose work has repeatedly
made use of archival images of police
violence and black bodies. Parts
of the museum staff and the local
artistic community are outraged
by what they consider to be an
inappropriate and insensitive artistic
proposition, a fetishization of
violence and alienation. The artist
is challenged to justify her body
of works but fails to answer the
questions, appease the anxiety,
the anger. Tension grows. These
images are reclaimed. Apologies
get written. Walls are built. Was it
the good place, the good time for
this exhibition? Who can talk for
whom? Whom do these images
belong to? How could we not build
walls? Are there a space and a time
for the exhibition of negative images?
The museum becomes a place for
intense discussions, it is alive, voices
are raised, spirits and ghosts are
somewhere near. The world listens.

OVERTURE

The narrator speaks about the city
where the story takes place, its recent
tragic events and the mobilization
that they have triggered. A young
black man has been killed by the
police, his dead body remaining
uncovered and exposed to anyone's
sight for a long, long time. Riots,
pain, anxiety, anger, activism and
protests followed, for months and
months. History repeats itself,
seemingly endlessly, but some
things change: images get to move
faster, mobilization gets to a higher
level, voices can be heard louder
and further.

ACT 1
BEFORE THE EXHIBITION

Museum staff
Parts of the museum staff express their
concerns and unease at the images
they have to install. They talk together
about the position they're in: they care
for works, install them, invigilate them,
but apparently, through the process
of bringing the show to a public, their
voices will not be heard.

Curator
The curator takes a walk outside the
museum in order to think about the
exhibition. She does not respond
to the museum staff's questions or
discomfort (maybe she doesn't notice),
but rather addresses some invisible
press person or audience – or even
herself – about the exhibition and the
publication that will accompany it.

Art critic
The critic eloquently sings about
the artist's work, about the
complexities of desire, fantasy and
love, about exhibiting and living
with images that constitute a mutual
and shared history. By comparison
with the curator's argument, which
is impersonal and distanced, abstract
even, the critic's song is personal,
emotional and lyrical.

ACT 2
EXHIBITION OPENING

Community
Some of the visitors react to
the works on display. They feel
uncomfortable in their presence,
they do not understand why this is
shown here, in this city, and at this
particular moment. They discuss
their exhaustion at seeing images
of police violence, bodies exposed
and fetishized. They read parts of
the curator's argument with disbelief.
They have so many questions.

Activist Artist
The activist artist voices her deep
disgust and rejection of the exhibition.

By comparison with the community's concerns and the way they are voiced – more with an incredulous, interrogative tone – the activist artist's position is more that of an unambiguous rejection of what is being shown. She convinces the community to stiffen their positions and demand answers to their questions, by attending the artist's talk and confronting her with the discrepancies of her work in the museum.

ACT 3
ARTIST'S TALK

Artist
The artist talks about her work in relation with consumption, with the circulation of images and images of bodies, with art history. The artist also thinks about all the things she doesn't want to talk about, or sing out loud: her childhood, sexuality, beliefs, desires. Why doesn't the artist want to share any of this, why does the artist remain so abstract? Doesn't the artist know that, to a certain extent, the personal is the political? Or does she refuse to justify the work from an emotional point of view?

Community and
Activist Artist
Questions!!! Questions!!! Questions!!! The community and the activist artist urge the artist to talk further about the provenance of these images, the context of this exhibition, its desired audience. The artist fails to answer, repeatedly.

ACT 4
WALLS

Activist Artist
The activist artist wants the show taken down. She thinks this exhibition should have never taken place. She is vocal and passionate, angry and implacable.

Museum staff
The museum staff inform the museum of their decision to stand in solidarity with the community and the activist artist. They will not perform their duties in relation with the exhibition of the artist's works.

Curator
The curator apologizes for failing to acknowledge the museum staff's concerns during the installation period and for being unable to answer the community's questions during the talk. She announces that the exhibition will not be taken down, but that walls will be built in order to partially conceal the works that caused the outrage.

Artist
The artist apologizes for being unable to provide answers and to appease the anger and anxiety her work has caused. She sings that she stands in solidarity with the communities she has offended, that her belief is that art can bring certain difficult memories, topics, images, at the centre of intense and necessary conversations and that her intention was to do so with these works. She sings about the walls her work has – somehow – created between herself and the community it has hurt. She sings about the walls that will be built to prevent her works being overtly exposed to any visitor's sight. The walls that will be built to prevent further pain. The soothing walls. The painful walls.

Lili Reynaud-Dewar, synopsis of the libretto of *Small Tragic Opera of Images and Bodies in the Museum*, 2017.

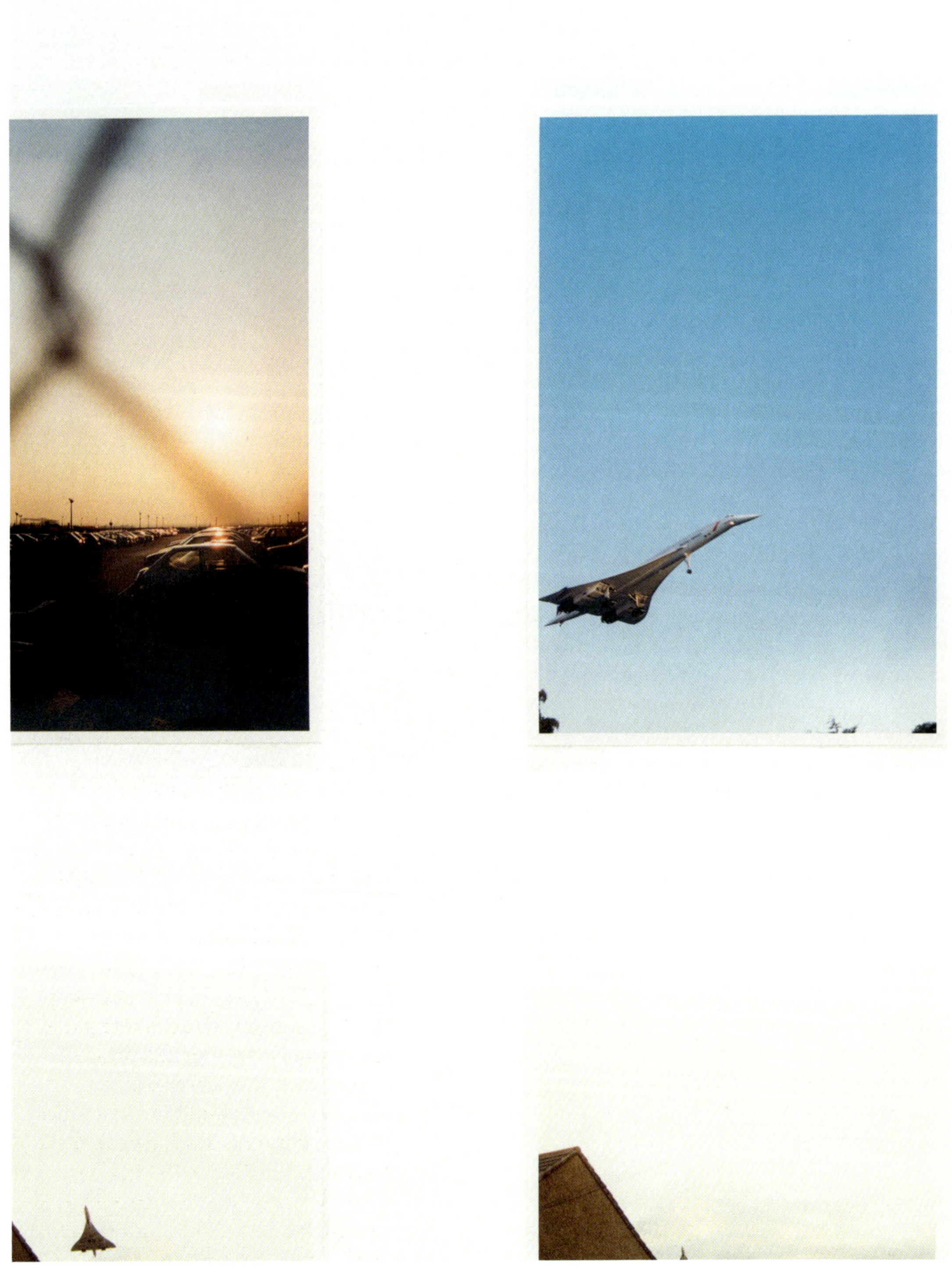

Wolfgang Tillmans, *Concorde Grid*, 1997, 159.5 × 444.5 cm, 56 chromogenic prints on paper.

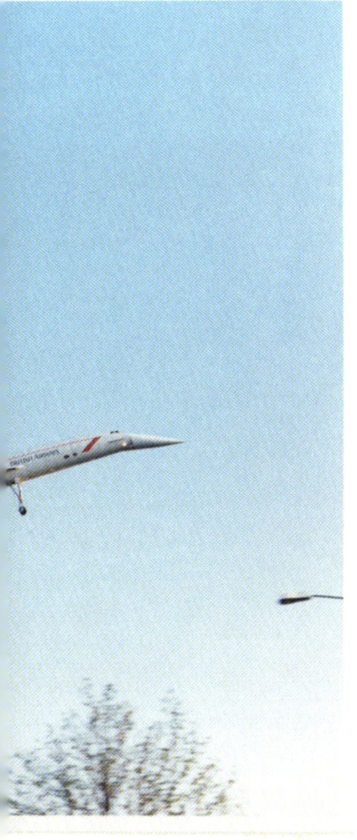

Concorde

Concorde is perhaps the last example of a techno-utopian invention from the 1960s still to be operating and fully functioning today. Its futuristic shape, speed and ear-numbing thunder grabs people's imaginations today as much as it did when it first took off in 1969. This environmental nightmare was conceived in 1962 when technology and progress was the answer to everything and the sky was no longer a limit. It flies at more than double the speed of sound, at a maximum of 2,333 km/h at an altitude of 16,000 m. Its empty weight is 85,900 kg and it uses up to 94,750 kg of fuel for a capacity of 100 passengers. Due to rising fuel prices and environmental pressures, supersonic travel never really became a reality. Only 14 Concordes, excluding prototypes, have ever been built and were flying between Paris, New York and London in just three and a half hours. For the chosen few, flying Concorde was a glamorous but cramped and slightly boring routine, while to watch it in the air, landing and taking off is a strange and free spectacle, a super-modern anachronism and an image of the desire to overcome time and distance through technology.

Wolfgang Tillmans, 1997

1

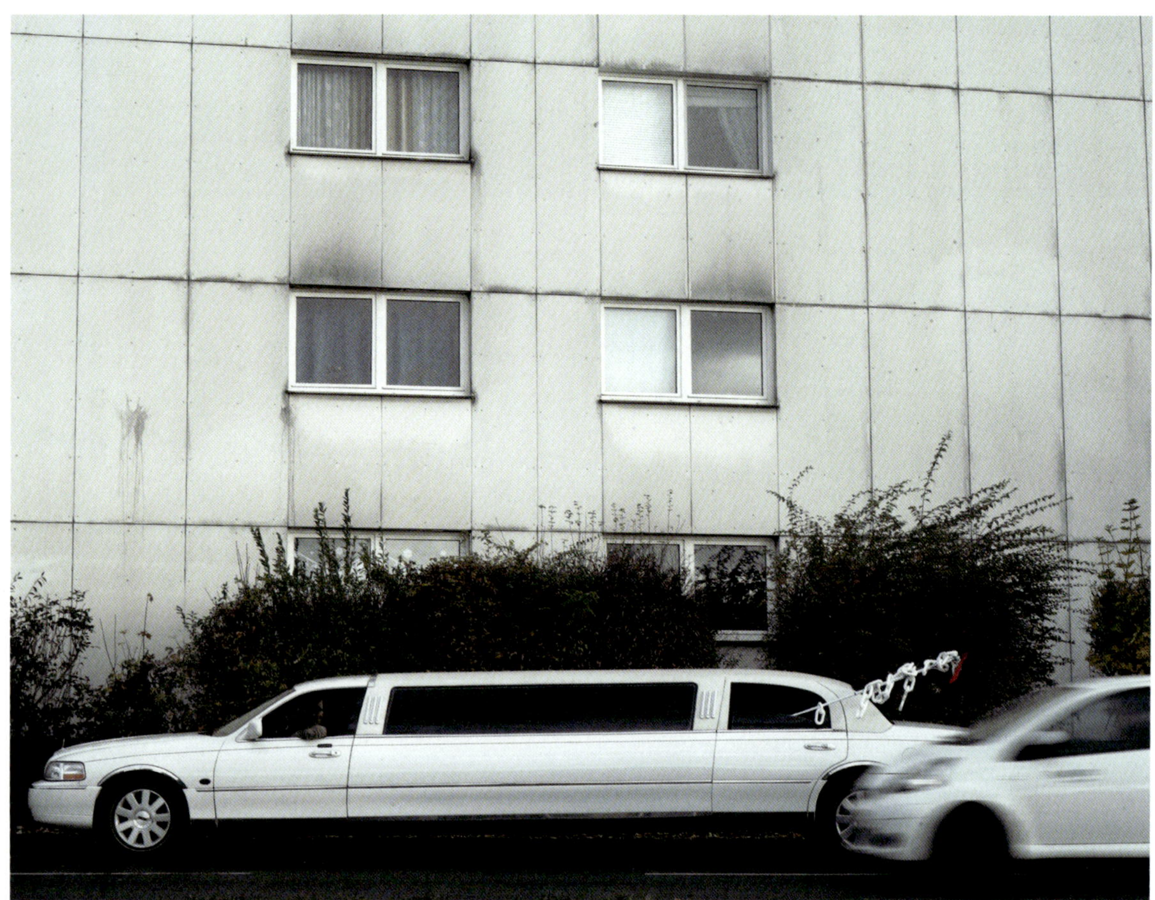

2

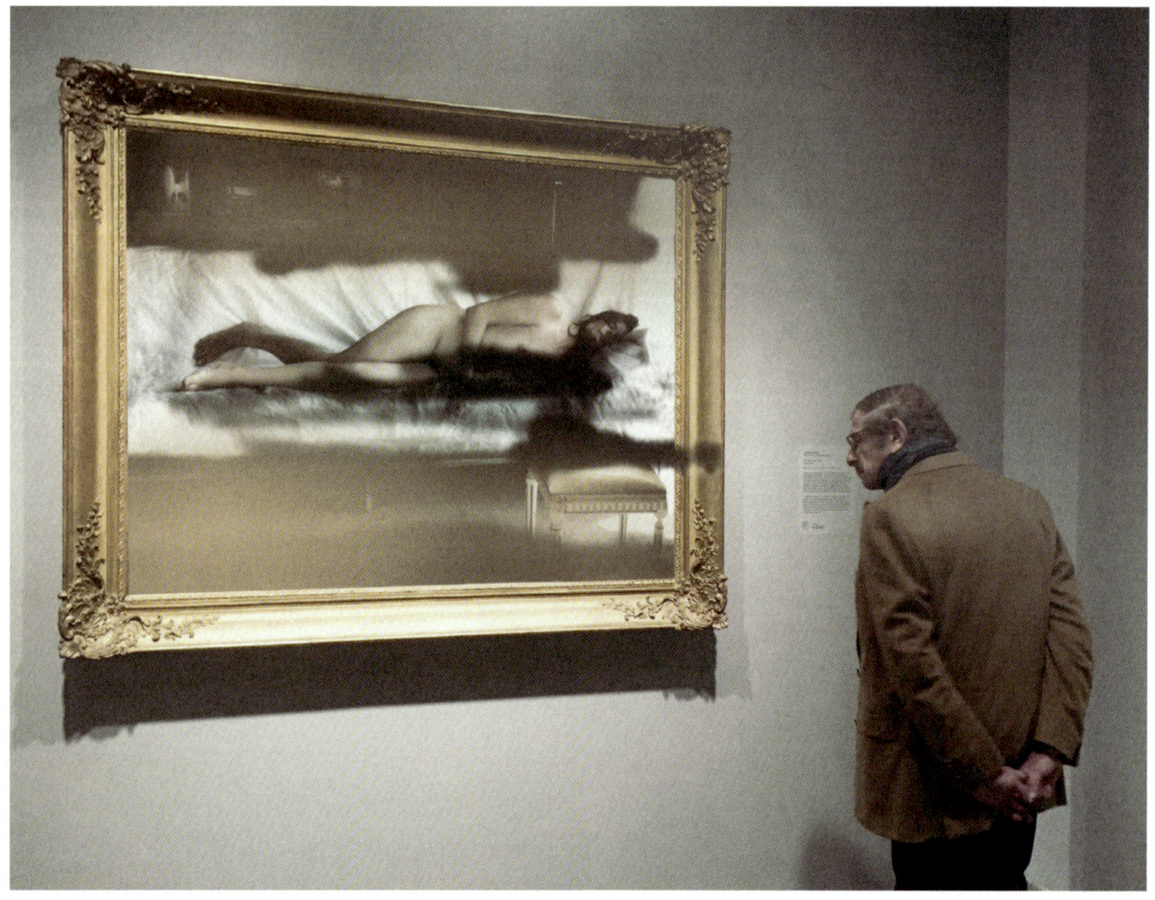

3

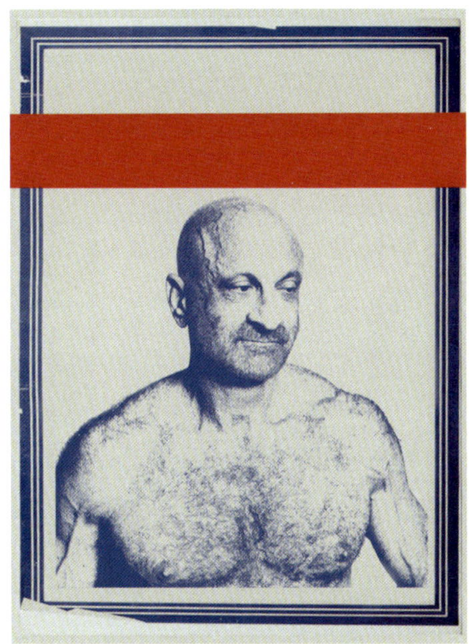

4

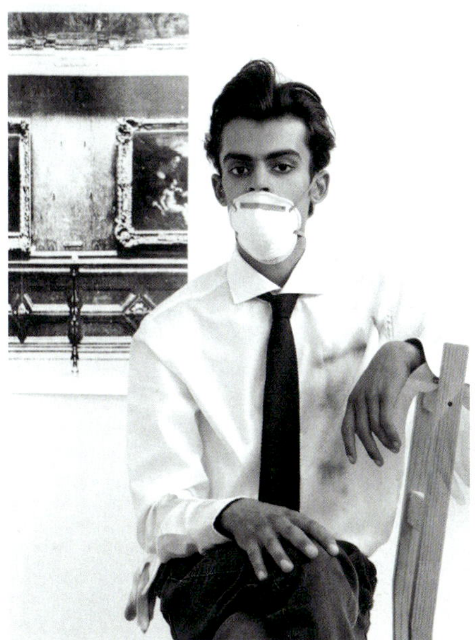

5

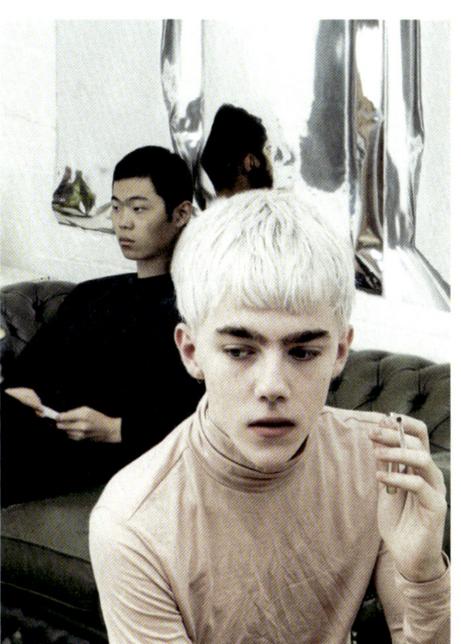

6

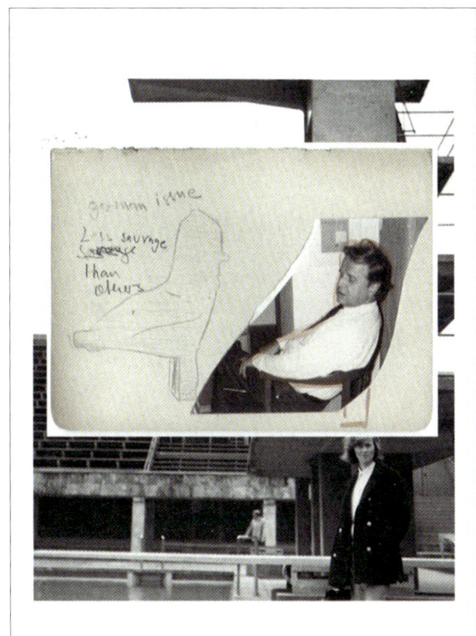

7

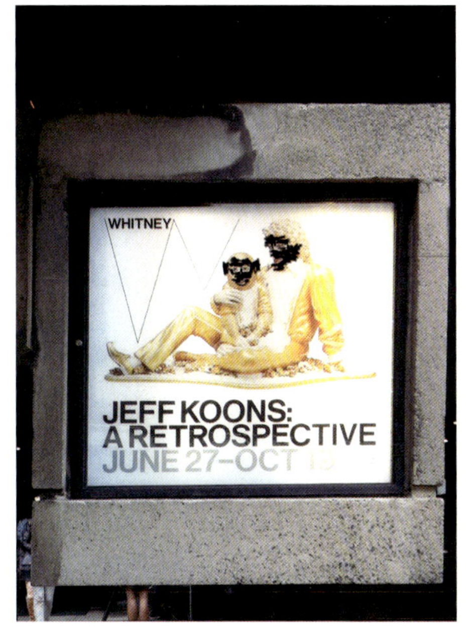

8

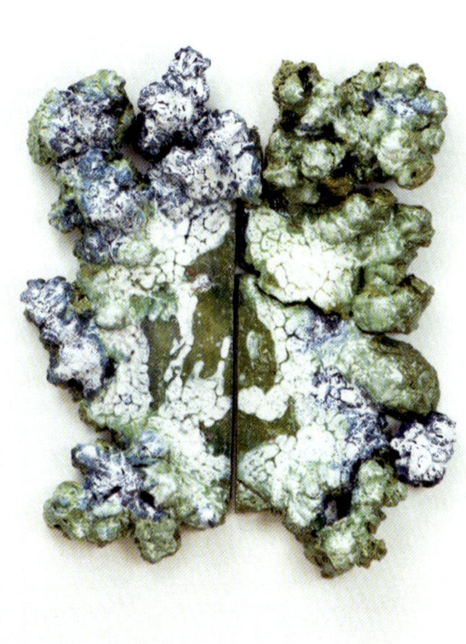

9

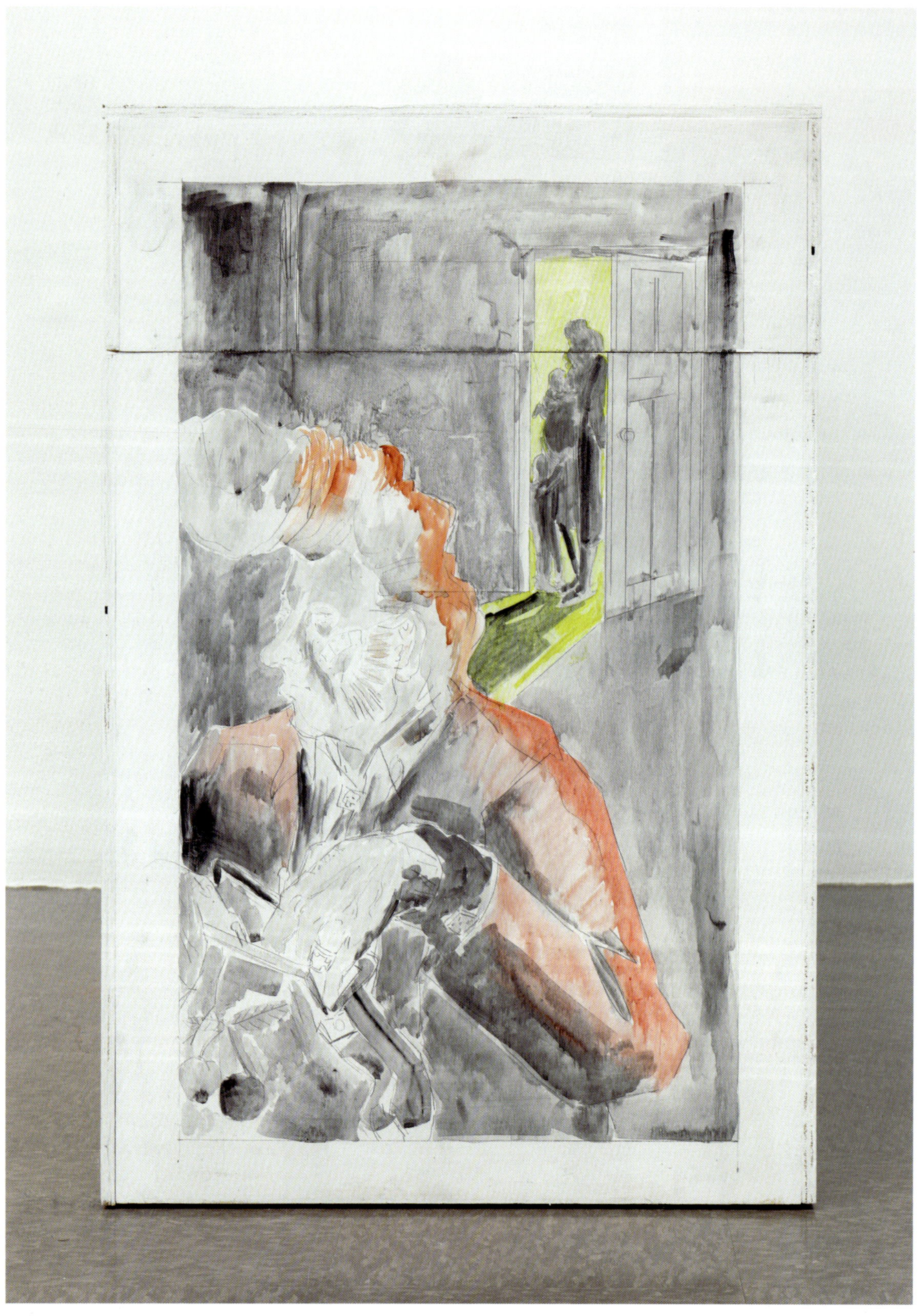

Peter Wächtler, *Teddy Boy 3: 'And I Said, Go Back to Bed'; A Winter's Day; Running through the Streets with the Boys, Enjoying Life*, 2016, 87.6 × 114.3 × 57.2 cm, watercolour and pencil on plywood box.

Peter Wächtler, *Teddy Boy 1: At the Doctor; Meeting The Pimps; Feeling Sick*, 2016, 87.6 × 114.3 × 57.2 cm, watercolour and pencil on plywood box.

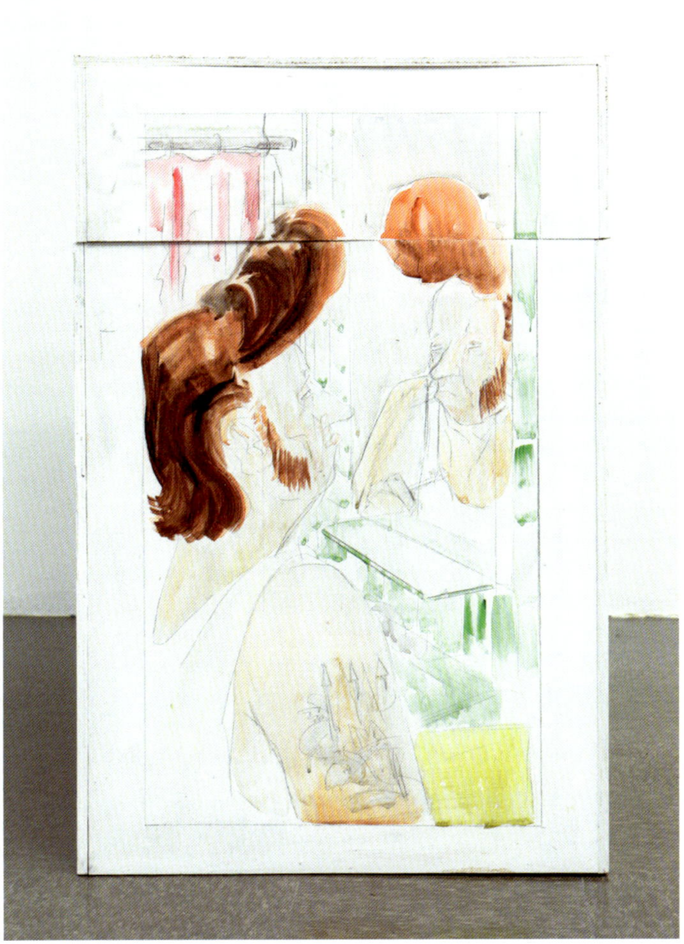

This Sporting Life

Exercising a wide range of techniques and media (ceramics, hand-drawn animations, aquarelles, bronzes, photography and, not least, short stories and occasional readings of them), Peter Wächtler's work is populated by a rowdy multitude of particular characters. They appear in different forms of sequential scenes and narrative formats. And though only a smaller part of Wächtler's work is animated in the true technical sense of the word, there's quite an amount of staged movement in his imagery. Movement is most certainly not the artist's prime or exclusive subject, but of recent works it is quite safe to say that if someone or something is not on the move, it must be out of plain refusal, or by higher arrest.

Almost everyone seems on and about, either involuntarily blown forward or dragging themselves just a couple of centimetres further. It's a busy world where movie trailers are rendered roundabout as bas-reliefs on ceramic pots, echoing classical Greek vases; there are long-distance runners and Teddy boys doing a jig; there are seagulls burdened under the weight of rocks they haul along. Most of these scenes – whether visual or written – are characterised by the particular conduct of their principal actors, and conduct brings up a question of intention and maybe even destination. Many of the actors seem to be hurdling and trudging towards nirvana or a something like a simpler and better life, and often they go in circles, encompassing a communal bankruptcy they attempted to escape (and conspiring sometimes appears as a variety of encompassing). Some others seem to be chased but then often tailgated by their own curiosity (the *Tom & Jerry* revolution), while others yet, more arrogant or opinionated, are hurriedly pushing and driving us forward, muttering something like 'Sorry to keep you waiting'. Sorry, as the sound of a whip. And though arrogant as the common *sorry* may sound, it cannot suppress the deeper connection to its moral and pious ancestor: the original Apology, as a defence of a cause or of one's beliefs and actions. In the end, most of the voices in Wächtler's work, even if they take on the guise of tearjerkers and blockbuster classics, are those of a modern moral subject. And with a loaded term like that, how to keep it frail yet hard enough, neither sentimental nor ironic? Where do you locate the aesthetics and power of melodrama in a situation like Paul Simon singing *The Sound of Silence* at Ground Zero on the tenth-year commemoration of 9/11?

For many of these individual creatures the question is not which way the journey is heading, but how to move about. And what is the morality in movement? Many centuries ago, *progress* merely indicated a general *moving forward* and not necessarily one heading towards a state of improvement. It could perfectly well be applied to the advancing state of a ruin or the plain downfall of a person. Then, by the end of the seventeenth century, the term became altogether obsolete in Britain, only to reappear in America in the early nineteenth century. It's tempting to speculate that *progress* acquired its exclusive value of improvement in the general vocabulary after a short colonial detour. It is tempting in the light of a European, Protestant fantasy about American settlers and their faith in the search for a better and simpler life.

Peter Wächtler's depictions of *progress* and his observations of pathetic downfall acknowledge our very ability to laugh at weakness, but all the same seem to wish or

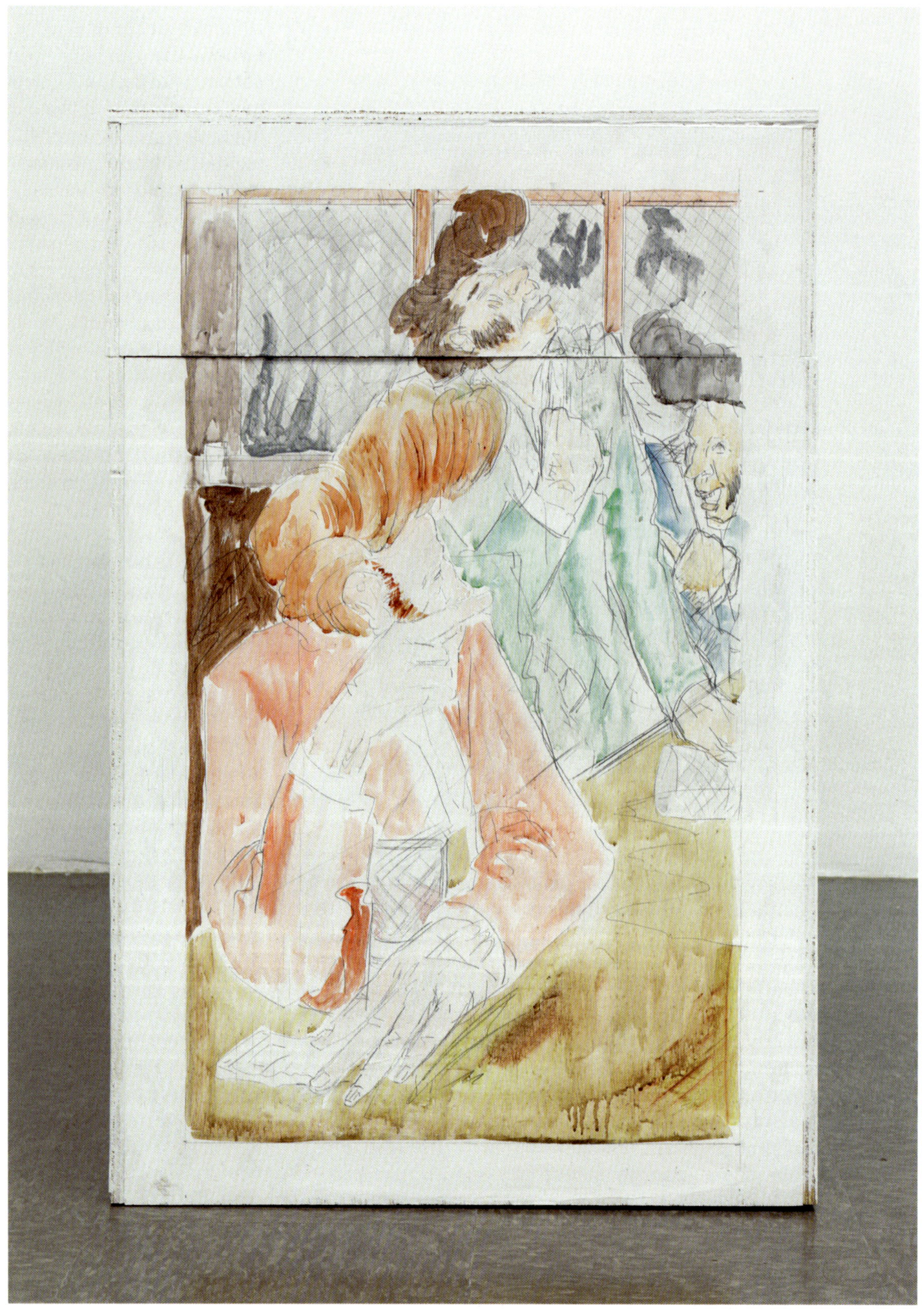

Peter Wächtler, *Teddy Boy 2: Goofing Around with Friends; Getting Betty back at the Headquarters of The Pimps; 'I Cannot Do It'*, 2016, 87.6 × 114.3 × 57.2 cm, watercolour and pencil on plywood box.

Peter Wächtler, *Teddy Boy 2: Goofing Around with Friends; Getting Betty back at the Headquarters of The Pimps; 'I Cannot Do It'*, 2016, 87.6 × 114.3 × 57.2 cm, watercolour and pencil on plywood box.

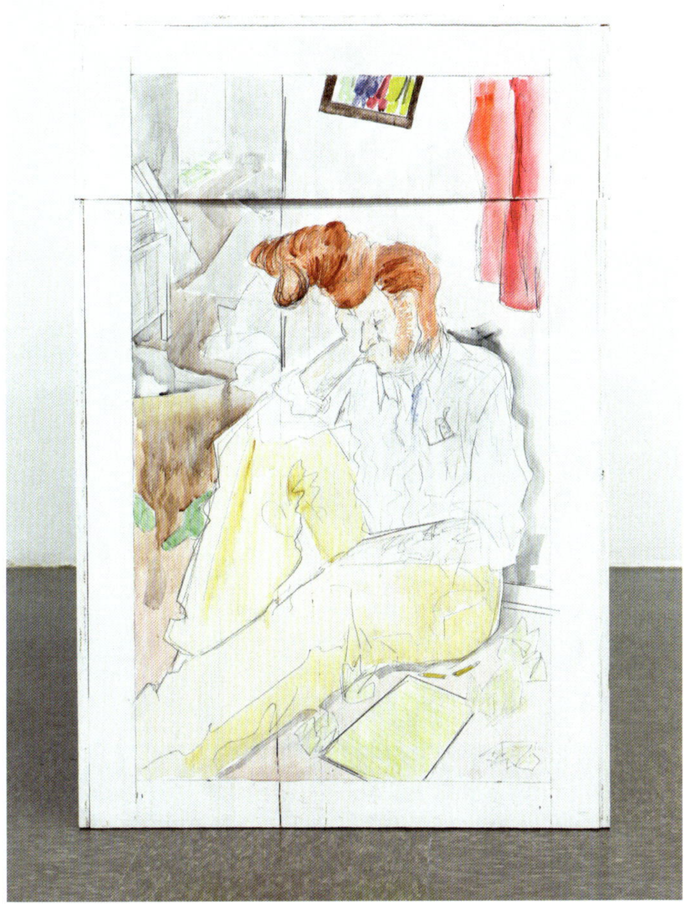

phrase by similarly breaking down the sentences and words. This variety of techniques lead to Baroque and vortical dynamics in some of his aquarelles, clean lines swift like the wind in others or stuttering staccato (now faster, but slower!) in some of the animations. And occasionally he's able to capture the effect of slow-motion in a still image, as with the herd of chasing bloodhounds, entangled in a gigantic flesh-eating plant, or the sequential aquarelles of drying laundry whose bulging embodies the different drifts of wind in the landscape.

The truly immobile works, then, often function as a complementary momentum to the more agile and sprightly pieces. The only thing standing, fair and tall like a flaunting sphinx, is the mascot that keeps the group together; like a talisman; a baseball cap, a leather feather. Many of Peter Wächtler's individuals are uncoordinated at playing in league but they've got spirit and play forward, knowing that this sporting life will be the death of them.

Michaël Van den Abeele, 2016

hope for this to be grounded within some form of morality. But then to turn such observation into a rare vintage, cynicism and irony have to be carefully averted.

Here's a storyteller who experimentally tries out a primary law of a narrative craft: that there's never a *plot* at the beginning. You just start to write; embrace your heroes and see what the effect of guilt does to them – then you carry on.

Notwithstanding the various artisan techniques Wächtler employs, he handsomely averts the craftsmanship's qualitative tradition, which is too post-rationalised for his purpose. It's mainly the *making it himself* and the close-contact concentration that goes with it that offers refuge. Refuge, in the way amateur-carpentry for example can offer a temporary peace treaty between a misanthrope and the rest of the world.

But the key technical question to all these dimensions of progression is how to visualise them. Fully embracing the exaggerated gestures of the theatrical, Peter Wächtler has skilled himself over the last couple of years in a particular captivation of action and locomotion that coincides and addresses the specific needs of the movement and conduct that characterises each of the sceneries.

Breaking down the movement is an important step in animating figures – evidently in the process of the hand-drawn animations (the limbs; the nodding head; the sagging shoulders) but Wächtler seems to have transferred this knowledge equally to the other media he uses. Another approach to this could be inspired by those pop songs or rock operas in which a (too) long speech is forced and bent into a melodious

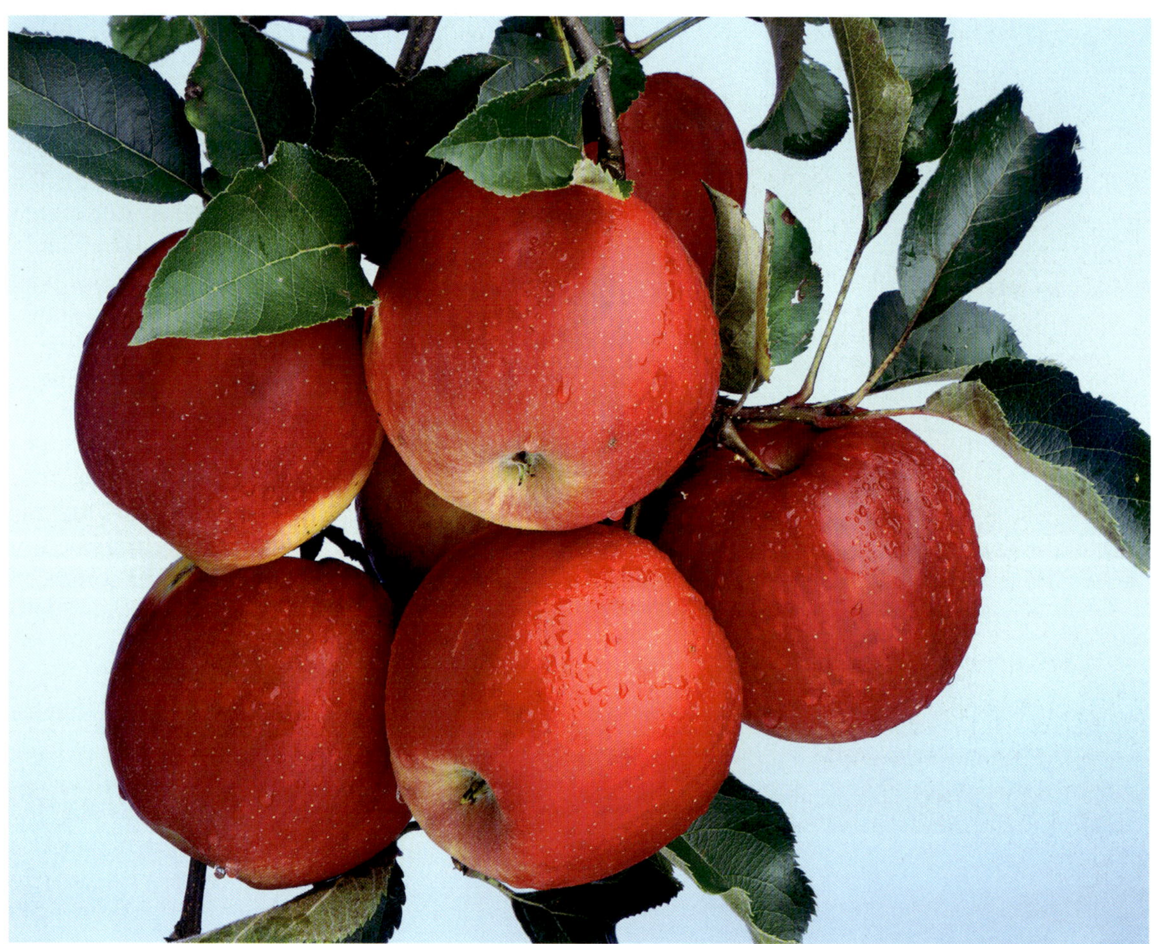

Christopher Williams, *Bergische Bauernscheune, Junkersholz / Leichlingen / September 29, 2009*, 2010, 50.8 × 61 cm (paper), 83.5 × 94.1 cm (framed), archival pigment print.

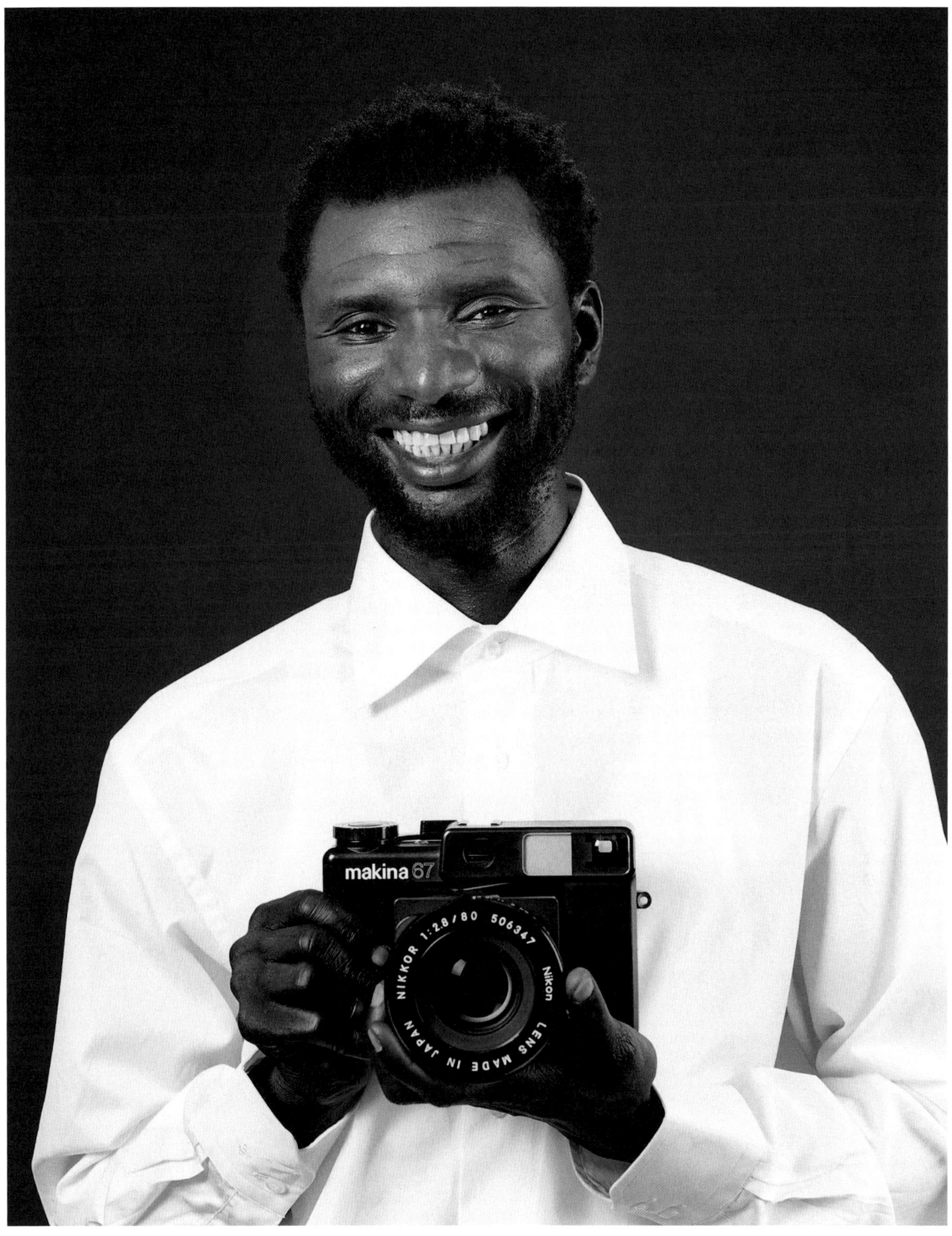

Christopher Williams, *Mustafa Kinte (Gambia) / Camera: Makina 67 506347 / Plaubel Feinmechanik und Optik GmbH / Borsigallee 37 / 60388 Frankfurt am Main, Germany / Shirt: Van Laack Shirt Kent 64 / 41061 Mönchengladbach, Germany / Dirk Schaper Studio, Berlin / July 20, 2007*, 2008, 50.8 × 40.6 cm (paper), 86.2 × 74.7 cm (framed), selenium toned gelatin silver print.

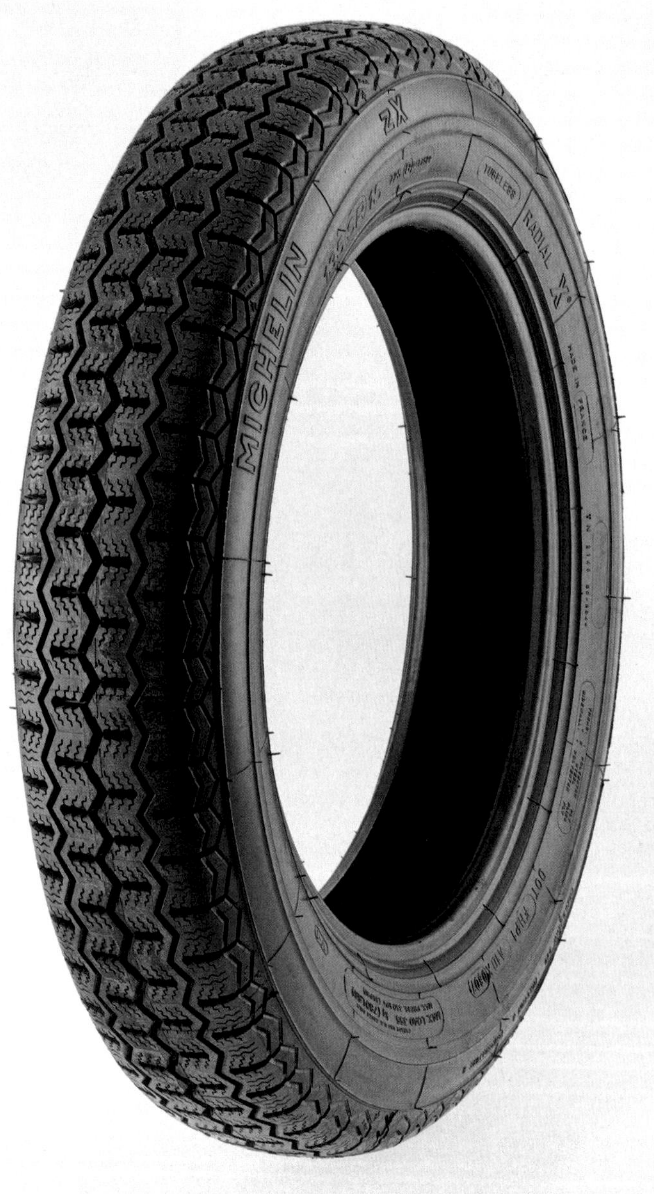

Christopher Williams, *Clockwise from Manufacturer Name (Outer Ring) / Michelin / X M+S 89 / Clockwise from Tire Size (Inner Ring) / 135 R 15 / 72 Q E2 0281541 / M+S / Tubeless / Radial X / TF 852 20-2044 / Tread: 1 Polyester Ply / + 2 Steel Plies / Sidewall: 1 Polyester Ply / Canada and U.S. Codes Only / Max Load 355 Kg (780 Lbs) / Max Press. 350 kPa (51 PSI) / V-1 / Photography by the Douglas M. Parker Studio, Glendale, California / January 03 – January 04, 2008,* 2008, 61 × 50.8 cm (paper), 94.7 × 83.4 cm (framed), selenium toned gelatin silver print.

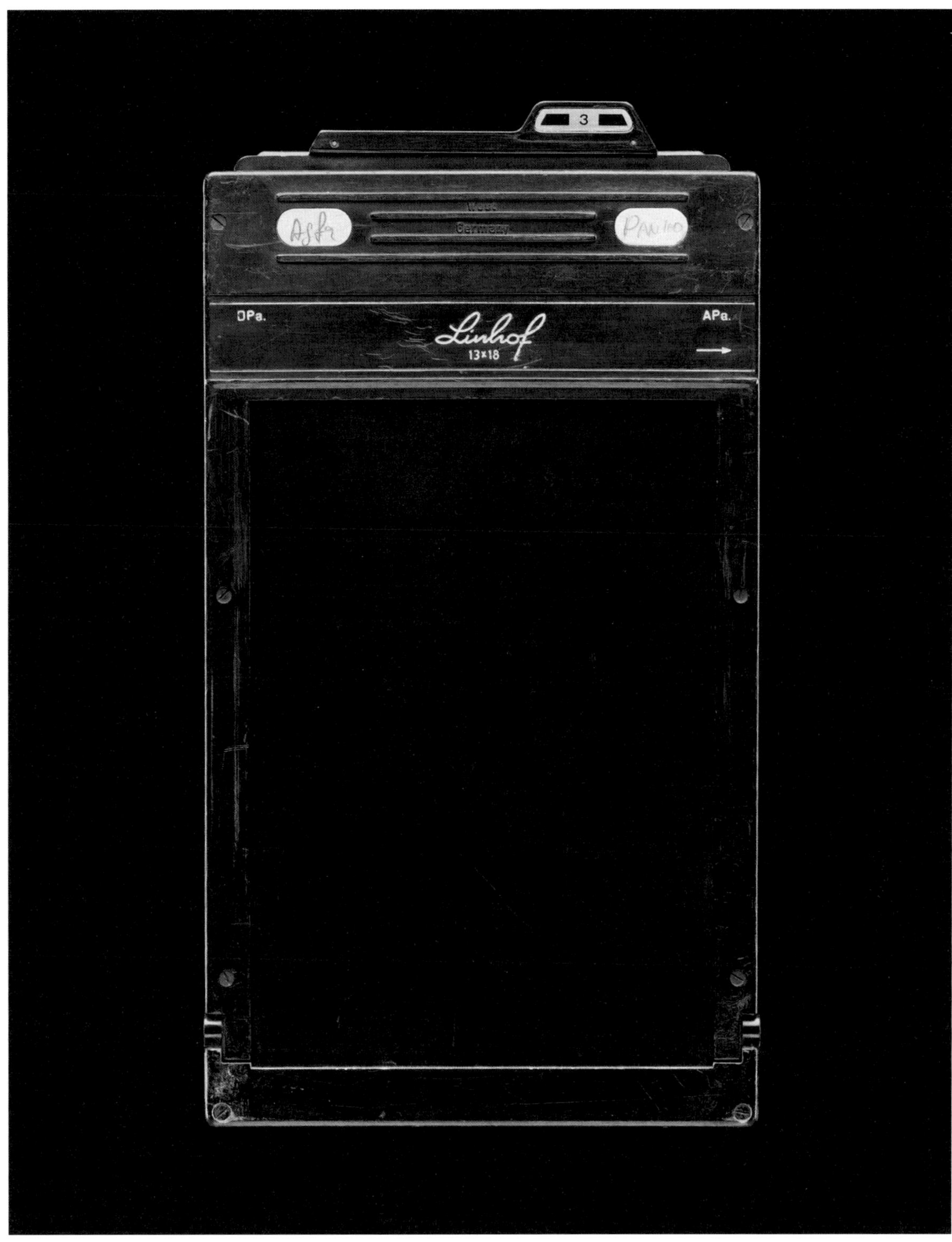

Christopher Williams, *Linhof 13x18 DPa. APa. / Doppelkassette/Double Plate and Cutflm Holder/ Châssis Double/Chasis Double / – YZDD – / Manufactured by Linhof, Nikolaus Karpf K.G. / Präzisions-Kamera-Werke, München 25, West-Germany / Studio Rhein Verlag, Düsseldorf / January 15, 2016*, 2016, 76.2 × 61 cm (paper), 112.6 × 95.6 cm (framed), selenium toned gelatin silver print.

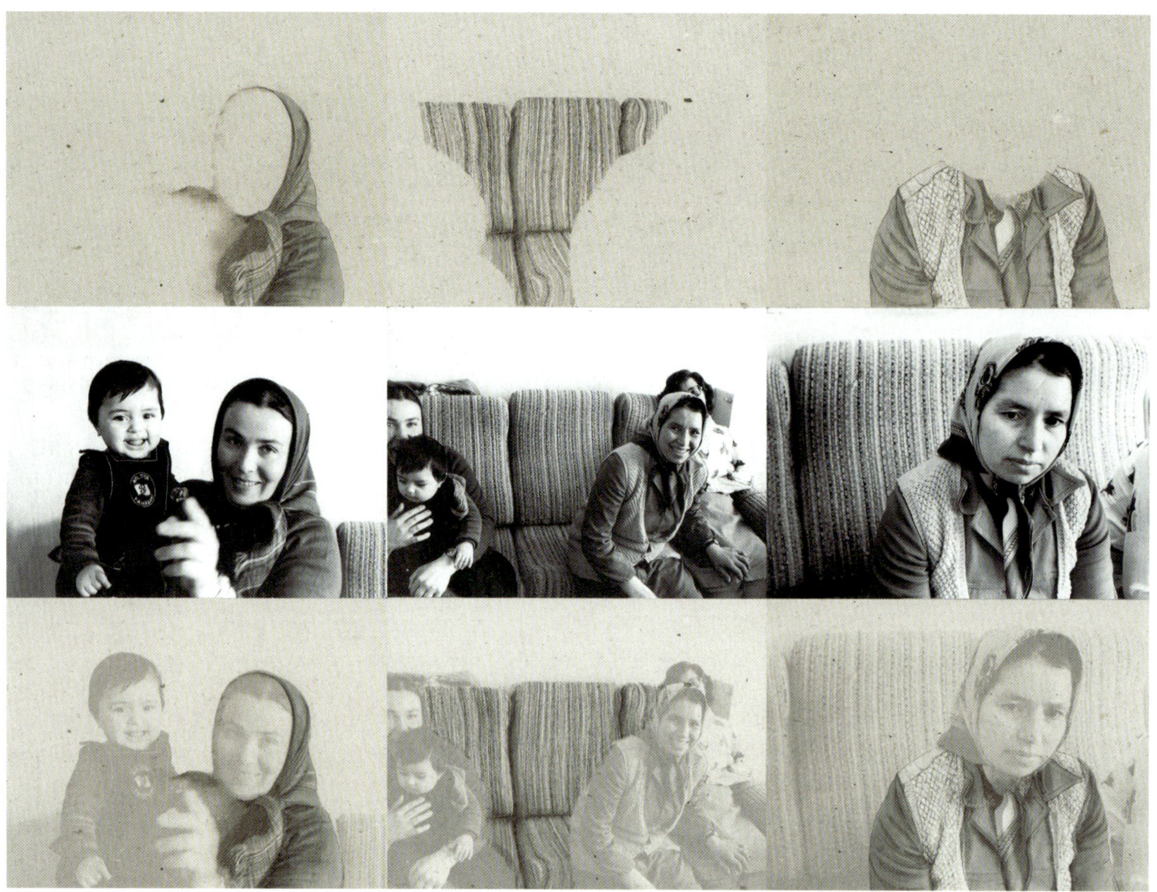

EXILE IS
A HARD JOB

Nil Yalter, *Turkish Immigrants #5. Two Women and Child*, 1977–, dimensions variable, poster.

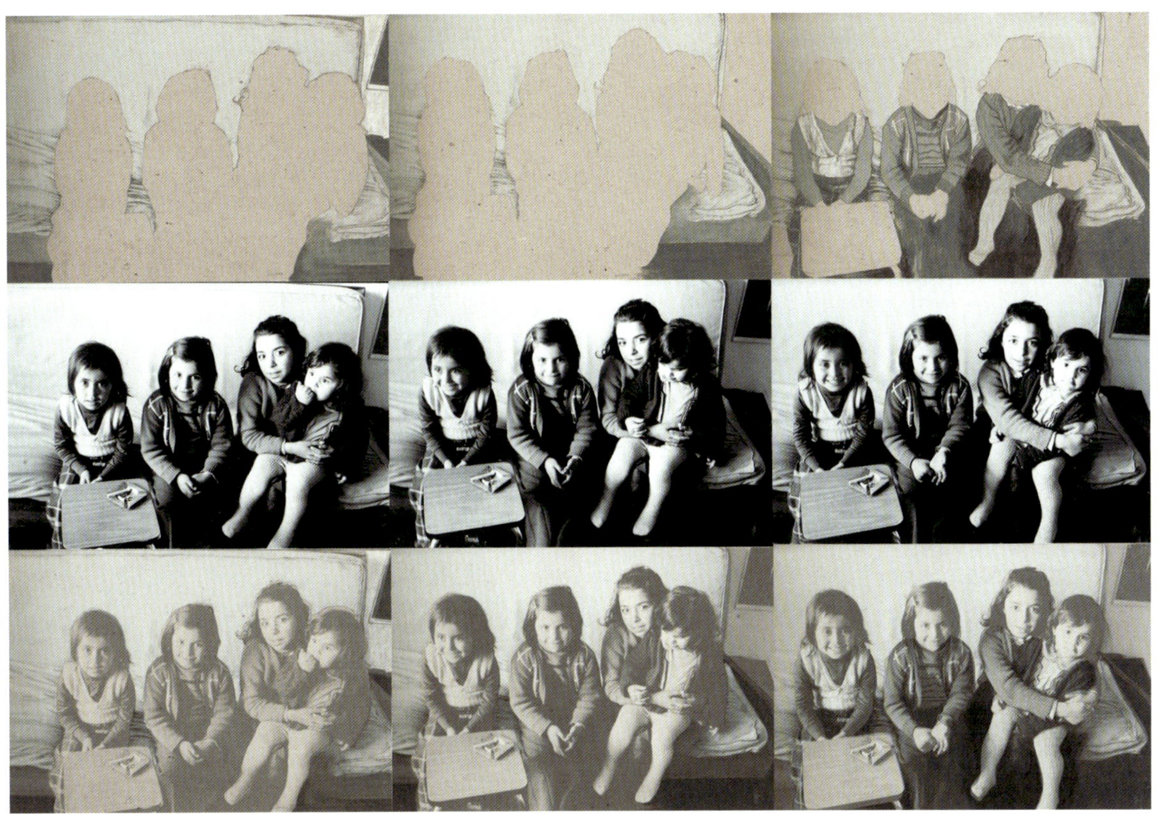

Nil Yalter, *Turkish Immigrants #2. Three Girls*, 1977–, dimensions variable, poster.

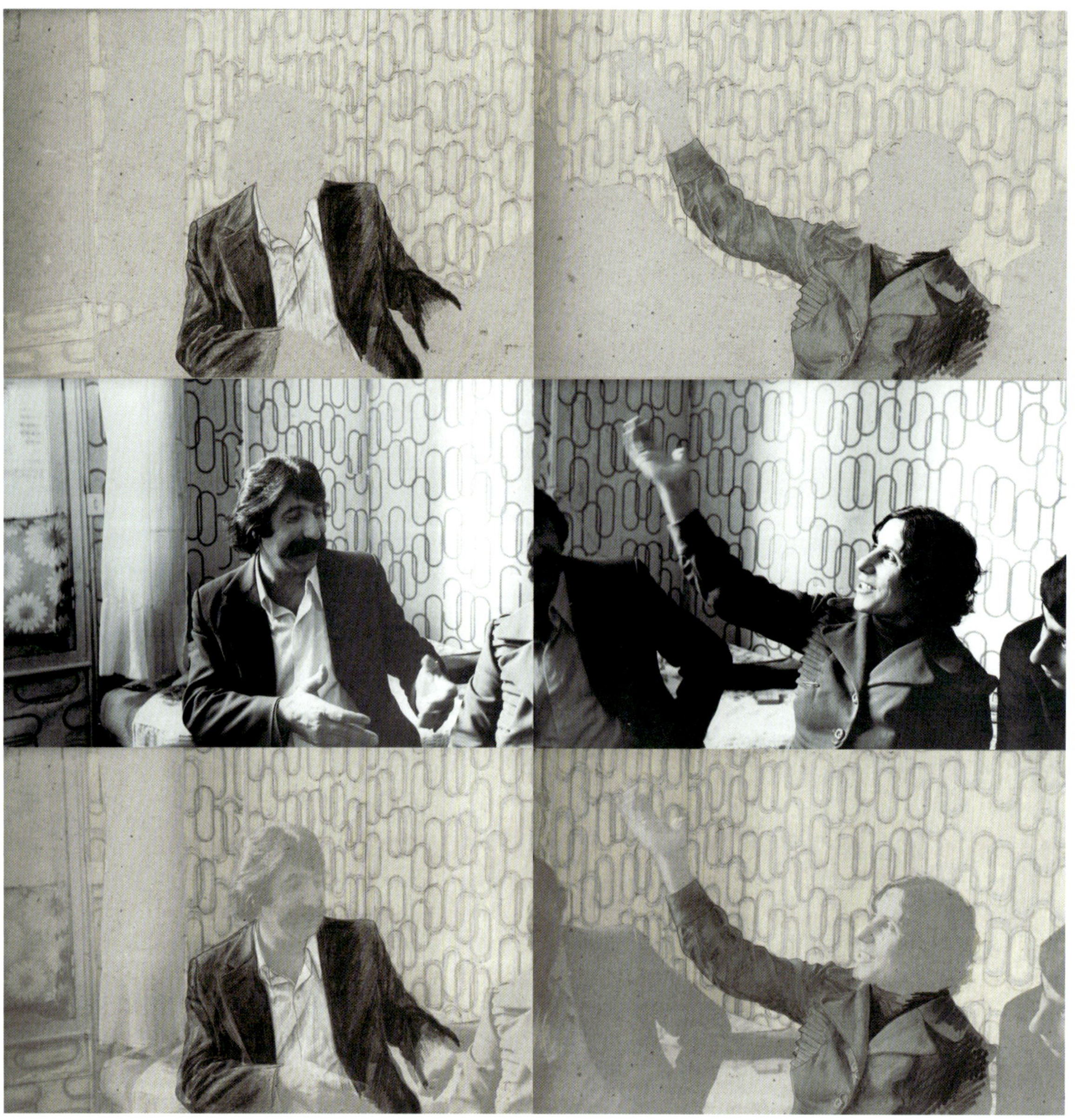

Nil Yalter, *Turkish Immigrants #1. Women and Man*, 1977–, dimensions variable, poster.

Nil Yalter

Franco-Turkish artist Nil Yalter uses social ethnology as a method for understanding human communities, their connection to the earth, to the cosmos, to objects, rituals, cultural practices and spiritual beliefs. *Topak Ev* (1973), a recreated nomad's tent, encourages the idea of meeting inhabitants of shanty towns, those accumulations of precarious shelters constructed by exiles and migrants, among others. Yalter seeks to understand how the 'migrant male and female workers, whom Europe needs but exploits, holds in contempt and shuts out as it pleases', deal with their situation. To this end, she is interested in the way in which members of a given population apprehend their everyday world, and the way in which they might change it through improved awareness and direct action.

The exhibit features videos, photographs, drawings, texts and objects, examining the frontiers between reality and fiction, myths or beliefs and convictions. Photographs of populations living in shanty towns or urban 'sink estates' are transposed as drawings. The photographs convey the state of the place whereas the drawings, through an obliteration of the faces and a creation of proximity filtered through the artist's imagination, immerse the viewer in the intimate experience of this exile – a tugging between the memory of origins and the integration into the culture of a new society. Equally, there is a constant oscillation between the filmed scenes – which, presented

with political statements, highlight the interiors and the body postures – and the spaces revealing the desires, wishes and explanations of the myths that shape the understanding of the exiles' world. The testimonies combine descriptions of these people's living conditions, their job reality, their employment situation, and the myths structuring their community loyalties and their understanding of the world, thus providing a framework for understanding. In this way, *Ris-Orangis* (formerly entitled *L'Immigration et la ville nouvelle*, 1979) and *C'est un dur métier que l'exil* (1983) bring together testimonies and images that overlay the exterior context onto the intimate environment. In order to communicate an idea of this entrenchment, Yalter films her protagonists in their apartments, surrounded by their familiar objects, going about their daily tasks, expressing themselves in their native languages. Yalter translates and then shows images of the exterior environment, the apartment blocks, at the same time as showing bodies and intimate spaces, merging the realities to dovetail, so to speak, the different ways of understanding the world they are given. This way of filming reflects the dichotomies between the country of origin and the receiving country, between the hopes and the hard, everyday struggle, between the protected family environment and the life on the estate in the suburbs, seen through the prism of myths and dreams preoccupying these immigrants.

Yalter has renewed her engagement with migrant populations, since the early 2010s, by producing posters that combine old drawings and photographs from the 1970s with the title of her second solo show, 'C'est un dur métier que l'exil / Exile Is a Hard Job', held at the Musée d'Art moderne de la Ville de Paris, in 1983. The title, borrowed from the Turkish poet Nâzım Hikmet (1902–1963), accompany testimonies from illegal immigrants working in the clothing industry around Paris's Rue du Faubourg-Saint-Denis, and whose destitution and misery are a far cry from their initial fascination with the West. The first fly-posting of the series *C'est un dur métier que l'exil / Exile Is a Hard Job* took place in Valencia in 2012, followed by Mumbai in 2013, Vienna in 2014, Metz in 2016 and lastly in Istanbul in 2016. These posters, with the slogan written across it in explosive red in the language of the respective country and those of its local immigrants, denounce the accusations made against migrants for taking advantage of the social welfare system, in Europe as elsewhere in the world. Whether protected or ripped and torn to pieces, these large display works provoke strong reactions.

FD

Manuel J. Borja-Villel

is director of the Museo Nacional Centro de Arte Reina Sofía in Madrid. He received his undergraduate degree in art history from University of Valencia (1980) and he has a doctorate from the City University of New York (1989). He has written about museums, institutions, and the relationship between art and politics, as well as modern and contemporary art and individual artists, including Antoni Tàpies, Hans Haacke, Nancy Spero, Lygia Clark and Marcel Broodthaers. As director of Barcelona's Fundació Antoni Tàpies, from its opening in 1990 until 1998, he organised exhibitions such as 'The Limits of the Museum' and 'The City of the People'. From 1998 until 2008 he directed the Museu d'Art Contemporani de Barcelona, where he curated 'Antagonisms: Art and Politics', 'Force Fields: Phases of the Kinetic', 'Art and Utopia: Limited Action', 'Theatre without Theatre' and 'Be-Bomb: The Transatlantic War of Images and All that Jazz, 1946–1956'. In his current position since 2008, he has programmed exhibitions such as 'Principio Potosí', 'Mixed Use, Manhattan', 'Atlas', 'The Movement of Workers Photography', 'Biographical Forms' and 'Playgrounds'.

Charles Esche

is a curator and writer. He is director of the Van Abbemuseum, Eindhoven, and co-editorial director of Afterall Journal and Books based at Central Saint Martins, London. In addition to his institutional curating, he has (co-) curated a number of international exhibitions, including 'Le Musée égaré', Toulouse (2016), Jakarta Biennale (2015), São Paulo Biennial, (2014); U3 Triennale, Moderna Galerija, Ljubljana (2011); Riwaq Biennale, Ramallah (2007 and 2009); Istanbul Biennale with Vasif Kortun (2005); Gwangju Biennale (2002). He teaches at Central Saint Martins, London, and the Jan van Eyck Academie, Maastricht. He is on the board of L'Internationale confederation and chair of Casco, Utrecht.

Dirk Snauwaert

is the founding and artistic director of WIELS in Brussels. He was formerly joint artistic director of the Institut d'Art Contemporain in Villeurbanne, where he programmed exhibitions and developed the Frac Rhône-Alpes collection. From 1996 to 2001 he was director of the Kunstverein München. From 1989 to 1995 he was curator of contemporary art at the Exhibitions Association of the Palace for Fine Arts in Brussels (currently BOZAR). He lectures and publishes regularly on art and visual culture. At WIELS he has curated the one-person exhibitions of Anne-Mie van Kerckhoven, Luc Tuymans, Francis Alÿs, David Claerbout, Rosemarie Trockel, Jeremy Deller, Joëlle Tuerlinckx, Walter Swennen, Ana Torfs, Stan Douglas, Edith Dekyndt and Duncan Campbell; and the group exhibitions 'Expats and Clandestines' and 'ReSiDuE' with Agata Jastrząbek. He also curated the Jef Geys Belgian Pavilion at the 53rd Venice Biennale (2009), 'Atopolis', an international group exhibition organised in collaboration with Mons 2015 – European Capital of Culture, and 'Ideolect', a thematic exhibition project for the 2010 Bruges Poetry Festival.

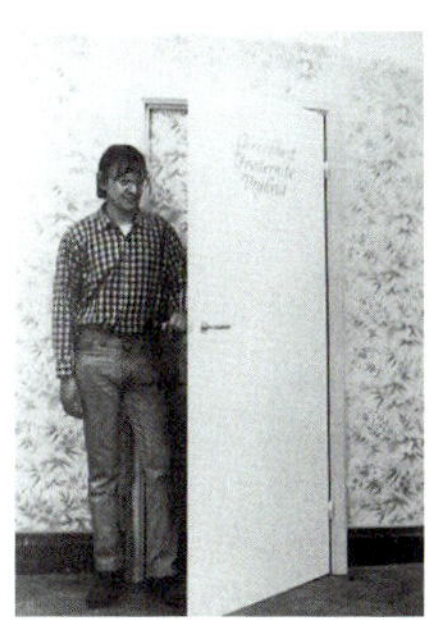

Jef Geys, *Gleichheit, Fraternité, Vrijheid*, 1986, 213.5 × 99 × 11.5 cm, wooden door and frame, paint. © Lieven Herreman

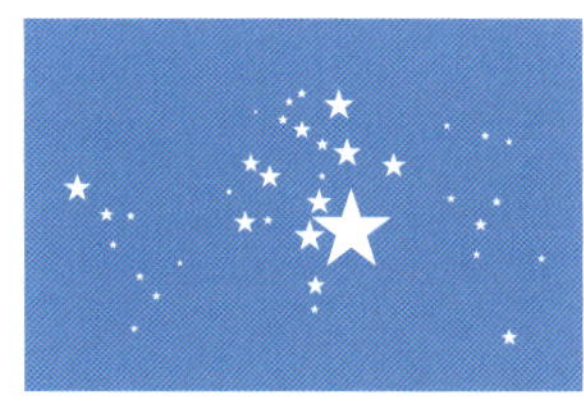

Flag of the Universal Embassy

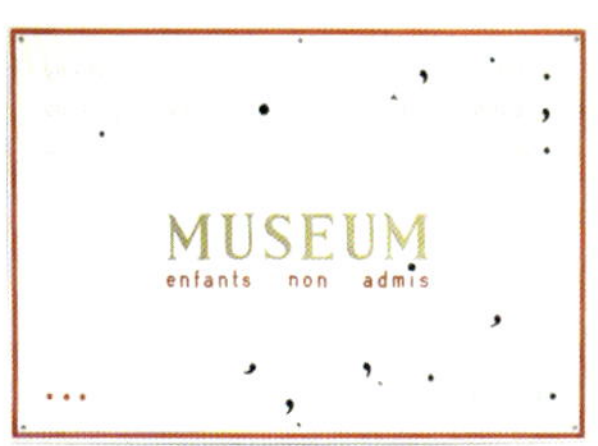

Walter Swennen, *We/They*, 2010, 90 × 70 cm, oil and acrylic on canvas. Collection Gaby and Wilhelm Schürmann, Herzogenrath

Marcel Broodthaers, *Museum enfants non admis*, 1968, 84 × 122 cm, painted vacuum-formed plastic plate © Estate Marcel Broodthaers

---

Anonymous

Le Mur
1968
6'42"
16 mm film transferred to HD video, black and white, sound
Collection Lutz Becker, London

Francis Alÿs

Born 1959 in Antwerp, Belgium. Lives and works in Mexico City, Mexico

1943
2017
(3 ×) 200 × 165 cm
Adhesive vinyl text in Dutch, French and English
Courtesy of the artist

Archives of the Universal Embassy

Universal Embassy was founded in 2000 in Brussels, Belgium, and remained active until 2005

Various documents and objects relating to the activities of the Universal Embassy, 2000–05; screening of Hito Steyerl's *Universal Embassy*, 2004, single channel video, 16:9 DV on DVD, 3'
Collection Etopia Centre for Private Archives, Namur

Younes Baba-Ali

Born 1986 in Oujda, Morocco. Lives and works in Brussels, Belgium, and Casablanca, Morocco

Être et ne pas avoir
2014
5' 54"
HD video 16:9, colour, sound
Courtesy of the artist

Jo Baer

Born 1929 in Seattle, USA. Lives and works in Amsterdam, The Netherlands

Red, White and Blue Gelding Falling to its Right (Double-Cross Britannicus/Tricolor Hibernicus)
1984–86
243.8 × 314.9 cm
Oil on canvas

Tis Ill Pudling in the Cockatrice Den (Là-Bas)
1987
244 × 244 cm
Oil on canvas

Memorial for an Art World Body (Nevermore)
2009
183 × 160 cm
Oil on canvas

All courtesy of the artist and Galerie Barbara Thumm, Berlin

Monika Baer

Born 1964 in Freiburg im Breisgau, Germany. Lives and works in Berlin, Germany

Untitled
2005
47 × 40.5 cm
Ink, ashes, oil on canvas
Collection Bernhard Martin, Berlin

Untitled
2005
50 × 40 cm
Watercolour, ashes, oil on canvas
Private collection

Untitled
2005
70 × 50 cm
Watercolour, ink, ashes, oil on canvas
Collection Heubi-Mishiev, Berlin

10 Euro
2005
50 × 40 cm
Watercolour, ashes, oil on canvas

Untitled
2008
58 × 45 cm
Watercolour, acrylic, oil on canvas, thread

Untitled (Stocking)
2008
50 × 39 cm
Watercolour, acrylic, oil on canvas, thread

Untitled
2008
119 × 86 cm
Watercolour, acrylic, oil on canvas, thread

Untitled
2008
70 × 56.5 cm
Watercolour, acrylic, oil on canvas, thread

Bay View
2009
83.5 × 71 cm
Watercolour, acrylic on canvas, thread

All courtesy of the artist and Galerie Barbara Weiss, Berlin

Sammy Baloji

Born 1978 in Lubumbashi, Democratic Republic of the Congo. Lives and works in Brussels, Belgium, and Lubumbashi, Democratic Republic of the Congo

Untitled
From the series *Mémoire*
2006
60 × 180 cm
Digital print on matt satin paper

Untitled
From the series *Mémoire*
2006
60 × 193.75 cm
Digital print on matt satin paper

Both courtesy of the artist and Galerie Imane Farès, Paris

Guillaume Bijl

Born 1946 in Antwerp, Belgium. Lives and works in Antwerp, Belgium

Sculpture trouvée
1980
200 × 84 × 108 cm
Wood, fabric, nails
Collection Els and Vincent Vlasblom, Hoorn

Project m.b.t. Kunstliquidatie
Project m.b.t. Kunstliquidatie
Project-Pleasure m.b.t. Rubensjaar ()
Project-Pleasure m.b.t. Rubensjaar (1)
Project-Pleasure m.b.t. Cultuurverspreiding
Project-Pleasure m.b.t. Conformistische praat (1)
1977
90 × 70 cm each
Prints on paper
Collection M HKA Antwerp, on loan from the Flemish Community

Dirk Braeckman

Born 1958 in Eeklo, Belgium. Lives and works in Ghent, Belgium

R.R.-D.R.-11
2011
180 × 120 cm
Gelatin silver print
Courtesy of the artist and Zeno X Gallery, Antwerp

Marcel Broodthaers

Born 1924 in Brussels, Belgium.
Died 1976 in Cologne, Germany

*Museum enfants non admis
Museum enfants non admis*
1968
84 × 122 cm each
Painted vacuum-formed
plastic plate
Courtesy Estate Marcel
Broodthaers

Door A
1969
85.2 × 118.5 cm
Painted vacuum-formed
plastic plate
Courtesy Estate Marcel
Broodthaers

*1. David 2. Courbet 3. Ingres
4. Ingres 5. Wiertz*
1971
120 × 86 cm
Painted vacuum-formed
plastic plate
Collection Thieck, Paris

*1. David 2. Courbet 3. Ingres
4. Ingres 5. Wiertz*
1972
119.4 × 83.8 cm
Painted vacuum-formed
plastic plate
Private collection

stanley brouwn

this way brouwn
1962
(3 ×) 24.5 × 32 cm
Felt-tip pen and stamp on paper
Courtesy of the artist and
Konrad Fischer Galerie,
Düsseldorf

this way brouwn
1963
24.5 × 31.5 cm
Felt-tip pen and
stamp on paper
Collection Helen and Raymond
Verbouwens, Uccle

this way brouwn
1963
(4 ×) 22 × 21 cm
Felt-tip pen and
stamp on paper
Collection Bruno van Lierde,
Brussels

this way brouwn
1963
(4 ×) 24.5 × 31.9 cm
Felt-tip pen and stamp on paper
Collection Frac Picardie,
Amiens

steps of pedestrians on paper
1963
(2 ×) 24 × 32 cm
Shoeprints on paper
Collection Moraes-Barbosa,
São Paulo

this way brouwn
1964
24.5 × 32 cm
Felt-tip pen and stamp
on paper
Collection Frac Nord-
Pas de Calais, Dunkirk

this way brouwn
1964
32.9 × 25.5 cm
Felt-tip pen and stamp
on paper
Collection Van Abbemuseum,
Eindhoven

this way brouwn
1964
24.5 × 32 cm
Felt-tip pen and stamp
on paper
Collection Eric Decelle,
Brussels

Daniel Dewar & Grégory Gicquel

Born 1976 in the Forest of
Dean, United Kingdom. Lives
and works in Brussels, Belgium
& Born 1975 in Saint Brieuc,
France. Lives and works in Paris,
France

Stoneware Vessel
2014
135 × 40 × 68 cm
High-fired stoneware
Courtesy of Jan Kaps, Cologne

*Stoneware Mural with Sink and
Soapdish*
2016
240 × 105 × 52 cm
High-fired stoneware mounted
on aluminium
Courtesy of Galerie
Loevenbruck, Paris

*Stoneware Mural with Two
Sinks and Two Soapdishes*
2016
240 × 210 × 52 cm
High-fired stoneware mounted
on aluminium
Courtesy of Galerie
Loevenbruck, Paris

Stoneware Mural with Carp
2017
224 × 784 × 3 cm
High-fired stoneware mounted
on aluminium
Courtesy of the artists

Marlene Dumas

Born 1953 in Cape Town, South
Africa. Lives and works in
Amsterdam, The Netherlands

Great Men
2014–
44 × 35 cm each
Ink, pencil and metallic acrylic
on paper
Courtesy of the artist

The Widow
2013
150 × 140 cm
Oil on canvas
Defares Collection,
Amsterdam

The Widow
2013
60 × 80 cm
Oil on canvas
Defares Collection, Amsterdam

Jimmie Durham

Born 1940 in Washington, AR,
USA. Lives and works in Naples,
Italy, and Berlin, Germany

*In the Air, Long Before
Archeology*
2008
230 × 400 × 80 cm
Scaffold, wood, bone, plastic
elements, chinaware, doll
Courtesy of the artist and
Galerie Barbara Wien, Berlin

In Europe
1994–2011
Variable dimensions
Slide projection of digitized
photographs
Courtesy of the artist

Jana Euler

Born 1982 in Friedberg, Germany.
Lives and works in Brussels,
Belgium, and Frankfurt-am-Main,
Germany

„ "
2016
210 × 210 cm
Acrylic on canvas
Defares Collection, Amsterdam

Untitled
2017
60 × 50 cm
Oil on canvas

Untitled
2017
70 × 60 cm
Oil on canvas

Untitled
2017
70 × 50 cm
Oil on canvas

Untitled
2017
65 × 50 cm
Oil on canvas
All courtesy of the artist and
dépendance, Brussels

Olivier Foulon

Born 1976 in Brussels, Belgium.
Lives and works in Berlin, Germany

Stehimbiss #1–9
2012
100 × 80 cm each
Xerox copies on canvas
Courtesy of the artist and
dépendance, Brussels

Michel François

Born 1956 in Sint-Truiden, Belgium.
Lives and works in Brussels, Belgium

Afrique
1988
63 × 86 × 74 cm
Wooden table, world map,
black paint
Collection Christine Duchiron
Brachot, Lot

*Pièces à conviction (Sandales
vache)*
2008
27 × 11 × 1 cm
Rubber, sandals
Courtesy of the artist and
Xavier Hufkens, Brussels

Fac-similé (Sandales vache)
2008
21 × 14.5 cm
Print on newspaper
Courtesy of the artist and
Xavier Hufkens, Brussels

*A Frozen Eagle Melting on the
Theatre of Operations (Asphalt)*
2017
Variable dimensions
Asphalt, ice, ink, cacti, bronze
Courtesy of the artist and
Xavier Hufkens, Brussels

Ellen Gallagher

Born 1965 in Providence, USA.
Lives and works in Rotterdam,
The Netherlands

Abu Simbel
2005
62 × 90 cm
Photogravure, watercolour,

colour pencil, varnish, pomade,
plasticine, fake fur, gold leaf
and crystals
Private collection

Dr. Blowfins
2014
188.2 × 202.9 cm
Ink, graphite and paper
on canvas
Private collection. Courtesy
of Hauser & Wirth

Dew Breaker
Dew Breaker
Dew Breaker
2015
188.2 × 202.9 cm
Pigment, ink, oil, graphite and
paper on canvas
Courtesy of the artist and Hauser
& Wirth

Mekhitar Garabedian

Born 1977 in Aleppo, Syria. Lives
and works in Ghent, Belgium

*Fig. a, a comme alphabet
(ayppenkeem)*
2009–
Variable dimensions
Marker, pen, pencil on paper
Courtesy of the artist and Galerie
Albert Baronian, Brussels

Isa Genzken

Born 1948 in Bad Oldesloe, Germany.
Lives and works in Berlin, Germany

OIL XV
2007
35 × 220 × 380 cm
2 mannequins, 3 plastic vessels,
metal foil, plastic, cloth

OIL XVI
2007
265 × 450 cm; 265 × 450 cm;
270 × 132 cm
23-part wall installation:
aluminium, metal foil, adhesive
tape, metal, paper

Both collection MMK
Museum für Moderne
Kunst, Frankfurt-am-Main,
acquired with funding from
the Freunde des Museums
für Moderne Kunst, the
Hessische Kulturstiftung,
private donation and the
Tischgesellschaft 2011

Jef Geys

Born 1934 in Leopoldsburg,
Belgium. Lives and works in Balen,
Belgium

Sterrendoek
1965
170 × 140 cm
Oil and pastel on canvas
Collection of the artist

*Gleichheit, Fraternité,
Vrijheid*
1986
213.5 × 99 × 11.5 cm
Wooden door and frame, paint
Collection of the artist

Jos de Gruyter & Harald Thys

Born 1965 in Geel, Belgium &
Born 1966 in Wilrijk, Belgium.
Live and work in Brussels, Belgium

*Keizer Ro: Het verslag van een
staatsgreep in onze gewesten*
1993
Dimensions variable
13 black-and-white prints on
wood, 3 videos (in loop, sound,
colour), documents, objects
and photographs in vitrines,
desk, mortar
Courtesy of the artists

Thomas Hirschhorn

Born 1957 in Bern, Switzerland.
Lives and works in Paris, France

Pixel-Collage n°35
2016
370 × 712 cm
Prints, tape, transparent sheet

Pixel-Collage n°41
2017
433 × 368 cm
Prints, tape, transparent sheet
Both courtesy of the artist

Pixel-Collage n°47
2016
33 × 29 cm
Prints, tape, transparent sheet

Pixel-Collage n°49
2016
37.5 × 43.5 cm
Prints, tape, transparent sheet

Pixel-Collage n°51
2016
33.5 × 48 cm
Prints, tape, transparent sheet

Pixel-Collage n°54
2016
28.5 × 61 cm
Prints, tape, transparent sheet

Pixel-Collage n°61
2016
31 × 42.5 cm
Prints, tape, transparent sheet

Pixel-Collage n°62
2016
47 × 41.5 cm
Prints, tape, transparent sheet

Pixel-Collage n°63
2016
33 × 50.5 cm
Prints, tape, transparent sheet

Pixel-Collage n°66
2016
28 × 50.5 cm
Prints, tape, transparent sheet

All courtesy of Dvir Gallery, Tel
Aviv/Brussels

Showcase for Thoughts
2017
540 × 90 × 110 cm
Vitrine in wood and Plexiglas,
documents

Banner
2017
390 × 840 cm
Spray paint on cloth
Specific installation for WIELS

Banner
2017
450 × 820 cm
Spray paint on cloth
Specific installation for BRASS

All courtesy of the artist

Carsten Höller

Born 1961 in Brussels, Belgium.
Lives and works in Stockholm,
Sweden

*The Baudouin/Boudewijn
Experiment: A Deliberate,
Non-Fatalistic, Large-Scale
Group Experiment in Deviation*
2001/17
24-hour performance;
8 May 2017, Palais de la
Dynastie/Dynastiepaleis,
Brussels
Re-creation commissioned
by WIELS and
Kunstenfestivaldesarts.
Originally organised by
Roomade and curated by
Barbara Vanderlinden

Cameron Jamie

Born 1969 in Los Angeles, USA.
Lives and works in Paris, France

Spine Stations
2010
Variable dimensions
Glazed ceramic
Courtesy of Gladstone

Gallery, New York/Brussels,
and Bernier/Eliades, Athens/
Brussels

Untitled
2009–13
207 × 54 × 59 cm
Glazed ceramic
Courtesy of Gladstone Gallery,
New York/Brussels, and Bernier/
Eliades, Athens/Brussels

Untitled
2009–13
206 × 45 × 50 cm
Glazed ceramic
Courtesy of Gladstone Gallery,
New York/Brussels, and Bernier/
Eliades, Athens/Brussels

Titania C.
2016
205 × 35 cm
Glazed ceramic
Courtesy of Gladstone Gallery,
New York/Brussels

Staxx Flora Maria
2016
125 × 40 cm
Glazed ceramic
Courtesy of Gladstone Gallery,
New York/Brussels

Ann Veronica Janssens

Born 1956 in Folkestone, United
Kingdom. Lives and works in
Brussels, Belgium

Volare
2017
Variable dimensions
Wood, metal, concrete, pigeons
Architect: Philippe Vander
Maren; pigeon consultants:
Mady and Alain Vekens
Rooftop sculpture for WIELS.
Courtesy of the artist

Martin Kippenberger

Born 1953 in Dortmund, Germany.
Died 1997 in Vienna, Austria

Untitled
1979
129.5 × 96 cm
Acrylic, enamel and spray print
on map on board in the artist's
frame
Collection de Bruin-Heijn,
Wassenaar

Untitled
1988
63 × 92 cm
Oil and coins on canvas
Collection Wilfried and
Yannicke Cooreman, Puurs

Goshka Macuga

Born 1967 in Warsaw, Poland.
Lives and works in London, United
Kingdom

*Before the Beginning and
After the End (Transhumanism
& The Destructive Nature
of Humankind)*
2017
Produced in collaboration with
Patrick Tresset
451.3 × 133.2 cm each
2 metal tables, conveyer belts,
motor, and biro drawings by
system 'Paul-n' on paper scrolls

Transhumanism features the
following works:

Anonymous
Okimono of a Skull with Snake
Japanese, Meiji period, late 19th
century
23 × 13.5 × 13.5 cm
Carved wood
Courtesy of Desmet Gallery,
Brussels

*Letter from Albert Einstein to
Sigmund Freud*
30 July 1932
27.3 × 18.8 cm
Facsimile, 7 pages
Reproduced with permission
of Manuscript Division, Library
of Congress, Washington, DC
Collection Goshka Macuga,
London

Albert Einstein, Sigmund Freud
Why War?
1933
22.3 × 16.5 cm
Published by the International
Institute of Intellectual
Co-operation, Paris
Collection Goshka Macuga,
London

Eadweard Muybridge
Animal Locomotion (Plate 348)
1887
40 × 50 cm
Collotype
Courtesy of Galerie Rodolphe
Janssen, Brussels

Claudio Parmiggiani
Che cos'è la tradizione
1997
34 × 20 × 14 cm
Wood, metal, lead cast of ear,
paper, iron
Courtesy of the artist and
Meessen De Clercq, Brussels

Mary Shelley
Frankenstein draft Manuscript,

*MS. Abinger c.56, fols. 60v, 61r,
61v*
c. 1816
26 × 18 cm
Facsimile, 3 pages
Reproduced with permission
of Bodleian Libraries,
The University of Oxford
Collection Goshka Macuga,
London

*The Destructive Nature
of Humankind* features
the following works:

Walter Benjamin
*Theses on the Philosophy
of History*
c. 1940
21.4 × 14.4 cm
Facsimile, 1 page
Reproduced with permission
of Manuscript Division, Library
of Congress, Washington, DC
Collection Goshka Macuga,
London

Ray Bradbury
Fahrenheit 451
1953
18.4 × 11 cm
Published by Ballantine Books,
New York
Collection Goshka Macuga,
London

Peter Fischli & David Weiss
Brick
2005
23 × 11 × 6 cm
Unfired clay
Courtesy of Sprüth Magers,
Berlin/London/Los Angeles

John Latham
*Book in Processed Oil Shale
from Bing*
1976
29 × 20 × 31 cm
Two books, rocks and canvas
gauze
Courtesy of the John Latham
Estate and Lisson Gallery,
London

Friedrich Nietzsche
Also Sprach Zarathustra
1883–85
20.3 × 16.6 cm
Facsimile, 1 page
Reproduced with permission
of Klassik Stiftung, Goethe und
Schiller Archiv, Weimar
Collection Goshka Macuga,
London

Panamarenko
Puk Bot, Archaeopteryx III
1991
23 × 35 × 10 cm

12 solar cells, tape, beads
Private collection

Mark Manders

Born 1968 in Volkel,
The Netherlands. Lives and works
in Ronse, Belgium

Silent Studio/Argile silencieux
2016–17
Variable dimensions
Painted bronze, offset print on
paper, wood, painted wood,
rope, iron, dry clay, pencil on
paper, plastic sheeting
Courtesy of the artist and
Zeno X Gallery, Antwerp

Lucy McKenzie

Born 1977 in Glasgow, United
Kingdom. Lives and works in
Brussels and Ostend, Belgium

In My Area (For Kato)
2017
37.25 sq m
Painted mural at Rue des
Chartreux/Kartuizerstraat,
Brussels.
Commissioned by Ans
Persoons, Deputy Mayor
for Dutch-language Affairs, in
charge of the Comic strip trail of
the City of Brussels and WIELS

Wesley Meuris

Born 1977 in Lier, Belgium. Lives
and works in Antwerp, Belgium

*Crocodile Range: A Freshwater
Swamp in the Wetlands*
2006
78 × 84 cm
Pencil and watercolour
on paper
Private collection

*Aqua Theatre: The Intelligent,
Acrobatic Moves of the
Bottlenose Dolphin*
2006
78 × 84 cm
Pencil and watercolour
on paper
Private collection

*Aqua Theatre: An Amazing Show
with Three Gigantic Walruses*
2006
78 × 84 cm
Pencil and watercolour
on paper
Belfius Art Collection, Brussels

*Aqua Theatre: The Elegant
Plunge of the Great White
Beluga Whale*

2006
78 × 84 cm
Pencil and watercolour on paper
Belfius Art Collection, Brussels

Nástio Mosquito

Born 1981 in Huambo, Angola.
Lives and works in Ghent, Belgium

*The Guided Tour – Once We
Shared Consequent Masturbation*
2017
Performance by Nástio
Mosquito et al.
Written and developed by Nástio
Mosquito and Bedwyr Williams.
Produced by ZZZZZ
Creation for
Kunstenfestivaldesarts
and WIELS

Jean-Luc Moulène

Born 1955 in Reims, France.
Lives and works in Paris, France

*Documents: Produits de
Palestine*
2002–05
(53 ×) 50 × 40 cm
Cibachrome under Diasec
Edition of 5
Courtesy of Galerie Chantal
Crousel, Paris and Thomas
Dane Gallery, London

Nœud 0.1 Varia 03
Nœud 5.2 Varia 01
Nœud 3.1 Varia 05
Nœud 4.1 Varia 05
Paris, 2010–12
20 × 15 × 150 cm
Green patinated bronze
Courtesy of Galerie Greta
Meert, Brussels

*Blown Knot 6 32 (Borromean)
Varia 04*
2012
32 × 23 × 21 cm
Glass
Courtesy of Thomas Dane
Gallery, London

Knot 5.1 Varia 03
2012
20 × 15 × 150 cm
Bronze
Courtesy of Thomas Dane
Gallery, London

Blown Knot 0.1 Varia 03
Blown Knot 3.1 Varia 04
Blown Knot 4.1 Varia 02
Marseille, 2012
21 × 33 × 121 cm
Glass, steel
Courtesy of Galerie Greta
Meert, Brussels

Blown Knot 6 32 (Borromean)
Varia 09
2013
28 × 32 × 25 cm
Glass
Courtesy of Thomas Dane
Gallery, London

Oscar Murillo

Born 1986 in La Paila, Colombia.
Lives and works in London, United
Kingdom

Human Resources
2016
Variable dimensions
Wood, fabric, papier mâché
Courtesy of the artist and David
Zwirner, New York/London

Otobong Nkanga

Born 1974 in Kano, Nigeria. Lives
and works in Antwerp, Belgium

*Contained Measures of Shifting
States 1/4*
2012–17
On-going performance;
installation of one table of
250 ø, aluminium metal strip,
electrical heating plate, glass
container on wooden cylinder,
wood and demineralized water
and metal legs
Courtesy of the artist and In
Situ – Fabienne Leclerc, Paris

Felix Nussbaum

Born 1904 in Osnabrück,
Germany. Died 1944 in Auschwitz,
Poland

Maler mit Maske
c. 1935
62 × 47.5 cm
Oil on canvas
Private collection

*St. Cyprien (Gefangene in Saint-
Cyprien)*
1942
68 × 138 cm
Oil on canvas
Collection Felix-Nussbaum-
Haus, Osnabrück, on loan
from the Niedersächsische
Sparkassenstiftung

*Soir (Selbstbildnis mit Felka
Platek)*
1942
87 × 72 cm
Oil on canvas
Collection Felix-Nussbaum-
Haus, Osnabrück, on loan
from the Niedersächsische
Sparkassenstiftung

*Vorzeichnung zu den
Verdammten*
c. late 1943
12.5 × 21 cm
Pencil on parchment paper
Collection Felix-Nussbaum-
Haus, Osnabrück

Willem Oorebeek

Born 1953 in Pernis, The
Netherlands. Lives and works in
Brussels, Belgium

*Monogrammatic Studies 1999-
2007-2016, #3A-B, #17*
1999/2016
Lithograph/offset print
mounted on Dibond
Courtesy of the artist

Marina Pinsky

Born 1986 in Moscow, Russia. Lives
and works in Brussels, Belgium

Influencing Machine (Lock)
2016
Steel

Polar
2016
Wallpaper

Door
2017
Metal, glass

Keyholes
2017
Synthetic polymers

All variable dimensions
All courtesy of the artist and
C L E A R I N G, New York/
Brussels

Lili Reynaud-Dewar

Born 1975 in La Rochelle, France.
Lives and works in Grenoble, France

*Small Tragic Opera of Images
and Bodies in the Museum*
2017
Performance: 40', libretto by
Lili Reynaud-Dewar. Score by
Nicolas Murer
Installation: variable dimensions,
glass, silk, metal, speakers, sound
Creation for WIELS and
Kunstenfestivaldesarts. Courtesy
of the artist and C L E A R I N G,
New York/Brussels

Gerhard Richter

Born 1932 in Dresden, Germany.
Lives and works in Cologne,
Germany

Hund
1965
62.2 × 46.9 cm
Screen print on a manually
applied ground on white
cardboard
1 edition of 8 (not numbered)
Collection Museum
Morsbroich, Leverkusen

Onkel Rudi
2000
96 × 58.5 cm
Cibachrome mounted
on Dibond
A.P. 4/10
Collection Gerhard
Richter Archiv, Staatliche
Kunstsammlungen Dresden

Bridge 14 FEB 45 (I)
2000
46 × 34.5 cm
Offset print on white cardboard,
coated with printer's varnish,
fixed on cardboard
A.P.
Collection Dietmar Elger,
Cologne

September
2009
66 × 90 cm
Digital print between two glass
panes
Edition 27/40
Private collection

Ulrike Meinhof
2015
51 × 50 cm
Giclée print on Hahnemühle
Photo Rag on Alu Dibond
A.P. 15/15
Collection Gerhard
Richter Archiv, Staatliche
Kunstsammlungen Dresden

Walter Swennen

Born 1946 in Brussels, Belgium.
Lives and works in Brussels, Belgium

Zij die hier zijn, zijn van hier
2006
40 × 50 cm
Oil on canvas
Collection of the artist

We/They
2010
90 × 70 cm
Oil on canvas
Collection Gaby and Wilhelm
Schürmann, Herzogenrath

Ceux qui sont ici, sont d'ici
2013
136 × 150 cm
Oil and acrylic on canvas

Collection Gaby and Wilhelm
Schürmann, Herzogenrath

Wolfgang Tillmans

Born 1968 in Remscheid, Germany.
Lives and works in London, United
Kingdom, and Berlin, Germany

Concorde Grid
1997
361 × 464 cm
Chromogenic prints on paper,
behind Plexiglas
Collection Charles Asprey,
London

Rosemarie Trockel

Born 1952 in Schwerte, Germany.
Lives and works in Cologne and
Berlin, Germany

Humus
2012
60 × 80 cm
Digital print on paper
on Alu Dibond

Art Brut
Question of Time
Walk on Water
2012
80 × 60 cm each
Digital print on paper
on Alu Dibond

Wearing Propaganda
2006/14
80 × 106 cm
Digital print on paper
on Alu Dibond

Maison roulante
One's Hero (Kricke)
Semelparous
2014
80 × 60 cm each
Digital print on paper
on Alu Dibond

L'amitié franco-allemande
2014
60 × 80 cm
Digital print on paper
on Alu Dibond

Ghost on Lemon Cure
Untitled
Aspen Time
Changing Studios
2014
80 × 106 cm each
Digital print on paper
on Alu Dibond

Queen Anne Is Dead
Redcross the Country
Melting into Eyes and Tears
Social Ladder

2014
80 × 60 cm each
Digital print on paper
on Alu Dibond

Depression Is Art
1995/2015
80 × 106 cm
Digital print on paper
on Alu Dibond

One Minute Fluida
2009/15
80 × 60 cm
Digital print on paper
on Alu Dibond

Fusion of a Painting and Stuff
Cat's-Eye
2015
80 × 106 cm each
Digital print on paper
on Alu Dibond

Demanding Person but
a Sublime Poet
Moma's Boy
2016
80 × 60 cm each
Digital print on paper
on Alu Dibond

Merry Mood
2016
105 × 90 × 18 cm
Ceramics, glazed

First Chlamydia
1966/2017
80 × 106 cm
Digital print on paper
on Alu Dibond

Jirili
1982/2017
80 × 106 cm
Digital print on paper
on Alu Dibond

Er kam und blieb
2009/2017
80 × 60 cm
Digital print on paper
on Alu Dibond

Art Nouveau Cliché
2015/17
80 × 106 cm
Digital print on paper
on Alu Dibond

Baywatch
Fingers Like Toes
First Come, First Served

Le château ambulant
2017
80 × 106 cm each
Digital print on paper
on Alu Dibond

Homesick
Impromptu
The Enchanted Students
Trade and Commodities 1
Trade and Commodities 2
2017
80 × 60 cm each
Digital print on paper
on Alu Dibond

From Smoke to Smother
2017
60 × 80 cm
Digital print on paper
on Alu Dibond

All courtesy of Sprüth Magers,
Berlin/London/Los Angeles

Luc Tuymans

Born 1958 in Mortsel, Belgium.
Lives and works in Antwerp,
Belgium

Secrets
1990
52 × 37 cm
Oil on canvas
Private collection. Courtesy of
Zeno X Gallery, Antwerp

Doha I
2016
147.4 × 231.8 cm
Oil on canvas

Doha II
2016
151.7 × 231.8 cm
Oil on canvas

Doha III
2016
154.6 × 232.8 cm
Oil on canvas

All courtesy of David Zwirner,
New York/London, and Zeno X
Gallery, Antwerp

Presence
2017
247 × 182.3 cm
Oil on canvas
Courtesy Studio Luc Tuymans

Richard Venlet

Born 1964 in Hamilton, Australia.
Lives and works in Brussels, Belgium

Exhibition architecture
'The Absent Museum'
Commissioned by WIELS

Peter Wächtler

Born 1979 in Hanover, Germany.
Lives and works in Berlin, Germany

Old Brain
2017
Video 16:9, colour, no sound
Courtesy of the artist

Christopher Williams

Born 1956 in Los Angeles, USA.
Lives and works in Cologne,
Germany, and Chicago, USA

Untitled (Study in Black/Afrique)
Photography by the Douglas
M. Parker Studio, Los Angeles,
California
March 20, 2006
2006
46.8 × 34.9 cm (paper)
86 × 72.5 cm (framed)
Selenium toned gelatin
silver print
Collection Dr. Claudia Orben

Clockwise from Manufacturer
Name (Outer Ring)
Michelin
X M+S 89
Clockwise from Tire Size (Inner
Ring)
135 R 15
72 Q E2 0281541
M+S
Tubeless
Radial X
TF 852 20-2044
Tread: 1 Polyester Ply
+ 2 Steel Plies
Sidewall: 1 Polyester Ply
Canada and U.S. Codes Only
Max Load 355 Kg (780 Lbs)
Max Press. 350 kPa (51 PSI)
V-1
Photography by the Douglas
M. Parker Studio, Glendale,
California
January 03 – January 04, 2008
2008
61 × 50.8 cm (paper)
94.7 × 83.4 cm (framed)
Selenium toned gelatin
silver print
Haubrok Collection, Berlin

Mustafa Kinte (Gambia)
Camera: Makina 67 506347
Plaubel Feinmechanik und Optik
GmbH
Borsigallee 37
60388 Frankfurt am Main,
Germany
Shirt: Van Laack Shirt Kent 64
41061 Mönchengladbach,
Germany
Dirk Schaper Studio, Berlin
July 20, 2007
2008
50.8 × 40.6 cm (paper)
86.2 × 74.7 cm (framed)
Selenium toned gelatin
silver print

Bergische Bauernscheune,
Junkersholz
Leichlingen
September 29, 2009
2010
50.8 × 61 cm (paper)
83.5 × 94.1 cm (framed)
Archival pigment print

Reinigung Ursula Schweyen
Lindenstr. 34, Köln
February 17, 2010
2010
60.3 × 50.5 cm (paper)
86 × 94.9 cm (framed)
Gelatin silver print

TecTake Luxus Strandkorb
grau/weiß
Model no.: 400636
Material: wood/plastic
Dimensions (height/width/
depth): 154 cm × 116 cm ×
77 cm
Weight: 49 kg
Manufactured by Ningbo Jin
Mao Import & Export Co., Ltd,
Nigbo
Zhejiang, China for TecTake
GmbH
Igersheim, Germany
Model: Zimra Geurts, Playboy
Netherlands Playmate of the
Year 2012
Studio Rhein Verlag,
Düsseldorf
February 1, 2013
(Zimra stretching)
2013
50.5 × 60.3 cm (paper)
86 × 95 cm (framed)
Selenium toned gelatin
silver print

Linhof 13x18 DPa. APa.
Doppelkassette/Double Plate
and Cutflm Holder/
Châssis Double/Chasis Double
– YZDD –
Manufactured by Linhof,
Nikolaus Karpf K.G.
Präzisions-Kamera-Werke,
München 25, West-Germany
Studio Rhein Verlag, Düsseldorf
January 15, 2016
2016
76.2 × 61 cm (paper)
112.6 × 95.6 cm (framed)
Selenium toned gelatin
silver print

Prototype
Studio Rhein Verlag,
Düsseldorf
March 20, 2016
2016
50.8 × 40.6 cm (paper)
86.1 × 74.4 cm (framed)
Selenium toned gelatin
silver print

*180HR15 Michelin XAS
Manufactured by: Tigar Tyres
d.o.o., Pirot, Serbia, Est. 1935
Parent Company: SCA
Compagnie Générale des
Établissements Michelin,
Clermont-Ferrand, France,
Est. 1889
Studio Rhein Verlag,
Düsseldorf
February 22, 2016*
2016
50.8 × 61 cm (paper)
86.9 × 95.8 cm (framed)
Selenium toned gelatin silver
print

*Untitled
Focal length: 180 mm
Aperture: f/5.6
Image ratio: 2:1
Distance lens to focal plane:
27 cm
Distance film layer to focal
plane: 81 cm
Bellows extension: 36 cm
Depth of field: 1.932 mm
Studio Rhein Verlag, Düsseldorf
August 13, 2016*
2017
45.7 × 45.7 cm (paper)
85.1 × 83.5 cm (framed)
Selenium toned gelatin
silver print

*Wall designed and constructed
by Dirk Ufermann, Head
Technician, Bonner Kunstverein*
2017
349 × 350.4 × 57.2 cm
Wood, screws, paint, ink on
PVC-free wallpaper, aluminum,
rubber

All courtesy of Galerie Gisela
Capitain, Cologne and David
Zwirner New York/London

Nil Yalter

Born 1938 in Cairo, Egypt.
Lives and works in Paris, France

*Turkish Immigrants #1.
Women and Man*
1977
6 parts
42 × 55.5 cm each
Graphite on paper and gelatin
silver prints
Collection Reydan Weiss, Essen

*Turkish Immigrants #2.
Three Girls*
1977
3 parts
42 × 55.5 cm each
Graphite on paper and gelatin
silver prints
Collection Reydan Weiss, Essen

*Turkish Immigrants #5.
Two Women and Child*
1977
3 parts
35.5 × 51.5 cm each
Graphite on paper and gelatin
silver prints
Collection Reydan Weiss, Essen

Turkish Immigrants #7. Meatball
1976–77
5 parts
43 × 79 × 3 cm each
Graphite on paper and gelatin
silver prints
Private collection
Immigrants
2016
Installation composed of
extracts from 6 video works:
Katran (1975); *Bidonville*
(1976); *Meatball* (1976);
Workers in Paris (1976);
L'Isle-d'Abeau (1977);
Workers in Ghent (1978)
Courtesy of the artist

*C'est un dur métier que l'exil/
Balling zijn is een zwaar beroep*
2012/17
Poster campaign in 5 language
versions: French, Dutch,
English, Arabic, Turkish
Re-creation for WIELS

Photographic Credits
Courtesy of
pp. 34–35: Guillaume Bijl/SABAM, Brussels; p. 37: Stadsarchief Turnhout; p. 39: Fox Photos/Hulton Archive/Getty Images (left) & English Heritage/Heritage Images/Getty Images. Photo by Eric de Maré (right); p. 41: Archives Galerie de France. Photo by Alberto Ricci; p. 42: Maria Gilissen; p. 43: © The Museum of Modern Art, New York. Photo by Peter Butler © 2017 Artists Rights Society (ARS), New York/SABAM, Brussels; p. 44: Photo by Philippe De Gobert; p. 45: Photo by Dirk Pauwels; pp. 49–53: © Felix-Nussbaum-Haus Osnabrück/SABAM, Brussels; p. 55: Francis Alÿs; pp. 56–59: © Gerhard Richter 2017; pp. 60–61: David Zwirner, New York/London and Zeno X Gallery, Antwerp; pp. 62 & 66: Zeno X Gallery, Antwerp: p. 63: Flemish Community/M HKA, Antwerp; p. 69: Erfgoedbibliotheek Hendrik Conscience, Antwerp, cat. no. B 25606; p. 70: Belga Archives; pp. 72–73: Walter Swennen and Xavier Hufkens, Brussels. Photos by Markus Wörgötter; pp. 74–77: © Estate of Martin Kippenberger, Galerie Gisela Capitain, Cologne. Photos by Dirk Pauwels (pp. 74–75) & Christie's Amsterdam (p. 76); pp. 78–79: Marlene Dumas: pp. 80–81: Zeno X Gallery, Antwerp. Photos by Peter Cox; p. 82: Museum Arnhem; pp. 84–85: Sammy Baloji and Galerie Imane Farès, Paris; pp. 86–89: Sammy Baloji; pp. 92–95: Etopia Centre for Private Archives, Namur; pp. 96–99: Photos by Maria Thereza Alves; pp. 100–03: Michel François and Xavier Hufkens, Brussels. Photo by Stuart Whipps/Ikon Gallery, Birmingham, 2014 (p. 102, above); pp. 105–06: Mekhitar Garabedian and Galerie Albert Baronian, Brussels; pp. 110 & 113: Photos by Ekaterina Kaplunova; pp. 111 & 112: Richard Venlet and Carlo Siegfried; pp. 116–18: Jo Baer and Galerie Barbara Thumm, Berlin; pp. 120–24: Monika Baer and Galerie Barbara Weiss, Berlin; p. 126: the artists. Photo by Lola Pertsowsky; p. 128: the artists and Galerie Loevenbruck, Paris. Photo by Fabrice Gousset; pp. 130–31 (2, 4, 5, 6, 8): Jana Euler and dépendance, Brussels. Photos by Sven Laurent; (1): Jana Euler and dépendance, Brussels. Photo by Stefan Altenburger; (3): Jana Euler. Photo by Stefan Altburger; pp. 132–33: Jana Euler and cabinet, London. Photo by Mark Blower; pp. 134–35: Olivier Foulon; pp. 136–39: © Ellen Gallagher. Courtesy the artist, Hauser & Wirth and Gagosian Gallery. Photos by Alex Delfanne (p. 138) and Kevin Richards (p. 139); pp. 140–41: MMK Museum für Moderne Kunst Frankfurt am Main. Photo by Axel Schneider; p. 142: Installation view Venice Biennale, 2007. Photo by Jan Bitter/SABAM, Brussels; p. 145: Jos de Gruyter & Harald Thys; pp. 147–51: Thomas Hirschhorn and Galerie Chantal Crousel, Paris. Photos by Florian Kleinefenn; pp. 152–53: Cameron Jamie; pp. 154–55: Photo by Sławomir Kowalewski, 2014; pp. 156–59: Goshka Macuga; pp. 160, 162, 163 (above): Mark Manders and Zeno X Gallery, Antwerp. Photos by Peter Cox; p. 163 (below): Mark Manders and Zeno X Gallery, Antwerp and Tanya Bonakdar Gallery, New York. Photos by Genevieve Hanson; p. 164: Photo by Kristien Daem; pp. 170–73: © Jean-Luc Moulène/ADAGP 2017 and SABAM, Brussels, courtesy of the artist, Galerie Chantal Crousel, Paris and Thomas Dane Gallery, London; pp. 174–77: Oscar Murillo and David Zwirner, New York/London. Installation views 'Flying Moths', Condo, Carlos/Ishikawa London, 2016; p. 179: Otobong Nkanga. Installation view, Carriageworks, 20th Biennale of Sydney, 2016. Photo by Document Photography; pp. 180–85: Willem Oorebeek; pp. 186–93: the artist and C L E A R I N G, New York/Brussels; pp. 196–97: Installation views, Stiftung Kunstsammlung, Nordrhein-Westfalen, Düsseldorf, 2013; pp. 198–201: Rosemarie Trockel and Sprüth Magers/SABAM, Brussels; pp. 202–05: Installation views, 'Secrets of a Trumpet', The Renaissance Society, Chicago, 2016. Photos by Tom Van Eynde/SABAM, Brussels; pp. 206–09: Christopher Williams, courtesy of the artist, Galerie Gisela Capitain, Cologne and David Zwirner New York/London.

Text Credits
pp. 6–14: Charles Esche, partially based on a lecture given on 6 September 2016 at the Valand Academy in Gothenburg, Sweden, in the context of Frank Forum Talks.

pp. 16–23: Manuel Borja-Villel, partially based on the lecture 'Museums of the South' given on 12 April 2010, organised by BAM and FARO, previously published in *Cahier: over collecties*, Brussels 2010, pp. 36–57.

p. 68: Carsten Höller, 'The Baudouin/Boudewijn Experiment. A Deliberate, Non-Fatalistic Large Scale Group Experiment in Deviation' (2001) in Claire Bishop, ed., *Participation*, London and Cambridge, MA 2006, p. 144–5. Revised version of the original advertisement in Dutch in *De Witte Raaf*, no. 91, May–June 2001, p. 6.

pp. 104–07: Mekhitar Garabedian, revised and abridged version of 'The Foreignness of Language' in *To a Stranger from a Stranger*, Ghent 2015, pp. 114–35.

p. 119: Jo Baer, excerpt from 'Tis Ill Pudling in the Cockatrice Den (La-Bas)' (1989) in *Jo Baer – Broadsides & Belles Lettres: Selected Writings and Interviews 1965–2010*, ed. Roel Arkesteijn, Amsterdam 2010, p. 129.

pp. 147–51: Thomas Hirschhorn, 'Why Is it Important – Today – To Show and Look at Images of Destroyed Human Bodies?' (2012) in *Critical Laboratory: The Writings of Thomas Hirschhorn*, eds Lisa Lee and Hal Foster, Cambridge MA and London 2013, pp. 99–104.

p. 197: Wolfgang Tillmans, *Concorde*, Cologne 1997, flap text.

p. 213: Fabienne Dumont, revised and elaborated excerpt from 'La Roquette, from Confinement to Emancipation' in *Une artiste engagée: variations sur Nil Yalter*, Paris 2016, pp. 92–93.

The exhibition and publication are generously supported by
The WIELS Patrons: Jean-Pierre and Katherine Berghmans, Michel and Virginie Cigrang, Emilie De Pauw, Pieter and Olga Dreesmann, Dean Johnson and James Van Damme, Catherine Lagrange, Sophie Le Clercq, Wolfgang and Martine de Limburg Stirum, Jean-Claude and Nicole Marian, Michel and Stéphanie Moortgat, Corinne and Alexandre Van Damme, Christian and Nathalie Van Thillo, Jean and Chantal Vandemoortele, and Sylvie Winckler

Willame Foundation: Luc Boellaert, Xavier Donck, Michel Delfosse, André Gordts, and Jacques Verhaegen

Fundación Almine y Bernard Ruiz-Picasso para el Arte, Mondriaan Fund, Kunststiftung NRW, Institut français and la Service de Coopération et d'Action Culturelle de l'Ambassade de France en Belgique, Embassy of the Kingdom of the Netherlands in Brussels, SAHA, Pro Helvetia, and Peter and Nathalie Hrechdakian.

We are grateful to our partners
Kunstenfestivaldesarts, General and Artistic Director Christophe Slagmuylder and Managing Director Valérie Wolters; Ans Persoons, Deputy Mayor for Dutch-language Affairs of the City of Brussels, responsible for the Comic strip trail, Karine Lallieux and Yvan Mayeur; BRASS, Director Frédéric Fournes and Charles Spapens, Deputy Mayor for Urban Renewal; la Maison de l'emploi de Forest/Vorst Jobhuis and Coordinator Natacha Giloteau; JCX Immo, Managing Director Sophie Le Clercq and Director of Legal Affairs Pascal Hanique; Visit Brussels, CEO Patrick Bontinck, Deputy CEO Geert Cochez, and Legal & Contemporary Art Product Advisor Olivia Battard; Toerisme Vlaanderen, CEO Peter De Wilde and Product Manager Helena De Brabandere; Radio Vibration.

We warmly thank the lenders to the exhibition
The artists, Charles Asprey, Galerie Albert Baronian, Lutz Becker, Belfius Art Collection, Bernier/Eliades, Collection de Bruin-Heijn, Galerie Buchholz, Galerie Gisela Capitain, C L E A R I N G, Wilfried and Yannicke Cooreman, Galerie Chantal Crousel, Thomas Dane Gallery, Eric Decelle, Defares Collection, Galerie De France, dépendance, Desmet Gallery, Christine Duchiron Brachot, Dvir Gallery, Latifa Echakhch, Dietmar Elger, Estate Marcel Broodthaers, Etopia Centre for Private Archives, Galerie Imane Farès, Felix-Nussbaum-Haus, Konrad Fischer Galerie, Flemish Community, Frac Picardie, Frac Nord-Pas de Calais, Gladstone Gallery, Haubrok Collection, Hauser & Wirth, Collection Heubi-Mishiev, Xavier Hufkens, In Situ – Fabienne Leclerc, Galerie Rodolphe Janssen, Jan Kaps, John Latham Estate, Bruno van Lierde, Lisson Gallery, Galerie Loevenbruck, M HKA, Bernhard Martin, Galerie Greta Meert, Meessen De Clercq, Collection Moraes-Barbosa, Museum für Moderne Kunst Frankfurt-am-Main, Museum Morsbroich, Niedersächsischen Sparkassenstiftung, Dr. Claudia Orben, Gaby and Wilhelm Schürmann, Sprüth Magers, Gerhard Richter Archiv – Staatliche Kunstsammlungen Dresden, Thieck Collection, Galerie Barbara Thumm, Van Abbemuseum, Els and Vincent Vlasblom, Helen and Raymond Verbouwens, Reydan Weiss, Galerie Barbara Wien, Zeno X Gallery, David Zwirner, and all those who wish to remain anonymous.

WIELS

Avenue Van Volxemlaan 354
1190 Brussels, Belgium
www.wiels.org

WIELS Board of Administrators

President
Pierre Iserbyt

Founding President
Herman J. Daled

Vice-President
Michel Moortgat

Members
Bruno van Lierde
Frédéric Rouvez
Sylvie Winckler

WIELS General Assembly
Board members
Inge de Bruin
Michel Cigrang
Bart De Baere
Chris Dercon
Ann Veronica Janssens
Dimitri Jeurissen

Sophie Le Clercq
Luc Tuymans
Richard Venlet
Jacques Verhaegen

WIELS is supported by
Vlaamse Gemeenschap
Fédération Wallonie-Bruxelles
Région de Bruxelles-Capitale/Brussels Hoofdstedelijk Gewest
Vlaamse Gemeenschapscommissie
COCOF
Loterie Nationale/Nationale Loterij
Duvel Moortgat
WIELS Patrons
WIELS Club
WIELS Business Club

This publication accompanies
the exhibition
'The Absent Museum: Blueprint
for a Museum of Contemporary
Art for the Capital of Europe',
conceived and produced by
WIELS, Brussels, presented from
20 April to 13 August 2017.

Publisher
Mercatorfonds (Managing
Director, Bernard Steyaert)
WIELS (Director, Dirk Snauwaert)

Edited by
Dirk Snauwaert

Foreword
Pierre Iserbyt

Essays
Manuel Borja-Villel
Charles Esche
Dirk Snauwaert

Catalogue entries and texts
Lutz Becker
Fabienne Dumont (FD)
Charlotte Friling (CF)
Zoë Gray (ZG)
Hicham Khalidi (HK)
Dirk Snauwaert (DS)
Michaël Van den Abeele
Bob Vanden Broeck (BVB)
Szymon Zareba

Coordination
Caroline Dumalin, WIELS
Charlotte Friling, WIELS
Wivine de Traux, Mercatorfonds
Ann Mestdag, Mercatorfonds

Translations
Annette David (from French)
Patrick Lennon (from Dutch)
Graham Thomson (from Spanish)

Editing
Lise Connellan

Book design and concept
Boy Vereecken
assisted by Antoine Begon

Pre-press, printing and binding
Die Keure, Bruges (Belgium)

© 2017 Mercatorfonds and
WIELS, Brussels and the authors

Distributed in Belgium,
The Netherlands and Luxembourg
by Mercatorfonds, Brussels
ISBN 978-94-6230-174-0
D/2017/703/17
www.mercatorfonds.be

Distributed outside Belgium,
the Netherlands and Luxembourg
by Yale University Press,
New Haven and London
www.yalebooks.com/art
www.yalebooks.co.uk

YALE ISBN 978-0-300-22914-1
Library of Congress Control
Number: 2017937959

Every effort has been made
to trace and credit all known
copyright or reproduction right
holders. The publishers apologise
for any errors or omissions and
welcome these being brought to
their attention.

Curated by
Dirk Snauwaert
with Zoë Gray, Frédérique Versaen,
Caroline Dumalin,
Charlotte Friling

Director
Dirk Snauwaert

Director of Administration
Sophie Rocca

Senior Curator
Zoë Gray

Education and Outreach
Frédérique Versaen

Public Relations and Development
Martine de Limburg Stirum

Curators
Devrim Bayar, Caroline Dumalin,
Charlotte Friling

Press and Communication
Micha Pycke

Registrar
Ari Hiroshige

Presentation and Production
Kwinten Lavigne, Cédrik Toselli,
Fredji Hayebin

Visitor Service and Mediation
Nadia Essouayah

Visitor Service and Bookshop
Nancy Junion, Wim Clauwaert

Events and Facilities
Alice Vanbiervliet

Administrative Assistant
Adèle Bonnet

WIELS Club
Michèle Rollé

*WIELS Club Assistant
and Residency Coordinator*
Eva Gorsse

*Public Relations and
Development Assistant*
Fran Bombeke

*Coordinator
SuperVliegSuperMouche*
Benoit De Wael

Assistant Registrar
Julie Anne

Interns
Maëlle Delaplanche,
Katrien Doms, Julie Roland,
Yaozheng Tan, Bob Vanden Broeck,
Caterina Zevola